BIG GAME SHOOTING
(VOLUME I)

BIG GAME SHOOTING
(VOLUME I)

CLIVE PHILLIPPS-WOLLEY,
ALFRED E. T. WATSON,
SAMUEL W. BAKER,
W. C. OSWELL, ET AL

ISBN: 978-93-5420-744-0

Published: 1894

LECTOR HOUSE LLP
E-MAIL: lectorpublishing@gmail.com

The Lion's Last Charge

C. Whymper
Page. 240.

BIG GAME SHOOTING
(VOLUME I)

BY

CLIVE PHILLIPPS-WOLLEY

**WITH CONTRIBUTIONS BY
SIR SAMUEL W. BAKER, W. C. OSWELL, F. J. JACKSON,
WARBURTON PIKE, AND F. C. SELOUS**

**EDITED BY
HIS GRACE THE DUKE OF BEAUFORT, K.G.**

ASSISTED BY ALFRED E. T. WATSON

**IN TWO VOLUMES,
VOL. I.**

**WITH ILLUSTRATIONS BY CHARLES WHYMPER, J. WOLF
AND H. WILLINK, AND FROM PHOTOGRAPHS**

1894

DEDICATION
TO
H.R.H. THE PRINCE OF WALES

Badminton: *May 1885.*

Having received permission to dedicate these volumes, the Badminton Library of Sports and Pastimes, to His Royal Highness the Prince of Wales, I do so feeling that I am dedicating them to one of the best and keenest sportsmen of our time. I can say, from personal observation, that there is no man who can extricate himself from a bustling and pushing crowd of horsemen, when a fox breaks covert, more dexterously and quickly than His Royal Highness; and that when hounds run hard over a big country, no man can take a line of his own and live with them better. Also, when the wind has been blowing hard, often have I seen His Royal Highness knocking over driven grouse and partridges and high-rocketing pheasants in first-rate workmanlike style. He is held to be a good yachtsman, and as Commodore of the Royal Yacht Squadron is looked up to by those who love that pleasant and exhilarating pastime. His encouragement of racing is well known, and his attendance at the University, Public School, and other important Matches testifies to his being, like most English gentlemen, fond of all manly sports. I consider it a great privilege to be allowed to dedicate these volumes to so eminent a sportsman as His Royal Highness the Prince of Wales, and I do so with sincere feelings of respect and esteem and loyal devotion.

Beaufort.

Badminton

PREFACE

A few lines only are necessary to explain the object with which these volumes are put forth. There is no modern encyclopædia to which the inexperienced man, who seeks guidance in the practice of the various British Sports and Pastimes, can turn for information. Some books there are on Hunting, some on Racing, some on Lawn Tennis, some on Fishing, and so on; but one Library, or succession of volumes, which treats of the Sports and Pastimes indulged in by Englishmen—and women—is wanting. The Badminton Library is offered to supply the want. Of the imperfections which must be found in the execution of such a design we are conscious. Experts often differ. But this we may say, that those who are seeking for knowledge on any of the subjects dealt with will find the results of many years' experience written by men who are in every case adepts at the Sport or Pastime of which they write. It is to point the way to success to those who are ignorant of the sciences they aspire to master, and who have no friend to help or coach them, that these volumes are written.

To those who have worked hard to place simply and clearly before the reader that which he will find within, the best thanks of the Editor are due. That it has been no slight labour to supervise all that has been written, he must acknowledge; but it has been a labour of love, and very much lightened by the courtesy of the Publisher, by the unflinching, indefatigable assistance of the Sub-Editor, and by the intelligent and able arrangement of each subject by the various writers, who are so thoroughly masters of the subjects of which they treat. The reward we all hope to reap is that our work may prove useful to this and future generations.

THE EDITOR.

CONTENTS

LIST OF ILLUSTRATIONS

BIG GAME SHOOTING

Springbuck, Steinbuck, Blesbuck and Reedbuck

1 *Springbuck.* 2 *Steinbuck.* 3 *Blesbuck.* 4 *Reedbuck.*

C. Whymper

CHAPTER I

ON BIG GAME SHOOTING GENERALLY
BY CLIVE PHILLIPPS-WOLLEY

It may be asked, as to these volumes, why 'Big Game Shooting' should find a place in a series devoted to British sports and pastimes, whereas, except the red deer, there is no big game in Great Britain?

It is true that there is no big game left in Britain; but if the game is not British, its hunters are, and it is hardly too much to say that, out of every ten riflemen wandering about the world at present from Spitzbergen to Central Africa, nine are of the Anglo-Saxon breed.

It may be asked, again, what justification there is for the animal life taken, and for the time and money spent in the pursuit of wild sport?

That, too, is an easy question to answer. Luckily for England, the old hunting spirit is still strong at home, and the men who, had they lived in Arthur's time, might have been knights-errant engaged in some quest at Pentecost, are now constrained to be mere gunners, asking no more than that their hunting-grounds should be wild and remote, their quarry dangerous or all but unapproachable, and the chase such as shall tax human endurance, human craft, and human courage to the uttermost.

If in these days of ultra-civilisation an apology is needed for such as these, let it be that their sport does no man any harm; that it exercises all those masculine virtues which set the race where it is among the nations of the earth, and which but for such sport would rust from disuse; that if the hunter of big game takes life, he often enough stakes his own against the life he takes; and if he be one of the right sort, he never wastes his game.

Incidentally, however, the hunter does a good deal for his race and for the men who come after him; something for science, for exploration, and even for his worst enemy — civilisation.

In Africa, hunting and exploration have gone hand in hand; in America the hunters have explored, settled, and developed much of the country, replacing the buffalo with the shorthorn and the Hereford; while in India, not the least amongst those latent powers which enable us to govern our Asiatic fellow-subjects is the respect won by generations of English hunters from the native shikaries and hill-men.

From Africa to Siberia the story of exploration has never varied. The world's pioneers have almost invariably belonged to one of two classes. It has been the love of sport, or the lust of gold, which has led men first to break in upon those solitudes in which nature and her wild children have lived alone since the world's beginning. Hunters or gold prospectors still find the mountain passes, through which in later days the locomotives will rush and the world's less venturous spirits come in time to reap their harvests and make fortunes in the footsteps of those who ask nothing better than to spend their strength and wealth in the first encounter with an untrodden world, living as hard as wolves, and content to think themselves rich in the possession of a few gnarled horns and grizzled hides. As for us who are Englishmen, it is well for us to remember that in most lands in which we shoot we are but guests, and the beasts we hunt are not only the property of the natives, but one of their most important sources of food supply. Bearing this in mind, we should be moderate in the toll we take of the great game, and considerate even of those who may not be strong enough to enforce their wishes. The recklessness of one man in a country where foreigners are few may suffice to damn a whole nation in the eyes of a prejudiced people, and it is worth while to recollect that any one of us who strays off the world's beaten tracks may serve for a type of his nation to men who have never seen another sample of an Englishman.

Looked at from any point of view, the wholesale slaughter of big game must be condemned by every thinking man. The sportsman who in one season is lucky enough to obtain a dozen good heads does no harm to anybody, and probably does good to the bands of game in his district by killing off the oldest of the stags or rams. But the man who kills fifty or a hundred foolish 'rhinos' (beasts, according to Mr. Jackson, which any man can stalk) in one year, or scores of cariboo at the crossings during their annual migration in Newfoundland, or deer and sheep by the hundred in America, shocks humanity and does a grave injury to his class.

The waste of good meat is quite intolerable; kindly natured men hate to hear of the infliction of needless pain, and waste of innocent animal life; good sportsmen recoil in disgust from a record of butchery misnamed sport, for, according to the very first article of their creed, it is the difficulty of the chase which gives value to the trophies. If there were no difficulties, no dangers, no hardships, then the sport would have no flavour and its prizes no value. The mere fact that a man can kill as many of any particular kind of animal as he pleases should be sufficient to make him let that beast alone, unless he wants it for food, as soon as he has secured (say) a couple of fine specimen heads. Finally, to look at this question from the lowest and most selfish standpoint, the wholesale slaughter of wild game in foreign countries should be discouraged unanimously by all who love the rifle, since men who kill or boast of having killed exceptionally large bags of big game in any country are extremely likely to arouse the natural and proper indignation of local legislators, who have it in their power to close their happy hunting grounds to all aliens for the fault of a few individuals, not by any means typical of, or in sympathy with, their class.

On the other hand, it would be well if some of those of our own race, who should know better, would be less ready to call other men butchers merely because they have killed large quantities of game. Everything depends upon the circumstances connected with the slaying. If a man needs and can utilise a hundred antelope, surely he has as good a right to kill them as if he were killing a hundred sheep for market. There are occasions when not only does the hunter's skill win the regard of savages who value nothing in friend or foe more than real manhood, but it is absolutely necessary to kill game in order to keep a native following in food. Without the hunter's skill, food would have to be bought or looted from hostile natives, a feud engendered which might end in the shedding of other blood than that of the beasts, and a serious obstacle be thus raised in the path of the pioneers of civilisation and trade.

Our big game sportsmen have made more friends than foes, have always contrived to feed their men, and the very greatest of them have never shed a drop of native blood. Where gallant Oswell or Selous have been, there are no blood feuds against the English to hamper an expedition of their countrymen.

So much for the ethics of Big Game Shooting; as to the practical side of it, let it be said at once that it is impossible upon paper to teach any man to become a successful big game hunter. Upon the hillside or in the forest, with an expert to guide him, with the floating mists to teach him something of the way of the winds, with game tracks or the game itself before him, each man has to learn for himself, and even then he learns more from his own mistakes than from anyone else. To be really successful a man wants so many things; he needs so many qualities combined in his own person. To be a good shot means but little. The man who can win prizes at Wimbledon *may* be a successful deer-stalker, but it by no means follows that he will be. He has one good quality in his favour, but even that quality varies with the varying conditions under which he shoots. With his pulses steady, his heart beating regularly, his wind sound, his digestion unimpaired, his eyes free from moisture, with the distances measured off for him, and with a bull's-eye to shoot at, he may make phenomenal scores; but when he has been living upon heavy dampers and strong tea taken at irregular intervals, his digestion may become impaired. When he has toiled all day and come fast up a steep incline at the end of a long stalk, his pulse will not be steady, his sides may be heaving like those of a blown horse, his eye may be dimmed by a bead of sweat which will cling to his eyelash and fall salt and painful into his eye just when it should be at its clearest. The distances are not marked for him, and the atmosphere varies so much at different altitudes, that it is not always easy to judge how far he is from his quarry, and that quarry, instead of being marked in black and white for his convenience, has an awkward trick of being just the colour of the hillside, with an outline which at 200 yards melts into the background and becomes one with its surroundings.

Many a man who shoots well at a mark is a poor shot in the woods; but luckily the converse of this proposition is also true. Again, strength and endurance, steady nerve and quick eyes count for much, but they alone will not make a man successful.

The strong young hunter is often the worst. Likely enough he does the work for the work's sake, laughs at mountain-sides, and, like a friend of our own, starts at dawn, travels all day, tells us at night of peaks at fabulous distances on which he has stood, but comes back empty-handed, simply because he is too strong, too fast, and runs over ground leaving behind him, or 'jumping' out of range, game which a feebler man might have seen when crawling slowly over the hillside or sitting down for a frequent rest. One really good Western sportsman we know advocates a very different system. 'Camp,' he says, 'near where game is, look out for likely places, and then go and sit about near them all day long. If the game comes to you, you'll probably get it; if it don't you won't, and you wouldn't any way. Somehows,' he generally adds, 'them bull elicks allus did have longer legs than mine, d—n 'em.'

Perhaps a knowledge of natural history is almost better than either great physical powers or exceptional skill with the rifle. If you watch a first-rate tennis-player, it will seem to you that tennis is a very easy game. The second-rate player performs prodigies of activity to get into the right place in time, but the first-rate man never seems to be obliged to exert himself at all. He always is where he ought to be. So it is with the good man to hounds. His place at the fence is the easiest, and yet he never seems to swerve or pick his place. In every case it is the same. Knowledge of the game helps all the men in the same way, and each in his own fashion picks his place; but he picks it long beforehand. The tennis-player knows where the return must come, the hunting man sees the weak place by which he means to go out at the very moment that he comes in to a field, and in like manner the big game hunter gets to where the big game is because he has calculated beforehand where it ought to be, and experience and knowledge of the beasts' habits, and a certain instinct which some men have, do not mislead him.

First, then, study the habits of wild animals generally. They are much the same all the world over, and a man may learn a great deal by the side of an English covert, when the rabbits and pheasants are running before the beaters, which he can turn to good use when hunting bigger game.

Why do you suppose some men always seem to get more shots than others; why do the birds always rise better to them than to you? Pure luck you think, and they perhaps don't deny it. Don't believe it. The true sportsman knows by instinct what tussock of grass will hold a rabbit as he goes by it, and if a rabbit is there he won't let it lie whilst he passes. You won't see *him* swing round, saving himself a bit and leaving the likeliest corner in a big field unbeaten. The birds would have sneaked down into the ditch and stopped there whilst you wheeled by thirty or forty paces off, but our friend puts them up; and if when those rabbits at the covert-side were bolting just out of range between you and him, you think he dropped his white pocket-handkerchief on the drive by mistake, you don't know your man. That handkerchief just turned them enough to bring them close by him, and he had awful luck you know, and fired six shots to your one.

That is the way in big game shooting too. Partly from experience, and partly by instinct, some men know where to look for a beast, and know the ways of it when found. Study then the habits of beasts generally to begin with, and then those of the particular beast you are going to hunt. Learn what it feeds on at different seasons of the year, and where its food is to be found; learn at what time of day it feeds, and at what time it lies down. Most animals feed early and late, just at dawn and just at the edge of night, sleeping when the sun warms them, using what Nature sends them instead of supplying the place of the sun with a blanket as we do. Many beasts are almost entirely nocturnal in their feeding hours, and these not only such as one would naturally expect to prowl by night—tigers, lions and suchlike—but ibex and mountain beasts which feed on nothing worse than grass. Just at and before dawn most beasts are up and feeding, probably because that is the coldest time in the twenty-four hours; the beasts become chilled and restless, and Nature warns them that food and motion are the best cures for the evils they are suffering from.

Learn too, with the utmost care for yourself, upon which of its senses each particular beast relies, for all do not rely upon the same sense. The sense of smell is perhaps the most universal safeguard of the beasts which men hunt, but all are not as keen of scent as the cariboo, nor all as wonderfully quick and long-sighted as the antelope, of whom Western men say that he can tell you what bullet your rifle is loaded with about as soon as you can make him out on the skyline. A bear is so short-sighted as to be almost blind on occasion, and no beasts seem capable of quickly identifying objects which are stationary, though all catch the least movement in a second. This of course is where the man who rests often gets an advantage. If a beast is stationary in timber, for instance, you may often look at him for a minute after your Indian has found him before making him out; but if he but flick his ear or turn a tine of his antler ever so little, it will catch your eye at once.

In still hunting for wapiti or other timber-loving deer, a broken stick will warn every beast within a quarter of an hour's tramp; but on a mountain-side, where stones are constantly falling from the action of sun and wind and rain, ibex, sheep and other mountain beasts will often take but little or no notice of the stones you dislodge during your climb. Only be careful that these stones do not fall too often or at too regular intervals.

A Close Shot

Major H. Jones

In Scotland stalking is almost the only form of hunting deer; in America and other wild countries there are two principal forms of sport—stalking and still hunting; the one practised in comparatively open country and in the mountains, and the other in those dense forests where, partly from choice and partly because it has been much hunted, most of the big game now harbours. In this series stalking has already been dealt with, so that with this form it is only necessary to deal briefly here. The wind is the stalker's deadliest foe, and in many of the countries known best to the writer (sheep countries for the most part) there are days in each week when it is wiser to stay in camp or hunt in the timber down below, rather than risk disturbing game when the winds are playing the devil in Skuloptin. Take your Indian's advice, and stop at home on such days as these; play picquet with your friend, look after your trophies, or write up your diary.

To any but the youngest hunters it seems superfluous to say that you must hunt up or across the wind; to remind them of what a score of authorities have said before about the lessons to be learnt from the drifting mist-wreaths; to warn them to take care that they see the beast before the beast sees them, and to this end to be careful in coming over a rise in the ground; to put only just so much of their head above the skyline as will enable them to see the country beyond, and even then to bring that small part of their body up very slowly and under cover of some friendly bush-tussock or boulder. In eighteen years' hunting the writer has met many men who might be forgiven for believing that wild game never lies down, for whenever they have seen it, it has been on its feet, looking at them. And no wonder, for some of them would even *ride* up to the top of a bluff before looking to see what lay in the valley beyond. And yet, even after such a mistake as this, there is a chance sometimes of retrieving your error if the wind is in your favour. If, for instance, in riding from camp to camp you suddenly come in full view of a stag, with a hind or two, walking in the early morning along the ridge of the next bluff to that upon which you and your Indians are riding, say a word to your men, and let them either ride slowly on or stop absolutely stationary in the same spot, whilst you slide out of your saddle and creep away on your belly amongst the grass. Above all, *they must keep in full view* of the stag, and if they do this, in nine cases out of ten the stag will not notice that you have gone, and whilst he stares intently at the strange objects which he knows to be at a safe distance from himself, you will have time to get round and make a successful stalk. Even the hinds will be too intent on watching the other men to keep a proper look-out in your direction. And this brings up another point. Take care of the hinds and of those lean grey-faced ewes. The ram and the stag are blunderers and reckless, especially in love-time; but the ewes are as suspicious and wary as schoolmistresses, and must always be watched carefully. If for a moment you see the grey faces turn in your direction, *keep still*; keep still as a statue, even though you have raised yourself upon your hands to peer over and have found out too late that your palms are pressing upon the thorny sides of a bunch of prickly pears. It will come to an end at last, though that fixed regard seems never ending; but in any case, if you want a shot you *must* be still, for if you try to lower your head and hide whilst they are looking at you, you might just as well go home. This rule applies in another instance. If you should by chance come upon a beast unawares, stand stock still at once; don't try to hide if it is a deer; don't try to bolt if it is something more dangerous. If you stand still, beasts are slow to identify objects, and your deer may not be badly scared or your bear may pass on with only a suspicious stare; but if you attempt to hide, your deer will certainly show you his paces over fallen timber, or your bear or tiger if bad tempered *may* charge.

Molopo River

Joseph Wolf

But you ought very seldom to run into beasts in this way, if you keep your eyes open for 'sign,' i.e. tracks, droppings, freshly broken twigs, and places where deer have been browsing, and if, as you ought to, you take a good long time to scan every valley carefully before you enter it. Of course you must not keep your eyes on the ground looking for tracks—this is a fatal trick of a 'tender foot'—but you can see tracks well enough with eyes looking well ahead of you; and indeed, if you are following a trail, you will find it more easily by looking for it yards ahead of you than you will by searching for it at your feet.

Again, in looking for game you have at first to learn what to look for. The deer you are likely to see will not be standing broadside on, with head aloft like Landseer's 'Monarch,' but will be a long blur of brown on a hillside, with head stretched out almost flat upon the ground in front of it, crouching (if it has seen you) more like a rabbit than a lordly stag, or else it will be but a patch of brown which moves between the boles of the pines, or a flickering ear, or a gleaming inch or so of antler, or, worse than all, a flaunting white flag bobbing over the fallen timber if it is a deer, or a dull white disc moving up towards the skyline if it is a sheep which you have stirred from amongst those grey boulders for one of which you mistook it.

Over the fallen Timber

A common error which men make is to depend too much upon the eyes of their gillie. That an Indian has better sight than a white man is an article of many a man's creed. I believe it to be a mistake. The Indian is trained, he knows what to look for, and is looking for it. The average white man who takes an Indian with him does not know what to look for, and is relying upon his Indian's eyes. Consequently the Indian sees the game first, tries to point it out to his master, who finds it just about the time that the beast has stood as long as it means to, and is on the move by the time that the white man, flurried by his Indian's oft-repeated 'Shoot! shoot!' has found out what he is to shoot at. Of course the result is a miss. If, instead of allowing his Indian to go ahead and do the spying, the gunner had gone ahead, he would in the course of a few weeks have learnt to find his own game, and when he had found it he would have secured for himself those first invaluable seconds when the beast was still standing uncertain of danger and for the moment at his mercy. If only a man is enough of a woodsman to find his way back to camp and to find again the game he has killed, he will do far better to go alone than with the best of guides. Two pair of eyes may be better than one, but one pair of feet make less noise than two, and the man who finds his own game, and chooses his own time to shoot, is far more likely to kill than the man who presses the trigger at the dictation of an excitable redskin. That 'Shoot, shoot' has lost many a head of game.

Don't be in a hurry when you have sighted game. If it has not seen you it is not likely to move, and if it has you can't catch it. Take your time. Light a pipe if the wind is right, and if it isn't the deer will object to your smell quite as much as to the smell of tobacco. Having lighted your pipe, con the ground over carefully, and plan out your stalk at your leisure. It may be that you have come across sheep in an utterly unapproachable position, lying down for their midday siesta. If so, lie down for yours too, keeping an eye open to watch their movements. Towards evening first one old ram will get up and stretch himself (and perhaps turn round and lie down again) and then another; but eventually they will feed off slowly over the brow, and then you can run in and make your stalk. If there is a good head in the band your patience will not be without its reward. Again, when you have made your stalk and are safe behind your boulder at 150 or 200 yards from your beast, don't be in a hurry. If your eyes are dim and you cannot see your foresight clearly, shut your eyes and wait. There is no more reason why the beasts should see you now than half an hour ago. Wait till your hand is steady and your eye clear; don't look too much at the coveted horns (as my gillies always said that I did); shoot *not* at the whole beast, but at the vital part behind or through the shoulder; and remember that you have worked days perhaps for the chance you will either take or miss in the next few seconds. Remember that a man shoots *over* three times for every once he shoots too low. Put your cap under your rifle if you are going to shoot from a rock rest; shoot from a rest whenever you can, and if you miss the first shot, do as the Frenchman wanted to when pheasant shooting, i.e. wait until he stops. If it is a ram or a deer, unless he has seen or winded you, it is a thousand to ten that he will stop within 50 yards or so to look back to see what frightened him before leaving the country. When he stops you will get another chance at a stationary object, and one shot of this kind is worth a good many 'on the jump.' If a beast does not look likely to stand again after the first shot, a sharp whistle will sometimes stop him.

You will hear, especially from Americans, who very often can shoot uncommonly well with the Winchester, and from Indians, who are the poorest shots in the world, of extraordinary shots at long ranges. Pay no attention to them. If you cannot get within 200 yards of game, except antelope in an open country, you are a poor stalker; and rely upon it more game is killed within 80 yards than is fired at over 200. Indians get what game they kill, not by their fine shooting at long ranges, but by their clever creeping and stalking. At the same time, there is a limit to everything, and if you attempt to get too close, a glimpse of your cap, which would only make a deer stare at 150 yards, will make him dash off as if wolves were after him at 50 yards.

Having dropped your stag, lie still (if you have wounded him only, this is still more necessary) and reload, as many a man has been terribly disappointed at seeing a deer which he considered was 'in the bag' get up and go off from under the very muzzle of an unloaded rifle. But your stalk may end without your getting a shot. Some puff of wind of which you had no suspicion may warn your quarry before you get within range of him, and if this happens, watch which way he goes, and do you go by another way, for he will put every beast he passes in his flight upon the 'qui vive.'

In case of wounded game do not be in too great a hurry to follow it. A wounded beast which is pressed will go on travelling just out of range of you until night falls, even though you can see a hind leg, broken high up, swinging loosely at every step he takes; but the same beast will lie down very soon if he has not seen or winded his enemy; his wound will stiffen, and in an hour he will be easy enough to stalk again and kill.

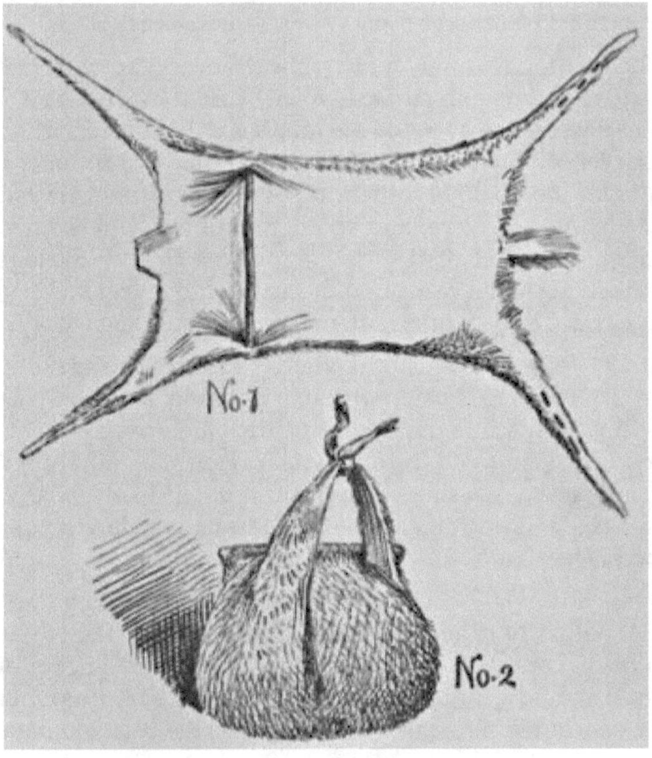

Skin and Pack

When you kill your stag, don't cut his throat, as a Tartar would do, high up, thereby spoiling the head for mounting, but plunge your knife into his chest. This will let out the blood and not spoil the neck. If, when you kill, you are far from home, and want to pack your venison home yourself, the Indian fashion of packing and carrying is the simplest that I know. It is done thus:—

After grallocking, skin your deer and cut off his head. Skin well down the legs, cutting off the feet at the fetlock joint, and spread the skin out with the hair downwards. Now cut from a bush near by a stick about as thick as your thumb, about three inches shorter than the width of the skin just behind the forelegs. Lay this on the skin and stretch the skin over it, driving in the points of the stick so as to hold the skin taut at the width of the stick. Next cut two or three little holes in the skin of each hind leg, and sew the two legs together by pushing a small twig through alternate holes in the skin of either leg. This will make the hind legs into a loop or handle. Now cut up what meat you want into joints of convenient size, pack them neatly on the skin behind the stick, fold up your pack and bring the stick through your loop, so that the ends of it overlap and hold against the loop; put the loop over your forehead or your shoulders, and there you are with a fairly convenient satchel full of meat on your back, the hairy side of the skin against your coat, and a sufficiently soft strap of skin across forehead or chest to carry the weight. All this can be done on the spot with no more adjuncts than your skinning knife and a bush to cut twigs from. The only difficulty is that the head must be arranged as an extra pack or must be called for on a subsequent occasion.

But your beast, though down, may not be dead, and apart from the caution already given to load before going up to a fallen beast, there is another worth giving. Many a man has lost his life by being too anxious to handle his prize. One instance of a fine young fellow maimed for life by a panther whose mate he had killed, and whom he was too anxious to handle without sufficient investigation of the position, occurs to me as I write, and an attempt of my own to turn over a wapiti which was not quite dead elicited such a vigorous kick from the leg I was hauling upon as sent me flying some yards into the scrub. If the deer had had free play for his leg, he might have done worse than make me a laughing stock for my Indians.

When you get your shot be careful where you place it, and if the beast is moving towards you, let him pass before firing, if possible. If it is only a deer, a raking shot, striking him even a little far back and travelling transversely through him, will be much more likely to go through vital organs and stop him than one fired from in front; and, besides, a shot of this kind is not so likely to reveal the shooter at once to the beast and elicit a charge, if the beast is a dangerous one, as when fired right into his face.

Don't, unless absolutely compelled to, fire at dangerous game above you. A wounded beast naturally comes down hill, and you are likely to be in its way if you fire from below; besides, a wounded beast will come quicker down hill than up. If your beast should charge you, stand still and go on shooting. Your chance may be a poor one, but in nine cases out of ten it is the best you have got.

Interlaced Antlers

From a photograph by J. Lord

But if after all your care, and even after you have heard (or think that you have heard) the bullet smack upon your stag's shoulder, he should show absolutely no sign of being hit, except perhaps a slight shiver or contraction of his muscles—if even he should turn and bolt at headlong speed—do not be at once discouraged; no, not even if you should follow him for many hundred yards without finding a single splash of blood upon the trail. Don't listen to your Indian, if you have reason to think that you held straight, even though appearances justify his assertion that you made a clean miss. That little spasmodic shiver is a hopeful sign. When you see your stag do this, you may be very sure that he is hard hit in a vital spot, and he will not go far. It he starts off at racing pace, he will probably pitch over on his head, dead, at the end of a hundred yards; and even if he does not bleed at first, follow him persistently: flesh wounds often bleed more freely than more dangerous ones, and it is quite on the cards that you will at last find that your stag was hit after all (far back, perhaps), and you may get him, although the shot hardly deserved such a prize. In any case it is your duty as an honest sportsman to do your utmost to find out whether you have wounded a beast, and, if so, to do all in your power to secure him and put an end to his pain, rather than leave him to take a better chance which may offer.

The greater part of what has been written so far applies either to shooting big game generally or to stalking: a word or two may well be devoted to still hunting—a form of the chase much practised in America and other well-wooded countries.

Still Hunting

Almost every fresh form of sport brings a fresh set of muscles, a hitherto little used sense or mental quality, into play, so that an all-round sportsman should be that very exceptional animal, a man in the full possession of all his faculties.

On the mountains a man depends upon his feet and upon his eyes; in the woods he has to place at least as much reliance upon his ears as upon his eyes; whilst his feet in still hunting are to the beginner the very curse and bane of his existence.

Except in wet weather or to a redskin, still hunting is an impossibility in any true sense of the term. When for weeks in Colorado there has not fallen one drop of rain, when sun and wind have parched the whole face of Nature, every twig and every fallen leaf upon the forest floor become absolutely explosive, and the merest touch will make them 'go off' with a report loud enough to be heard in London.

Damp weather is, then, the first essential for successful still hunting; but even then, when the leaves crush noiselessly under foot and fallen twigs bend instead of snapping, the utmost patience and care are necessary.

With a pair of good shooting boots, English made, with wide welts and plenty of nails in them—boots, for choice, which would run about two to the acre— with his rifle over his shoulder, and a handful of loose change in the pocket of his new American overalls, any average young man may go confidently into the best woods in America, certain that in a fortnight of hard work he will see nothing except what Van Dyke calls 'the long jumps' (i.e. tracks of startled deer) or those waving white flags popping over the fallen logs which those gunners only may hope to stop who habitually shoot snipe with a Winchester.

The man who is generally successful as a still hunter is he who knows the haunts and habits of the deer, who travels slowly in the woods, constantly stopping to listen and look ahead, who not only takes care to wear clothes of the softest material, with moccasins or tennis-shoes upon his feet, but who always has a hand ready to move an obstinate briar or obstructive rampike gently out of his way before it has time to rasp against his clothes or trip him and pitch him upon his head.

The first thing to remember in entering upon this sport is that every live thing in the woods is watching and listening at least three parts of its waking life, and that your only chance of success is to catch it off its guard in those rare moments when it is either feeding or moving, and therefore making a noise itself. A moving object is more easily seen than a stationary one, therefore do you stand or sit still from time to time among thick cover on some ridge or other commanding position, and watch the woods, peer through the thickets, and make certain that they are untenanted, before you blunder through them. When a log upon which your eyes have been dwelling idly for several minutes gets up as you move, and goes off with a snort, before you can get your rifle to your shoulder, you will realise more thoroughly how hard it is to distinguish stationary game in cover. Keep your ears, too, on the alert: a bear will move through a dry azalea bush, when he pleases, almost less noisily than a blackbird, and his great soft feet make far less sound on the dead leaves than yours do. Slow ears are almost as bad as slow eyes in still hunting; but do not condemn either your eyes or ears as worse than the natives' until the eyes have learned from experience what to take note of, and the ears which are the sounds worth listening to. In time the language of the forest will become plain to you, whether it is spoken in the voices of birds and beasts, in the rustlings and scurryings amongst the bushes, or written in tracks upon the great white page of new-fallen snow at your feet; but at first your ears will send many a false message to your brain.

In the intensity of the stillness the fir cones which the squirrels drop make you start, expecting to see the bushes divide for a bull moose at least to pass through them: at night, when you are watching by the river for bear, you think that you hear distinctly the 'splosh, splosh' of the grizzly's feet as he wades down the shallows towards you. Not a bit of it: it is only a foolish kelt who has run himself aground and is trying to kick himself off again into deep water. On the other hand, that grating of one bough against another which you fancied that you heard may have been a 'bull elk' burnishing his antlers against a cottonwood-tree, that far-away whistle of the wind may have been a fragment of a forest monarch's love-call, and that angry squirrel across the canyon was actually chattering *not* because he had seen you, but because he was disturbed by a bear passing by the log on which he was sitting.

But the language of the woods can only be learnt by residence amongst them, and this is especially true of the written language of tracks, which is to my mind one of the few things utterly beyond a white man's powers ever thoroughly to master. Such proficiency as a man may acquire in tracking he must acquire for himself in the woods, since any essay upon it would need more illustrations than words to make the meaning plain.

Fishing is said to require patience. Believe me, still hunting requires more. Although you have toiled all day and seen nothing; although you are hot, 'played out,' and therefore intensely irritable (perhaps you have even a touch of fever upon you); although every log on your way home 'barks' your shins, and every tendril clings to your ankle—you *must* keep your temper; and even when that thorny creeper hooks you by the fleshy part of your nose, you must not swear—at least, not aloud. If you do, at the very moment that the words leave your lips, the only beast you have seen all day will get up with a contemptuous snort from *the other side* of the bush in front of you.

But when all is written that can be written upon 'still hunting,' there is still much which can only be taught in the woods—or, if on paper, then it has been done already, as well as man could possibly do it, in the pages of the best book ever written by an American, Van Dyke's 'Still Hunter.' I am glad to have a chance of acknowledging my indebtedness to this author. Whatever I know of still hunting I have learned from his book and from experience, and have never yet known my two teachers disagree.

There is only one word which I would add here, but it is the most important that I shall write. There is one danger in still hunting in the woods more terrible than any other which the big game hunter can encounter: the danger, I mean, of accidentally shooting his fellow-man.

Make a rule for yourself before you go into the woods, and keep it as the first of sylvan commandments: Never, under any pretence whatever, pull your trigger until you know not only *what* you are shooting at, but also *at what part of* your beast you are shooting.

Once in a while the observance of this rule may lose you a beast which you might have crippled, and eventually secured if you had taken a snap shot at the grey thing which you saw moving in the bushes. But, on the other hand, instead of killing a bear or a buck, it is much more likely that your snap shot will wound some poor devil of a hind, who will sneak away to die in anguish somewhere in the thick covert where none but the jackal will benefit by her death; or else you may do as I once actually did—hit a bear in the seat of his dignity, thereby arousing his very righteous indignation in a way that is dangerous to the offending party; or, worse still, you may (as I *nearly* did) fire upon your own gillie or friend, whose moccasined footfall is very like a bear's tread, and whose sin in wandering across your beat would be too severely punished by death.

In all seriousness, it has always seemed to me that any man who, whilst out shooting, kills another in mistake for game deserves to be tried for his life, unless he be a very young beginner—and young beginners should hunt by themselves. There is no excuse for shooting a man. If the shooter could not tell that that at which he fired was a human being, much less could he tell at what part of his beast he was shooting, and a random shot 'into the brown' of a beast is unsafe, unsportsmanlike, and brutally cruel.

Finally, do not be tempted to use complicated sights in still hunting. When you have followed deer under pines heavy with snow, through sal-lal bush which looks like deep billows of the same, only to find, the first time, that your Lyman sight is down, and the second time that though erect the peephole is full of ice, you will recognise the merits of a Paradox with the simplest sights for wood shooting in any weather as thoroughly as the writer does, and whilst admitting the merits of the Lyman sight for long-range shooting in the open, eschew all but such simple sights in timber.

There are, of course, other ways of hunting big game besides those already dealt with. Almost any game may be driven, from lions in Somaliland and tigers in the Terai to chamois in the Alps and sheep in North America, and there is no doubt that sufficient excitement and a good deal of sport may be got out of the day's work; but, after all, the beaters who out-climb the Spanish ibex (as described by Mr. Chapman in his 'Wild Spain') and the natives who risk their lives in the driving, have always seemed to the present writer to be the men who did the work, and were principally responsible for the success of the day's sport. To the guns who are posted by the organiser of the beat little advice can be given, except to obey orders, stick to their posts, be careful not to shoot at anything until it has passed them—or, at any rate, at anything which is in such a position with regard to the beaters and other guns as to make it unsafe to fire—to keep their attention concentrated upon the business in hand, to make all arrangements for concealment and ease in shooting directly they are posted, and then to keep quiet. There is not quite enough in this form of sport for the gun to do to please some men, but *de gustibus non est disputandum.*

Night shooting is another form of sport, sometimes rendered necessary by the shyness and nocturnal habits of such beasts as the grizzly and the Caucasian ibex. There are charms in night watching peculiar to the hour, which appeal particularly to the naturalist and lover of outdoor life; there is a certain fascination in the mystery of the night, the gloom of the great woods, and the awful stillness of the white peaks; while the children of the forest always seem more natural and less suspicious at night than at any other time. But it needs every charm which the night can boast to tempt a man to sit hour after hour in the shadow, without stirring, without speaking, without even thinking of anything except the sport in hand, whilst the rain runs down his spine in a strong stream, or a cold wind catches his body, heated by the tramp to the ambuscade, and slowly freezes it. If you must shoot at night, be careful about the wind: find out as well as you are able from what quarter you may expect your bear, and take care that your wind does not reach him before he reaches the carcase by which you are hidden. Choose a spot where you have some chance of making out his outline against the sky if he should come, and whether you are watching by a carcase or by a salmon pool, be satisfied with a *distant* inspection of the bait, i.e.—don't go and walk about all round it, &c.

Bears are especially shy of returning to a carcase when they know that men are about, one grizzly that I know of in British Columbia having defeated a very well-known Indian sportsman by making a circuit round the carcase before coming in to feed. If in that circuit he caught no taint of human kind upon the night air, he used to come in and sup; but if he found that I——y was on guard, he used to go quietly home to a canyon down below, and wait for a more favourable opportunity. The tracks in the morning told the whole story, of course, as plainly as if the unfortunate sportsman had been a witness of the performance.

The principal difficulties in this kind of shooting are to keep sufficiently quiet to induce your bear to come, and to see your sights sufficiently to kill him, even at short ranges, when he has come.

Go to the spot as lightly clad as possible, carrying any spare things you can on your arm; don't hurry or overheat yourself on the way to your ambush, and put on a spare flannel shirt or coat, or whatever it is you are carrying, before you begin to feel chilled. Take a little sheet of macintosh with you to secure you a dry seat, and if you have no fancy night sights on your rifle, you can make a rough but serviceable one by twisting white string or cotton with a large knot in it round the muzzle of your rifle, while the thumb and finger of your left hand, as they embrace your rifle barrels, may be held a little apart to make a very coarse backsight. This is only a more or less clumsy Indian device, but it is considerably better than nothing if you get caught in the dark with no better appliances. After all, a sport which keeps you up all night, and in camp without any exercise all day, and which depends for success so entirely upon the good will of the bear, is not one to hanker after.

By the way, when you have shot your bear (if you should shoot him), and when you have taken his hide off, be careful how you pack it upon any ordinary pony. A spark applied to a powder magazine is hardly more astounding in its effects than the application of a fresh bear-skin to the back of some of the meekest of cayuses. A perfect Dobbin which belonged to the writer shook his faith in horse-flesh for ever by cutting his legs from under him as if they had been carried away by a round shot, merely because Dobbin had been asked somewhat suddenly to carry the hide of a two-year-old black bear.

Poor Old Sam

C. Whymper

In all American sport, dogs are used from time to time by the trappers and meat hunters who make hunting a business, and a thoroughly broken collie, such as accompanied the writer and Mr. Arnold Pike in an expedition to Colorado, would be invaluable to any still hunter, as this dog would not run in without orders, would precede his master at a slow walk in timber, regularly pointing in any direction from which he got wind of a deer, would take his owner up to it at a walk, would run a wounded beast to bay, follow and worry at the heels of a bear, and keep the camp secure from the inroads of inquisitive strangers or the all-devouring burros of our train. But such dogs as 'Pup' are rare, and the old gentleman to whom he belonged informed me that an offer of $500 for him would not be entertained, though his own whole ambition in life was to make double that sum to buy a farm and settle down, as at 65 he was beginning to think that he was almost too old to stay all the year in the woods. Poor old Sam! When one is too old for the woods, it should be almost time to 'turn in' for that last sleep.

Vignette

H. Willink

CHAPTER II

SOUTH AFRICA FIFTY YEARS AGO

BY W. COTTON OSWELL

WILLIAM COTTON OSWELL:
A BIOGRAPHICAL SKETCH BY SIR SAMUEL W. BAKER

One man alone was left who could describe from personal experience the vast tracts of Southern Africa and the countless multitudes of wild animals which existed fifty years ago in undisturbed seclusion; the ground untrodden by the European foot; the native unsuspicious of the guile of a white intruder. This man, thus solitary in this generation, was the late William Cotton Oswell. He had scarcely finished the pages upon the fauna of South Africa when death seized him (May 1, 1893) and robbed all those who knew him of their greatest friend. His name will be remembered with tears of sorrow and profound respect.

Although Oswell was one of the earliest in the field of South African discovery, his name was not world-wide, owing to his extreme modesty, which induced him to shun the notoriety that is generally coupled with the achievements of an explorer. Long before the great David Livingstone became famous, when he was the simple unknown missionary, doing his duty under the direction of his principal, the late Rev. Robert Moffat, whose daughter he married, Oswell made his acquaintance while in Africa, and became his early friend.

At that time Oswell with his companion Murray allied themselves with Livingstone to discover a reported lake of the unknown interior, together with Mrs. Livingstone and their infantine family. This expedition was at the private cost of Oswell and Murray; but, in grateful remembrance of the assistance rendered by Livingstone in communicating with the natives and in originating the exploration, Oswell sent him a present of a new waggon and a span of splendid oxen (sixteen animals), in addition to a thorough outfit for his personal requirements.

Livingstone, in the 'Zambesi and its Tributaries,' dwelt forcibly upon the obligation imposed upon him by Oswell's generosity; but, having submitted the manuscript to his friend for revision, Oswell insisted upon disclaiming the title of a benefactor. After the discovery of the Lake 'Ngami by Livingstone and his party, Oswell received the medal of the French Geographical Society; he was therefore allied with Livingstone, who was the first explorer of modern times to direct attention to the lake system of Africa, which has been developed within the last forty years by successive travellers.

Oswell was not merely a shooter, but he had been attracted towards Africa by his natural love of exploration, and the investigation of untrodden ground. He was absolutely the first white man who had appeared upon the scene in many portions of South Africa which are now well known. His character, which combined extreme gentleness with utter recklessness of danger in the moment of emergency, added to complete unselfishness, ensured him friends in every society; but it attracted the native mind to a degree of adoration. As the first-comer among lands and savage people until then unknown, he conveyed an impression so favourable to the white man that he paved the way for a welcome to his successors. That is the first duty of an explorer; and in this Oswell well earned the proud title of a 'Pioneer of Civilisation.'

As these few lines are not a biography, but merely a faint testimony to one whose only fault was the shadowing of his own light, I can sincerely express a deep regret that his pen throughout his life was unemployed. No one could describe a scene more graphically, or with greater vigour; he could tell his stories with so vivid a descriptive power that the effect was mentally pictorial; and his listeners could feel thoroughly assured that not one word of his description contained a particle of exaggeration.

I have always regarded Oswell as the perfection of a Nimrod. Six feet in height, sinewy and muscular, but nevertheless light in weight, he was not only powerful, but enduring. A handsome face, with an eagle glance, but full of kindliness and fearlessness, bespoke the natural manliness of character which attracted him to the wild adventures of his early life.

He was a first-rate horseman, and all his shooting was from the saddle, or by dismounting for the shot after he had run his game to bay.

In 1861, when I was about to start on an expedition towards the Nile sources, Oswell, who had then retired from the field to the repose of his much-loved home, lent me his favourite gun, with which he had killed almost every animal during his five years' hunting in South Africa. This gun was a silent witness to what its owner had accomplished. In exterior it looked like an ordinary double-barrelled rifle, weighing exactly ten pounds; in reality it was a smooth-bore of great solidity, constructed specially by Messrs. Purdey & Co. for Mr. Oswell. This useful gun was sighted like a rifle, and carried a spherical ball of the calibre No. 10; the charge was six drachms of fine-grained powder. There were no breech-loaders in those days, and the object of a smooth-bore was easy loading, which was especially necessary when shooting from the saddle. The spherical ball was generally wrapped in either waxed kid or linen patch; this was rolled rapidly between the hands with the utmost pressure; the folds were then cut off close to the metal with scissors, and the bullet was again rolled as before. The effect was complete; the covering adhered tightly to the metal, which was now ready for ramming direct upon the powder-charge, without wads or other substance intervening. In this manner a smooth-bore could be loaded with great rapidity, provided that the powder-charge was made up separately in the form of a paper cartridge, the end of which could be bitten off, and the contents thrust into the barrel, together with the paper covering. The ball would be placed above, and the whole could be rammed down by a single movement with a powerful loading rod if great expedition should be necessary. Although the actual loading could thus be accomplished easily, the great trouble was the adjustment of the cap upon the nipple, which with an unsteady horse was a work of difficulty.

This grand old gun exhibited in an unmistakable degree the style of hunting which distinguished its determined owner. The hard walnut stock was completely eaten away for an inch of surface; the loss of wood suggested that rats had gnawed it, as there were minute traces of apparent teeth. This appearance might perhaps have been produced by an exceedingly coarse rasp. The fore-portion of the stock into which the ramrod was inserted was so completely worn through by the same destructive action, that the brass end of the rod was exposed to view. The whole of this wear and tear was the result of friction with the 'wait-a-bit' thorns!

Oswell invariably carried his gun across the pommel of his saddle when following an animal at speed. In this manner at a gallop he was obliged to face the low scrubby 'wait-a-bits,' and dash through these unsparing thorns, regardless of punishment and consequences, if he were to keep the game in view, which was absolutely essential if the animal were to be ridden down by superior pace and endurance. The walnut stock thus brought into hasty contact with sharp thorns became a gauge, through the continual friction, which afforded a most interesting proof of the untiring perseverance of the owner, and of the immense distances that he must have traversed at the highest speed during the five years' unremitting pursuit of game upon the virgin hunting-grounds of Southern Africa. I took the greatest care of this gun, and entrusted it to a very dependable follower throughout my expedition of more than four years. Although I returned the gun in good condition, the ramrod was lost during a great emergency. My man (a native) was attacked, and being mobbed during the act of loading, he was obliged to fire at the most prominent assailant before he had time to withdraw his ramrod. This passed through the attacker's body, and was gone beyond hope of recovery.

There could not have been a better form of muzzle-loader than this No. 10 double-barrel smooth-bore. It was very accurate at fifty yards, and the recoil was trifling with the considerable charge of six drams of powder. This could be increased if necessary, but Oswell always remained satisfied, and condemned himself, but not his gun, whenever a shot was unsatisfactory. He frequently assured me that, although he seldom fired at a female elephant, one bullet was sufficient to kill, and generally two bullets for a large bull of the same species.

Unlike Gordon Cumming, who was accustomed to fire at seventy and eighty yards, Oswell invariably strove to obtain the closest quarters with elephants, and all other game. To this system he owed his great success, as he could make certain of a mortal point. At the same time the personal risk was much increased, as the margin for escape was extremely limited when attacking dangerous game at so short a distance as ten or fifteen paces. When Oswell hunted in South Africa, the sound of a rifle had never disturbed the solitudes in districts which are now occupied by settlers. The wild animals have now yielded up their territory to domestic sheep and cattle; such are the rapid transitions within half a century! In those days the multitudes of living creatures at certain seasons and localities surpassed the bounds of imagination; they stretched in countless masses from point to point of the horizon, and devoured the pasturage like a devastating flight of locusts. Whether they have been destroyed, or whether they have migrated to far distant sanctuaries, it is impossible to determine; but it is certain that they have disappeared, and that the report of the rifle which announces the advance of civilisation has dispersed all those mighty hosts of animals which were the ornaments of nature, and the glory of the European hunter. The eyes of modern hunters can never see the wonders of the past. There may be good sport remaining in distant localities, but the scenes witnessed by Oswell in his youth can never be viewed again. Mr. W. F. Webb, of Newstead Abbey, is one of the few remaining who can remember Oswell when in Africa, as he was himself shooting during the close of his expedition. Mr. Webb can corroborate the accounts of the vast herds of antelopes which at that time occupied the plains, and the extraordinary numbers of rhinoceros which intruded themselves upon the explorer's path, and challenged his right of way. In a comparatively short period the white rhinoceros has almost ceased to exist.

Where such extraordinary changes have taken place, it is deeply interesting to obtain such trustworthy testimony as that afforded by Mr. Oswell, who has described from personal experience all that, to us, resembles history. He was accepted at that time as the Nimrod of South Africa, 'par excellence,' and although his retiring nature tended to self-effacement, all those who knew him, either by name or personal acquaintance, regarded him as without a rival; and certainly without an enemy: the greatest hunter ever known in modern times, the truest friend, and the most thorough example of an English gentleman. We sorrowfully exclaim, 'We shall never see his like again.'

INTRODUCTION
BY W. COTTON OSWELL

I have often been asked to write the stories of the illustrations given in the chapters on South Africa, but have hitherto declined, on the plea that the British public had had quite enough of Africa, and that all I could tell would be very old. As I now stand midway between seventy and eighty I trusted I might, in the ordinary course of nature, escape such an undertaking; but in the end of '91 the best shot, sportsman and writer that ever made Africa his field—I refer to my good friend Sir Samuel Baker—urged me to put my experiences on paper; and Mr. Norton Longman at the same time promising that, if suitable, he would find them a place in the Badminton volume on 'Big Game,' I was over-persuaded, made the attempt, and here is the result.

The illustrations are taken from a set of drawings in my possession by the best artist of wild animal life I have ever known—Joseph Wolf. After describing the scene, I stood by him as he drew, occasionally offering a suggestion or venturing on two or three scrawling lines of my own, and the wonderful talent of the man produced pictures so like the reality in all essential points, that I marvel still at his power, and feel that I owe him most grateful thanks for a daily pleasure. Many of the scenes it would have been impossible to depict at the moment of their occurrence, so that even if the chief human actor had been a draughtsman he must have trusted to his memory. Happily I was able to give my impressions into the hands of a genius who let them run out at the end of his fingers. They are rather startling, I know, when looked through in the space of five minutes; but it must be remembered that they have to be spread over five years, and that these are the few accidents amongst numberless uneventful days. I was once asked to bring these sketches to a house where I was dining. During dinner the servants placed them round the drawing-room, and on coming upstairs I found two young men examining them intently. 'What's all this?' one asked. 'I don't know,' the other replied. 'Oh, I see now,' the first continued, 'a second Baron Munchausen; don't you think so?' he inquired, appealing to me. We were strangers to each other, so I corroborated his bright and certainly pardonable solution; but they are true nevertheless. I have kept them down to the truth: indeed, two of them fall short of it. I am very well aware that there are two ways of telling a story, one with a clearly defined boundary, the other with a hazy one, over which if your reader or hearer pass but a foot's length he is in the realms of myth. I think I had my full share of mishaps; but I was in the saddle from ten to twelve hours a day for close upon five seasons, and general immunity, perhaps, induced carelessness. I may say now, I suppose, that I was a good rider, and got quickly on terms with my game. I was, however, never a crack shot, and not very well armed according to present notions, though I still have the highest opinion of a Purdey of 10-bore, which burnt five or six drachms of fine powder, and at short distances drove its ball home. This gun did nearly all my work. I had besides a 12-bore Westley-Richards, a light rifle, and a heavy single-barrelled one carrying two-oz. belted balls. This last was a beast of a tool, and once—I never gave it a second chance—nearly cost me my life, by stinging, without seriously wounding, a bull elephant. The infuriated brute charged nine or ten times wickedly, and the number might have been doubled had I not at last got hold of the Purdey, when he fell to the first shot. We had no breech-loaders in those days, save the disconnecting one, and that would have been useless, for we had to load as we galloped through the thick bush, and the stock and barrel would soon have been wrenched asunder or so strained as to prevent their coming accurately into contact again.

The Purdey gun has a second history which gives it more value in my eyes than the good work it did for me. I lent it to Baker when he went up the Nile, and it had the honour, I believe, of being left with Lady Baker to be used, if required, during her husband's enforced absences. Baker returned it to me with a note apologising for the homeliness of the ramrod—a thornstick which still rests in the ferrules—adding that having to defend themselves from a sudden attack, his man Richarn, being hard pressed whilst loading, had fired the original ramrod into a chief's stomach, from which they had no opportunity of extracting it.

I am sorry now for all the fine old beasts I have killed; but I was young then, there was excitement in the work, I had large numbers of men to feed, and if these are not considered sound excuses for slaughter, the regret is lightened by the knowledge that every animal, save three elephants, was eaten by man, and so put to a good use. I have no notes, and though many scenes and adventures stand out sharply enough, the sequence of events and surroundings is not always very clear. If my short narrative seems to take too much the form of a rather bald account of personal adventure, I must apologise; and I may add that the nature and habits generally of the animals I met with are now so well known, and have over and over again been so well described by competent writers, that my relations with a few individuals of their families must be the burden of my song.

I spent five years in Africa. I was never ill for a single day—laid up occasionally after an accident, but that was all. I had the best of companions—Murray, Vardon, Livingstone—and capital servants, who stuck to me throughout. I never had occasion to raise a hand against a native, and my foot only once, when I found a long lazy fellow poking his paw into my sugar tin. If I remember right, I never lost anything by theft, and I have had tusks of elephants, shot eighty miles from the waggons, duly delivered. One chief, and one only, wanted to hector a little, but he soon gave it up. And with the rest of the potentates, and people generally, I was certainly a *persona grata*, for I filled their stomachs, and thus, as they assured me, in some mysterious way made their hearts white.

There is a fascination to me in the remembrance of the past in all its connections: the free life, the self-dependence, the boring into what was then a new country; the feeling as you lay under your caross that you were looking at the stars from a point on the earth whence no other European had ever seen them; the hope that every patch of bush, every little rise, was the only thing between you and some strange sight or scene—these are with me still; and were I not a married man with children and grandchildren, I believe I should head back into Africa again, and end my days in the open air. It is useless to tell me of the advantages of civilisation; civilised man runs wild much easier and sooner than the savage becomes tame. I think it desirable, however, that he should be sufficiently educated, before he doffs his clothes, to enjoy the change by comparison. Take the word of one who has tried both states: there are charms in the wild; the ever-increasing, never-satisfied needs of the tame my soul cannot away with.

But I am writing of close upon fifty years ago. Africa is nearly used up; she belongs no more to the Africans and the beasts; Boers, gold-seekers, diamond-miners and experimental farmers—all of them (from my point of view) mistakes—have changed the face of her. A man must be a first-rate sportsman now to keep himself and his family; houses stand where we once shot elephants, and the railway train will soon be whistling and screaming through all hunting-fields south of the Zambesi.

FIRST EXPEDITION TO AFRICA

Reduced from 12 st. 2 lb. to 7 st. 12 lb. by many attacks of Indian fever caught during a shooting excursion in the valley of the Bhavany River, I was sent to the Cape as a last chance by the Madras doctors; indeed, whilst lying in a semi-comatose state, I heard one of them declare that I ought to have been dead a year ago; so all thanks to South Africa, say I! I gained strength by the voyage, and, shortly after reaching Cape Town, hearing that a Mr. Murray, of Lintrose, near Cupar Angus, had come from Scotland for the purpose of making a shooting expedition to the interior, I determined to join him. The resolve was carried out early in the spring of 1844 (the beginning of the Cape winter); we started out from Graham's Town to Colesberg, buying on the way horses, oxen, dogs, waggons, and stores, crossed the Orange River, and set our faces northwards. We were all bitten in those days by Captain—afterwards Sir Cornwallis-Harris, whose book, published about 1837, was the first to give any notion of the capabilities of South Africa for big game shooting, and, Harris excepted, 'we were the first that ever burst into that "sunny" sea'-as sportsmen. Murray was an excellent kind-hearted gentleman, rather too old perhaps for an expedition of this kind, as he felt the alternations of the climate very much; and no wonder, for I have known the thermometer to register 92° in the shade at 2 P.M., and 30° at 8 P.M. I was younger, and though still weak from the effects of fever, the dry air of the uplands daily gave me vigour, and the absolute freedom of the life was delightful to me. Just at first I had to become accustomed to the many little annoyances of missing oxen, strayed horses, &c.; but when our waggons became our *home*, and our migratory state our life, all anxious care vanished. Things would be put right somehow; there was no use worrying ourselves; what had been yesterday would be to-morrow. What though the flats between the Orange and Molopo Rivers were full of sameness, they were also full of antelope, gnu, and quagga. These, with the bird and insect life, were all fresh, and made the world very bright around us. These upland flats have been so often described, that I will not bore the reader unnecessarily with an account of them, and besides, I am not writing of the country or its appearance, but have merely undertaken to try and give some idea of the game that once held possession of it; and, indeed, I doubt very much if I could convey any notion at the present time of what it was some fifty years ago, for all the glamour of the wildness and abundant life has long passed away.

On these plains the springbucks were met with in vast herds; for an hour's march with the waggons—say two and a quarter miles—I once saw them to the left of the track, along a slightly rising ground, thicker than I ever saw sheep. I suppose they must have been *trek bokken*; that is, a collection of the herds over an extended area on the move for pasturage. The Hottentot waggon-drivers shot many of them, frequently killing two at a time, they were so closely packed. They were to be counted only by tens of thousands. Formerly, they used often to invade the northern outlying farms of the Boers, and destroy their crops; and though shot in waggon-loads, they would still hang about as long as there was a green blade of anything. They were nearly as bad as the locusts, a flight of which we saw, by the way, a few days after leaving Kuruman, near the 'Chooi,' or large natural salt-pan. We were at breakfast, when far down on the south-east horizon I noticed a wreath as of dark smoke rising rapidly, broadening as it advanced. In a very short time it enveloped us in the form of a locust storm; the whole earth and air were full of them; tens of myriads settled, and myriads of myriads rode on clanking in mimicry of armed cavalry, and crackling like a flame devouring the stubble. Look which way you would—nothing but locusts; they did not hide the sun, but they so obscured his rays that you could look straight at him. No simile seems so apt to me as that of a heavy snow-storm with large flakes, and this uninterruptedly for two or three hours. Though the land before them was not exactly as the Garden of

Eden, verily behind them it was a desolate wilderness. As the cold of night came on, they collected on the bushes in enormous masses, eight or ten feet through, for warmth, weighing them completely to the ground, and they took flight again the next morning after the sun was well up. For two days my oxen never put their heads down; there was nothing found for them to eat. The swarms pass through waste and cultivated land alike, bringing dearth and destruction, and men's hearts fail; but the adversary has arrayed his forces against them, and through the dense flights sweep the wedge-shaped squadrons of the *springkhän vogel*, or locust birds: dark and long of wing like swifts, with white patches beneath the pinion. As squadron after squadron wheels and passes over you, the husks of the locusts fall like hail. The birds are in very large numbers and do their work deftly; before long the air above you is clear, and though the evidence of the curse is upon the earth, and remains, the locusts themselves are soon got rid of, for everything on two legs and four eats them. The Bushmen follow the flights, feed on them, dry them, and keep them in store. One night, Livingstone and I lost our way, and seeing the light of a fire, made for it. Around it sat a family of Bushmen; so, heralding our approach from a safe distance, for fear of a flight of arrows, we introduced ourselves. They welcomed us, and offered us guides and a snack of dried locusts. I ate two or three, and they were not so nasty; something like what old shrimp-shells without the insides might be. These insects are bad enough in their winged, but worse in their early wingless, form, when, as the dreaded *'foot-gangers'* of the Dutch farmer, they roll in living waves over his land, defy all attempts at extermination from their multitude, climb walls, quench lines of small fires placed in the hopes of turning them, cross rivers, millions jumping in, and millions getting over on the living raft. In both the winged and wingless state they are wonderfully described in chapter ii. of Joel.

On these choois, of which there are many, some of them twenty miles long and half as broad, the effect of mirage is more wonderful than I have ever seen it elsewhere. What seems an antelope grows into an elephant, and with the waving of the gauze returns to its actual form—a bush. By nearly all these salt-pans there is a spring which may perhaps have once played its part in their formation, or be the relic of the cause.

At one period of its history, Africa must have been a better watered country than it is now. In the driest tracts, in the waterless woods, you light unexpectedly on deep eroded channels, coming no whither and going nowhere. It gave me the impression that there had been a gradual uplifting of the surface, and a consequent sinking away of the old torrents and streams. The Bushmen and the elephants dig in these courses for water, which is now never seen on the surface, though the sides are sometimes worn away by its former action, twenty feet down. Over a large area the rainfall is exceedingly small, and in it the trees and grass have adapted themselves to their surrounding conditions. The former all send down long tap-roots through the upper soil to the close substratum, utilising them as the Bushman does the reed in his sucking-holes mentioned elsewhere; the latter grows with fleshy roots, and from the joints are thrown out delicate fibres ending in small tubers which, through the excessive drought and heat, act as reservoirs of moisture, thus sustaining vitality and enabling a bright green carpet to be spread two days after the fall of the rain. The animals, instinct led, follow the waterfall of the storm, and migrate to and fro in narrow zones. The birds do likewise; one beautiful hawk—happily called from his graceful movement *Molela shoquan*, 'he flows as he turns'—is a most assiduous attendant in the green-room of nature. But the thunderstorms are very partial. For two days I have passed through country so drought-stricken that the bushes were leafless, the twigs dry, the grass dust, the ground iron, and all animal, bird, and even insect life completely absent. In those two days we felt and knew the abomination of desolation, and so did our poor beasts.

Nothing particular happened during our journey between the two rivers. We shot and trekked—one day much like another—and stopped a short time at Kuruman, the station of that grand old patriarch of missionaries, Mr. Moffat, where we received all the kindly hospitality, attention and advice possible from him and Mrs. Moffat—verily the two best friends travellers ever came across. I shall never forget their affectionate courtesy, their beautifully ordered household, and their earnest desire to help us on in every way. He advised us to go to Livingstone, who was then stationed at Mabotsé, 220 miles or so to the northward, and obtain from him guides and counsel for our further wanderings.

We were once nearly in trouble, however, after leaving Kuruman. We had crossed a little stream called, I think, the Meritsani, and one of our men, while cooking some tit-bit of an antelope Murray had shot far away from the camp, carelessly set the grass on fire. Luckily we saw it two miles off, and by clearing the ground, and burning the stubble round the waggons, we escaped. It was a wonderful sight to watch the wall of smoke and flame as it licked up the grass and bush and coiled itself in folds about the tree stems; birds, insects, and beasts fleeing before it. As it approached our clearing, the heat was intense, and we had some difficulty in restraining the frightened horses and oxen; but the roaring rolling flame came within thirty yards of us, and then as it touched the edge of our charmed circle died away into nothingness, its disappointment seeming to goad it onward to right and left.

The flat open country held till we reached the Molopo River. The sketch very correctly represents this little stream when we first saw it, and gives a good general idea of the 500 or 600 miles we had come. Seven different kinds of animals were within view, some, especially the quaggas and the buffaloes, in large herds—springbucks, hartebeests, gnus, &c., filling in the picture; together there could not have been fewer than 3,000. I shot a couple of buffaloes for the camp, and then inspanning passed ahead towards the ridge of low hills, fifteen miles beyond, and running east and west; they told of a coming change of scenery, and the next day we stood on the top of them—to the south 600 miles of rolling plain, very similar to that immediately below, lay between us and the southern sea; but to the north the scene was changed, the well-wooded and watered valley of the Ba-Katla, a broken country full of game, was stretched out before us—in those days a hunter's paradise. For the first time tracks of rhinoceros, giraffe, and other unknown creatures were abundant, and we longed to cultivate the closest relations with them.

Without any just cause I thought myself a better sportsman than my companion, and determined to seek my game alone, in the hope that I might be the first to bag a rhinoceros. All day long I followed, with an attendant Hottentot, a trail of one of these animals, neglecting inferior game, but my experience in African woodcraft was small then, and I believe now that the spoor may have been a week old. At last, tired and disgusted with my want of success in not coming up with the object of my search, I shot an antelope, and returned rather earlier than usual to the waggons, which had been ordered to outspan under the range of hills. It was still daylight when I reached them, and there sat my friend Murray, quiet, cool and calm, very calm indeed. He greeted me with a nod and a smile, and asked me what I had killed? 'A buck,' I answered. He said nothing, but kept on smiling serenely. Presently I noticed a group of Kafirs sitting round their fire, and eating as only Kafirs can eat. 'What are those brutes gorging themselves with?' I asked my quiet friend. 'Oh, only some of the rhinoceroses I shot this afternoon.' I noted the plural, the iron entered into my soul, but I merely said: 'Ah! indeed!' in an easy nonchalant way I flattered myself, as if the shooting a rhinoceros was a matter of supreme indifference to me in those days, and walked to my own waggon.

Next morning at breakfast my friend offered to show me where the rhinoceroses lived. I was quite meek now, and ready to be introduced to this entirely imaginary locality. At that time we had not to go far to find, and had hardly left the camp a quarter of an hour, when the leading Kafir pointed out a great ugly beast rubbing itself against a tree eighty yards from us. I was off my pony in a second, determined to get to close quarters as soon as, and if possible sooner than, my companion. We both stalked to within twenty yards without being seen, and knelt down, I with the stump of a small tree before me; we fired together, and while the smoke still hung, I was aware of an angry and exceedingly plain-looking beast making straight at me through it. Luckily he had to come rather uphill to my stump, and his head was a little thrown back, when, within five feet of the muzzle of my gun, he fell, with a shot up his nostril, the powder blackening his already dingy face. This was a *borili* (or sour-tempered one); as a rule, the only really troublesome fellow of his family. I remember thinking my first introduction promised a stormy acquaintance, and hoping there might be gentler specimens, who rather liked being shot, or at all events did not resent it so violently. I got two or three times into serious trouble with these lumbering creatures; but the stories shall be told as they crop up. I may mention here, however, that success in rhinoceros shooting depends very greatly upon the sportsman's kneeling or squatting. I lost many at first by firing from a standing position. The consequence was, that the ball only penetrated one lung, and with the other untouched the beast runs on for miles, unless, of course, the heart happen to be pierced; whereas, fired from a lower level, the ball passes through both lungs, and brings him up in 100 or 200 yards. A rhinoceros very seldom drops to the shot. Of all I killed, but two fell dead in their tracks. Exclusive of the Quebaaba (*R. Oswellii*), which was probably a variety of the mahoho, (*R. Simus*), and of which we killed three and saw five, there were three kinds—the Mahoho, the *R. Africanus*, and the *R. Keitloa*.[1] I say 'were,' for whilst I write I hear that the dear old mahoho is extinct. I am very sorry. He was never, I believe, found north of the Zambesi, but between that river and the Molopo, of which we have just spoken, he was formerly in great force. Poor old stupid fellow, too quiet as a rule, though, when thoroughly upset (like a good-natured man in a passion) reckless, he was just the very thing for young gunners to try their 'prentice hand on, and directly the Kafirs got muskets he was bound to go; though, considering the numbers there used to be, I hoped he would have lasted longer. He had no enemies to fear, save man and the hyæna, and the first without firearms would have made but little impression on him; for, although sometimes taken in the pitfalls, he was never, so far as I know, killed by spears. The hyæna, when hard pressed for food, would occasionally attack the male, who is formed like the boar, and eat into his bowels from behind; but it was a long business, and not by any means always successful. The 'Cape wolf' must have been very hard set before he attempted it.

I have seen these long-horned, square-nosed creatures in herds of six and eight, and when in need of a large supply of meat for a tribe, have shot six within a quarter of a mile, with single balls. They had a curious habit which helped the sportsman, and has no doubt led to their too rapid extinction. If you found four or five together, and wounded one mortally, he would run off with the others until he fell, and then the survivors would make a circular procession round him until the gun was again fired, and another wounded. Off they would go again, halting and repeating the performance when the second fell, and so on to the end. The female was an affectionate mother, never deserting her calf, but making it trot before her, until she was mortally wounded, when she seemed to lose her head and shot on in advance, and we then always knew she would not go fifty yards further. Though they were a very meditative inoffensive lot, there was a point at which they drew the line. I once saw Vardon pull a mahoho's tail; this, however, was taking too great a liberty, and if I had not been near he might have suffered, but, as the heavy brute swung round to give chase, a ball at very close quarters stopped him. We have often been obliged to drive them from the bush before camping for

[1] Another seems to have been evolved recently, if I may draw that inference from a highly-coloured print I see in the shop-windows intituled: 'An African rhinoceros hunt.' A gentleman, on a fiery rearing steed, is engaging the enemy at very close quarters, and, unless he is a left-handed gunner, on the impossible side, as he is riding in the same direction as his quarry, and at its *near* shoulder. He may not be answerable for this position of affairs; it looks awkward, but he appears content, and holds his gun firmly by the middle, muzzle in air. The rhinoceros is the interesting figure in the picture, for he is *mailed*, like the Asiatic variety, and is either a late discovery, or an escaped specimen from the travelling show of some African Wombwell.

Rhinoceroses are puzzles to others besides artists. An old yeoman farmer, many years ago, lay dying near my house; to amuse him I sent some sketches and odds and ends, and received a message thanking me, but putting me straight as to those *two*-horned creatures being rhinoceroses; the rhinoceros had but *one* horn, he had seen it in a book, and it was no use my saying it had two, for it hadn't. I suggested to him that we wanderers, who went far afield for hunting and shooting, had a hand in making the books, but he wouldn't have it, and died a firm believer in one horn.

the night. They apparently mistook the waggons for some huge new beasts, and were very troublesome; but this hallucination was not confined to the mahoho. A borili in a great passion away to the east of the Limpopo, charged Livingstone's waggon, smashing his iron baking-pot. The borili is fidgety, apparently always in bad health, and constantly on the look out for a tree to scratch his mangy hide against. He has, too, an evil habit of hunting you like a bloodhound. He is the smallest of the three, with a short, snubby head, and a well-defined prehensile lip.

The keitloa, or more equal horned variety, is a mixture in form and temper between the mahoho and the borili; much larger than the latter, with differently shaped body, head, and horns, and less development of lip. The mahoho and quebaaba live on grass, the end of the latter's horn from its downward curve being abraded by contact with the ground as he feeds. The borili eats bush alone, and the keitloa a mixed diet of grass and bush.

I could never understand the great power and strength of a rhinoceros' horn. It is sessile on the bone of the snout, but not part of, or attached to it; apparently it is only kept in its place by the thickness of the skin, and yet, as I mention hereafter, a white rhinoceros threw me and my horse clear up into the air. Of course, the enormous muscles of the neck bore the brunt of the lift, but the horn did not suffer in any way. It is quite intelligible that the fact of it not being cemented to the bone would render it less liable to fracture at the base, and in itself it is tough enough, though consisting only of agglutinated hair; but I am only wondering that, attached as it is, it should possess the necessary rigidity for the work it does. It is occasionally used in the most determined way by rhinoceroses who have mutual differences to adjust. The Kafirs pare it down into hafts for their battle-axes. Of strips of the hide we made horse-whips, as the Egyptians do man-whips of that of the hippopotamus.

For his bulk the rhinoceros, especially the borili, is a quick mover in a hard trot and sometimes a gallop. The whole tribe are heavies, taking their pleasure, if any, very sadly. The hippopotamus, an even more ungainly beast, has the decency to remain most of his time in the water, but the 'chukuru' thinks it behoves him to bask in the sunlight and parade his ugliness. Standing motionless is the routine of his life, a scrub now and then against a tree his *délassement*—a very solid, stolid brute!

These creatures appear to me to be out of time, to have belonged to a former state of things, and to have been forgotten when the change was made. Often have I sat upon a ridge and looked at them as they moved solemnly and clumsily on the plain below, wondering how they still came to be in this world, and it has occurred to me how delightful it would have been to watch the pre-Adamite beasts in the same way, and learn their manners—which, I fear, were bad—as they came and went, no other man to interfere with your preserves, the world all to yourself and your beastly companions! How they would fight, and wallow, and roar, and how very cunning you would have to be to escape being eaten! I am afraid in my dreams two or three large-bored, hard-hitting guns have figured as *desiderata*; indeed, under such circumstances, I should not see the fun of doing king with a celt for a sceptre and half a dozen flint-headed arrows as a standing armament.

The rhinoceros would be even easier of approach than he is were it not for his attendant bird, a black slim-built fellow very like the king crow of India, who, in return I take it for his food, the parasitic insects on the chukuru, watches over his fat friend and warns him of the coming danger by springing up in the air and alighting smartly again with a peck on his back or head. This puts him on the alert, and he does his best, by sniffing and listening, to find out the point from which he is threatened, for his ears are quick and his scent excellent; but, as you are below wind of him, sound and smell travel badly, and his vision is by no means first rate. The natives by a figure transfer the connection between the bird and the beast to themselves, and when they wish to emphasise the great affection they bear you, or the great care they intend to take of you, address you as 'my rhinoceros,' an elliptical expression by which they mean to convey that they are your guardian birds. They are not always quite unfailing. Going out from Kolobeng after elephants I had heard of in the neighbourhood, I passed an old rain-doctor, whom I knew well, making rain with his pot on the fire, and his herbs and charms on the bubble. 'Chukuru ami, where are you going?' he asked. 'To shoot elephants,' I replied. 'I was just making rain, but as you are my chukuru, I put it off till to-morrow.' Is it necessary to say I was wet through in half an hour? A fine heavy thunderstorm was brewing whilst he was boiling. This rain-making is the Kafir's pet superstition—the power is hereditary—believed in by the maker and his fellow-countrymen. Conditions difficult to keep are imposed, such as that the women are not to speak one word when at work in the fields: if the rain fails, why of course the women spoke!

We travelled very slowly towards Mabotsé, Livingstone's station, and on our arrival there received every kindness and attention from him and Mrs. Livingstone, guides to the country to the north, with advice as to route, &c. Livingstone had not long got over his lion mishap—get over it altogether, indeed, he never did—the overlapping end of the broken humerus was visible enough when the body was brought home. The story of the accident was fresh with him and the Kafirs when we reached Mabotsé. A lion had killed an ox near the village, and the Ba-Katla turned out, as they always did when the lion deserted his game, and attacked their herds. Each man, as is usual in a hunt of this kind, carried two or three assegais and a plume of ostrich feathers on a pointed six-foot stick. The lion was tracked to his sleeping place, and the men made a ring round it, gradually closing the space between man and man as they advanced. Presently the quarry was roused and sat up, and then a spearman, taking a few steps in advance, threw his assegai. The thrower is generally charged, but the animal's attention is immediately taken off by a second spearman and second assegai, and so on until, poor beast, it is killed. Accidents seldom occur in fairly open ground, as the men support one another very coolly and effectively. In rocky places the sport is dangerous; sometimes, however, even in favourable spots, the man is pressed closely by the beast, and he then as he runs plants the stick with the plume firmly in the ground and dodges away from it; the lion, half-blinded by rage, sees something before him, and springs at the ostrich feathers, giving the man a chance of escape. In Livingstone's case they had lost the lion after wounding it, and were looking for it; the dear old Doctor caught sight of its tail switching backwards and forwards.

Up and off went a gun that would hardly have killed a strong tomtit. Livingstone was spun over eight or ten feet, and the lion was standing over him. The brute took his arm in its mouth and put a heavy paw on the nape of his neck, from which he pushed it off, for, as he said, 'It was so heavy, man, and I don't like to be stamped on'—neither did he! The lion was then driven off and killed. Livingstone was so quiet and imperturbable that he would have made a capital sportsman, but he could neither shoot nor ride (except on oxback)—this was not his business. I am afraid he despised the *rôle* of a sportsman, and no doubt believed, as he has stated, that the Kafirs looked upon us as weaklings to be used for providing them food. Perhaps he was right; but I think he overlooked that we, with no knowledge of the language, would have found it very difficult to make our way, if we had only come to see the country, without shooting. He could talk to the Kafirs' ears and hearts, we only to their stomachs; and I would fain believe that his grand work was occasionally made a little smoother by the guns.

An incident highly creditable to Kafir womanhood occurred just as we reached Mabotsé. The women, as is their custom, were working in the fields—for they hoe, and the men sew—and a young man, standing by the edge of the bush, was chatting with them. A lioness sprang on him and was carrying him off, when one of the women ran after her, and, catching her by the tail, was dragged for some little distance. Hampered with the man in her mouth and the woman behind her, she slackened her pace, whereupon her assailant straddled over her back and hit her across the nose and head with a heavy short-handled hoe till she dropped her prey and slunk into cover. This man was her husband! Would Mrs. Smith do as much for Mr. Smith? Could she do more?

We pushed on from Livingstone's station and hunted through the country of the Ba-Katla, the people amongst whom he was living. It was then full of game, and put me in mind of the children's pictures of Adam naming the beasts in the Garden of Eden—more animals than bushes. The first giraffes fell here, Murray again scoring, and killing No. 1. We seldom shot these beautiful-eyed, gentle-looking creatures—only a cow as a dainty now and then, for the flesh of the female is the most excellent eating, a kind of venisony beef. They were to be seen nearly every day in herds of from five to thirty. Shooting them on foot was a difficult matter, their great height giving them an extended view. I never stalked but two—a delicate head peering over a mimosa-tree nearly always detecting the coming danger before I could get within reasonable distance with my smooth-bore. There is no difficulty in riding them down (as we had, of course, sometimes to do for the men when other game was scarce) provided you are a light weight and a fair rider, for a horse requires more driving up to this animal than to any other. The towering height and the ungainly sawing motion appear to terrify him; and to these must, I think, be added the scent. Horses have very sensitive noses, and try to avoid giraffes, as in India they do camels. A good-couraged beast soon conquers his fears, but I have had regular fights with faint-hearted ones. Get as good a start as possible, press your game as much as you can for 300 or 400 yards—for press them you must, or you may ride after their tails all day—and you are alongside; a shot in the gallop with the gun across the pommel brings the poor thing to the ground, and you are ashamed of yourself if it has been done wantonly. Eland hunting, from horseback, may be classed with giraffe, as very tame after the novelty is over.

I would utter two words of warning with regard to hunting the giraffe. Do not ride close behind him, for in his panic he sometimes lashes out most vigorously—I have had his heels whiz very ominously within a few inches of my head; and my friend Vardon, in pistolling one that was standing wounded, only just missed what might have been serious injury from a vicious stamp of the forefoot—and be careful after you have fired to slacken speed at once, or pull your horse to the right, lest your victim fall on you.

I have measured bulls quite 18 feet—6 feet of leg, 6 feet of body, 6 feet of neck. For their peculiarity of shape, shared by other African animals, there must be a reason. Now we can understand that 'a deer with a neck that was longer by half than the rest of his family—try not to laugh—by stretching and stretching became a giraffe,' to the detriment of his hind-quarters. But what about the sasaybye, hartebeest, and elephant—why are they so low behind? The lion, too, is weak-quartered in comparison with his forehand, and even the hyæna has thought it necessary to follow the fashion. The animals of South Africa, indeed, are a queer lot—all countries have their specialities, but Africa is all speciality—distinct are the giraffes, the gnus, the hippos; adapted *plus æquo* are the elephants, rhinoceroses and antelopes.

Buffaloes were abundant, the bravest and most determined of all animals when wounded and at bay; courage is the instinct of the buffalo family. Look at the wild cousin in India, who will charge home upon a line of elephants, and even at his tame relations in the same country. In Collegal, an outlying talook of the district of Coimbatoor, in the Madras Presidency, I have seen the village buffaloes drive a full-grown tiger helter-skelter up the hills, pursuing him far beyond their feeding grounds. Again, I have known a misguided tiger spring into the midst of a herd penned up for the night; he was stamped and gored to death, and when taken out from amongst the half-maddened beasts in the morning he was a pulp. The *Bubalus caffer* is a stirring fellow when his blood is up; you may shoot a dozen on a flat or in open ground, taking your own distance for dismounting and shooting, and think them oxen; but wound one in thickish bush and follow him, and if alive he'll let you know it! The Kafirs will hunt a blood spoor of elephant, lion, rhinoceros, or any other animal right ahead of you like hounds; but put them upon wounded buffalo tracks, they will *follow* you at a respectful distance; they know the ways of him and his character. Wounded in bush he runs straight on for some little distance, then turns back and takes a line close to and parallel with his up-tracks, lying down or concealing himself behind a patch of cover. With his eyes on the ground the sportsman is picking out the trail, when a hard grunting bellow to right or left makes him look up, and he had better beware and hold straight now if ever, for down comes the wounded bull, and nothing but death or a disabling shot will stop him. I have seen one with entirely paralysed hind-quarters attempt to carry out his rush to the bitter end by dragging himself along with his forefeet. His pluck is splendid; no single lion will face him, though, attacked by stealth or numbers, he occasionally falls a prey. Once I went out in one direction and Murray in another to shoot elands for fat to make candles—we carried wicks and tin moulds amongst our stores. I turned homewards early to throw off my load, and within a mile or two of the waggons put up six lions on a flat surrounded by bush; in riding after them for a shot I drove up a couple more, so I had a 'flock' of eight before me. Pressing them, the hindmost, a fine black-maned fellow, who seemed willing to sacrifice himself for his friends and relations, turned on me, thus giving the others time to continue their retreat. Twice I dismounted to shoot him, but before I could get the chance I wanted, I was obliged to remount, for the whole of his companions, seeing their rearguard cut off and in difficulties, bore down upon me. One was all very well, but I felt I was not the man for the eight; they were not very far from bush when I first saw them, and before I could get upon anything I thought equal terms they reached cover without a shot.

I found Murray already in camp. He had come upon an ostrich's nest, and making his after-rider take off his trousers and tie up the bottoms, he had carefully packed the eggs in them, put them across a horse, and, with heart set on omelet, had returned to the cookery pots. Unfortunately, he had not broken an egg, but taken them in faith, and they all contained young birds, which the Kafirs were joyfully stirring round in our big baking-pot preparatory to a feast when I appeared on the scene. My readers may naturally say, 'What has eland fat and ostrich eggs to do with the courage of buffaloes?' Well, these are just the incidents of daily camp life, which have brought up another recollection illustrative of my point.

Death of Superior

J. Wolf

That night, half a mile from the waggons, from dark to dawn a fight was going on. The air rang again and again with the short snapping bark of attacking lions and the grunting snorts of buffaloes on the defensive; and, as soon as it was day, we went to the field of battle. None of the combatants were to be seen, but the whole story was clearly told by the trampled ground. A herd of 40 or 50 buffaloes had evidently been attacked by a number of lions—the Kafirs said nine, from the spoor—but the ground was so torn and trampled I could not pretend to count. They had taken up a position in front of a very dense patch of thorns, on a curve, and shifted backwards and forwards as their flanks were threatened; the bulls and cows had come to the front, the calves had been placed in the rear, and they had held their own throughout the night without the loss of a single calf! The lions I had seen in the afternoon were probably the baffled marauders.

We had been unsuccessful up to this time in killing buffaloes handsomely. More than half those hit got away—chiefly, I think, from our not having as yet adopted the squatting position; but this may be a fad of mine, and our bad shooting have been the cause. Two days after leaving the camping ground I have just spoken of, whilst the waggons were moving slowly through the low bush, three bulls crossed the line of march. I was on my horse, Superior, and, with a shout to Murray that I intended to make sure of a bag this time, galloped after them, and singling out one, got alongside of him within five feet and fired. He pitched upon his head and lay perfectly still. Making sure he was dead, I would not give him the second barrel, and turned the horse to ride after the two others which were still in view; but, before I could get my animal into his stride, the wounded beast sprang up and struck him heavily. I felt the thud, but the horse did not fall, and cantered on for twenty yards, when the whisk of his tail dabbled my trousers with blood, and, on getting off, I found a hole thirty inches deep, and nearly wide enough to get into, in his flank, for the horn had been driven up to the base. The bull was too weak to follow up the attack, and died where he stood; the horse crawled on for a few yards, and then, seeing it was a hopeless case, I put a ball through his head.

This lesson early in shooting experiences made me cautious in buffalo-hunting throughout the whole of my time, though I have had a narrow escape or two. Coming homewards one afternoon, we stumbled into the middle of a herd asleep in the long grass. Our sudden appearance startled them from their dreams, a panic seized them, and away they galloped in the wildest confusion. One old patriarch had been taking his siesta apart from the rest, in a dense patch of bush to the right: the sound of the gun and the rush of his companions roused him, and with one barrel loaded, as I ran after his relations, I found myself face to face with him, within ten yards. He was evidently bent on mischief. We stared at one another for a second. I fired at his broad chest; it was the best I could do, for his nose was up, and the points of his shoulders were not exposed. He plunged at me instantly. I fortunately caught a projecting bough of the mimosa-tree under which I was standing, and, drawing my knees up to my chin, he passed below me. I have heard of people avoiding a charge by quickly stepping on one side, but the ground must have been in their favour, and they must have been very cool, and only resorted to this instinctively, I think, as a last resource. A buffalo, it is true, drops his head very low, but only just before he closes, and he can strike desperately right and left from the straight line, so you ought to secure four or five feet side room. I have never been obliged to try this lateral movement, and fear I should have made a mess of it, though I know it is possible; for I once travelled down the west coast of South America with a bull-fighting man and woman, and they explained to me how, when the 'toro' charged, they stepped aside and stuck the banderillos into his neck; but they had no bush or smoke to contend with. I have often, however, had to dodge animals round a tree, and once escaped from a borili by catching a bough, as in this instance.

On our first journey to Lake 'Ngami, when within a hundred miles, the oxen wearied, so we selected twelve of the freshest and started with my waggon only, and some of the men, leaving the rest to encamp themselves and await our return. During our absence the drivers had to supply the party with meat. One of them wounded a buffalo, which immediately charged. The man, dropping his musket, climbed a tree just in time. For four hours the buffalo watched that tree, walking round and lying down under it. How Piet got to *terra firma* again I do not remember. Probably the animal grew tired of waiting, though they are generally very patient, and willing to bide their time for retaliation. The following short story illustrates the vengeful nature of the beast; it is told, I think, in Moffat's 'Missionary Travels,' but I have not the book by me, and cannot vouch for the exact words: A native, sitting by the water at night, wounded a buffalo, but not mortally. It made for the shooter, who ran and lay down under a projecting rock. Unable to get its horns to bear, but not to be baulked, with its long, rough tongue it licked off the flesh of the exposed part of the man's thigh down to the bone, and then left its victim, who died early in the morning.

The smell of blood seems to madden these beasts; they will turn on a wounded and bleeding companion and gore him most savagely. As I write recollections come back of scenes that had left no vivid pictures in my mind, because nothing untoward happened; but why not, and how not, now one thinks of it, is wonderful. Stalking an antelope, or I know not what, I found myself in an immense herd of buffaloes. The bush was full of them, I was surrounded, and had nothing to do but stand still. They dashed about me like rooks after the wireworms in a newly ploughed field. I had the sensation of drawing myself in very tightly about the waistband. Till they thinned out into a tail I could not begin to shoot, but there were such numbers that even then I knocked over six at exceedingly close quarters. The danger was, being run over or butted down in the headlong stampede. The same thing has happened to me, and, I dare say, to many all-round shots, with elephants. How they avoided or missed you—for they didn't seem to try to avoid—you can't tell. You come out of it without a scratch, and therefore, as a rule, think no more of it.

If I were to write our daily life and shooting, it would be weary reading. In a few chapters of this kind, all I can do is to take my readers into some of my scrapes, and let them fill in the blanks; but perhaps, once for all, I may put the abundance of the game in those days in some way intelligibly before them, if I say that in most parts, with horses, one gun could easily have kept 800 men—600 we tried—

fattened, and supplied with a store sufficient to last for months. Fortunately, in consequence of the excessive dryness of the climate, meat, cut into long thin strips and hung over the bushes to dry in the sun, will keep quite good for a long time. It needs soaking before cooking, and loses much of its flavour, but it holds body and soul together.

Leaving the valley and rocky hills of the Ba-Katla, we moved slowly onwards towards the Ba-Wangketsi; before reaching them, an event occurred which coloured my whole African life, and will colour my life as long as I live. It is no story of big game, and perhaps ought not to find a place in these pages; but it is so bound up with all my shooting, all my pleasure in Africa, that I would ask to be forgiven for telling it. I should feel a traitor to the memory of a dead friend if I did not.

We were trekking through some low sand-hills covered with scrub, when three lions crossed about fifty yards ahead of the oxen. Snatching up a gun, I jumped from the waggon, calling upon someone to follow me with a heavy rifle which was always kept loaded as a reserve battery. I pressed so closely on the leisurely retreating trio that the largest stopped short. I squatted, intending to take his shoulder as he turned, looked round for my second gun, and heard the bearer, who was close to me, whisper in Dutch, 'You can get nearer by the ant-hill.' The move lost me the lion, as he broke away after his companions; and then for the first time I took notice of the cool, tall, handsome lad who had offered me advice, and recognised in him at once the stuff to make a henchman of. From that day forth he was my right-hand man in the field, and never failed me.

John Thomas was an Africander, born at the Cape, of parents probably slaves; but as a grand specimen of manhood, good nature, faithfulness, and cheerful endurance, I never met his equal, white or black. Plucky to a fault, he was the least quarrelsome of men, the life and light of our camp fires, and the pet of the Kafirs, who seemed at once to understand his quiet unpretending nature, and always made their requests to me through 'bono Johnny.' To tell his good deeds through a five years' wandering would very often be to show up my own faults; let it be enough to say that he was a perfect servant to a very imperfect master, who, now that his friend is dead, feels that he did not value him half enough, though he never loved man better. His worth, to those who know the troubles and difficulties of African travelling, may be outlined by the following little story.

When Livingstone and I made our journey in search of Lake 'Ngami, we held out to our followers that if we were successful we would not attempt to press on further. They were, as a rule, a timid folk, dreading the unknown, too ready to listen to any tale of danger and difficulty that might be in the world beyond, and always eager to turn colony-wards. After some hard work we reached the lake, and success bred in us the wish to do more; but we were bound to stand to our agreement. At last the desire of penetrating deeper into the land became so strong that I suggested calling a meeting of the servants and trying what our eloquence might effect. After putting before them that we fully recognised our promise of not constraining them to go with us any further, I told them that the Doctor and I had made up our minds to give them one of the waggons with sufficient stores, supplies and ammunition for their homeward journey, while we ourselves had decided to push on ahead. I further explained to them that they would have no difficulty in reaching the colony, as they knew the waters, and had the wheel-tracks. I paused for a minute, and then added, that though we could not ask them to accompany us, yet that if any one of them was willing to do so, we should be very glad. I rather enlarged upon our ignorance of the country in advance, for we did not wish to influence them unduly to join us. For a few moments there was silence, and blankness of face; then out stepped John, and speaking in Dutch, as he always did when his feelings were touched, though he at other times spoke English perfectly, said: 'What you eat I can eat, where you sleep I can sleep, where you go I will go; I will come with you.' The effect was instantaneous. 'We will all go!' was the cry. Do you think after that it was much matter to us whether our brother was black or white?

Time wore on. I was obliged to return to England. John accompanied me to the Cape. I told him, in part, how I valued his services, and asked him if I could in any way repay my debt of gratitude. I had taught him to read, in the bush, but that was the only good I had ever done him. His answer came, after some hesitation. He had heard so much of England that he should like, of all things, to go with me there. Two days later we were on board ship together. He, as usual, was everything to everybody—helping the steward, attending the sick ladies, nursing the babies; the idol of the sailors, to whom he told stories of bush life, the adored of the nurses. John, with all his virtues, was a flirt—the admirer and admired of all womankind. On arriving in England, I left him in London and went down to my brother's. He hesitated about my henchman, thinking a real live black man would hardly suit the household of a country clergyman. But his coachman fell sick. Could John drive? I should think so. He was the best eight-in-hander in Cape Town. Down he came, and in half an hour he was perfectly established in the family. My brother declared he never had such a coachman, and was very kind to him, timidly at first. The cook taught him writing; the lady's-maid went on with his reading. I shall not forget meeting him with the two women, one on either arm, chatting with them in the most accomplished style. His stay in England was limited to six months, as we had agreed, and he went back to the Cape with a friend of mine, who wrote most highly of him.

Two years passed away; I was a wanderer again; and at the beginning of the Crimean War found myself carrying secret-service money to Colonel, now Field Marshal, Sir Lintorn Simmons, political agent at Shumla. On my return to the coast I fell in with a cavalry regiment and the 60th Rifles encamped near Devna, a few miles from Varna. A sergeant of the latter regiment saluted as I passed, and asked for news from the front. Silistria was then besieged. I turned myself half round to the right on my saddle to talk with him, and presently felt a hand placed very *gently, lovingly,* on my left foot. John stood by my stirrup, his face a picture of affectionate triumph at having caught me again. He had taken service with an officer of the 60th. We threw ourselves down under a bush and renewed old memories. The Major, near whose tent we were, called John, and, finding from him who I was, most courteously entreated me, telling me how beloved John was by the regiment, and how well, through him, they knew my name. I had letters to deliver at Constantinople, and went on. John, I believe, sickened, and was invalided to England; but for two or three years I heard no more of him, for I was away in South America and elsewhere. Shortly after my return home a letter came to me, asking if I could recommend a black man named 'John Thomas' as a butler! He had referred the writer to me. I was obliged to say I knew nothing of his capabilities in this line, but added that, as a staunch ally in a fight with an elephant and an absolutely trustworthy man in all the relations of life (save that of a butler, in which I had not tried him), I could most highly recommend him. My friend engaged him, and had an excellent servant, for such was John's power of adapting himself to circumstances that nothing ever came amiss to him. But the dark day was coming on; and, in the midst of his affectionate service, beloved from the head of the house to the youngest child, trusted and never found wanting, always ready and always willing, this fine, noble fellow died. I heard of his sickness too late to see him alive on earth, but I trust that master and man may hereafter meet as brothers in Heaven.

We had been shooting in this Ba-Wangketsi country for a fortnight, and the work had been very hard. One morning after breakfast, my companion, who was busy cleaning the head of a koodoo, said he would have a day of rest, and finish what he was about. His laziness was catching. I ordered my horses to be unsaddled, and was idling about the camp when our head man told me there was no food for the twelve or fourteen dogs, our night watchmen; so I took up my gun, which was only loaded in one barrel, and strolled out on the chance of a shot; but as, kill or miss, I intended to return immediately, I did not carry any spare ammunition. A reedy pond lay close in advance of the waggons in a little opening; beyond this, as on every other side, stretched a sea of bush and mimosa-trees. Two hundred yards from the outspan I came upon a clump of quagga and wounded one, which though mortally hit struggled on before falling. I followed, and marking the place where it fell, set my face as I thought towards the waggons, meaning to send out men for the flesh. No doubt of the direction crossed my mind—the pool was certainly not more that 400 yards in a straight line, and I thought I could walk down upon it without any trouble; so taking no notice of my out tracks, which had bent slightly in following the quagga, I started. It was now about 10 A.M.; little did I think that 5 P.M. would still find me seeking three vans nearly as large as Pickford's, and half an acre of water.

In my first cast I cannot say whether I got wide or stopped short of the mark I was making for, and it was not until I had wandered about carelessly hither and thither for half an hour, feeling sure that it was only the one particular bush in front of me which hid the waggons, that I very unwillingly owned to myself that I was drifting without bearings in this bushy sea. The sun was nearly overhead, and gave but slight help as to direction, and the constant turning to avoid thick patches of thorns rendered it nearly impossible, in the absence of any guiding point, to hold a fixed course through this maze of sameness.

I tried walking in circles in the hopes of cutting the wheel tracks, but though on a previous occasion this plan had succeeded, it now failed. As with empty gun I plodded on, occasional small herds of rooyebuck and blue wildebeest, evidently very much at home, swept and capered by me, and, stopping and looking at me with wondering eyes, increased my feeling of loneliness. I had no doubts of regaining my party next day at latest, and cared but little for passing a night in the jungle; but, bewildered and baffled, I envied the instinct of the so-called brutes, which, careless of their steps, were nevertheless quite sure of their ways. Twilight near the tropics is very short. Just before the sun set, therefore, I followed a game track which I knew would lead to water, as it was still early in the season, and the rain supply had not yet dried up in the hollows. At dusk I reached a pool similar to the one I had quitted in the morning. After a good draught I began collecting firewood, but for once it was very scarce, and the night closed in so rapidly, that a bare hour's supply was all my store. Partly to save fuel, and partly in the hope that as the night crept on signals would be made from the waggons, I climbed a tree which stood by the side of the water, and had not been long perched before I heard, though so far off that I could hardly catch the sound, the smothered boom of guns. Alarmed at my absence my companions suspected the cause, and were inviting my return: but it required a very pressing invitation indeed to induce a man to walk through two miles of an African wood in those days on a dark night.

This particular spot, too, was more infested with lions than any other, save one, I was ever in; and, though harmless and cowardly enough as a rule in the day, they were not likely to prove very acceptable followers at night. But I had been walking all day under a tropical sun, my clothing was wet with perspiration, and it now froze hard—for freeze it can in Southern Africa—and I was bitterly cold. I determined to come down and light my fire. I knew it would last but a short time, but thought I would make the best of it, and thaw myself before attempting to return. I got to the lowest bough of my tree, and had placed my hand beside my feet before jumping off, when from the bush immediately under me a deep note, and the sound of a heavy body slipping through the thorny scrub, told me that a lion was passing. Whether the creaking of the tree had roused his attention and caused him to speak so opportunely I don't know, but without the warning, in another half-second I should have alighted on his back. I very quickly put two or three yards more between the soles of my feet and the ground. Presently, from the upper end of the pool came the moaning pant of a questing lion; it was immediately answered from the lower end—their majesties were on the look-out for supper, and had divided the approaches to the water between them. It was much too dark to see anything, but from the sounds they seemed to walk in beats, occasionally telling one another of their whereabouts by a low pant; of my presence I think they were not aware.

This went on for an hour or more, and I got colder and colder; my beard and moustache were stiff with frost. I could not much longer endure the cramped position in my scraggy tree, and I felt I must get down and light a fire, when, suddenly up came the blessed moon, and right under her the sound of three or four muskets fired together. With the help of her light and partial direction in case my companions got tired of firing, I was not going to stay up a tree to be frozen. Waiting, therefore, until she was about 'one tree high,' and until the lions were far asunder, on their separate beats, as well as I could make out from the sound, I came down, and capping—it was all I could do; for, as I said, I had started without powder and ball—my empty gun, which was standing against the tree, I passed at the double round the end of the water and dived into the bush on the opposite side. I have no doubt my desire was to get on as quickly as possible, but reasons for a cautious advance soon made themselves heard on all sides. An African forest was then alive at night. I only thought of the lions, and especially of the two I had left, or perhaps not left, at the water; but every little nocturnal animal that stirred kept me on the stretch—the less noise the more danger. The movement of a mouse might well be mistaken for the stealthy tread of the king of the cats. Among the trees the moon gave but scanty light, and nearly every minute I had to stop and listen as some un-seen animals passed near me. Sometimes I could recognise them by their cry, but mostly it was 'a running that could not be seen of skipping beasts' that troubled me. The only animal I really saw that night was a rhinoceros that, with head and tail up and in a terrible fuss, crossed a few yards before me. A sound in front, and I strained my eyes into the shadowy darkness in advance; the rustling of a leaf told of life to the right or left; and the snapping of a twig of possible death in the rear. But I struggled on for an hour, I should think, when, stooping to clear a low bough, four or five muskets fired together within fifty yards told me I was at home again. I hope I was thankful then; I know I am now. Two of my Hottentot servants and a batch of Kafirs had come some distance into the bush in the hope of meeting me, and escorted me to the fire in triumph. As I held my still only half-thawed hands over it, the baulked roar of a disappointed lion rang through the camp. He had not been heard before that night. 'He has missed you, Tlaga,[2] by a little this time,' said my black friends. 'Let him go back to his game.' They were right, for in the morning we found his spoor on mine for a long way back. Whether he had come with me from the water or I had picked up a follower in the bush I never knew. My constantly stopping and listening probably saved me, for a lion seldom makes up his mind very suddenly to attack a man unless hard pressed by hunger. He likes to know all about it first, and my turning, and slow, jerky progress had probably roused his suspicions.

Two nights before this we had met with a sad misfortune. The oxen were 'kraaled'—surrounded, that is, by a hedge of thorn-trees, and bushes strong enough to keep them in and lions out, we hoped—a mode of defence we always adopted if there was wood enough close to the outspan, or we intended staying any length of time in the same place; though occasionally, when we only halted for the night and were distant from water, and therefore likely to be free from lions, the oxen were instead made fast to the leathern rope, or 'trek tow,' by which they draw the waggon, each pair—there were five to each waggon—to their own yoke in the order they worked in the team, so that they were ready and in right position for inspanning in the morning. We were lying on this occasion by a large Wangket-si village, and the cattle had been kraaled rather to prevent them getting mixed with those of the Wangketsi, as they were taken out to graze at sunrise, than from any apprehension of an attack. The three waggons were drawn up as usual on one

---

[2] To my face the Kafirs always called me 'Tlaga,' which, I believe, means 'on the look-out,' wary, like game; behind my back, I have been told, I was called 'Bones,' from my leanness.

side of the enclosure, and the Kafirs were by their fires on the other. I was asleep, but was roused by shouts, the discharge of a musket, and the sudden rush of our pack of dogs. I found a lion had sprung over a weak place in the thorn fence on to the back of an ox, and, scared by the shouting, had jumped back again the same way. According to tradition I know the ox ought to have been in his mouth, but it wasn't. A lion will drag an ox by the nape of its neck anywhere, but he can't carry it, much less jump a 6-foot hedge with it in his jaws. It was quite dark, but by the gleam of the fires the men, aroused by the panic of the oxen, caught sight of him, and one of the Hottentot drivers had taken a flying shot. The dogs pressed hard upon him; directly he gained the cover he stood to bay. I suppose the poor things got hampered in the bush, for presently two crawled up to us mangled and dying. The hubbub went on for some minutes, and then the lion, frightened probably by the firing and yelling—we could give no other aid to our allies—broke bay, and ten dogs returned exclusive of the two that had come in to die; two were still missing—one of them a brindled bull terrier, which we all knew must one day come to grief, for he was a most reckless, determined brute, game to go in to anything. A few days before, feeling offended at a puff adder—the worst of the Cape snakes—hissing at him, he had seized it, and notwithstanding the snake striking him on the head with its fangs, had stuck to and killed it. His head swelled to an immense size, but he pulled through and recovered. With day we went to the place where the scrimmage of the night before had occurred, and there lay 'Tod,' as the Hottentots had named him, with the other absentee, both dead. 'Tod' had apparently run straight into the lion's mouth, for the marks of the teeth were visible enough over his back and loins. He was a rash fellow, but he died an honourable death. The loss of dogs was a very serious one, for it was through their fidelity and watchfulness we were able to sleep in comparative ease and safety. At the first sound or smell of danger they went to the fore, and walked barking round and round with the lions, just keeping clear of their spring or sudden rush, showing them they were detected and that the camp was not all asleep. In the times I am writing of I don't think it would have been possible, save with a large number of armed watchers and fires, to have kept your oxen in anything like safety without dogs. You went to sleep in peace as soon as the dog-watch was set and the fires made up for the night. Firewood was abundant after passing the Molopo. A store of huge logs was collected directly the waggons halted, and the blaze was kept up throughout the night, the fires being shaken together and replenished by anyone who chanced to wake; and as their own safety depended on it, the men were zealous in this part of their duty.

By this time we had shot most of the kinds of game to be found away from the rivers, in large numbers—Harris's black buck potoquan (*Aigoceros niger*), and the beautiful hill zebra (*Equus montanus*) excepted. The former I only saw once during my five years in Africa, and never got a chance at, and the latter I would not have shot if I could—he is such a pretty, tiny, thoroughbred-looking thing, the size of a small Shetland pony, and the most playful little fellow imaginable, springing about the rocky hill-tops with the surefootedness of an ibex. We had not yet fallen in with elephants or even seen their tracks. Three years after the time of which I am writing I killed them frequently to the south, but now they were away to pastures new for the time, and we decided on going on north to the Ba-Mungwato country in the hope of finding them.

A Night Attack—Lupapi

On our way we halted at a small spring at the bottom of a slight depression. It looked as if the water had once been much larger, and might have occupied the best part of the area. There was a trickling overflow, which, after running a few yards, tumbled into a hole and disappeared; hence its name 'Lupapi,' or the 'Mouse.' This was the very worst place for lions I ever knew; not so much from their number as their insolent audacity. I stopped here on three separate occasions, and each time was molested more than sufficiently. On this, the first, we had made, luckily, a very strong kraal. The fires would not burn brightly, as there was a misty rain falling. At 10 P.M. or half-past we had only just turned in when we were attacked in force by two lions and a lioness. Our vedettes, the dogs, were driven in, and the enemy charged down upon the cattle enclosure. The noise, of course, woke us all, and dogs, Kafirs, Hottentots, Murray and myself had our work fully cut out; our assailants kept just outside the firelight, making savage rushes at the dogs, but never giving us the chance of a shot. I stood for a long time in very scant attire (someone brought me a jacket and trousers later on), my first entrance to the scene being anything but noble, for on running from the waggon to the front my foot caught in a creeper, and I fell heavily. The Kafirs behaved admirably, never yielding an inch, though the lions were very determined. After half an hour or so we nursed the fires into brighter glow, and increased the circle of light around us, and things grew rather calmer. We could hear every breath and angry purr, though as we were looking into the dark we could see nothing. For some time I made a Kafir stand beside me and throw brands into the darkness, hoping by a gleam to get sufficient indication of the whereabouts of our foes for a shot—but in vain. I fired frequently as near as I could guess on the spot where the purring seemed to come from, and could hear the angry beast make a dash at the pinging ball. But I struck nothing save the ground. However, we had checked the onset, and now had only to keep on the alert. Just before the day broke the siege was raised, and I was on horseback to look out a better camping-ground for the next night. As I cleared the low jungle which lay around us, a lioness broke away from the edge of it and took across an opening beyond. She was eighty yards from me, rather too long a shot for the old Purdey; but there was cover ahead from which I could not cut her off, and I was savage enough at her unwished-for attentions during the night, for she was, no doubt, one of the three, and oh! how glad I was when I heard the ball thud, and saw her stride short. I mounted and rode her to a standstill in a couple of hundred yards, when she squatted in front of a bush. I got within twenty or twenty-five yards of her, intending to dismount, but found I had fired all my loose balls away during the night, and that the one in the barrel was all I had to rely on. I have a weakness for a second bullet, and backing my pony a little further off I told my after-rider to go to the waggon and bring me a fresh supply. He was only absent a few minutes, I keeping watch on the lioness meanwhile. On his return I loaded the empty barrel, and, getting off for a steady shot, found to my dismay that, although I could see her well enough whilst sitting on my horse, the long grass hid her entirely when on my feet. I could not remount, for the after-rider had removed the horse, and it is not probable the lioness would have allowed me to do so without interference. For a moment I was in a fix, but about ten yards to my left I saw a dead mimosa-tree with a fork in it five feet from the ground. It appeared my only chance, though a risky one; and I wonder to this day that the beast did not charge when she saw the scrub moving as I passed through it. She did not, however, and I gained my fork and could now see her quite plainly, and she me likewise, for she never took her eyes off for one second. Her head was full front. I aimed between her eyes, but a twig must have turned the ball, for I was firing from a rest, and it only bored a clean hole through her ear. She struck it angrily with her paw, and then faced me again. The second shot was more successful, and she dropped dead. I had hit her the first time very far aft, but I think she must have been more crippled than I had supposed, or she would never have allowed me to move about so clumsily without attempting a diversion.

The second attack, a year afterwards, was not so prolonged, but the lions pressed the men so hard that they had to take refuge between the fires and the hedge of the kraal, and the beasts twice crossed the line of firelight in pursuit. The third imbroglio at this water was more serious, but the initiative this time was with me. John, my after-rider, woke me very early one morning to tell me a lioness and her cub were drinking at the spring, from which we were lying only 200 yards distant. Ordering him to saddle two horses—they had not yet been loosed from the waggon-wheels to which we always made them fast in pairs—I slipped on my clothes and, jumping on the back of one of them, galloped towards the spring, followed by John, half a dozen Kafirs, and the dogs, hoping to cut off mother and child from the thick bush behind them. But they beat me; and the dogs, taking the scent, followed them. The Kafirs had come with me, partly to see the fun and partly, in case of my shooting the lioness, to catch the cub, which, when it is quite young, they manage to do by chasing and dodging it, and throwing their short skin carosses over it. They then roll it up like a baby in swaddling clothes, with only its head out at one end and its tail at the other; round the bundle they wind a leathern riem or strap, and pass the snarling though now harmless little beast from one to another, saying pretty things of its father and mother, aunts and uncles, &c.

Post equitem sedet "fulva" cura' — The Lioness does the scansion

The dogs very soon brought the lioness to bay, and I got within thirty yards, but from the thickness of the bush could neither see them nor her. I shifted my position once or twice in the hope of making out what was going on, standing up in my stirrups looking for an opening, that I might dismount and get a shot. Suddenly the barking of the dogs and snapping snarl of the lioness ceased, and I thought she had broken bay and gone on, but in a second I heard a roar on the horse's right quarter, in a different direction from that into which I had been peering, and, looking round, saw her with her mouth open, clearing a rather high patch of bush twenty yards from me. There was no time to get off the horse, and no possibility of a shot from his back, for the charge was on his *right* flank, and you cannot shoot to the right. I did the only thing that I could—jammed the spurs in and tried to make a gallop of it; but my follower was too close, and before I could get up full speed I heard her strike the ground heavily twice in her bound, and with the third she sat up behind me. She jumped short, however, and failed to get hold with her mouth, but drove her front claws well into the horse's quarters, and a hind foot underneath him, and so clung, but only for a moment; for the poor beast, maddened by fright and pain, and unable to stand up under the extra weight, became unmanageable, threw his head up, and swerved under the projecting bough of a tree which, striking me on the chest, swept me from the saddle against the lioness, and we rolled to the ground together. A sharp rap on the head, from my having fallen on a stump, stunned me for a minute or two, and I woke to life to find John kneeling alongside of me, asking me if I was dead, which was a needless question, seeing I was at the time sitting up rubbing my eyes. 'What's the matter?'I said, but at the same instant I heard the dogs again baying fifty yards off, and recollection came back. Rising to my feet, I staggered like a drunken man, rather than walked towards the sound, and propped myself up against a tree, for I was still weak and dazed; indistinctly I could occasionally see both dogs and lioness. Presently, something broke through the thinner part of the bush, and I fired and wounded one of the dogs. And the lioness, tired by the protracted worrying, and startled perhaps by the sound of the gun, bounded off and escaped without a shot. I have been often asked by those who have seen the sketch, 'Oh, but why did you not turn round and shoot her from the saddle?' And all the answer I could or can give is, 'It's easy to say but difficult to do,' and that in a second we were on the ground together. The men told Livingstone that the dogs came out so close upon the lioness that she, rather flustered at being swept from the horse's back, turned to fight with them, and took no notice of me. We caught the horse four miles off, and I sewed up and cured his wounds, but he was never fit for anything again, bolting dangerously at a stump or other dark object. A hard spin after a straight-horned gemsbok killed him.

It was here at Lupapi that I first saw the wild dogs hunting. I had gone towards the water on the chance of a shot, late one afternoon, and as I got into the little flat in which the spring lay, an antelope broke through the bush on my right, panic-stricken and blown. Thirty yards behind it came the wild dogs; before it had gained the middle of the open space they ran into it, and though I was within 100 yards, they had torn it nearly to pieces when I got up. They then retired a short distance, sitting down and watching menacingly whilst I cut away part of the hind quarters, and the moment I turned my back swooped down on their prey, dismembering and putting it out of sight in an incredibly short time. They are ugly-looking brutes, more like jackals than dogs, with great endurance in running, and great grip of jaw. Three or four head the pack, holding the scent. As they tire, three or four others take their places, the pack running loosely after the leaders.

We reached the kraals of the Ba-Mungwato, but met with a surly reception. The chief wished to play the part of the great potentate, and declined seeing us, sending messengers for presents and specifying what they were to be. His envoys, however, returned empty-handed, with a reply that we were not in the habit of giving without expectation of some return; that if we could not see him we would go to the next tribe; that we had come to hunt elephants in his country, and to feed his people; but that if he did not wish us to do so, or would not help us in our hunting, neither would we send him any gift in anticipation, or on the chance of changing his mind, adding that we should mention his politeness to other white men, who would henceforth avoid him. So the day passed. Two or three lounging fellows of the tribe told my men yarns of Secomi's power and of the retaliation he took upon his enemies, mentioning *inter alia* that we were encamped, having been led to it by his orders, upon the very spot where last year he had disposed of a party of Matabili who had come on an embassage. Hottentots are open to swaggering stories, but in this instance their credulity was confirmed when shortly before sunset they rambled out in advance of the waggons, and found that we were in a *cul de sac*, the hills closing in round us 300 yards off and offering no passage through them, and, horror of horrors! on the ground lay a number of human skulls.

They came back in great fear, and told us the result of their explorations. We were not much disturbed, but I thought it wise to take precautions against surprise, and served out ammunition to the men, bidding them sleep with their muskets handy and take their cue from us. The night, however, passed quietly. About 7 in the morning news was brought me that the great man was approaching with a number of his warriors. I ordered the horses to be made fast to the waggon-wheels and the oxen to be tied, ready for inspanning, to the trek tow, and then allotted to each man his tree, intimating very clearly that, in the case of a disturbance, they were to follow, not set, an example, and that if anyone fired a shot before I did, I would shoot him.

Secomi came up with his spearmen, and sat down opposite me, fifteen feet from our fire, where we were taking our morning coffee. Livingstone had sent a very fine old Bechuana fighter with us as a kind of head man, a most dignified superior fellow, by name Syami (*Anglicè*, I believe, 'stand firm'), who had won great renown in many a fight, and once, when wounded badly and left for dead, on coming to had broken off the shafts of the assegais, and crawled three miles on hands and knees to a friendly village, with the irons still in him. This man we put up as our champion, and for an hour and a half did he argue in our interests, speaking with all the untrammelled fluency of uncivilised man. We understood but little of what he said, and that only by signs, not words; but he was evidently very eloquent. The chief at first would hardly listen to him, but was by degrees brought to treat upon the matter, making suggestions as to what presents would be likely to assuage his wrath; but we firmly refused to budge an inch from our original lines, until he should give us a guide to the next tribe, for after his conduct we told him we were determined not to shoot in his country. There was no active sign of hostility. The position Secomi had placed himself in with respect to the muzzle of my gun, which lay across my knees, exercised perhaps a calming influence; but he would not help us in any way, and steadily refused guides. We were wearied of the long discussion, and I called to the Hottentots to inspan the oxen and loose the horses; this operation was watched intently, without remark, by the chief and his followers. I then gave orders to turn the waggons, for I had the night before ascertained the direction of the Bakaa Hills. As the oxen slowly brought the heavy carts round and faced the other way, I gave the order to trek, and the faces of the Ba-Mungwato were a sight to see. Throughout the preliminary operations they had watched us eagerly, believing us ignorant of the trap into which we had been inveigled, and hoping that we should go further on into it. I do not think they would even then have attacked us, but their feelings would have been relieved by our disappointment and the success of their arrangements. The bird had, however, seen the snare and escaped out of the hand of the fowler. They stood stupefied and crestfallen, and the waggons moved on without a word or sign of opposition. I brought up the rear with the loose oxen and horses. We had gained 300 or 400 yards from the camping ground, which was still in sight, when I heard the sound of running behind me, and turning saw a man coming on at the top of his speed after us. He threw up his hands to show he was carrying no arms, and I grounded my gun and waited for him. 'What is it?' 'I am sent by the chief to take you wherever you like to go!' 'Lead on to the Bakaa then!' and thus ended our first and only difficulty with the natives.

On our arrival we found this people in a pitiable state; the crops had failed, and they were starving. The chief welcomed us warmly, asked what we had come for, and on receiving answer to hunt elephants, besought us to take his people and feed them, putting his country and his services at our disposal. On condition that *his* people during their stay with me were to be *my* people, I accepted 600 men, women, and children in the most terrible state of starvation. No white man, emaciated as these poor fellows were, could have walked ten yards—the two bones in the lower arm and leg were distinctly visible, and you could see them working in the joints and attachments; in truth, nearly the whole party were bones covered with skin, and poor skin too, for from poverty of blood you could hardly have found a sound patch large enough to lay a crown piece on. The chief introduced three of the head men to me, and bade me hold them responsible for the rest, and I did—and never had the very slightest trouble.

We started for the hunting grounds next morning, and were among the elephants in a day or two. There have been discussions as to who is king among the beasts, and to this day the lion is generally given the title. But look down that narrow game-track. A lion is coming up it from the water. As he turns the curve in the winding path he sees that a rhinoceros or buffalo is coming down to drink. He slinks into the bush, lies very low, gives them the road, lets them pass well by, and then resumes his interrupted way. If this is the king, he is exceedingly courteous to his subjects—one might even think just a little in awe of some of them. King of the cats in Africa he may be, and is; but king of the beasts he is not.

Come with me to a desert pool some clear moonlight night when the shadows are deep and sharply cut, and the moon herself, in the dry, cloudless air, looks like a ball. All is nearly as bright as day, only the light is silver, not gold. Sit down on that rock and watch the thirsty animals as they drink—buffalo, rhinoceros, antelope, quagga, and occasionally, if the water is large, lions too. But what has frightened the antelope and quagga that they throw their heads up for a second and fade away into the shadows? The other beasts, too, are listening, and now leave the sides of the pond. Nothing but the inevitable, irrepressible jackal, that *gamin* amongst wild things, remains in view. As yet your dull human ears have caught no sound, but very soon the heavy tread, and low, rumbling note of an oncoming herd of elephants reaches you. They are at the water. The jackals have sat down with their tails straight out behind them, but not another creature is to be seen.

The king drinks. Not a sound is heard. He squirts the water over his back, makes the whole pool muddy, and retires solemnly, leaving his subjects, who now gather round, to make the best of what he has fouled. This is the king in the opinion of the beasts. You may think him a nervous monarch, subject to panic, and I do not know that you are not right; but he has weight in the animal world, you may be assured.

This African elephant is an uncomely, ragged fellow, with his bad facial angle, huge ears, long forelegs, sliced off quarters, and generally untidy appearance; but he carries fine tusks, and often gives you a lot of trouble. I have ridden nearly twenty miles on his spoor before coming up with him, and liked him all the better for it. He is wanting in ready wit, but is a wise, thoughtful being in his ponderous way, and a great hand at combination. He wishes to feed on the top of a tree, finds it too strong for him alone, calls on a friend or two, and, with an all-together swing, they bring it to the ground. When at bay, he has a fancy for pushing down a tree on your head and charging through the branches. His friend tumbles into a pitfall—by the way, males very seldom do, for, fearing no other animal, they carry their trunks down; the sensitiveness of that organ warns them of the danger, and they will walk securely amongst a nest of these traps and neatly uncover them, throwing the reeds and grass into the air with scorn. The cows, however, are frequently taken, for, anxious about their calves—which are often attacked by lions—they carry their trunks in the air, feeling for a chance scent of the enemy. The Kafirs sometimes lie in wait by the water near to which the pits are dug, and after the elephants or other game have drunk, raise a shout, and in the hurry of the retreat the living graves reap their harvest.

These pitfalls are 10 feet long by about 9 deep and 4 wide at the top, narrowing as they deepen, so that a large beast gets jammed in them; they are made larger specially for elephants, and are most skilfully covered with reeds, grass, and a few handfuls of sand. I have ridden into them horse and all, and I have walked into them; in the first instance, I shook my feet out of the stirrups in time to prevent my legs being crushed, and managed to scramble out from the horse's back. In the second, walking on the high bank of the Zouga River, I was rating one of my drivers in the river-bed below for punishing his oxen, when I suddenly felt the ground give way beneath me, and amidst a shower of dust and broken reeds thought I could catch the sound of laughter from the waggon—let us hope I was mistaken. Luckily this one had no stake at the bottom, as many have. But we have left our elephant in the trap too long; let us return to him. His friends at first run off panic-stricken, but often come back affected by his piteous calls for help; and, swinging their heavy forefeet, strike the sandy soil with the front part, cutting away earth from the end or side of the pitfall, quicker than a navvy could with a spade, and at last successfully freeing their companion, who stamps all the débris of the broken-down sides beneath his feet, by helping him with their trunks up the rough kind of incline they have made. This occurred one night within 300 yards of our waggons; we, of course, did not see the operations, but we heard them being carried on, and the elephants talking to one another, and these were the inferences the Kafirs drew next morning from the foot-marks and appearances, and they assured me the case was not uncommon. If the wariness of these heavy animals among pitfalls is wonderful, not less to be admired is the way in which they manage to clamber up trackless heights, and come down by impossible-looking paths. A wall of rock 300 feet high is before me; immediately along the edge runs a shelf five or six feet wide, in places so precipitous that you could only slip down it, and even that at considerable risk, but over it, in Indian file, come eighteen or twenty elephants making their way to the jungle below. As they reach the sharp inclines they sit down, and thrusting their hind legs straight out under them, as far forward as they can, they 'go it,' as Albert Smith used to say of the Alpine tourist, and everyone comes safely to the bottom. They take readily to deep water, displacing so much that only the ridge of the back, and upper part of the head down to the eyes, show above the surface; they carry the trunk up and swim strongly. I have known them come to the opposite side of a river, and finding the bank too steep to climb, at once begin pounding it with their forefeet until they had established a firm resting-place for one gigantic rammer, and then starting from their fresh point of departure, go on making steps till the flight was complete—this was in India.

In elephant country we were always obliged to be very careful, for a single shot at night will sometimes drive a herd far away. Unlike the rhinoceros and buffalo, elephants seldom drink twice at the same place in a river. This is partly due to caution, though perhaps it may chiefly depend on their soon eating up a district, and having to seek new feeding grounds. With this object they frequently travel great distances—fifty miles or more—in a night. This will not appear so remarkable if it is considered that the bulls often stand fifteen miles from the water, and walk to and fro in the hot nights without missing, though during the colder season they are contented with alternate nights. In India, where vegetation is rank and the forests dense, elephants hold on to the same locale.

The ears of the African elephant are enormous—six feet in length, and broad in proportion, though I never measured the breadth. The lower end just touches the point for the side shot. I was once hunting these animals in the Ba-Quaina country, and had killed three, when a tiny dark wreath on the horizon warned us of a coming thunderstorm. A South African sky is for nine months quite free of cloud; for 300 out of the 365 days of the year the sun rises as glowing copper, and sets as flaming gold, without a framing of any sort. A happy thought struck me: I ordered the Kafirs to cut off an ear from one of the dead elephants, and, lying curled up beneath it, I escaped a wet jacket, though the rain came down in waterspouts, and I stood six feet. The scientists of the future may find occupation for some time to come in developing the cause of abnormal ears, sloping backs, thorns at the ends of lions' tails, and a number of other little peculiarities in beasts, birds, insects and fishes; but they ought not to delay, for many types are already on the wane.

The elephant's head is wonderfully constructed. If it were great masses of bone and muscle, the ligaments of the neck would need to be of extraordinary power to support it; but between the larger bones, and in all admissible parts of the skull, the spaces are filled in with a cellular, bony structure, fulfilling both requirements of strength and lightness.

I believe some people suppose the Carthaginians tamed and used the African elephant; they could hardly have had Mahouts Indian fashion, for there is no marked depression in the nape of the neck for a seat, and the hemming of the ears,[3] when erected, would have half-smothered them. My knowledge does not allow me to raise any argument on this point; but might not the same market have been open to the dwellers at Carthage as was afterwards to Mithridates, who, I suppose, drew his supply from India, where they have been broken and made to do man's work from time immemorial? *Vide* friezes, carvings, pictures, stories, myths innumerable—the last running back into obscurity—the elephant holding in them the position of the 'gin' in the Arab tales. Half the world has at one time been the *habitat* of this great pachyderm or its congeners. Siberia, with its fossil ivory mines, and Europe everywhere, are its tombs. Destroyed or driven south by some climatic change, India and Africa are its present homes; but in Africa the place thereof shall soon know it no more, and to our great-great-grandchildren the old 'tlou' will be as the mammoth is to us.

The elephant's age is a disputed point; but, as no one has quite decided, let me put it down at 200 years, upon these two grounds: 1st, that most animals live four or five times as long as they take to attain maturity, and an elephant is certainly not a 'man' till he is fifty; 2ndly, that I had charge for the Government of a large take of elephants caught in a 'coopum' in India. They were sometimes, while being broken, very troublesome, and if they got beyond the control of the men a tame elephant, 'Lachmé,' was called in to 'whip' them. Lachmé had been a pagoda elephant sixty years; we had the record of her capture as a full-grown female. That makes her upwards of a hundred, and she was then, in 1847, quite in her prime, without a sign of old age, and I dare say is very much the same still. The young calves, too, are the smallest beasts for the size they afterwards attain, and must take a long while growing. Such tinies are they that I have had them run under my pony, and touched their little pinky bodies with my foot—poor morsels! I never could shoot the female with any satisfaction, and I think I never did at all but twice; males were plentiful enough.

Men differ as to the height of the African elephant. I have seen thousands, and shot the largest one I ever saw. I measured him, and he was 12 ft. 2 in. I have *heard* of one 17 feet high, but I did not see him, and it is long ago, so perhaps he was the last of the giants! A tusk was exhibited in the African Exhibition in Regent Street, in 1890, by Sir Edmund Loder. It weighed 180 lbs. odd, and was by far the heaviest single tusk known, I should suppose; but I have been shown a pair, 303 lbs. and 9 feet in length. My largest trophy was rather under 8 feet long, and the pair weighed between 230 and 240 lbs. They belonged to a bull I killed on the Zouga; he was the smallest old one I shot in Africa-not more than 9 feet high. I went out with John one bitter morning to provide food for the camp, and, having dropped a white rhinoceros, made for the waggons to get hot coffee and breakfast. On the way we came across an elephant, its head entirely hidden by a thick bush. Think-

---

[3] I know in the representations on the medals of Faustina and of Septimius Severus the ears are African, though the bodies and heads are Indian; but these were struck nearly 400 years after Carthaginian times, when the whole known world had been ransacked by the Romans for beasts for their public shows; and I still think it possible that the Carthaginians—the great traders and colonisers of old—may have obtained elephants through some of their colonies, from India.

ing, from its size, it was a cow, I was passing it unnoticed, when John, with the desire, I suppose, of adding to his collection of tails, begged me to shoot it. I fired, and down went the bush, as, with a shrill trumpet, the elephant trampled through it, disclosing nearly six feet of naked ivory, over the curve; so long were the tusks, and so diminutive their owner, that the points barely cleared the ground. A second ball finished him.

The drier the country the smaller the elephants. On the Limpopo the average height of the bulls was 11 feet, on the Zouga and through the Kalahari 10 feet. The ivory of the smaller kind was larger and, I am told, closer in grain. These tusks, which are deposited by a gum, are very slow of growth; and the molar teeth, to ensure a supply for a long life, have always a young tooth growing at the back of the alveolar process which pushes out the old ones as they become worn.

Most of my elephants were killed from horseback with the shoulder-shot; the cover is rarely thick enough to allow you to get within reach on foot. Besides, on foot you can seldom dispose of more than two at a time; whereas from horseback, under favourable conditions, you may double or even treble that number. Sometimes you must crawl in, and then, of course, you take the head shot if you can get it; but you ought to be within fifteen yards, on a line parallel with your quarry, just a trifle in advance, and then a ball in the lower depression, or temple, will, nineteen times out of twenty, be instantly fatal. I see Sir S. Baker does not believe in the front shot for Africans; but, though as a rule I agree with him entirely, I certainly have killed them by this. Their heads slope so much backwards, however, that it often fails. In tolerable ground there is but little difficulty; but in thick bush there is always some danger, more especially if you are particular in choosing your tusks; and in riding the bull you select out of the herd there is a certain amount of knack—you settle to him and then press him individually, disregarding the rest of the herd for the time. He shoots ahead of his companions, or turns round on you and charges; in either case you have gained your object—separation. If he charges, put the horse to the gallop and let him follow you, the farther the better. Watch as he slacks off, keeping about twenty yards ahead, and pull up sharp when he comes to a stand. He is too blown to charge again, and when he turns to go after his mates he must give you his side; one or two shots properly placed at short range are enough, and you are away again after the flying herd. The oftener you attack the easier the victory, for the heavy beasts get tired, and in consequence are much less difficult to kill.

The little elephant is an amusing imitator of the ways of his elders. I have come upon cow herds with a number of very small calves. As the mothers move off, disturbed and trumpeting, the little fellows fancy it their business to follow suit. Up goes each tiny trunk with a penny trumpet and a fussy waving to and fro. When frightened they run under their mothers, and peer out in the most old-fashioned way; and if you have been unfortunate enough to kill the parent, they will often follow your horse—poor little beggars!

The mothers, I think, as a rule, do not show so much affection for their young as might be expected. They are too nervous and easily affected to remain mistresses of themselves, and, so far as I have experience, forget their offspring in troubled times. You have occasionally striking instances to the contrary, but they are the exceptions. In a large herd of females I once shot a young bull, believing him a good tusked cow; as he dropped, a gaunt old lady, presumably his mamma, fell out from the herd, and charged me at once. I was on horseback and galloped away from her, as she had shabby stumpy tusks, and though I was that day shooting for the pot, there were plenty of others to choose from. She turned back to the dead elephant, which lay in the opening through which I had to pass to get at the others, and stood guard over it, charging in the most determined way every time I attempted to get by—which I had to do at last by allowing her to follow me and then doubling on her. This scene I remember more clearly than I otherwise perhaps should because of an extraordinary sight. When I caught the elephants again they were slinging down a hillside. Dismounting, I killed three of them, two pitching on their heads and rolling over like rabbits.

We shot through the country of the Bakaa for about seven weeks, north and south of the rocky hills on which they lived, and I was here first introduced to that giant tree, the baobab. I was following elephant spoor on foot, with three or four men, through thick thorns, when I found that they had led me off the tracks; and on looking up for a reason why, quite close to me stood what at first I took to be the body of an elephant, I threw my gun into my left hand to be in readiness, to the amusement of my followers, who, knowing I had never as yet fallen in with the baobab (*Adansonia digitata*), had led me a little aside to grin at my astonishment. These quaint, enormous trees seem to have belonged, like many of the animals of Africa, to a bygone world, and, finding the present doesn't suit them, they are taking their leave. A few of the old ones still remain, but I never saw a young one. The largest I measured was 74 feet girth at four feet from the ground, and the smallest 45 feet, but I perhaps overlooked smaller specimens.

We had very good sport, unbroken by accident or anything remarkable. Our starvelings had fattened day by day, and were now shining and very merry and happy in their new skins. Uncivilised man does not take long to pick up; he only wants food, and plenty of it. Shall I be believed if I say that Kafirs will eat, if you give it them, from 12 lbs. to 15 lbs. of solid meat in the day? It appears, I know, an impossible feat, but I can vouch for it and partly explain it, too; for in a short journey with Livingstone, between the Chobé and Zambesi rivers, two or three years after this, we had no sort of meal with us, and were consequently obliged to live on meat alone. And I certainly thought the dear old Doctor was very greedy, for he would eat 4 lbs. for his breakfast and the same or more for his dinner. On telling him my opinion of his performance, he retaliated, 'Well, to tell you the truth, I've been thinking just the same of you!' The fact is that a very large quantity of meat is required if nothing else is eaten. When I got back to the waggons I tried giving two or three of the men a handful of beans with their rations, and found they could not possibly eat more than 3 lbs. of flesh, the smaller mixed diet meeting all the requirements of the system.

We had harried the country of the Bakaas a good deal, and decided on seeking a new field along the banks of the Limpopo, where we heard the game—elephants especially—were in great abundance; so, setting our heads about E. by S., we journeyed onwards, and, travelling slowly, came to it on the third or fourth day—the last twenty-four hours without water for the cattle.

This day ought to be marked with a very large though dull-coloured stone in my shooting annals. Murray made a long *détour* to the N.E., intending to strike the river lower down and follow it up to the encampment. I kept within easy distance of the waggons, as I was anxious to see the cattle watered and well cared for. I shot two large bull elephants and a rhinoceros, and one of the drivers killed a giraffe and a quagga. I think we must have been near the river, for men were left behind to cut them up and dry the flesh, and I do not remember any other water within reach. It was about 3 P.M. when we drew up on the bank, and I was sitting down and enjoying the pleasant sight of the thirsty beasts taking their fill, when I heard three shots in quick succession three-quarters of a mile down stream. It could only be Murray, for there were no guns in the country in those days except our own and those of the Boers far away to the eastward, and my Kafirs would have told me soon enough had any stray party of these been about. Again came shot after shot, and thinking Murray was either in trouble or had fallen in with a herd of buffalo, the spoor of which was very plentiful, I caught one of the ponies, and putting the bit in his mouth, kicked him along as fast as he could go in his waterlogged condition.

Immediately opposite the sound of the guns the bush was so thick I could not get through with the horse; so, tying him to a tree on the outside, I crawled in, and came upon a kind of backwater from the main river, very deep, 150 yards long by fifty wide, with high banks, especially the one opposite me, on which sat the dear old laird blazing away right merrily—his after-rider helping him keep up the cannonade by loading one of the guns. 'What is it?' I shouted. 'Look at those beasts,' he replied—*bang*. 'There again'—*bang*. 'Look!' he cried. The pool was alive with monstrous heads, and though this was the first time I had seen the hippopotamus in the flesh—fat, perhaps, I ought to say—for we had then no friendly hippo in the Zoo—there was no mistaking him.

I opened fire at once from my side at heads which showed for a second above water and then disappeared below, again to reappear; and Murray kept pounding away from his. This went on for a quarter of an hour, and nothing came of it; though the hippos were hit every time, not one of them seemed to die—there was, apparently, the same amount of snorting, puffing, and blowing—but no results of the thirty or forty shots that had been fired, and yet the animals were within twenty or twenty-five yards of us. 'Have you killed any, old fellow?' I shouted, and the answer came back to me, 'No!' At the same moment a big bull made straight for the part of the bank on which I was standing. Letting him get his forelegs clear of the water, I fired within three feet of his head, blowing him back, as it seemed, into the stream. 'Well, I'll swear I hit him!' I roared to Murray. 'Oh, I've hit all I've fired at,' was his reply. The evening was closing in, and just before we started for the waggons one hippopotamus floated up dead on Murray's side. We looked at one another, and did not say much of our shooting. Next morning, however, on the surface of the creek lay fourteen huge bodies—a hippopotamus sinks to the bottom when killed, and only floats when the gas distends the stomach; at least, that was our reading of the riddle. It is the poorest of sport, and I never shot another except for food. The young are very good eating, the flesh resembling the most delicate pork.

We knew nothing about the tusks when we shot this first batch, and so lost some valuable ivory. Large hippopotamus' teeth were then worth 20s. a lb., when elephant ivory would bring only 5s. 6d., the former, I believe, being used for the finest sort of inlaying and artificial teeth.[4]

The hippopotamus and crocodile live together in the same rivers, and keep the peace, though on what pact I know not, for the young of the former would be sucking-pig to the latter; I suppose there is a mutual agreement of bear and forbear. The hippopotamus looks more like a retired publican than a fighter, but whether he can bite or not, ask the canoes. The little calves stand on the broad backs of their mothers as the school moves from one feeding ground to another, and this may be a precautionary measure, for I fear 'Brer' Crocodile is not a very honourable fellow. I may mention as a curious fact that once or twice I found his armoured skeleton fifteen feet up in the trees by the river's bank. The Kafirs assured me that it was thrown there by an elephant who had come down to drink, and on whose trunk the crocodile had fastened, whereupon the elephant in his fright and fury had kneaded him to death and then, with a toss from his tusks, treed him. I could see, and can suggest, no better explanation of his position—high above even flood mark.

Next morning our now plump Bakaa came as a deputation, assured us we had made their hearts quite white, and requested leave to return to their kraals. It was granted, of course, and a few days later, after drying their strips of meat and making it up into large faggots, having requisitioned as carriers a number of Ba-Lala—a kind of poor Kafirs who hang on the outskirts of the more powerful tribes like pariahs or mean whites, and whose position I could never exactly make out—they set out for their villages, each man, woman, and child staggering under as much meat as he or she could possibly stand up under. This one day's shooting of elephants and hippos had given them over 60,000 lbs. They had large stores beside, and every few days had sent back men with loads to their chief throughout the whole time of their being with me. They *all* went to their homes. Out of the 600 not one was missing, sick or feeble.

We shot down the river for a month or five weeks. On one of the last days, Murray and I rode out together. We usually took our separate beats, and this is, as a rule, by far the best plan, for men get jealous shooting against one another—the camp fires dull; in this way, too, you learn more of the country through which you are travelling. We had pottered about, shot a giraffe, and some smaller game, when accidentally we lighted upon a herd of elephants. Now you very seldom come across elephants by chance; you have nearly always to follow them for miles from the water; but here they were, and eight fine bulls too—nothing very large in tusks, but all good. Though startled, they stood and fronted us. We each took one

---

[4] Sir S. Baker tells me these prices are altered now, and that in 1892 elephant ivory fetches from 12s. to 18s. a pound, and hippo's only from 5s. to 10s., as the dentists have given up using it.

of the flankers, firing at the point of the shoulder. With a flourish of trumpets the whole eight charged in a crescent—it was a grand sight—we turned and galloped right and left, the bulls pressing after Murray, and in their course driving up an old mahoho, who puffed and snorted, and putting on full steam managed at last to get clear, in great alarm. We only bagged a couple; in after years with more knowledge I should have got at least four single-handed.

The season was drawing on, and we set our heads southward and westward towards Mabotsé, and, shaking the dear old Doctor and Mrs. Livingstone by the hand, went down to the Colony, I to refit for next year, Murray to return to England. I should have managed very well with the stores I had, but from December to April you cannot keep your horses alive—the horse sickness kills every one. This mysterious illness, though an epidemic at the Cape, is endemic through the old hunting grounds. It is said to be peripneumonia, and to arise from the rank vegetation springing up after the first rains; but I think some other explanation of its cause than this must be found, as the horses suffered just the same once when I was crossing the Bakalahari desert rather too early in the season, for I lost six in nine days. Bleeding to exhaustion seems the only remedy, and one or two I certainly managed to pull through by opening the veins at both sides of their necks at once, and letting the blood run till I could push them down with my hand. Had it not been for this we should never have taken the trouble of the long journey to and fro, but have remained quiet for the hot months, and then resumed the campaign when the weather became cooler.

CHAPTER III

SECOND EXPEDITION TO SOUTH AFRICA

BY W. COTTON OSWELL

Murray returned to England. I threw off my ivory at the nearest frontier town, and laying in such fresh supplies as were needed, and buying half a dozen horses to fill up the gaps, was by the middle of April on my way to the Mariqué River, a small tributary of the Limpopo, intending to shoot down it to its junction, and then follow the main stream as far as I might be able. The game was very numerous, and John was already well on with his frieze of elephant tails round the inside of my waggon. He always cut off the 'tips' from the elephants I shot, as a kind of tally; and now that we did much of the tracking alone, he was besieged on his return to camp by the Kafirs, to find out how many tails he had, and whether the late owners were fat! They ran heel the next morning and left men to cut, dry, and despatch the flesh to their respective kraals; a large number, and all the head men, remaining with me.

One morning, before I started, a Kafir came in with a letter fastened in a cleft-stick, from 'a white man shooting on the Limpopo, three days up stream from the junction of the Mariqué'; it was from a Major Frank Vardon, of the 25th Madras N.I., who, hearing I was within a short distance, proposed to join parties and shoot together. I had been one whole season and part of another at the work, and I thought that a new comer of whom I knew nothing might not be the most desirable of companions; he would very likely wish to stop when I wished to go on, and *vice versa*, and I sent an answer in this spirit; but, 'thanks be praised,' I repented of my churlishness in an hour after the departure of the messenger, and wrote a second letter, begging Major Vardon to ignore the first, pardon my selfishness, and join me as soon as possible; and to the end of my life I shall rejoice that I did so, for in three days the finest fellow and best comrade a man ever had made his appearance.

I had been fortunate in finding elephants early, had shot three fine bulls, and in consequence of having had a very long ride the day before, after a herd we never came up with (we started at 8 A.M. one morning and only reached the waggons again next day at 7 A.M.), I returned to camp about 3 P.M., and introduced myself to my new companion, who had just arrived. I will not attempt to describe him—let every man picture for himself the most perfect fellow traveller he can imagine, and that's Frank; brightest, bravest-hearted of men, with the most unselfish of dispositions, totally ignorant of jealousy, the most trustworthy of mates; a better sportsman, and better shot than myself at all kinds of game save elephants, and only a little behindhand in that, because he was a heavy weight and poorly armed with a single-barrelled rifle; yet he was always rejoicing in my success, and making light of his own disappointments—and this man I had all but missed!

Sometimes we would take a day together after elephant or buffalo, and occasionally we met by accident, our beats cutting one another, and the sound of the guns showing our whereabouts. Once having come together in this way, we saw the finest struggle of brute force I ever witnessed. We were making tracks back to the camp, walking our horses slowly along the bank of the river, when Frank got off to shoot a waterbuck (*Aigoceros ellipsiprymnus*). A shout followed the report of his rifle. Dismounting, for the bush was thick, I soon joined him. In stalking the waterbuck he had come across buffalo, and had wounded one, which with two others was still in view. I started in pursuit and soon outran Vardon, for he was stout, one Kafir holding with me. Presently I was abreast of his animal, which was leaning, hard hit, against a tree. I gave it a widish berth, not wishing to finish Frank's work, and pressed on after the others; but, just as I passed, it made a plunge forward, and began to run again; at the same instant the bush was streaked with yellow, and calling out, 'Come along, there's a lion!' I put on a spurt to get first shot, carrying the gun at the trail, for one had to stoop often under the branches of the thorns. After going a hundred yards, I could distinctly hear the sharp snort of the buffalo, and muffled growl of its assailant, and knew that the latter had got hold. I still ran on, looking out for a sight of the combatants, when suddenly the man who had kept up with me put his hand on my wrist, and, pulling rather harder than he intended, stooping forwards and running as I was, down I came over-balanced. 'What is it?' I asked angrily. 'Look!' he answered. Within twenty-five yards a magnificent fight was going on. Two other male lions had joined the one I had first seen, and run blood-spoor till they had overtaken and stopped the buffalo. They were now all standing rampant on him, teeth and claws both at work, the gallant old bull doing his utmost to hold his own against odds. He tried to gore them, but they hugged his side, putting their bodies parallel with his, and so escaping the thrust; he swung the lion on his right completely off his legs, as you swing a child by his arms. It was only by glimpses that you saw anything, for it was an enfolding cloud of dust, out of which came every now and again the black hide of the bull and the fulvous coats of the lions. Every muscle of the attackers and attacked was on the stretch. You felt rather than saw the terrible strain. Had the buffalo been unwounded, even with the odds of three to one against him, he would have left his mark. It did not last much more than a minute—perhaps not even that—and then the grand, old 'Naàri' came to the ground, killed by the ball, not by the lions.

Odds—3 to 1

Joseph Wolf

The one of these which had attacked on the right came round to his fellows, and they all three stood with their forepaws on the carcase, and roared and growled their pæan of victory. Frank had come up; we were too near to speak, but I motioned him to take the lion on the left, while I covered the middle one. We fired together; his fell dead with a broken back, filling its mouth with bush as it rolled over: my shot was rather a slanting one, went in through the back ribs, and out somewhere forward; at all events, it was not fatal on the spot, for the lion sprang over the buffalo without stopping to inquire where it came from; the third never moved, but kept on shaking the dead bull till I had loaded again and killed him. I wish we could have picked up No. 2, but the evening was closing in too rapidly to allow us to track him any great distance, and we did not therefore bring him to bag, as we must under other circumstances have done, for he was wounded to his death. It was my clumsy first shot that was in fault, and Frank's want of a second barrel. When a lion has fast hold of his prey with his mouth, his eyes are nearly closed, and you may get quite close to him, the folds of the skin of the face being driven up by the constriction of the muscles of the jaws against the lower lids: the Kafirs all recognise this fact.[5] Vardon was a very deliberate shot, and used to take me to task for snapping too much. But our weapons were different, his a finely-sighted rifle, mine a very open-sighted smooth-bore.

He gave me quite a jobation one day, in the presence of a living lion, not ten yards from us, when he delivered his text. It happened on this wise. The waggons were halted for the night, on the bank of a deep 'nullah.' There were no elephants to alarm in the neighbourhood, so I strolled out on the chance of a shot. It was late in the afternoon, 4 P.M., and I could hear Vardon talking to his men two hundred yards off, as he came back to camp. Whether roused by his voice, or by sight of me I don't know, but a lion broke from the bottom of the nullah, and scrambled up the opposite bank. It was a longish shot, and I think I missed. In two or three minutes, exactly at the spot the lion had gained the bank, Vardon and his party appeared; I ran through the hollow, and telling him what had just happened, we put the Kafirs on the trail and followed. We had not gone a hundred yards before one of the men made signs to us to stop, and through the very patch of bush in which we were standing the beast came heading down again to the thickly-wooded ravine. He really was not more than eight feet from us, but a dry bush was between. I dropped on my knee, and when he was slightly in advance fired. It is always better to let a *passing* lion get a trifle ahead of you; there is more chance of a kill, less of a charge. The ball struck well behind the shoulder and went right through him. He bounded on, dabbling the bush on either side with blood, and then dear old Frank began to blow me up for firing too quickly. In this instance, I really had not done so, but he had not got his rifle off, not having a clean sight, or he was desirous that the game should get clear of the partially covering scrub. We never picked up this lion, for a wind arose in the night and blurred the spoor, and he had not died in the long grass, for we burnt it; his loss was always scored against me.

---

[5] Mr. Wolf's sketch does not quite bear out this statement; when he was drawing it I forgot to mention the peculiarity. I am, however, able to indicate it in the illustration, thanks to the courtesy of Mr. Caterson Smith, who altered the plate in accordance with my suggestion.

Opinions are very various about lions. There is the young lady's lion, a noble generous animal, that always kills his own mutton, and refuses all butcher's meat; and the young gentleman's, whose experience, perhaps, began at Wombwell's, and ended at the Zoo. His is a cowardly, sneaking brute, a regular cur. There must be lions and lions. Those I have met with are not above eating what may be before them, asking no questions for conscience sake; but as a rule, if you will take my advice, you will hold as straight as you can when you pit yourself against a lion; and if you accept all chances without picking and choosing, you'll now and again find yourself in a warm corner. Lions are not so plentiful as black-berries, or even as buffalo, and perhaps it's better so. I do not think his rush is so quick or so resolute as a tiger's, and he has a much better head to hit; still, he looks ugly enough when, with mane standing out as if electrified, and with a short, barking roar, he comes down to the charge. He will not, except when hard pressed by hunger, or when accustomed to feed off human carcases lying about after fights and raids, attack man in the daytime unprovoked. A surly beast, awakened suddenly from sleep, or disturbed while feeding, might be nasty; but he nearly always retreats before man, for the fear and the dread of one of Noah's family are still a tradition with wild beasts. But even in the cases above mentioned his conduct very much depends on yours. In the daylight wild animals, especially the wildebeest and quagga, show but little fear, running up to within fifty yards, and gazing at him as if fascinated.

In my first journey I hunted for many weeks with a party of Bushmen, and gained many valuable hints about beasts and their ways from them; and, with regard to the lion, I learned that if you came unarmed on one, your best chance was to stand still and he would move off, but that if you turned and ran, he was nearly sure to make after you. Three times in my shooting life have I tested this advice— once on horseback, twice on foot. On the first occasion, without a gun, I came quite unawares upon a sleeping lion. He woke, stood up, and we looked at each other for a few seconds. Then he turned, walked away very slowly for thirty or forty yards, as if he wished to convey the idea that he was only moving to get out of such low society—throwing his head first over one shoulder, then the other, to see what impression he was making—and directly he thought he was out of sight broke into a lumbering gallop. If he shows an inclination to hold his own when met, the Bushmen stoop, and, with their hands resting on their knees, begin to walk very slowly towards him. He raises his head and watches the man suspiciously, trying to find out what he is about, and then, turning, retreats. I would not say that this plan would be always successful, but I firmly believe it is the best to try when you are unarmed. I have even stood thus twice opposite a *wounded* lion with an empty gun. Had I fallen back I feel certain my *vis-à-vis* would have attacked, for he was in neither case so crippled as to be unable to follow and overtake me. When the cubs are very small the male will show fight, to give the lioness a chance of making off with them, but this is rather a demonstration than real business.

I do not think our South African lion can be nearly so formidable as the North African, for I had the pleasure of once meeting the famous French sportsman, M. Gérard, and the animals he described far exceeded any I ever met with in size and ferocity; perhaps the climate and the constant badgering they get from the Arabs may be sufficient to account for the differences. Of course, if you take the war into his camp, he will fight, and he is a very dangerous opponent, from his quickness and strength. I see Sir Samuel Baker believes that he possesses more power in his paw than the tiger. I would not be understood as disputing such excellent authority; but a tiger can give a tidy pat, too—I have seen him smash in an ox's head at a blow. Again, I have spoken of the lion as less resolute in his charge; but Sir W. C. Harris asserts that he is never stopped. This is not my experience, for I have sometimes known him brought up short by comparatively trifling wounds, and one actually by the cutting away of an eye-tooth by the bullet. He has two very distinct cries besides his roar and charging bark, one when questing, the other when full. Lying by the fire at night, Kafirs will start up at once and pile on wood if they hear the low panting moans of the first; of the second they take no notice, unless you call their attention to it. 'Oh, he's full; he's going home singing.'I have once or twice taken the grunting of the cock ostrich for the note of the lion. It is much shallower; but it has deceived me. The Kafirs never make the mistake.

People looking at the original sketches of the pictures which are engraved in this book have often asked me how I felt at the time of the accidents. Much as other men would, I suppose, is all I can reply. We all belong to the same family. When trouble threatens, you shoot very straight, your muscles are rigid and steely *for the time*; if you come to grief the whole of your mind is bent upon getting away, and on that only. Some men have more of their wits about them than others, no doubt; but all pale faces must yield to the black skins in this particular. A man was cutting long grass to thatch one of Dr. Livingstone's outbuildings when he came upon a buffalo, which charged. The man ran some little distance, but noting a slight depression on the ground, like a shallow ditch, threw himself down flat into it, holding on to the bush and grass with his hands. The points of the buffalo's horns turn in, bowing out the middle—there was, from the man's position, a difficulty in getting the points to bear, and before the bull could arrange matters satisfactorily to himself his nose came close to the Kafir's body; in an instant he had hold of it, and pinched and wrung it sharply. The nose is the buffalo's tender spot, and this happy thought of the native was sufficient to rid him of his assailant. Livingstone told me this story. I did not see it enacted, but I believe it; and it is illustrative of such presence of mind as would hardly be found in the European—living amongst wild animals and inheriting from generation to generation the instinctive knowledge of their natures, it would be surprising if the blacks were not in such things our superiors.

The buffaloes were in immense herds along the Mariqué River. As we were coming home one night rather later than usual from hunting, a white rhinoceros with a calf insisted on stopping the way. It was bright moonlight, and easy to shoot her; but the country was full of elephants, and I was very unwilling to scare them. We tried every way to get her to move, but no, she would not. We pelted her with pieces of wood, abused her roundly, and the men threatened her with their assegais, all to no purpose. At the last, very unwillingly, I was obliged to fire. She ran a little distance and dropped dead; but the report of the gun had awakened the whole forest to the left of us into life, unheard, unseen before. I rode up to the edge, it was a mass of struggling buffaloes jammed together. The outside ones, startled by the shot, and having got sight of our party, bore back upon the main body; hoof and horn, horn and hoof, rattled one against another, and for some distance I rode parallel with a heaving stream of wild life. I cannot pretend with any accuracy to guess their numbers, but there must have been thousands, for they were packed together like the pictures of American bison, and any number of 'braves' might have walked over their backs, so far as I could see, for any distance. In the moonlight, I could only, to be sure, make out my side of this seething river.

Two marches from the junction of the Mariqué we found elephants in such large herds that we halted a week or ten days, and the ivory as it was brought in was piled up under my waggon. Once whilst here, after a long day's tracking, the night caught us and we had to lie out. We found water, but had no food—for you never shoot on elephant spoor for fear of disturbing your game, or losing your men, who settle down like vultures to eat. Kafirs hunt best hungry. It was a bitterly cold night, and how the men without clothes got through it I don't know. I had no extra covering, it is true, save my saddle-cloth, a square of blanket 3 feet by 3; but we made a large fire, and lay all round it like the spokes of a wheel, and I don't remember feeling much inconvenience, though I was a little stiff in the morning, for the fire had burnt low, and the ground, except where we had lain, was white with frost. One of the men had kindly roused me about midnight, with an invitation to partake of a tortoise he had caught and was stirring tenderly in its shell among the warm ashes. I declined with thanks. We were all quite fresh and merry when the sun thawed us, and as we neared our waggons we heard shot after shot in the bush around, every now and then catching sight of a buffalo. I thought Vardon had turned out with the drivers for an early 'battue'—very much against his custom, certainly—but who else could it be? The mystery was solved directly I reached our encampment, for on the opposite bank of a small stream, which here ran into the Limpopo, I saw two waggons unmistakably Dutchmen's. I was disgusted enough that anyone should dare to come poaching on our manor. But what was to be done? They were many, nine or ten, and we were but two. After breakfast one of my Hottentots, who had been herding the oxen in the direction of the Boers' waggons, brought a message, or rather an order, that I was to go over to them. I returned for answer that if they wanted anything they could come to us. They took it quite in good part, and about ten o'clock, after ascertaining from my boys of what our party consisted, seven or eight of them crossed the stream and made their way up to our camp, having the good taste to leave all their roërs behind. We had a friendly chat, coffee and tobacco playing a considerable part in it, and filling up the gaps in my rather incomplete Dutch. Dear old Frank could never be induced to believe that Dutch was anything but bad English, and would occasionally put in a word or two of this latter in the worst grammar and pronunciation he could improvise. We smoked and we drank coffee, and we were amicable exceedingly, when one of my guests chanced to see the ivory under the waggon. They all got up to look at it—where did it come from?—who shot it? I said I had, and during the last few days. Alone? Yes, alone. 'That must be a lie. A poor lean fellow like you could never have shot such a splendid lot of tusks.' They appealed to my drivers for the truth, and when we returned to our coffee-pot, made an astonishingly liberal proposal that I should join and shoot with them, and take half the ivory killed by the whole party. They were in earnest, and I had the greatest difficulty in getting off; but I have reason to believe it was through the account of these Boers, and of another party I met at Livingstone's station at Mabotsé, that I received the most courteous message from Prœtorius, who was then their chief, that he hoped I would visit Mahalisberg, and that I should find a hearty welcome throughout Boerland. They had a wholesome dread of traders, who for ivory might supply the natives with muskets and ammunition, and thus render them recalcitrant, and they had found out I didn't and wouldn't trade; indeed, the story among them was that on a native bringing a tusk to my waggon for sale I threatened to shoot him then and there!

Vardon was the most enthusiastic rhinoceros hunter; he filled his waggon with horns as I did mine with ivory; he used to shoot four or five every day, and there was always a freshness about the sport to him which seemed remarkable. He was an all-round shot, but best at rhinoceros. The mahoho is not bad eating—by the way, his hump is excellent—but there is a good deal in the cooking of pachydermata. We had a capital cook at the waggons, and had eaten elephant's trunk many and many times. Two or three days farther down the river the men told me they had heard of a fine herd of bull elephants, about thirty miles off; as there was little water, or at all events not sufficient for the oxen, they begged me to take only a couple of horses and sleep two nights away from the waggons. John and I started accordingly with our guides, and at 5 P.M. reached the small spring where we were to halt. Early next morning news came of two tuskers being close by, and it was proposed I should begin with them and go after the large herd next day. I soon found and shot them. One, a very fine bull with large tusks, charged viciously after getting a ball through the thick end of the heart. The men brought it to me to look at when they opened him. We took a lump of the trunk, and returned to our sleeping place—only one woman had remained, the rest were off to the dead elephants. We were hungry, and John proposed we should cut part of the trunk into small lumps and boil them. On the fire they went, and on they were still three hours afterwards. John, who was a very hungry fellow, kept prodding the pieces with a pointed stick to see if they were fit to eat, but they were still springy. At length we voted them done and tried to chew them, but they were exactly like bits of india-rubber, and we could make no impression. The woman, seeing our difficulty, made us scrape a hole under the fire, roll the trunk up in its skin, put it in the hole and draw the ashes and fire over it, and in two or three hours it was done to a turn and excellent food.

Next day, about 4 P.M., we came up with the herd we were looking for—eleven bulls, all well furnished with ivory. It was so late in the day that we were in doubt whether to attack or leave them till the morrow, but as there was no water for the horses, I decided to go in at once, the more so as the elephants were standing lazily among thin bush in an easy country. Looking for the finest tusks, I rode out and killed the first bull without any trouble, but the next two gave plenty, and took more time than I had reckoned on, and the night closed in so rapidly that I was obliged to give up further attempts; had there been sufficient daylight I always thought I should have shot them all, for they were so tired and disinclined to run that they walked sulkily a little distance and then stood again. The men never forgave the want of light, and often asked me afterwards to press a herd till they were done up and then shoot them all, a programme difficult of execution as a rule—this *might* have been the exception.

I had dismounted, and we were making our fires when an elephant trumpeted fifty yards from us. He had probably lost his friends in the scrimmage and was trying to find them. I got within twenty-five yards of him, but could only see very indistinctly a mass of something, though he stood in rather an open place. There was no chance of my stalking any nearer. I might have run forward and got a shot, but it was too dark to play tricks. John squatted with the second gun and whispered to me to do the same, and, gazing steadily against the sky, I could now make out the elephant enough to tell his head from his tail-end. I fired—a shoulder-shot—and, stumbling a length or two, down he came. It was a good day's work, though it might, as I have said, have been better; but four first-rate bulls and at least 500 lbs. of ivory lay within a space of three or four acres, and there were, besides, the two I had killed the day before, one of which had very heavy teeth.

We lit our pipes and smoked quietly for a time, and then remembered that we had breakfasted early and that we ought to be hungry and thirsty. The Kafirs suggested that as the elephants had probably come from the water in the morning, we should find some in their stomachs, and they immediately set to work and opened a large tusker that was lying close to our bivouac. They found what they sought and, after a good pull, invited me to partake. I was very thirsty, and they seemed to have enjoyed their drink, so, by their directions, placing a small bunch of grass as a filter, I took a mouthful, but—well! I immediately got rid of it—it was simply nitric acid. As the elephant was opened, however, the men were not going without dinner, and though I dare say it was horrible, there was at the same time something grand in the sight of the dark forest, lit sufficiently by the ruddy firelight to deepen the gloom beyond, with the naked savages, their blazing torches in their hands, walking about inside the cavernous ribs. A few choice morsels from the undercut of the sirloin broiled on the embers made a palatable supper, and, putting our feet to the blaze, we all fell asleep.

Whiz! 'tao!' *whiz!* woke me some time during the night, and, sitting up, I found the Kafirs throwing brands from the fire and shouting. A lion, no doubt attracted by the smell of blood, was tearing at the inside of the disembowelled elephant. I just got a glimpse of him, but it was too momentary for a shot. We slept, and were not again disturbed. I gave the dead beasts to the Ba Lala who had brought the information, telling them to send me the tusks, and returned to my waggon. The dozen were duly delivered in four or five days' time, though the waggons had gone fifty miles farther down the Limpopo. It was always so. Once the chief of a large tribe of Bushmen came running—as we were inspanning for the march— with a request that I would shoot two elephants, which he had just seen coming up from the river, for him and his people. I was very unwilling to stop the trek; telling the men therefore to go on, and saying I would overtake them, I jumped on a horse and went off with my Bushman, he keeping well in front, though I was making a sharp canter of it. Through the bush, on to the open plain, and the game was in view. I dashed ahead. One had good tusks, and I settled down to him. He soon turned on me. I had been shooting buffalo the night before, and as there was only an ordinary charge in the gun, wishing to get rid of it, I fired at long range—forty yards, I dare say. The horse was fidgety, and the ball struck eight or ten inches below the backbone; to my astonishment, the bull took one stride and settled down quite dead. The bullet had cut the aorta. His companion had such small teeth I let him go free, and, making the carcase over to my Bushman, who was astounded at the easy way the animal had been disposed of, and telling him to keep the tusks till I returned, I galloped after my waggons. Three months passed before I was again in the neighbourhood; but while yet thirty miles off, the man, hearing that I was coming on, brought the ivory to me. I was delighted to gladden his heart and reward his honesty with a present of beads and brass wire.

Death of Stael

But the saddest of days was at hand. I had one preeminently good horse, the very pick of all I ever had in Africa—fearless, fast, and most sweet-tempered. Returning to camp one evening with a number of Kafirs, tired and hungry after a long day's spooring elephants, which we never overtook, I saw a long-horned mahoho standing close to the path. The length of his horn, and the hunger of my men, induced me to get off and fire at him. The shot was rather too high, and he ran off. I was in the saddle in a moment, and, passing the wounded beast, pulled up ten yards on one side of the line of his retreat, firing the second barrel as he went by from my horse, when, instead of continuing his course, he stopped short, and, pausing an instant, began to *walk* deliberately towards me. This movement was so utterly unlooked for, as the white rhinoceros nearly always makes off, that, until he was within five yards, I sat quite still, expecting him to fall, thinking he was in his 'flurry.' My horse seemed as much surprised at the behaviour of the old mahoho as I was myself, and did not immediately answer the rein, and the moment's hesitation, cost him his life and me the very best horse I ever had or knew; for when I got his head round, a thick bush was against his chest, and before I could free him, the rhinoceros, still at the walk, drove his horn in under his flank, and fairly threw both him and his rider into the air. As he turned over I rolled off and fell in some way under the stirrup-iron, which scalped my head for four inches in length and breadth. I scrambled to my knees, and saw the horn of the rhinoceros actually within the bend of my leg; but the animal wavered, and, with the energy of self-preservation, I sprang to my feet intending to run, for my gun was unloaded and had fallen from my hand. Had I been allowed to do so this story might never have been told, for, dizzy as I was from the fall, I should have been easily caught. Tottering a step or two, I tripped and came to the ground a little to the right of the creature's track. He passed within a foot without touching me. As I rose for the second time my after-rider came up with another gun. I half pulled him from his pony and mounting it caught and killed the rhinoceros. The horn now hangs over the entrance to my front door.

That day Frank happened to be again hunting in the same direction as myself, and, hearing the reports of my gun, hoped I might have come up with the elephants I had started after in the morning. He found me sitting under a bush, hatless, and holding up the piece of my scalp with the blood streaming down my face, or, as he afterwards described it to Livingstone, 'I saw that beggar Oswell sitting under a bush holding on his head.' A few words told him what had happened, and then my thoughts turned to Stael. That very morning, as I left the waggons, I had talked to him affectionately, as a man can talk to a good horse, telling him how, when the hunting was over, I would make him fat and happy, and I had played with him and he with me. It was with a very sore heart I put a ball through his head, took the saddle from his back, and started waggonwards, walking half the distance (ten miles), and making my after-rider do likewise. Unless a man has been situated as I was then, it is difficult to make him understand all that the loss of a good horse means. You cannot even fill up his place in quantity, let alone quality. In this part of Africa, at all events, your success depends enormously upon your steed, for the country is generally too open for stalking, and he carries you up to your game, in most instances, as near as you like, and it is your fault if you don't succeed. Had I been the best shot that ever looked along a rifle, and made of steel, I could have done but a trifle without horses, in comparison with what I accomplished with them. Armed as I was with a smooth-bore not very true with heavy charges at over thirty yards, it was a necessity to get as near my game as possible. I am not vain of my shooting—I can do what I intend pretty well at from ten to twenty-five yards—but I would have given the best shot in the world without horses very long odds; besides, from the saddle you see so much more of the country, and are so much more at your ease, and your attention for everything that surrounds you is so much more free.

On horseback your whole day is a pleasure to you, mind and body, whereas on your legs it is often a wearisome, unsuccessful tramp. Men going into Africa for shooting should be very careful in the selection of their mounts, and get the aid of some local friend or trusty acquaintance in their purchase, remembering always that five good horses are worth ten moderate ones and five brutes. For a season's shooting eight to ten trustworthy animals, and five not quite so costly for your after-rider, will, with luck, be an ample provision. The number seems large, but there are accidents, sore backs, hard fare, and hard work to be taken into account. You may sometimes do with fewer no doubt, but there ought to be a margin for loss. Men who go to Africa with the idea that the game will come to them to be shot will find their mistake; 'Dilly, dilly, come and be killed' is not sufficient to fetch the African fauna.

Among my horses, I had many unbroken for riding; they had, I fancy, all been driven. I once bought a whole team—eight—out of a waggon. On my way up from the colony to the shooting ground I used to amuse myself by breaking them in. The method was expeditious, though primitive. We saddled a quiet old stager and tied the young one to him, neck to neck, allowing about two feet length of coupling, by the riem, or leathern thong which every horse habitually wears for knee haltering, or fastening up at night. By degrees, with coaxing, we got the saddle and bridle on, and then I mounted the young one over the back of the old, on which John or one of the Hottentots got astride. There was a little trouble at first with the pupil, but as he could neither rear nor back, and might kick as long as he liked, I sat quietly until he was tired, and then, putting the broken horse into a slow walk, persuaded him to follow suit; he generally did so, and after a mile or two, when he had become accustomed to my weight and movement in the saddle, I lengthened the coupling, little by little, and once or twice I have cast it off altogether and let him go free alongside the other in the first day's march; but generally two or three lessons are necessary, and it takes a week or two to give him anything of a mouth. The principal trouble with the Cape horses is the *inbred* trick of bucking, of which I think they are hardly ever cured; they may behave well for a time, but just when you want them at a pinch, the vice recurs, and they leave you in a hole. Some, when hard worked and brought low, will go peaceably an ordinary journey, but anything unforeseen happening is apt to upset them. I had a very good-looking chestnut I bought out of a team, and broke to saddle myself, and he went well and steadily. One day something put him out, and he began bucking, not in the straightforward style of the trained horses of the Wild West Exhibition, which is difficult enough to sit, but in what we at the Cape call the half-moon, which is much worse, when a horse, without any warning, while going quite quietly, suddenly puts his head and neck well down between his forelegs and bucks right or left in a semicircle. I have heard many men say they can sit it, and perhaps, if expecting it, you might do so; but, in my experience, you nearly always part company. At all events, I and my chestnut did, four times, in as many minutes. The first time I was encumbered with the gun, but the three others were fair spills. I am sorry to say I lost my temper and meant shooting him, but thought better of it, and rode him down thin, keeping him so with work, till he was killed by the fly. Greys are not common at the Cape, and unless first rate, don't buy one for elephant hunting;

you will be seen sooner and longer, and pursued further in the charge. I had a cream-coloured dun, and sometimes it was very difficult to shake off his followers.

I found a very light S-cheeked curb bit, single-reined, work well—you often need to turn quickly. I wore hunting-spurs, and kept my hands quite free for gun and rein. The horses were unshod and sure-footed. Introduce them, if possible, gradually to their work by letting your after-rider use them a few times. He is always out of danger, and if once accustomed to the sight of an animal at a respectable distance, they can soon be driven up alongside of it, and get as eager in pursuit of elephant and large game as their riders.

By neglecting this rule, I very nearly came to grief on an afterwards capital pony. It was his *début*, and a wounded elephant charging with a scream, so terrified him that he was paralysed with fear, and stood stock-still after turning round; spurs had no effect, and how we escaped I cannot now tell. The bull came within a few feet of his tail and then wheeled. I can only suppose he got the scent of the human being, for he was quite near enough to have swept me from the saddle with his trunk. By a little careful treatment this pony became a very valuable one, and I once in after days shot 120*l.* worth of ivory from his back in half an hour. Have nothing to do with a vicious or uncertain tempered horse. If you find you have been taken in with such a one, shoot him; the first loss may not be so bad as the last. Never ride a stumbler up to anything that bites or butts. I had one, and he twice fell with me before a charging elephant. Luckily I did not come off, and pulled him up just in time to escape. Horses used to be cheap enough, but I dare say the price has risen. I mounted myself well from 7*l.* 10*s.* to 15*l.* apiece. Your ponies—for they are hardly more—ought to be quick getting their legs, and a turn of speed is desirable; for though in the open it is easy sailing away from an elephant, in bush or broken ground for 200 yards he will sometimes press a slow horse.

I was once, in particular, hard put to it by a smart though rather small bull. I had fired both barrels, and on he came. I might have had twenty yards' start, but for the first 100 he gained on me, and I had to ride as if in a close finish. A good Hantam horse is an exceptionally tough beast. Whilst at 'Oologs Poort,' a farm then in the occupation of a Mr. Nelson, I was buying mounts, when a Hottentot riding a neat round-ribbed bay came in with a return-letter from the town of Cradock, as far as I remember, seventy miles distant. The horse's appearance pleased me much, and though I found the owner, a Mr. Cock, at first unwilling to part with him, I at last purchased him for 15*l.*—a large price then; but he was worth it. He had just done his 140 miles in thirty hours, including five hours off saddling at Cradock. I was unfortunate with my horses, and lost this one early in the campaign. I had shot an eland or two just beyond the first chooi, and, being alone, had tied 'Vonk' (spark), as the men called him, to a tree whilst I gave the *coup de grâce* to the game. This done, I walked up to loose him and remount; but as I thoughtlessly placed my hand on the rein he got scent of the blood, and suddenly starting back, broke away. I followed him a long while, every moment hoping to catch him, as he let me come quite close and then trotted on, feeding quietly till I came up to him again. At length I grew weary and angry, and twice covered him with the gun, that I might at all events save my saddle and bridle; but twice I relented—the creature was too good and too tame to shoot, and there was a chance that I might find him next morning if he were not killed by a lion during the night. So I let him go, and just before sundown set my face towards the waggons, the encampment lying ten miles off. I walked really, I think, for once by instinct; it was soon dark, and after three hours, afraid of going astray, I decided upon making a fire and camping out, knowing I should find the wheel-tracks next morning if I did not overshoot them. I took out my tinder-box and trying to strike a light, dropped the flint, and was on my knees feeling for it on the ground with my head down, when a muffled shot, which I at first took for a lion's pant, made me start to my feet, and within 100 yards of where I was standing, though hidden by a belt of thorns, by a second shot I was directed to the waggons. I had come quite straight down upon them through the night. We searched for the horse next morning in vain; his spoor was over-trampled by a large herd of quaggas, and for two years I never heard any more of him; when I ascertained a wandering party of Barolongs had found him in the veldt, and, unable to catch him, had driven him before them for thirty miles to their kraal, and had killed many giraffes and other game from his back, one or two of the tribe who had gone into the colony for work having learnt to ride.

Round the dead elands there was a typical African breakfast party—two lions, a dozen jackals, five or six hyænas, and an innumerable company of vultures. The lions, having fed to the full, were lying down close to the carcase, the jackals intently watching them, one of their party every now and then, when he thought the lions' eyes were turned upon his companions or partly closed, running in for a hasty mouthful till a growl sent him to his seat again. A shambling hyæna, after many tries, for the beast wants dash, gets hold of one of the outside strings of the entrails and, pulling it taut, backs as far as he possibly can. Two or three of his friends invite themselves, and, rushing into breakfast, tug different ways. Vultures of various kinds stalk about tearing with beak and claw, and good right have they, for the invitations to the feast have all come through them. High up in the blue, entirely beyond your ken, they saw the game killed, and before you left the spot, if you had looked up, you might have seen the air alive with them. Soaring very high for an extensive view of anything going on for their advantage upon the earth be-low, their keen sight has comprehended the situation at a glance. Those immedi-ately over the spot begin to descend, the message of there being something 'down' has been aërially communicated from battalion to battalion among the circling brotherhood, and through miles and miles of ether a game of follow my leader is going on. It is sight, not scent. An animal killed in a nullah, or in thick bush and covered up at once, escapes. The jackal, hyæna, and lion follow the birds. When the beasts of prey do not find the carcase—it may have been shot far from water—and the animal is thick-skinned, like the rhinoceros and elephant, and even the giraffe and buffalo, the beaks and claws cannot for some time make an entrance into their larder supply, and the birds sit about in solemn funereal state on the sur-rounding trees waiting for the softening of putrefaction, which is well established in two days, solacing themselves meantime with an eye or the inside of the mouth if they can get at it.

In this neighbourhood and between Lake Kamadou and the Zambesi the works of the ants are marvellous. One variety builds a dome-shaped nest, which makes a first-rate oven, for it is hollow inside, and by smoking out the inhabitants and lighting a fire it becomes thoroughly heated, and bakes well. So much has been written about the white ant that it needs no description from me; but though I was in India for years I never remember seeing their earthworks half the size they are in Africa, where I have come across them ten to twelve feet high, and so large and firm that I have ridden about the roofs, in and out amongst the pinnacles and minarets, which give them an appearance, let us say, of Milan Cathedral on a small scale! And all this is the work of blind architects, who are obliged to protect themselves from the sun and from enemies by a covered way they build between their nests and any of the trees around, which may have dead wood or branches. How their instinct leads them my reason cannot tell, for they are eyeless. Where there are no chairs or stools, one sits and lies upon the earth, and sees much of the kingdoms and communities of the insect world. Here is the ant-lion lurking at the bottom of his inverted cone of a hole, ambushed and ready to spring upon the incautious insect that, stepping on the edge of his trap, is carried to the bottom by the loose, unstable grains of sand; here the hard-biting, plunger-looking red ant, whose holes have been stopped when the breakfast was prepared and the surface swept for the skins on which we lie. Up he comes, having wired his way through his closed front door, sits on end, strokes what would be his moustache if he had any, and then, with a number of his fellow-sufferers and friends, walks straight to the nest of a large black species of his own family, and each throwing one of the blacks—about twice his own size—over his back, away they go to their own holes, and, pointing out the work to be done, stand with a fierce countenance over their slaves until all is put right, when the inferior race retire. Trapdoor spiders, too, were very numerous, with their cunning arrangements.

But I have wandered from the Limpopo.

The Bechuana are not of much account in hunting elephant with the spear, though they talk and brag a good deal about it; indeed I have known them fairly beaten and forced to come to me for assistance. I can see a young bull now, walking about quite strongly, with forty assegais in him, scattering his assailants by trumpeting and half-charges. 'Would "Tlaga" come and shoot him for them?' Tlaga did. The elephant looked like a porcupine, but they would never have bagged him, though he might have died afterwards. It is not so with the Bushmen. They are past-masters of the art of hunting, though here I would mention that there are Bushmen and Bushmen. Those found near the colony and spread over the barren Kalahari country are a small, stunted race, dwarfed probably by scarcity of food and hard usage. The others are upright, tall, sinewy fellows, who with their skill in hunting and the abundance of game never suffer hunger, and who are looked upon, though small in number, with a certain amount of fear by the Bechuanas. I was very fond of the Bushmen. They tell the truth, which the Bechuana do not, and instead of being mere pot-hunters they are enthusiastic sportsmen, enjoying the work as much as yourself. When you are hunting with them, it is true, they leave all to you, and greatly delight in watching a tough fight with a savage bull, giving you full credit for your weapon and your use of it; but their tactics when alone are as follows. Taking up the spoor of, say, five or six tuskers, they follow on until they see their quarry, which, with their splendid sight, they do a long way off. A handful of dust thrown up gives them the wind. Some half-dozen or more men conceal themselves in pairs not far apart in the line they hope the elephants will take. Two or three of the others, making a long *détour*, give them their wind, and as they move off, try to head them in the direction of the ambush. The moment an elephant comes within reach of one of the pairs a man springs up and, running towards him, throws a very heavy hafted-spear—twelve to fifteen inches in the iron head—not straight, for it would not penetrate—but in a sort of curve, and the descending weapon buries itself by its own weight. The man is in full view, the irritated beast usually makes for him, and though fleet of foot the hunter would very often be caught were it not for his mate, who, immediately the elephant charges, runs up behind him as close as he can, and sounds a shrill whistle, made generally of the leg-bone of a crane, which each wears hung round his neck by a leathern thong. The elephant hears it, and, cautious even in his rage, stops suddenly to find out what danger is in his rear. As he turns, another spear is thrown; another charge, and another whistle; and this goes on until the animal is exhausted and winded, when the final *coups* are given by men running in and stabbing him behind the ribs, while their companions occupy his attention in front. In this manner a dozen Bushmen will often kill two or three out of a herd.

The Boers have an effective, though cruel, way of killing them. Their legs are solid, not hollow with marrow, like those of most animals; they need to be strong, for a large bull weighs all six tons. The jägers come upon the herd and wish to bag as many as they can; they are not fond of getting too near, and bombarding effectively from a distance is a work of time, so they take the first shots, if opportunity offer, at the forelegs of two or three. The ball splinters and weakens the limb; the sagacity of the animal tells him this at once, and he instantly stands immovable, lest his weight should break it. The hunters follow the rest of the herd and shoot one or two perhaps, and then return to the cripples, who fall an easy prey to the roërs at close quarters. Nine times out of ten the elephant refuses to stir, but if goaded into attempting a charge, the bone snaps directly weight in motion is thrown upon it, and the poor brute falls. It is a most pitiful sight to see these fine, intelligent monsters quietly awaiting death—standing, sadly conscious of their inability to make an effort for attack or escape. I witnessed this butchery but once, and, willingly, would never again.

In the open country the Bechuana, though muffs at elephant hunting, catch large numbers of animals in the hopo. The Ba-Quaina and Ba-Wangketsi, especially, were clever at this kind of work. The hopo is a large pit dug in a favourable spot, generally just the other side of a slight rise, in neighbourhoods where game is abundant, and is often used year after year. From the sides of it stiff, diverging hedges of bush and branches are run out for a considerable distance, and the beaters, sweeping a large area of country in a crescent, open at first, but gradually contracting its horns as the game approaches the hedges, manage to drive slowly forward large masses of antelope, quagga, and wildebeest. Men are suitably placed here and there outside the range of the fences, to indicate gently to the game the way they are expected to take. When they are well within the lines the men bear down on them, and by shouts urge them forward *pêle mêle* to the hopo, which by the rise in the ground is hidden from the leaders until too late; for the weight of the scared body behind them, always pressing on, carries the foremost ranks into the pit, which, in a successful drive, is soon filled with a heaving mass of struggling life. Numbers of the driven escape through the hedges and through the crowd, by this time close up, many of them, the quagga especially, charging the drivers, who, sitting or kneeling, cover themselves with their shields, and ply their assegais as opportunity offers, from beneath them. I should have said that some of the hunters are ambushed near the hopo, and these dispose of any animals that, coming to the surface, seem likely to escape. The southern tribes manage some-times to kill the hippopotamus by suspending a heavy spike of iron, or of wood burnt and sharpened to a point, and weighted with a large stone. This, by an in-genious contrivance, is fastened to the branch of a tree overhanging the animal's path as it leaves the water at night to graze, by a rope attached to a catch, the other end of the rope being brought down, fixed about a foot from the ground, across the path, and tied to one of the trees opposite. As the animal presses against the rope the catch is freed, and down comes the spike. The northerners, who live on the shores of the lakes, Kamadou particularly, kill them from canoes with spears like harpoons, which, once firmly fixed, serve to show by their shafts the direction taken by the wounded beast, and enable the men to follow him and repeat the at-tack until, utterly weakened from loss of blood, he is secured by ropes and drawn ashore. This plan, which seems to me to have its drawbacks and dangers, is not attempted on the rivers, and I was never an eye witness of it, even on the lakes; but I have two or three of the harpoon assegais, and this was the story of the hunting as told to Livingstone.

On the low Siloquana hills near this we made our acquaintance with the Tsétsé fly, which we were the first to bring to notice; Vardon taking or sending to England some he caught on his favourite horse. They have now been thoroughly discussed entomologically, and I would only very lightly touch upon them. The *Glossina morsitans* is a dusky grey, long-winged, vicious-looking fly, barred on the back with striæ, and about the size of the fly you so often see on dogs in summer. Small as he is, two to three will kill your largest ox, or your strongest horse—for the poi-son introduced by the proboscis is zymotic; the victims sicken in a few days, the sub-lingual glands and muscles thicken, the eyes weep, a defluxion runs from the nostrils, the coat stares, and in periods varying from a fortnight to three months death ensues. On examination after death the blood is found to have diminished wonderfully in quantity, to have become gelatinous in appearance, and to have parted with its colouring property. You may plunge, your hands into it and it runs off like tapioca, without staining them. The vital organs, lungs and heart, are flaccid and anæmic, but show no further sign of disease. The flesh has a peculiar glairy appearance. Wild animals are not affected, but all domesticated ones are, save the ass and the goat, and the calf as long as it sucks. Man escapes scot free. The flies settle on and bite him sharply, but no results follow.

Supposing the poison to be alkaline, is it not possible that the creic—an acid known to be present in the blood of all wild animals and to disappear as they become domesticated—may act as an antidote, more especially as man, on whom the poison is innocuous, shares with the donkey, &c., this prophylactic acid? This pest, like all others, is held in check by an antagonist, one of the ichneumons—a rakish-looking creature which catches and sucks it out on the wing, dropping the empty cases much as the locust bird does the locusts.

These tsétsé have caused me sad searchings of heart. The Geographical Society of Paris honoured me with their medal, 'pour la découverte du lac 'Ngami,' and I, in acknowledging their highly valued distinction, sent them a short sketch of the country through which we had passed, and a small bottle of the flies, with an account of their habits, habitat, and the poisonous nature of their bite. This account—probably from my confused style—was entirely misunderstood, and when the copy of the Proceedings of the Society reached me I found I had been made to attribute the death of a native chief, Sebitoani, to the poison of these insects, and also to state that the oxen were maddened by their attacks, whereas the poor things took their deathbites quite calmly—with a whisk of their tails, as is their custom with other flies—and, as I have already stated, human beings suffer no ill. I have tried to correct this impression, but fear I may not have succeeded.

When I came home I happened to meet Dr. (now Sir Richard) Quain, the great toxicologist, and by him to be introduced to Dr. Spence, to whom I told the story of the tsétsé, the result being that I was invited to attend a meeting of the Entomological Society. Doubting my power of giving any clear account before such an august assembly by word of mouth, I wrote the few particulars I had to communicate. When I entered, rather late, a gentleman was explaining the abnormal and interesting peculiarities of a beetle, which had an extra tarsus—at least I think that was the peculiarity—and that tarsus was actually fimbriated! A great deal of very learned talk and discussion followed, and I thought what a fortunate fellow I was to have written my description; but alas! my turn came, and the same savant, after holding my scrawl at every angle in the hope of deciphering the cacography, at last gave it up, saying he regretted he could not make it out, but fortunately the writer was in the room, and would perhaps kindly tell them the history of the flies of which he had sent a specimen. I longed for a repetition of the days of Korah, Dathan, and Abiram just to swallow up that old gentleman and his scarabæus; but I had to get up and explain that I was sorry if they expected me to address them in the very erudite way I had been listening to for the last hour, as I really had no idea how many (if any) tarsi my fly had, and, moreover, I was supremely ignorant whether their tarsi (if existent) were fimbriated or not. They kindly begged me to tell my tale in my own words, declaring they should much prefer it, and I did so, and was dealt with in a most friendly manner. I certainly would rather have stood the charge of a couple of lions at once than laid myself open to a catechism on tarsi and fimbriæ.

We pushed down the Limpopo beyond the Siloquana ridge four or five marches, and then crossing the river near a high rocky hill returned to the Mariqué without anything of much interest occurring; but half-way between the junction of that river with the main stream and the place where we left it to get to Livingstone's station, I was again in trouble.

It was three in the afternoon. We had followed a herd of elephants since 8 A.M., and the traces of the dew of the previous night were still visible on the trail. Our chances of coming up with them were so small that we abandoned the pursuit and turned in the direction of the waggons. After an hour or two the natives began to make pathetic appeals to the state of their stomachs, suggesting that they had met with hard usage, and that, as we had not found the elephants, they were not above breaking their fast upon quagga, giraffe, or even rhinoceros. I tried to persuade them that elephant was the only dish worthy of them or likely to fill those almost bottomless cavities to which they had alluded; that we might have better luck the next day, and that they might put off dining till then. If you wish to be successful in hunting for large tusks, it is as well to keep your men on an elephantine diet and not pamper them with dainties, or they become lazy and careless in seeking the larger game. Whether on this particular occasion I was unusually tender-hearted, or their appeals were too touching, I do not remember; but whilst with my very poor stock of Sechuana words I was trying to explain my views, in an open glade of the forest through which we were passing, their hungry eyes fell upon two rhinoceroses of the keitloa variety, and the eager cry of 'Ugh chukuru, mynàar!' — the last word a corruption of the Dutch mynheer, lengthened plaintively into a kind of prayer — was too much for me, and I dismounted to do their pleasure. Fifty yards before the animals ran a scanty fringe of dwarf thorn-bushes, on outliers of which they were feeding away from us. I made a long *détour*, and came out a hundred yards in front of them, the little scrubby cover lying between us. A handful of sand thrown into the air gave the direction of the wind; worming my way I gained the thorns, and, lying flat, waited for a side chance.

The rhinoceroses were now within twenty yards of me, but head on, and in that position they are not to be killed except at very close quarters, for the horns completely guard the brain, which is small and lies very low in the head. Though alone on the present occasion, I was travelling with the best rhinoceros shot I ever knew, and his audacity, and our constant success and impunity alone and together in carrying on the war against these brutes, had perhaps made me despise them too much. I had so frequently seen their ugly noses, when within eight or ten yards of the gun, turn, tempted by a twig or tuft of grass to the right or left, and the wished-for broadside thus given, that I did not think anything was amiss until I saw that if the nearer of those now in front of me, an old cow, should forge her own length once more ahead, her foot would be on me. She was so near that I might possibly have dropped her with a ball up the nostril, and, had she been alone, I should probably have tried it; but the rhinoceros, when he charges, nearly always makes straight for the smoke of the gun, even though the hunter is concealed, and I knew that if No. 1 fell, No. 2, who was within four or five yards of her, would, in all probability, be over me before the smoke cleared. In the hope that my sudden appearance from the ground under her feet would startle her and give me a chance of escape, I sprang up; the old lady was taken aback for a moment and threw up her head with a snort. I dashed alongside of her to get in her rear; my hand was on her as I passed; but the shock to her nerves was not strong enough, for before I had made ten yards she was round, and in full chase.

Feeling both Horns of a Dilemma

Joseph Wolf

I should have done better to fire into her as I went by, but it had not occurred to me, and it was now too late; in my *anxiety* to escape, to put it as mildly as may be, I had neglected my best chance, and paid the penalty. I was a fast runner; the ground was in my favour, but in thirty yards from the start she was at my heels. A quick turn to the left saved me for the moment, and, perhaps, by giving my pursuer my flank instead of my back, my life too. The race was over in the next; as the horned snout came lapping round my thigh I rested the gun on the long head and, still running, fired both barrels; but with the smoke I was sailing through the air and remember nothing more, for I fell upon my head and was stunned.

The day was fast drawing to a close when, though in that addled state which prevents a man from deciding whether to-day is yesterday or to-morrow, my brain seemed stirring again in a thick fog. By degrees I became aware that I was on my horse, that a native was leading it, and another carrying my gun beside my stirrup. It all appeared strange, but with the attempt to think it out the mist came eddying thicker, and I was content to let it be. Presently a dim confused impression that I was following some animal was with me, as in a dream; the power of framing and articulating a sentence returned, and I drowsily asked the nearest Kafir which way the trail led. He pointed in the direction we were going; his manner struck me, but I had had my say, and no other remark was ready. Men met us; among them I recognised two of my Hottentot drivers carrying a 'cartel,' or cane framework, which served as a swinging bedstead in my waggon. 'Where are you going?' I asked in Dutch. They stared stupidly; 'Why, we heard you were killed by a rhinoceros!' 'No,' I answered. Without a thought of what had occurred, my right hand fell faintly from the pommel of my saddle to my thigh; with the restlessness of weakness I drew it up again; a red splash of blood upon my cuff caught my eye. I raised my arm to see what was the matter; finding no wound on it, I sought with my hand for it down my leg, through a rent in my trousers, and, so numbed was all sensation, that I actually dabbled down to the bone in a deep gash, eight inches long, without feeling any pain—the smaller horn had penetrated a foot higher up, but the wound was not so serious as the lower one. The limb stiffened after I reached the waggons, and, unable to get in and out, I made my bed for nearly four weeks under a bush—the rip, healing rapidly, covered with a rag kept constantly wet.

The rhinoceros, as I afterwards learnt from the men who were with me, was running so fast when she struck me and lifted me so high, that she had shot ahead before I fell, and, on their shouting, passed on without stopping. The horns, as is generally the case in this variety, were of nearly an equal length, so that one to a certain extent checked the penetration of the other—as it would be more difficult to drive a double-spiked nail than a single one. The bone of the thigh, however, providentially turned the foremost horn, or it must have passed close to, even if it had not cut, the femoral artery.

CHAPTER IV

LATER VISITS TO SOUTH AFRICA

BY W. COTTON OSWELL

Vardon went home to England, I think, and I returned to India to finish my time before taking furlough in 1847. Early in 1849 hearing that Livingstone intended making an attempt to reach Lake 'Ngami, Murray and I again left England to join him. The Doctor had quitted his old missionary station, and was now with Sechélé at Kolobeng. As we neared this place, whilst we were lying at a small spring called Le Mawé, or the needles, from some pointed rocks which overhang it, the Kafirs told me there was a shorter way to Kolobeng through the hills, but they doubted if it would do for the waggons; so I volunteered one afternoon to examine it, and report for the onward move of the next day. I started at 2 P.M. on a good old horse, and had followed a winding track through the stony hills around us for an hour or more, and, as it seemed likely to answer, was thinking of returning to camp. We were at a slow walk when a low grumbling growl woke up man and beast, and on looking back I saw a lion within fifteen yards, coming up at his wicked slouching trot. He was too near to give me a chance of dismounting, and I spurred into a gallop; but he gained on me, and, in the hope of checking him, I fired a shot Parthianwise from the saddle. The bough of a tree swept off my hat, and, as it fell, the lion made a spring at it, giving me a moment's law. Fifty or sixty yards ahead there was a small, rocky, but otherwise open space, and to this I pressed at best speed. I pulled up, as I could see well around, intending to load the barrel I had fired, and bring my friend to account; but my foot was not out of the stirrup before he was again on me. I was alone, and the horse was so scared I could hardly hold him; but, freeing my foot, I caught the reins over my left arm, faced the oncomer, and threw the gun up to fire; just as I covered him, and my finger began to press the trigger, I was violently pulled back, and my arm jerked up. The lion still came slowly on, with his body sunk between his shoulders, and his brisket nearly touching the ground. When within twelve yards, I shouted at him, instinctively, hoping to stop him. The human voice acted like a charm; he stood, and made as if he would turn away. The horse, seeing that he no longer advanced, left off tugging at the rein, and I snatched the opportunity and fired my remaining barrel. The bullet struck the point of the shoulder, and rolled him off the little rocky plateau into the bush below, where he lay roaring, without my being able to get sight of him. I went forwards to look for and settle him, but had to give it up, for my horse, which I had tied to a tree, did not at all approve of being left alone, and tried to break his *riem*. I coaxed him, and as long as I stood by him he was quiet, but directly I turned to leave terror seized him. I could not afford to lose him, so I mounted, and attempted to ride him near enough to get a sight and shot; but the tremendous noise was too much for him, and neither spur nor hand had any effect. He stood up on his hind legs, and broke into a white lather of sweat. I persevered for a time, but had to give it up, and, breaking a few twigs and leaves from the trees to make myself a kind of substitute for my lost hat, got back to camp.

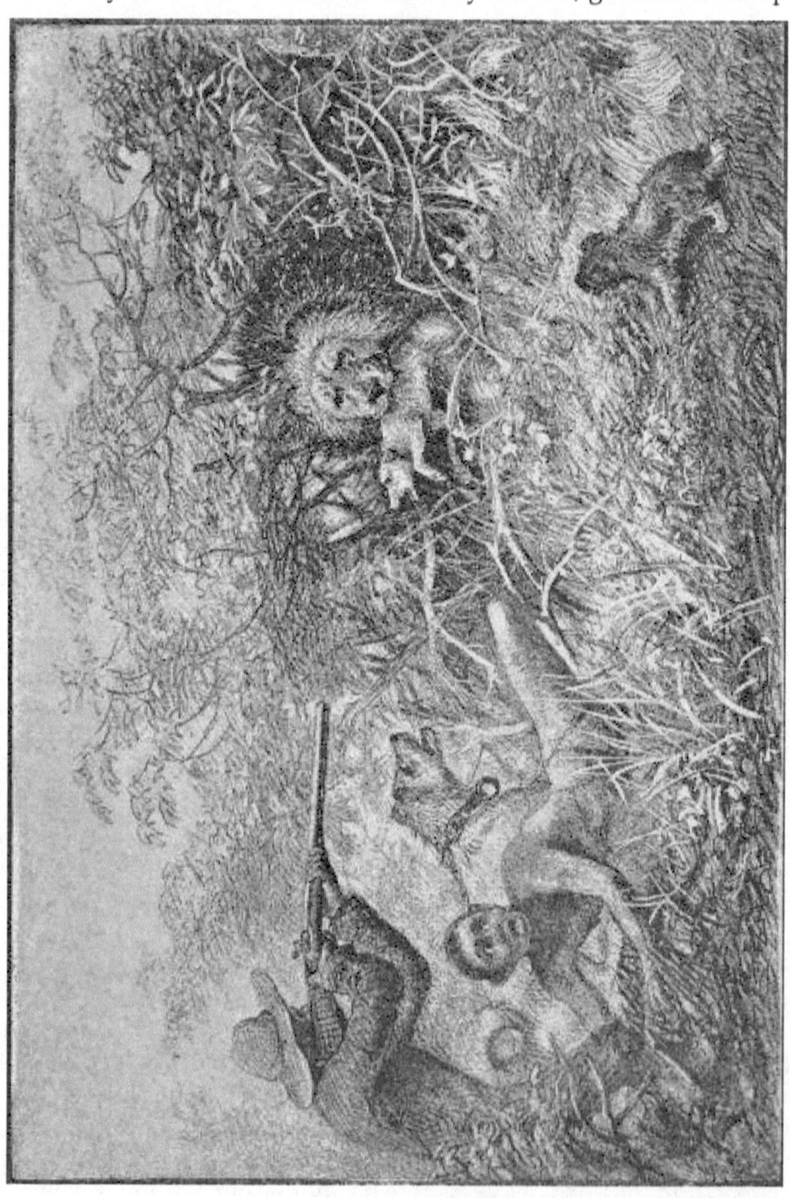

The Drop Scene

Joseph Wolf

Next morning, after putting the waggons on the path I had looked out the day before, Murray, I, two Kafirs, and three dogs[6] went on ahead to pick up the lion. We had just reached the place where my hat had been torn off by the tree, and I turned round to tell the Kafirs that he must be hard by, when an angry growl to my left and then the shriek of a man told me that something had gone wrong. Jumping off my pony, I ran into the scrub, guided by the sound. I had hardly got fifty yards when, bursting through a thicket in front of me, a man, covered with blood, fell at my feet, crying out that he was killed by the lion, and at the same instant I caught sight of the beast close up on three legs, his mane as if electrified into an Elizabethan collar, with the Kafir's dog in his mouth. As his head came clear of the bush I put a ball through it, and he dropped dead by the native's foot. I looked to the yelling victim, and found he was terribly bitten in thigh and arm; so, tearing my shirt into strips, I bound him up as well as I could, never expecting him to live, for large surfaces were mangled, and I had to replace much a good deal at hazard. As I finished the waggons came up, and, lifting the wounded man on a blanket into one of them, I took him home, made him over to his wife, gave her a handful of beads and a yard or two of brass wire to purchase food whilst he was laid up, summoned the chief, said I was very sorry an accident should have happened to one of his men, received his assurance that it was not of the slightest consequence, especially as I had killed the lion, and then, as there was no water for the oxen, I moved on. In seven weeks I returned to this village. The first to meet and welcome me was my wounded friend, quite well and sound, and about to start on a journey. He brought back the blanket on which we had carried him—I had left it at his hut—cleanly washed; and when I told him to keep it his joy was so great that I think he would have had the other leg bitten for a like reward. The recuperative power of the wild man is marvellous. A European must have died of the wounds, or the consequent fever. The native, it appeared, had stopped behind, as we came through the pass, to mend his sandal, and, taking a short cut to rejoin us, had chanced upon the wounded lion, which first seized him by the large back muscles of the thigh, and on his striking him over the head with his fist, shifted his grip to the arm, which was munched up to the elbow, though no bones were broken. I have before said, lions do not attack men in daylight without strong cause. I opened this one, and found the stomach and nearly the whole of the intestines absolutely empty! The beast was starving—he had evidently bled all night, and was very weak, a fact which may account for the man's getting off easier than one would expect.

My journey with Livingstone to Lake 'Ngami, and my subsequent visit to the Zambesi in the same company, have been fully described by the Doctor himself, and though on both occasions I had to kill game for the camp, they do not fall

[6] I have said but little of our dogs, but they deserve mention. I never shot with them; but besides guarding the camp from surprise, they were invaluable, as in this instance, in helping us to pick up a wounded lion, or in telling us the whereabouts of a hard-hit ambushed buffalo—in this illustration the dog in the lion's mouth was the Kafir's, and the other two were the best I ever had (the likenesses are admirable). I have known them hold a lion at bay for nearly an hour, the larger one heading him continually, and the little rough Skye-looking fellow running in at intervals, nipping him in the rear, and then scuttling off at full speed.

within the category of shooting expeditions. They were made with other ends in view, and would be out of place in a narrative of this kind; it will be sufficient to say we were successful in introducing two new antelopes[7]—the 'Nakong and the Leché. The latter, of a dark fawn-colour, with horns annulated and curved like the waterbuck's, only smaller, was found on the flats between the shallow lake Kamadou and the Seshéké plains, west of the Zambesi, the former about Lake 'Ngami, and in the marshy land and pools of one of its affluents, the Teoge River. It is a veritable swamp-liver, about the size of a goat, with long, brownish hair, and horns resembling those of the koodoo in miniature. The abnormal elongation of its hoof enables it to skim over the surface of morasses into which other antelopes would sink. I have one, which I have just measured, very nearly four inches long—if it were in the ratio of the animal's size, one and a half would be its proportion. On hard ground the 'Nakong runs with difficulty—the swamp shoe is a hindrance. Instead of escaping by flight or concealment in the bush, this antelope, on being disturbed, makes straight for the water, sits down in it, and submerges all but the nostrils until the danger be overpast.

When Murray and I reached Kolobeng in 1849 we found, for some reason or other, Livingstone had already started, but we caught him up beyond the Ba-Mungwato, with the chief of which tribe we had again a little difficulty. By the way, six or seven miles south of his kraals we found a hot, brackish spring, which bubbled up as if laden with gas.

Our trek to the lake was a hard one, and we were very anxious to see some of the dwellers of the desert, that we might gain information of the path and waters in advance; but messengers from Secomi, chief of the Ba-Mungwato, had gone through the land ordering all Bushmen and Balala to keep out of our way, and by no means to give us any assistance. If they happened to be anywhere near our line of march, they had instructions to step heavily on their toes, and, pressing the sand behind them, to make as good an imitation as they could of frightened wildebeest or quagga. We noticed these tracks, but were never able to use them to our advantage, though we saw through them, for in that land of thirst we could not afford time to follow the trail of people hostile to our advance, with perfect knowledge of the country and its hiding places, and likely to lead us in their flight as far from water as they possibly could. That they were often about us, even quite close, we knew; but we never sighted one. A little dog strayed one day into our camp: we caught it, and covered it with rings of beads, brass wire, and tinder boxes, then loosed it with a sudden crack of the waggon whip, in the hope of its running back to its ambushed masters and giving evidence of our friendly intentions; but nothing came of it. Again, I tried to lure our unseen watchers through that most sensitive organ, the stomach. Elephants trooped down one night to drink; in the morning I took up the spoor and shot one immediately, but after wounding a second had much trouble with him in the thick bush, the horse falling before the charging bull, and I only just escaping. Months afterwards, on our return from Lake 'Ngami, when there was no further object to be gained by opposition, we

[7] We *heard* of a third antelope which was said to burrow, but we never saw it. Has any later traveller anything to say about it? or is it a myth? The Kafirs were precise enough in their description.

were encamped at the same pool, and were soon surrounded by the children of the wilderness, who recounted and acted the story of the elephant hunt; how they had followed and found number two, which escaped at the time, and eaten him; how they had witnessed it all as invisible spectators; and now, turning actors, they enjoyed the play vastly: trumpeted like the elephant, fell like the horse, and imitated my attack and retreat, and the noise of the gun.

During this journey, when very hard up for water, I offered to sacrifice a pony and ride on in advance of the slow-moving waggons, which were to follow on my spoor, on the chance of finding what we needed so sorely. John and three or four Kafirs accompanied me, and we had travelled I dare say twelve miles when I saw a patch of high grass wave as if something were passing through it. Thinking it might be a lion, and if a lion then water was near, I cantered to the head of the 'Jheel,' dismounted, and watched the line of movement. It came to the edge, and some living thing broke from it. I covered it, and only just in time saw it was a woman running, or rather crawling, very fast on all fours. I mounted in an instant, and shouting to the Kafirs to follow, I headed her and made signs to her to stop. She fell upon her knees, and in Sechuana begged me not to kill her. She had never seen horse or white man before, and evidently took me for a hippogriff. I calmed her apprehensions, cut the metal buttons off my waistcoat, presented them to her, and asked where the water was. 'There is no water,' she said, 'I was just making something to drink' (she was mashing a watery tuber in a wooden bowl) 'when I saw the pitsi (horse).' Bushmen—she was of that people—we knew, lived for months without real water, but I thought it worth while trying the experiment of offering her beads and brass wire if she would guide us to some. It succeeded. 'Well, if you won't kill me, I'll show you where the elephants drink,' she replied; I bade her go ahead, and made her walk just in front. Never did any old lady step out through prickly bush as did my dame. Her bare legs were scratched by the thorns; but what was that to her, expecting instant death if she stopped a moment? On she went. Presently we came upon an elephant. She suggested by signs that I should kill it, but I answered, 'Water, then elephant.' We entered a belt of high trees. I pressed even more closely on her, lest she should dodge among them and escape; my pony's nose nearly touched her, and so we went through two miles of wood.

As we break into the open again, what do I see? The Lake! Can it be that I am the first to catch a glimpse of it? We had voted it mean to stand upon an ant-heap for the chance of a first view, and here was I engaged on a work of love for the public weal. I was the happy discoverer, and under 'creditable circumstances.' As far as the eye could reach, without limit rippled the bright blue water. Up went my old wide-awake, and I shouted for joy; down went the old lady on her knees begging for dear life: she feared the hour of sacrifice had struck. The Kafirs who were with me looked astonished, and thought I had gone mad. 'What is it; what is it, Tlaga?' 'The Lake!' I replied. 'Where?' 'Here—under our feet—close by.' 'Why, that's only a chooi!' and so it was. The low sun cast a slanting beam over the incrustations of salt, and they looked like ripples—indeed, a moment before I would have sworn it was water. The bush-woman showed us the usual spring by the side of the pan, and we got water enough for the cattle; she was bountifully rewarded, but she bolted during the night.

As the waggons came up I watched to see if Livingstone would make the same mistake as I; but one of the Kafirs had told him the story before, so he posed as Solomon and I was chaffed. The Lake was still 200 miles distant. These choois are remarkable features in South African lands. This one was fifteen miles long by, say, about four broad; one to the immediate north was much larger. The wild animals visit them as 'licks,' and the Kafirs get their salt from them.

In 1850 I hoped to bring a boat, but found it impossible to carry it through the drought and heat, and launch it in serviceable condition on the inland waters. The Doctor and I had arranged to start together, but he had already left Kolobeng a month when I arrived, Mrs. Livingstone with him. There was no chance of overtaking him this time, so I decided upon getting on to the Zouga, the river running out of Lake 'Ngami, and having a quiet shoot by myself. This was our second journey across the Bakalahari, and knowing the waters, we made our arrangements accordingly, crossed without much trouble, and reached our destination.

Let me here record my gratitude for the nearly absolute perfection of the copper caps I used—Joyce's. I might very ungratefully have forgotten my debt but for a rather narrow escape on this journey from *the only* miss-fire I ever had in thousands of shots. In mid-desert, attracted perhaps by the water we had opened, a fine bull elephant came close to the waggons. I rode to meet him, and fired, but failed to do any serious damage, though he pulled up. I reloaded and manœuvred for his shoulder; but before I could get a shot he charged, and the cap of the right barrel snicked—fortunately the left stopped him with the front shot, and he fell dead. I dismounted and then looked on the ground. I was amongst a nest of pitfalls—how the horse and the elephant had avoided them I don't know. On the Zouga the game was abundant, and the shooting, as it nearly always was, peerless.

Eight or ten days from Lake Kamadou the camp had been made, 150 yards from the river, just outside the thick fringe of trees, and all was quiet for the night; even the dogs were sleeping, I believe, for once, for I had not been roused since I turned in, when about midnight we were awakened suddenly by a tremendous noise, higher up stream, coming towards us. Crashing trees and a general rushing were the only sounds we at first heard, but presently the screams and trumpetings of panic-stricken elephants mingled in the din. The herd came tearing and breaking its way through the dense jungle straight for us; luckily they caught sight of the gleam of the fires and made a sharp bend to the left, but the outsiders were within a few yards of my waggon. On they passed into the darkness, and in five minutes all was again still. By coaxing and speaking to the horses, which were as usual tied two and two to the waggon-wheels, we calmed them down; but every ox had broken his tethering *riem*, for, as luck would have it, they were fastened to the trek-tow. The two teams with all the spare beasts had vanished no one knew whither, and five hours must pass before we could do anything to find out.

Making the best of it I turned in again, and did not wake until the sun rose, when John, putting his head into the waggon, told me the oxen were on the flat, with a lion after them. I was up in a moment, and unslinging a gun from the side of the waggon tent, went in hot pursuit. Interrupted in his pastime, the would-be cattle-lifter turned quickly to bay, and as he gave me a fine open front shot at fifty yards, I fired for his chest; but I had been after elephants the day before, and the heavy charges were still in the barrels. For accuracy at the distance I had too much powder by half, and the gun threw up, the ball striking his neck, and down he came on me with a grunting bark. I waited till he was within twenty yards and fired the second barrel, but it was a poor shot, the gun kicking violently, and it struck the upper part of the near foreleg. Two more bounds, snap went the bone, and pitching heavily forward he lay six yards from me. I had run out in a hurry, and had neither powder nor ball. John and another man stood a short distance off. Keeping my full front to the lion and never taking my eyes off for a moment—a compliment he returned in kind—in an undertone I told one of the men to go back for ammunition. He may have been away two or three minutes, but it seemed a long time. When he returned the difficulty was to get what he had brought to me. There were two or three small trees on the spot. I was standing beside one of them, and he managed somehow to climb into it, and, leaning forward from a bough, to put the powder and balls into my hand, which I held behind me. I began very cautiously to load, by feeling not by sight, for I knew I must keep my eyes fixed. Fortunately the balls went home easily, though every little push I had to give with the ramrod brought a twitch and a growl from my neighbour. At last all was finished except putting on the caps, but this was the crux. Directly I raised the gun to fix them the lion began to show signs of waking up in earnest. It was a touchy operation, and oh! the relief when it was done! The first shot rolled him over, and the second finished him.

I had now time to look about me, and found the ground trampled by elephants into broad roads. Going back along the line of the stampede of the previous night, I met a poor little yearling calf elephant, torn badly by a lion, but still alive. I put it out of its misery. This was doubtless the cause of the last night's scare. After a cup of coffee and a damper I started on the tracks. The herd was of cows, but I was induced to follow it, as to my surprise there were two or three bulls consorting with them—a most unusual circumstance, for as a rule they herd apart like stags. But there could be no mistake—there were the great tell-tale feet.

Elephants—Zouga Flats

Joseph Wolf

The line of retreat kept widening from the numerous small parties that had joined the main body till at length it was two hundred yards broad, and I and John cantered merrily along it over the flat for ten miles, when we entered a dense belt of bush, into which we had not penetrated far when our progress was obstructed by a young bull with small tusks, who seemed inclined to make himself unpleasant. I did not want him and tried to drive him off, but he wouldn't go, and at last charged down on our horses. This was too much, and I shot him. We pressed on as quickly as possible to the open park-like country of which I could now and again get glimpses, fearing that the shot might have disturbed the rest of the herd if they were within hearing. But I need not have troubled myself, for as I got clear of the bush I came upon at least 400 elephants standing drowsily in the shade of the detached clumps of mimosa-trees.[8] Such a sight I had never seen before and never saw again. As far as the eye could reach, in a fairly open country, there was nothing but elephants. I do not mean in serried masses, but in small separate groups. Lying on the pony's neck I wormed in and out looking for the bulls whose spoor we had been following, and while doing so was charged by a very tall, long-legged, ugly beast, who would take no denial, and I was obliged to kill him. He was *the* bull, but, alas! he was without tusks, and probably being defenceless had been driven from the bull herd and taken up with the cows. I did not want any of them, and turned waggonwards, rather disappointed at not getting ivory, but well satisfied with the sight my ride had given me.

In the evening a straight-horned gemsbok (*Oryx capensis*) coming up from the river passed near the camp; her horns struck me as unusually long, and with some of the dogs I gave chase on foot; she moved very slowly, soon stood to bay, and dropped to the shot. She was evidently very old and worn out. I introduce her to air a theory.

In many of the Bushman caves the head of the oryx is scratched in profile, and in that position one horn hides the other entirely. In Syria, even up to the present day, I am told, a very near relation of the *Oryx capensis* is found; it is the habit of man in his hunting stage to try his hand at delineating the animals he lives upon. Probably the rocks or caves of Syria may show, or formerly may have shown, glyphs of the oryx resembling the work of the African Bushmen, and an early traveller may easily have taken them for representations of an animal with one horn, and have started the idea of the unicorn, Biblical and heraldic. With regard to the former, the word in the Hebrew in our version rendered unicorn is 'reem'; in some old English Bibles, indeed, 'reem' has been preserved in the text untranslated. Again, I am told that the Syrian congener of the Cape oryx is called by the Arabs of to-day ريم 'reem.'[9] Is it not likely then, that the Biblical Unicorn is the

---

[8] Here, again, my description must have been defective, and Mr. Wolf had not then been introduced to Jumbo, or the forelegs of the elephants would have been longer, the backs more sloping, the ears larger, and the facial angle less; but it is a beautiful piece of drawing and reproduces the surroundings and heated atmosphere most wonderfully.

[9] Since writing the above I find this subject has been discussed by the learned, and a decision arrived at unfavourable to the oryx; but I let my remarks stand, for I do not know that anything has been said on the glyphs in profile theory: the idea was first started in my mind by a conversation with the son of a late Bishop of Jerusalem.

same as the 'reem' of the Arab? As an heraldic beast, the gemsbok lends himself most gallantly to the theory; he is a strongly marked equine antelope, and is the one of his family that frequently lowers his head to show fight, it is said even with the lion—and this is confirmed in song, though he certainly got the worst of it in poetry, as I very much think he would in real life.

The gemsbok is scarce, and hardly met with save in the barren open stretches of country like the Bakalahari desert; there were more near the colony in my day than further in. He can do without water for a long time certainly—indeed I believe altogether. He digs and eats watery roots such as luhoshé, a large tuber, and the bitter desert gourd; if rain falls, or he comes across water, he drinks, no doubt, but he does not need it to support life. His country is also the stronghold of the Bushmen, who can, as I have said before, live for months under the same conditions, but who generally obtain water by boring with a long pole through the sand, in hollows well known to them traditionally, down to the hard substratum. Enlarging the bottom of the boring as much as they can, by working their pole on the slant, and then tying a small bunch of grass to a long reed and inserting it in the hole, they suck up the water.

These maminas, or sucking holes, are common throughout the desert, and wherever we found the reeds we found water; in two instances, indeed, by digging to a depth of nine feet we were enabled to supply all our horses and oxen, for though the water never stood more than eight or ten inches, yet the oftener the well was emptied the quicker it filled again, obstructions to its free flow being removed by the continuous trickling.

Maneless Lions

I have mentioned how much the elephants of the Zouga differ from those of the Limpopo, and the more southern and eastern districts; the lions too are, I suppose, influenced by the drier climate and surroundings, for very few of the males grow manes. I thought at first this might depend on their age, as the lion of the south is only furnished in this particular in full lionhood; but one day whilst lying on the Zouga, a few days' march from Lake 'Ngami, a horse of mine fell into a pitfall, and in broad daylight three lions invited themselves to lunch. I was at the waggons, and ran out with a trader of the name of Wilson to get a shot at them. They saw us, and, leaving the horse, got into cover; as they had retreated very leisurely and were by no means scared, we took for granted they would come again. A low mound was within twenty yards of the pitfall, and gave an excellent standing-place behind a double-stemmed tree. Wilson took the right, I the left, and from our slightly raised position we commanded the only approach the lions could well return by. I can say that my eyes were never off that opening, and yet so quietly and glidingly did a lion fill it that I did not see him till he had come—the coming was a blank to me; he was looking at me. A ball in the chest killed him. A second closed the gap, halted inquiringly by his companion, who was stretching in the death spasm, and raising his head caught sight of us. I covered him, but let Wilson fire—the ball raked him from chest to tail, and he dropped dead alongside his mate. After watching some time vainly for the third, we walked up to the carcases; they were both males; the one I had shot was the longest I ever killed, teeth, claws, skin, perfect, in his very prime; the other the oldest, most worn-out specimen, no teeth, no claws, stumps only, his grizzled hide mangy and full of the scars of old wounds; in fact, he was, as the Kafirs said, 'Ra le tao,' the father of lions. Neither had a sign of mane.

A poor young fellow who had come out to shoot, but was utterly unfitted for the work, lost his companion on one of the lower reaches of this river, near where we now were. From the natives' account, it appeared his friend had fired at a goose, which fell in the river. He stripped to go in after it, though they begged him not, as there were alligators; he would not listen to them and swam out. When two or three yards from the bird he was observed to strike sideways, as if he saw something, and in another instant rearing himself half out of the water, with a cry, he sank. There was no doubt what had happened. I first came across the former of these two travellers in a pass not many days' trek from Kolobeng, Livingstone's station; but the interview was a short one, as I was inspanned and on the move. Next morning I found all his men, they were Ba-Quaina and knew me, had followed my waggons, and upon my questioning them they said they really could not stay with that white man, as he starved them. They had found him elephants two or three times, but he never killed any; he only rode after their tails, expecting them to fall off. Of course I insisted on their going back, and shot a rhinoceros on their promise of doing so, just for the present distress. Here was a country swarming with animals, a man with guns and ammunition in abundance, and yet he couldn't 'keep his camp.' I would not blame him for that; but why did he not give up at once when he discovered, as he must soon have done, his utter incapacity? My friend Vardon had interviewed him before he started, at the Cape, I afterwards learnt, and asked him what he had come out for. 'To shoot a lion,' he replied.

'Was that all?' he was asked; and he replied, 'Yes; if he did that he should be quite content.' 'You'd better have given 200*l*. and shot the one at the Zoo; it would have been cheaper, less trouble, and less dangerous too.' Poor lad! he picked up another mate and started on another journey, goodness knows what for; and on my second return from the Zouga we found his skull with a bullet-hole through it, and some small articles of dress, near an old camp-fire two or three marches only from where we first met. The hyænas had dragged away the rest of the bones. Rightly or wrongly, his death was attributed to his companion, and strangely enough this man, subsequently joining himself to an expedition, met a similar fate himself. I never could get full particulars of this sad story.

The way in which, according to the Kafirs, the native dogs worked the alligators on this narrow Zouga River amused us. Three or four of them wished to cross, either for better fare, or to see their friends on the other side; but, though alligator is very partial to dog, dog is not so fond of alligator. Assembling on the banks, they would run, barking violently, a quarter of a mile up stream in full view; halt; join in a chorus of barking, yelping, and baying; suddenly pull up in the middle of the concert, and dash at the top of their speed, absolutely mute, out of sight on a lower level, to the point they had started from, jump into the water and swim across, selling the alligators, who, hungry after their 'course of bark,' were eagerly expecting their dinner at the spot where they had had the largest dose. Whether this was eyes or ears, or both, I could not make out. One beast has wits, another power; and so the balance is pretty fairly kept.

While still in the desert, during our first trip, Livingstone called my attention to a wonderful bit of instinct in a bird—he mentions it in his works, but it is worth telling a second time. We had been a couple of days without water, and I was enjoying watching the cattle swell themselves out in a chance thunder-shower pond we had just come to, and sitting dabbling my feet, when to me the dear old Doctor, 'I say, what do you think is the greatest proof of conjugal affection you ever knew?' 'Go along, I'm not occupied with such matters.' 'Don't be cross; come here. Do you see the chink in that tree, and that large horn-billed bird going backwards and forwards to it? What do you think he's doing?' 'Oh, making a fool of himself generally.' 'No, he's feeding his wife and his children, who are shut in behind it.' And it was so. The ornithological name of the bird I don't know, but he's something between a toucan and a hornbill, neither one nor the other, about the size of a large pigeon, though, if I remember right, more like a woodpecker in build. After marriage the birds select a hole in a tree, and gather a few sticks for a nest; the hen takes some feathers off her breast to line it and lays her eggs. When this is done, and incubation begins, the male bird goes to the nearest pond, and brings wet clay, with which he stops up the hole at which his wife went in, leaving one narrow opening in the centre, and through this the excellent fellow feeds mamma and little ones, until the latter are fledged and ready to leave the nest, then he and she, from outside and in, jointly peck away the clay, which has by this time under the dry heat become as hard as a brick, and madame and her family make their *début*. The poor monsieur is a rickle of bones, madame as round as a ball; the Kafirs, knowing this, always dig her out as a tit-bit whenever they find the nest. And what's it done for? An African wood is filled with all sorts of cats, and without a protection the toucan (that's not right, but let it stand) family would soon be improved off the earth, for a hole in a tree comes handy to a cat; but the clay very soon gets too hard for his claws, and the bird hatches in security. Now come with me towards a Kafir kraal, such as those of the Ba-Quaina or Ba-Wangketsi, permanent tribes. We walk through the outskirts; there's our friend the toucan again, but there's his wife too, and they keep alternately flying to and from that hole in the tree, out of which many gaping mouths are protruded at each visit. They are the same birds, but the house-door is open. Within a radius of five to six miles of every large kraal no cat exists. The Kafirs kill everything that runs upon four legs for food or clothing, the best *carosses* are made of cat-skins (I have one with thirty-six pussies in it), and the birds have found this out—instinct? or reason?

I wandered on at my leisure, and on my return from the higher reaches of the river unexpectedly came upon the waggons of Mr. Webb, of Newstead Abbey, and Captain Shelley, and a companion who, I believe, was travelling with them and trading on his own account. We exchanged friendly greetings, they going towards the Lake, I homewards. I was returning earlier than need be, for I was very nearly run out of lead, and though J knew they were amply provided I had not the face to ask them for metal more valuable than gold in the middle of Africa. Next morning, however, I shot three elephants, and it occurred to me that I might exchange their tusks for lead with Mr. Webb's companion, and I accordingly sent John on horseback with a note to Mr. Webb, asking him to mediate for me, and telling him John would put his Kafirs on our tracks from the elephants and they might run heel, and take the tusks out. John overtook them twelve or fifteen miles off, and came back to camp with his horse laden with bars of lead and the prettiest and most courteous letter from Mr. Webb, who would not hear of my buying lead with ivory, and sent me a bountiful supply and a number of kind words. It was a most generous help, most graciously rendered, and enabled me to enjoy my homeward march. Without it I should have been troubled to feed my followers for 1,400 miles, for I had only a very small reserve.

These were the only elephants I shot that were not eaten, and I hope some wandering Bushman, vulture led, may have come across even them. I missed Livingstone. He was driven back by fever breaking out amongst his party, and returned on the other side of the river, to which I myself crossed over after a time, but he had then gone by.

Inspanning one morning whilst here, a shout of 'Ingwe' from the men, a rush of the dogs, and up jumped a leopard in the midst of us, and made for a large tree, which he climbed. I was beneath it in a minute with a gun, and for half an hour with three or four men searched for him along the branches without avail. At last we gave it up, and went after the waggons, thinking he must have managed to get away unseen by us. One man however stopped behind for a minute to tie up his bundle, and before we were a hundred yards off the cunning beast raised his head from a bough, came down, and made away too quickly for us to get back, on the man's halloo, in time to shoot him—he did wondrously in hiding himself. Leopards were not common thus far in; they clung to the rocks and hills in and near the colony. I only saw four or five of them, but one performed a cleverish trick. The Kafirs were sitting round their fire under a large tree, when, climbing along an overhanging branch, he dropped into the circle, caught a dog, cleared the ring at a bound, and got safely away. Towards the Colony, where the baboons are plentiful, the leopard preys on them, though, when in large herds, the old dog baboons will frequently drive him off; their canine teeth are formidable weapons. Most amusing fellows are these noisy ancestors of ours, especially when feeding, spread about, picking up what they can find, lifting stones, and seizing anything that may be under them, and popping it into their cheek pouches with a smack. Three or four experienced veterans keep guard, to give warning of the approach of danger. They cannot forage for themselves, so they have an eye for the pouches of their brethren, and now and then make a spring, take a young fellow by the ear, and cuff him well, until he allows them to put their fingers into his pouch, and transfer its contents to their own. The hunting leopard, too, was seldom seen. I once roughly tested his tremendous speed. I was on horseback, and caught sight of one in such a position that he must pass close to me, if I could gain a point fifty yards off. To upset my plan he had a hundred and fifty yards to run, and he beat me hollow, though I went at a full gallop.

The game was plentiful on this north side of the river, but the country in places was very ugly for hunting from the dense thickets. Lying lazily one day on a high bank of a beautiful reach, I was watching the otters below me as they paddled and fished down stream, when a troop of Bushmen from a neighbouring kraal came to the watering-place, to fill their gourds and ostrich shells, before starting for the elephants I had killed the previous day, which were as usual some twelve or fifteen miles from camp, in a dry and thirsty land where no water was. After filling their vessels with a supply sufficient to last them for the two or three days it would take them to cut up and dry their meat, they proceeded to fill themselves—a most remarkable process; each one, whether at the moment thirsty or not, pouring down a cargo of water to the utmost limit of his holding capacity, to economise the store he carried at his back. Like Mr. Weller at Stiggins' tea party, 'I could see them swelling wisibly before my very eyes,' until their usually shrivelled bodies became shining and distended all over; and man, woman and child waddled away—so many different sized water balloons. The last of the long line had disappeared in the dense forest—my otters were all gone—the country was not a tempting one for hunting, the thorns by the river being almost impenetrable, and the jungle further off so matted and bound together with creepers and monkey-ropes that I had determined not to try it again. The noonday heat had stilled the earth of all distinguishable sounds, though the unbroken monotonous hum of insect life, the never-failing accompaniment of a piping hot day, seemed to fill and load the head and sultry air. I had nothing to watch, less to do, and was not sleepy; the silence burdened me: and at length, to break it, I shouted to my after-rider, who was enjoying his siesta some distance off under the waggons, to saddle the horses, and taking my gun, I mounted and rode along one of the narrow game tracks into the thicket, picking up a Bushman who had remained behind at the encampment. For some time the only living thing we saw was an old bull buffalo, which with lowered head seemed inclined to bar the road until, threatened by the Bushman's spear, he sulkily withdrew. We had no need of him, and were content to let him go in peace. A shot would have disturbed the elephants we thought we might fall in with, for though we were not on a trail, the fresh footprints which were ever and again crossing the track, and the broken branches with the sap yet undried, told us they had been there very lately. Into the thorny barriers on either side of the way we could not have followed them with our horses, even had we wished, so we stuck to the path and kept our eyes open. Presently the ground to our right with its sea of thorns rose in a long low swell, and as it sank into the little hollow beyond, five or six colossal bodiless legs stood out amongst the bare lower stems of the closely woven branches. I slipped from my pony, and crawling on hands and knees, got within twenty yards of the legs, without being able to see anything more of the owners. A large tree was in advance, round whose stem the thorns did not press quite so pertinaciously as elsewhere. Slowly and cautiously I gained its side. An elephant was close to me, but though I could now see his body he was stern on. I broke a twig to attract his attention: his head swung half round, but was so guarded by the bush that it would have been useless to fire at it. His shoulder was more exposed. There was no time to wait, he was on the move, and the dust flew from his side as the heavy ball struck him. Screaming angrily, he turned full front in the direction of the tree by which I stood motionless. I do not think he made me out, and the bush was too thick for me to risk giving him further information by a second shot. For a moment we confronted one another: and then, the rumbling note of alarm uttered by his companions decided him on joining them, and the stiff thorns bent before the weight of seven or eight bulls, as a cornfield in the wind.

I regained the path and rode along the line of their retreat, which, as shown by the yielding bush, was parallel to it. After a time the thorns thinned out, and I caught sight of the wounded elephant holding a course of his own a little to the left of his fellows; and when he entered the tropical forest beyond I was in his wake, and very soon compelled to follow where he broke away. Lying flat on my pony's neck and guiding him as I best might by occasional glimpses of the tail of my now slowly retreating pioneer, I laboured on in the hope that more open ground might enable me to get up alongside of him. A most unpleasant ride it was. My constrained position gave me but little chance of using my hands to save my head; I was at one time nearly pulled from the saddle by the heavy boughs, and at another nearly torn to pieces by the wicked thorns of the 'wait-a-bit,' which, although no longer *the* tree of the jungle, were intolerably scattered through it. I have killed elephants on very bad ground, but this was the worst piece of bush I ever rode into in my life. A little extra noise from the pursuers caused the pursued to stop; and whilst clinging like Gilpin to the calender's horse and peering at the broad stern of the chase, I saw him suddenly put his head where his tail ought to have been. The trunk was tightly coiled-an elephant nearly always coils his trunk in thick bush for fear of pricking it—forward flapped the huge ears, up went the tail, and down he came like a gigantic bat, ten feet across. Pinned above and on either side, by dismounting I could neither hope to escape nor to kill my opponent. I therefore lugged my unfortunate animal round and urged him along; but I had not taken into account with what great difficulties and how slowly I had followed the bull.

He was now in full charge, and the small trees and bush gave way before him like reeds, whereas I was compelled to keep my head lowered as before and try and hold the path, such as it was, up which we had come. I was well mounted, and my spurs were sharp. Battered and torn by branch and thorn I managed a kind of gallop, but it was impossible to keep it up. The elephant thundered straight through obstacles we were obliged to go round, and in fifty yards we were fast in a thick bush and he within fifteen of us. As a last chance I tried to get off, but in rolling round on my saddle my spur gored the pony's flank, and the elephant screaming over him at the same moment, he made a convulsive effort and freed himself, depositing me in a sitting position immediately in front of the uplifted forefoot of the charging bull. So near was it that I mechanically opened my knees to allow him to put it down, and, throwing myself back, crossed my hands upon my chest, obstinately puffing myself out with the idea of trying to resist the gigantic tread, or at all events of being as troublesome to crush as possible. I saw the burly brute from chest to tail as he passed directly over me lengthways, one foot between my knees, and one fourteen inches beyond my head, and not a graze! Five tons at least! As he turned from chasing the pony-which, without my weight and left to its own instinct, escaped easily to my after-rider's horse—he swept by me on his way to rejoin his companions, and I got another snap shot at his shoulders. As soon as I could I followed his spoor, but must have changed it in the thick bush, for in five minutes I had run into and killed a fresh elephant in a small open space. The Bushmen found the first, next morning, dead.

Out of all my narrow escapes this is the only one that remained with me in recollection for any time. On four or five other occasions I was half or wholly stunned, and therefore not very clear about my sensations; but on this I was well aware of what was going on and over me. One hears of night-mares—well, for a month or more I dare say, I had night-elephants.

My reader will be glad to know that this is the last mishap I am going to tell him of, and that my contribution to the Big Game of Africa is finished. I beg his pardon for not making it more interesting, but I began a new trade too late in life. At starting I only proposed to give the stories of the illustrations; this I have done as well as I am able, but I have coupled them together with remarks not strictly within the subject of 'Big Game,' because in writing of African animals I could not quite get rid of African surroundings; and, besides, entirely by themselves they looked too bare. I hope I may be excused, therefore, for going a little beyond the limits prescribed for this 'accidental' sketch.

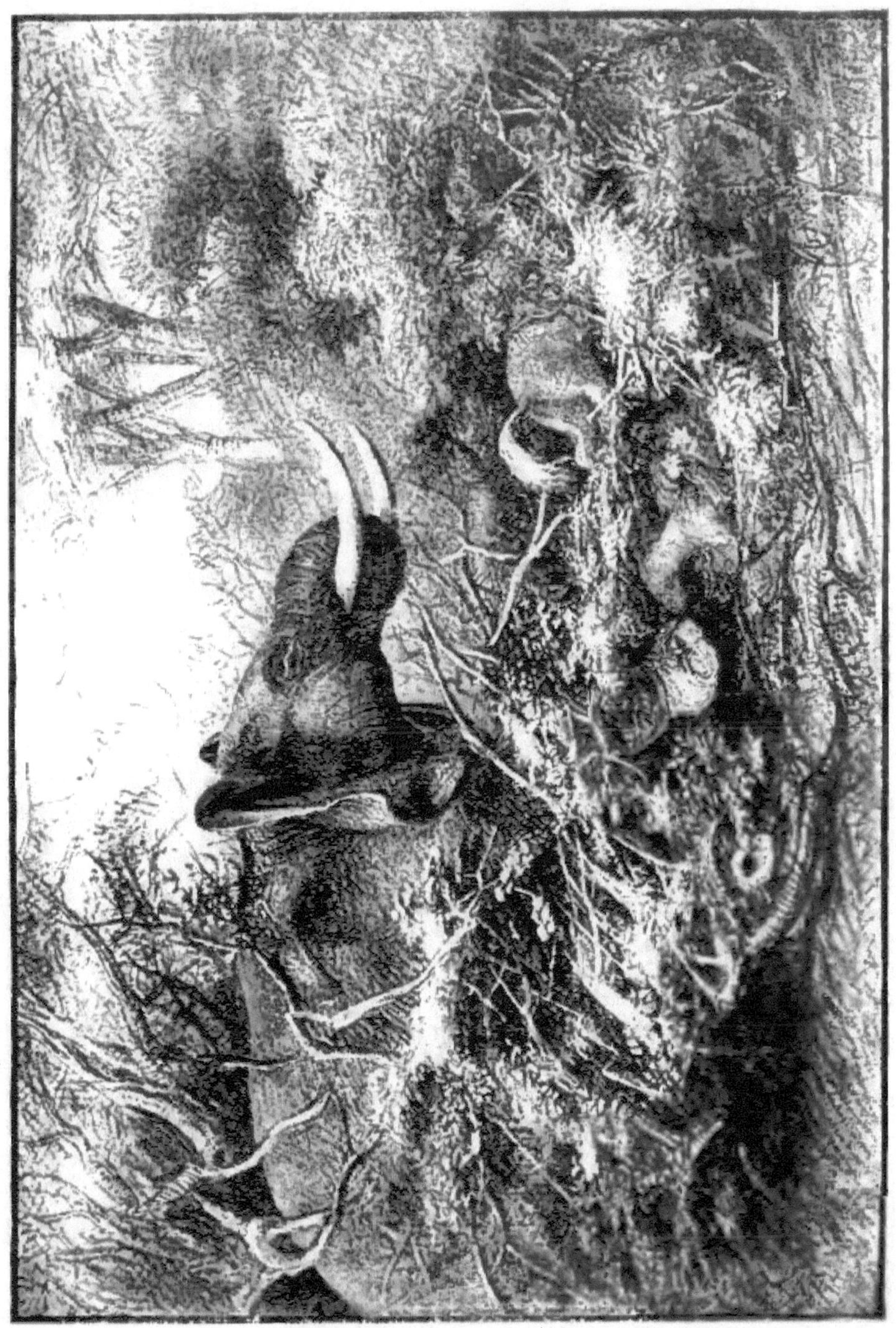

Threatening of Elephantiasis

Joseph Wolf

CHAPTER V

WITH LIVINGSTONE IN SOUTH AFRICA

BY W. COTTON OSWELL

[The Editors are fully aware that the following cannot be considered as coming strictly under the head of Big Game Shooting. It is, however, the special wish of the late Mr. Oswell's family that the whole MS. should appear as he left it, and the Editors willingly comply with the request. — ED.]

A few lines about my companion in my Zambesi journey. The description of the route taken may be found in his book, and of the man himself two Lives have been written. But I knew him well personally, and there was one trait in his character which, *me judice*, has never been made enough of — a kind of firm persistence to do whatever he had set his mind on. In an Englishman we might, I think, have called the phase obstinacy, but with Livingstone it was 'Scottishness.' It was not the *sic volo sic jubeo* style of imperiousness, but a quiet determination to carry out his own views in his own way, without feeling himself bound to give any reason or explanation further than that he intended doing so and so. This was an immense help to him, for it made him supremely self-reliant, and if he had not been, he could never have done half that he did. He was the Fabius of African travel. *Vicit cunctando* might well be his epitaph. He believed, as I do, that the way was to be won, not forced, if any good results were to follow. I have sat seven weeks with him on the bank of a swamp because he was unwilling to run counter to the wishes of the people. I pressed him to move on with the horses; no active opposition would have been offered, but he would not wound the prejudices of the natives — and he was right. We had our reward, for, after satisfying themselves that we meant no harm, we were given free passports, and even helped on our way, journeying, as an Indian would say, on 'the back of an elephant.' With his quiet endurance, and entire lack of fussiness and excitability, content to wait and let patience have her perfect work, quite satisfied that the day should bring forth what it liked, he was eminently the *'justum et tenacem propositi virum,'* on whom man or elements make but slight impression, yet strangely withal very enthusiastic. This nature fitted him for the successful traveller and trustworthy companion. His inner man and noble aspirations belong to the histories of his life. We were the firmest of friends, both a trifle obstinate, but we generally agreed to differ, and in all matters concerning the natives, I, of course, waived my crude opinions to his matured judgment. I had the management of trekking and the cattle, after he, with his great knowledge of the people and their language, had obtained all the information he could about the waters and the distances between them. This worked well.

When we reached the Chobé River, Sebitoani was on an island thirty miles down stream, but sent his own canoe with twelve paddlers to bring us to him. It was a pleasant trip, the men going with the current about eight miles an hour. At three in the afternoon we reached our destination and landed. Presently this really great chief and man came to meet us, shy and ill at ease. We held out our hands in the accustomed way of true Britons, and I was surprised to see that his mother-wit gave him immediate insight into what was expected of him, and the friendly meaning of our salutation; though he could never have witnessed it before, he at once followed suit and placed his hand in ours as if to the manner born. I felt troubled at the evident nervousness of the famous warrior, for he had been, and still was, a mighty fighter, with very remarkable force of character. Surrounded by his tribesmen, he stood irresolute and quite overcome in the presence of two ordinary-looking Europeans. Livingstone entered at once into conversation with him, and by degrees partly reassured him; but throughout that day and the next, a sad, half-scared look never faded from his face. He had wished us to visit him, had sent an ambassage to Livingstone at Kolobeng, but the reality of our coming, with all its possibilities, dangers, and advantages seemed to flit through the man's mind as in a vision. He killed an ox for us, and treated us right royally; he was far and away the finest Kafir I ever saw in mien and manner.

He had been told that Livingstone and I occasionally wrote a letter to one another, if by chance we were separated for a day or two and wished to communicate or arrange a meeting at a certain point, and asked us if his information were true that we could make one another hear when far apart, and if we could give him an example of our power. Livingstone took a man out of even Kafir earshot, four or five hundred yards away, and then whisperingly asked him his own and his wife's name, and writing them on a scrap of paper sent him to me. 'Well, Ra'chobe, and how is Seboni your wife?'I asked. The chief and his headmen, who were gathered expectant round, were amazed and somewhat frightened, taking it for magic, though they soon got over it.

It does not do to introduce Kafirs too suddenly to the common things of civilised life. I once lost an admiring audience by an act of this kind. A laughing circle was round me, and I was dispensing beads, brass wire, and tiny looking-glasses to ingratiate myself with a new tribe, the Macoba, when by way of amusing them I took a burning-glass from my pocket and ignited a pinch of gunpowder strewed on the waggon-box, telling them what I was going to do, and preparing them for it. With the puff, man, woman, and child, vanished; it was days before I could regain their confidence, and throughout my stay with them I was looked upon with awe as the wizard of the sun.

Sebitoani had allotted to us a bright clean kotla for eating and sleeping in, and after supper we lay down on the grass, which had been cut for our beds by the thoughtful attention of the chief. In the dead of the night he paid us a visit alone, and sat down very quietly and mournfully at our fire. Livingstone and I woke up and greeted him, and then he dreamily recounted the history of his life, his wars, escapes, successes and conquests, and the far-distant wandering in his raids. By the fire's glow and flicker among the reeds, with that tall dark earnest speaker and his keenly attentive listeners, it has always appeared to me one of the most weird scenes I ever saw. With subdued manner and voice Sebitoani went on through the livelong night till near the dawn, his low tones only occasionally interrupted by an inquiry from Livingstone. He described the way in which he had circumvented a strong 'impi' of Matabili on the raid, and raised his voice for a minute or two as he recounted how, hearing of their approach, he had sent men to meet the dreaded warriors of 'Umsilegas, feigning themselves traitors to him in order to lure them to destruction by promising to guide them to the bulk of the cows and oxen which they said, in fear of their coming, had been placed in fancied security on one of the large islands of the Chobé; how the Zulus fell into the trap, and allowed themselves to be ferried over in three or four canoes hidden there for the purpose, and how when the last trip had been made the boatmen, pulling out into midstream, told them they could remain where they were till they were fetched off, and in the meantime might search for the cattle; how, after leaving them till they were worn and weak with hunger, for there was nothing to eat on the island, he passed over, killed the chiefs, and absorbed the soldiers into his own ranks, providing them with wives, a luxury they were not entitled to under Zulu military law until their spears had been well reddened in fight. Then he waved his hand westwards, and opened out a story of men over whom he had gained an easy triumph 'away away very far by the bitter waters,' and to whom, when they asked for food, wishing to bind them with fetters of kindness, he sent a fat ox, and, '"Would you believe it? they returned it, saying they didn't eat ox." "Then what do you eat?" I asked; "*we* like beef better than anything." "We eat *men*," said they. I had never heard of this before. But they were very pressing, so at last I sent them two slaves of Macobas—the river people—who, as you know, are very dark in colour, but they brought them back, saying they did not like *black* men, but preferred the redder variety, and as that meant sending my own fighting men, I told them they might go without altogether.' This was the only intimation we ever had that cannibalism existed in our part of Africa.

This chief afterwards died close to our waggons from pneumonia set up by the irritation of some old spear wounds in his chest. He was beloved by the Makololo, was the fastest runner and best fighter among them; just, though stern, with wonderful power of attaching men to him. He was a gentleman in thought and manner, well disposed to Europeans, and very proud of their visiting him. Had he not died he might have been of the greatest use in civilising and missionary work. His kingdom has, I am afraid, melted away. The sceptre descended to his daughter, who thought, as man took a plurality of wives, a queen might allow herself like liberty in the way of husbands. Bickering and strife arose, and though the rule went to her brother after her resignation, he was not of the same calibre as his father, and disintegration of the heterogeneous elements of the carefully put together and wisely ruled kingdom soon set in. The nation lost its unity, and resolved itself into its separate nationalities—in the course, I believe, of a very few years. Such has been the fate of all African kingdoms; one great man has made and held them together, and at his death they have returned to the several petty tribal royalties out of which they were welded.

And now, having had my say on Big Game, one word on the 'biggest beasts' of Africa—the slave traders—and one on the country, and I have done. It was on the Chobé that we first came across the slaver's work. We had travelled all night through the sleeping flies. I was in advance with the gun and half a dozen Kafirs with axes, with which they had been clearing the way. In the very early morning we reached the river, narrow, but deep, with steep banks. I asked the guide if we could cross it. 'Do they swim?' he asked, pointing to the waggons. 'No,' I answered; 'where's the ford?' There was none, he said. 'Are there tsétsé here?' I inquired, and he replied that there were plenty. 'What are we to do with the animals?' and he told me to drive them as near as possible to the water, into the reeds, as the flies were not there, only in the bush. The pests were beginning to buzz about as the sun rose, so we took the man's advice, and while the others lay down for a rest of an hour or two I volunteered to keep watch. Putting my back against a tree, I kept my eyes steadfastly fixed on my charge for a time, and then I suppose I must have closed them, though of course I should deny that I was asleep.

Suddenly I was roused from my reverie by a salutation in Sechuana—'Rumélá.' I looked up, and before me stood a tall stalwart Kafir, clothed in a lady's dressing-gown. It came scantily to his knee, and in other parts seemed hardly to have been made for him, and his appearance was so queer that I burst into a laugh. I saw the blood rise in his dusky face as he asked what I was laughing at. 'Why, you have got on a woman's dress from my country,' I told him. 'I don't know about that,' he said, 'but I gave a woman for it last year.' We had come unaware upon the southern limit of the slave trade. It was months since we had last seen any products of European manufacture except those we had brought with us, and here they were in 18° S. Lat., in the middle of South Africa, 1,500 to 1,800 miles from any sea. Livingstone woke up, smoothed down my visitor, and inquired what we could do with the cattle. We could not leave them where they were; they would find nothing to eat, and besides, when the sun got hot the flies would find their way to them. We must drive them across the river, as there were no tsétsé there, the man told us; and we found it was so, the narrowest lines frequently defining the limits of safety and danger. Nothing, however, would persuade them to take the jump from the bank into the deep black water. Our friend whistled, and from the fringe of reeds on the opposite side four or five canoes full of men shot across the narrow channel. As they landed they presented the most motley appearance. They had evidently dressed to astonish us, and each bore about his neck or shoulders some article of European manufacture. Here was a fellow with a yard and a half of green baize or red drugget tied with a leathern thong about his throat, the ends streaming away behind him; another with a yard or two of some cheap gaudy cloth with a hole cut in the middle, wearing it *à la poncho*; two yards of calico of the commonest adorned the person of a third; it was a most ridiculous sight, but was evidently considered most impressively overwhelming. Still the cattle resisted our united efforts. At last, a canoe was paddled over to the other side, and in three or four minutes appeared again with a tiny cow and a most diminutive calf as passengers. The little cow was lifted on to the bank, and the canoe paddled back with the calf; we got our oxen as much together in a lump as we could, close to the river, surrounded them on three sides, loosed the lowing little mother, who instantly took a header into the water, and then by shouting, pushing, and twisting tails induced our oxen to follow the example set them, and they were safe. The horses gave no trouble.

On questioning these Kafirs and their chief (Sebitoani) afterwards as to the mystery of the fine clothes, this was the interpretation. 'Do you see that little hill? A number of men with hair like yours and with guns came from the eastwards and sat down on that hill. We sent to ask them what they wanted, and they said "to buy men." We explained we had none to sell; it was the first time they had ever come to us, though we had heard of them before. Wouldn't they buy ivory or ostrich feathers? No, they didn't want anything of that sort; they had beautiful cloths, which they showed us.' 'I told them,' said Sebitoani, 'that I thought it was an "ugly" thing to sell men, but they sat there day after day, and showed us fresh cloths so beautiful that you would have sold your grand-mother for them. Then I somehow remembered there were men whom we had taken in our last raid. And I at length consented to part with them. But they were not many, and they wanted more. I said I had none; if I sold now it must be my own people, and I would not do that. Then they asked, "Don't you want oxen?" What could I say—doesn't a chief always want oxen? "Well, as we came here, about five days off we passed through a country where the oxen were like the grass for number. Lend us 400 or 500 of your warriors, and we will help with our guns, and let us attack that tribe. We will take the men and women, and you shall take the oxen." What could I say? This appeared a very good plan to me, so we attacked. They got two great tens (200) of men and women, and I got all those cattle,' pointing to a plain on which a herd of these diminutive little creatures were feeding. I forget whether Livingstone described them, but they were most remarkably small things, like sturdy Durham oxen three feet high. There was not the least difficulty in carrying them about bodi-ly; we put one into a waggon, hoping to bring it out, but it died. Pretty little gentle beasts, I wish I had taken more trouble to secure specimens. When the men milked them they held them by the hind leg as you would a goat. On the other hand, by the shores of Lake 'Ngami, a gigantic long-horned breed is found, stolen in a raid from the Ba-Wangketsi thirty years before our visit. They were originally remark-able for their heads, but in four or five generations, from feeding on the silicious coated reeds and succulent grasses near the lake, had developed wonderfully in horns and height. Through Livingstone I obtained one 6 ft. 2 in. high, with horns measuring from tip to tip 8 ft. 7 in. and 14 ft. 2 in. round from one point to the other taking in the base of the skull. We had cleared a way for the waggons through the bush, but had in many places on our return to widen it for my ox. I hoped to have brought him home and to have presented him to the Zoological Gardens, but after driving him 800 miles the grass got very short, and his horns coming to the ground before his nose, prevented him feeding. I was obliged to shoot him, and his head now hangs over the sideboard in my dining-room.

These slave-dealers, with their devilish counsels and temptations, were Mam-bari, a kind of half-caste Portuguese, who fifty years ago were agents for the export slave-trade. When the survivors of the gangs reached the coast they were packed away in a slave-ship, like herrings in a cask, and transported. Through the vigilance of English cruisers this iniquitous traffic has been greatly reduced, and, but for the refusal of the right of search by the French, would be very small and unremunerative; but the Arab curse still continues, and though, now that the sea-board is partially occupied by Europeans, greater difficulty will be placed in its way, I am of opinion that through the avarice and cupidity of man—African and European— it will not entirely disappear so long as there is any ivory left. That once exhausted, is there anything else worth bringing a ten-mile journey to the coast?

In the late very cool partitioning of Africa we may congratulate ourselves in having obtained possession of Mashonaland, a district healthy enough for colonisation, and apparently rich enough to repay it. The tsétsé, that great enemy to the cattle-breeder, will disappear before the approach of civilisation, and the killing off of the game, especially the buffalo, its standing dish, as it has done many times already in African lore. I am speaking of the tracts south of the Zambesi. Of tropical lands to the north I know nothing, save from what I read and am told, and I cannot yet see how they are to be settled. Fever and general unhealthiness must weight immigration heavily, and even if the country is capable of supplying the needs of the world in the future, what philanthropic society will subsidise the workers until the industries are developed? It must be remembered the greatest prophylactics in an evil climate are movement, and its consequent excitement, and change of scene—the settler dies where the traveller lives. The railway, if made, will help to suppress slavery, by giving carriage for the ivory, its only cause at present—no ivory, no slavery. May the venture turn out better than many another has done, and not end in that very questionable blessing, a rum-civilisation!

The influx of immigrants into Mashonaland will, in time, with the gold and diamond seeking population further south, tend to minimise the power of the Boers over the native tribes. Dutchmen are slow colonists, and will not be able to hold their own with the incomers in enterprise, or in a few years in numbers or power, and the evil influence and oppression they have at times exercised upon the black race will be at an end. I hope no worse *régime* may come in with the new rule. There were many good points in the Dutch farmers, and I think they compare very favourably with English squatters in other lands. Where antagonistic races are brought together, the minority, the whites, if they are to hold their ground, are almost inevitably forced for very existence to terrorise the black majority that would otherwise overwhelm them. I am not arguing that their conduct is moral or legal, but it has been, and will continue to be, the rule where whites settle in black men's lands uninvited. We may hold up our hands in a Pharisaical way, and when we are once secure, I grant we try to improve our subjects; but they must be our subjects first. But would Englishmen under similar conditions have done much better than the Dutchmen? I think not. Without the pale of law, they would hardly have been so much of a law unto themselves. No doubt the Boers have many faults, and with respect to the native races have shown great cruelty—my contention is they could hardly have held their own without. We must not be too hard on them because they have twice got the better of us in the field, and twice in diplomacy. Englishmen have not forgotten Laings Nek and the Majuba Hills. Diplomatically, too, we were twice worsted: the Boers had very troublesome neighbours, and sought the suzerainty of our Queen for their own ends, not by a unanimous vote I know; but there are 'oppositions' everywhere, and at all events the seekers were the majority. The troublesome neighbours, now we are masters, call upon us to rectify the frontier line, which had been greatly encroached upon by the Boers. We refuse, or delay, to set matters right. Boers' troublesome neighbours become ours. The Zulus are conquered with some difficulty, and the Boers, relieved from their anxieties, demand and obtain the withdrawal of the suzerainty. This is not my opinion alone. The Zulus were our fast friends till we refused to undo the wrongs they had suffered at the hands of the Dutchmen—the whole story, including the subsequent withdrawal of our troops, is a page that one would like to tear out of our annals.

The character of the country in its different stages is well given in the illustrations. There are no striking features; no mountains, no large river, except the Zambesi, and only one rather uninteresting lake, 'Ngami; no great forests, no tropical vegetation; the rains are scanty, the soil dry, the plains large. What you see one day you may see for a week. In most countries you would have to describe nature in her many phases, but in South Africa one might take a paint-brush and give a broad, general idea of the land, with four or five streaks of colour—the widely extending, ascending, nearly treeless flats from Kuruman to the Molopo River; the broken, fairly clothed region of the Bakatla; and the open park-like scenery between them and the rocky homes of the Bakaa and Ba-Mungwato. Throughout this area the prevailing trees are mimosas; the flowers are of the same genera and orders, undisturbed by man—sheets of different kinds are often spread out side by side, parterre fashion, in separate beds, not mingling even at the edges. They have fought the battle out amongst themselves, and it has ended in the survival of the fittest, aliens less suited to the particular border being crowded out by the stronger natives.

From the Ba-Mungwato, however, as you dive into the Kalahari desert by the Bushmen sucking-holes of 'Serotli, thirty yards of sand suffice to change the growth and families of trees and flowers. On the side we struck the hollow, they were old friends; on the other, entire strangers—not even recognised by the Kafirs who had accompanied us from the south.

We had turned over a fresh leaf in Nature's book, and it lasted us until the sluggish waters of the Zouga River and Lake Kamadou came in sight, with their lonely palm-trees, and, on the upper reaches of the river, unusually thick bush. You thence passed through a country cut up with narrow sleepy streams, or by the dry barren road, eastward of Lake Kamadou, to the open flats of the Zambesi, the approach from the side of the Chobé being studded with euphorbia-trees, quaint of growth, and excellently named candelabra. Throughout these parts you hardly see a hillock; so rare, indeed, is the sight, that one tiny, isolated mound is named 'Sisalébue'—'we are still looking at you'—by the Kafirs, in recognition of the scarcity of even such haycocks. Beyond the Zouga the wonderful abundance of animal life is not maintained. There is game, but not in large herds. The happy hunting grounds in my time began at the Molopo and ended at the Zouga.

Throughout South Africa the sparseness of the population has favoured the increase of the game, coupled with the fact that the people were not adequately armed for its destruction. The massing of animals in particular localities, dependent on the waters, which are few and far between, may perhaps have led to an exaggerated idea of the sum total; but put it as you will, after all real and imaginary deductions from whatsoever cause, there never was a land so full of wild life since antediluvian days. It will die out before guns and civilisation, and that quickly, though the fly may bar the way to *mounted* sportsmen, for there are no dense jungles or inaccessible ranges of mountains for the beasts to fall back upon.

Dead Buffalo

From a photograph by E. Gedge

CHAPTER VI

EAST AFRICA—BATTERY, DRESS, CAMP GEAR AND STORES

BY F. J. JACKSON

The pursuit of big game in the Africa of fifty years ago has already been graphically described in the foregoing pages by the late Mr. W. C. Oswell; but, as the editor of these volumes considers that something ought to be written here of more modern sport in that country, and as the style of hunting has altered somewhat since my collaborator's time, I have accepted an invitation to describe East African sport as it is to-day, and to furnish such advice and guidance as may prove serviceable to others contemplating a shooting expedition to my old hunting grounds.

The nature of the big game in East Africa can have altered little, except in those parts of the country which have, within the last few years, been visited by European sportsmen. In these places, particularly in the district round Kilimanjaro, and in the vicinity of well-beaten caravan routes to the interior, the game has naturally become more cunning and more difficult to approach than it used to be. Little or nothing has ever been done or can be done in East Africa without patience and perseverance, and perhaps the pursuit of big game in that country will test these virtues more than anything else. Disappointments in such a country are, of course, numerous, and some of them are unavoidable, but there are others which might be avoided by the exercise of a little patience and knowledge.

First among the matters requiring the sportman's consideration is his battery.

Without entering into the details of the merits and demerits of the different rifles and their respective charges, about which so much has been written, I strongly recommend sportsmen intending to visit East Africa to arm themselves on the principle that a big beast, and more particularly a dangerous one, requires a heavy bullet, and the great shock such a bullet gives to the system, to disable or kill it, and not to allow themselves to be carried away with the idea that a .450 Express bullet is good enough for anything. There is no doubt whatever that the very largest and toughest of game can be killed by a .450 or .500 Express, and there are several well-known and very experienced sportsmen who use nothing else. But as it is more than probable that the majority of those men who use, and advocate the use of, small rifles for all kinds of big game used heavy rifles when they first began, and while learning by experience what they now know of the habits of the beasts, their anatomy, and their most vital spots, I should recommend beginners to use what these experienced hunters began with, i.e. heavy rifles for big game. This chapter is written more particularly for sportsmen who, though they may be excellent shots, and possessed of good nerve under ordinary circumstances in the open, have had little or no experience with big and dangerous game. Approaching a beast which is quite unconscious of the stalker's presence, even out in the open where there is little covert, although exciting and often rather difficult work, is rarely, if ever, dangerous; but following the blood spoor of a wounded buffalo, rhinoceros, or elephant into places where there is little chance of seeing the beast excepting at close quarters is quite another thing; and it is possible that a man might lose his nerve or become unsteady through over-excitement when the result of a badly placed small-bore bullet might end in disaster. The use of heavy rifles, however, reduces to a minimum the danger of following up such dangerous game into thick bush or long tangled grass. A large-bore spherical bullet driven by plenty of powder, even if it should not strike a vital spot (owing perhaps to the position of the beast when fired at, or to the stalker being unable in the thick covert to make out what part of the animal he is aiming at), will inflict such a tremendous shock upon the system that the creature is far less likely to charge than when hit with a small bullet. A big bullet might knock the beast down, and would also knock out of him any inclination he might have to charge, whereas a small bullet under the same conditions would have little chance of knocking him down, but would only inflict further pain and increase his inclination to charge.

The following is the battery used by myself, and it is one which I have found satisfactory:—

A single 4-bore rifle, weighing 21 lbs., sighted for 50, 100, and 150 yards, shooting 12 drams of powder and a spherical bullet.

A double 8-bore rifle, weighing 15 lbs., sighted for 100 and 200 yards, shooting

12 drams of powder and a spherical bullet.

A double .500 Express, sighted for 100 and 200 yards, bored for long bottle-shaped cases, 'Magnum,' shooting 6 drams of powder and long bullets of three kinds—solid, small-hole, and copper-tube.

A 12-bore shot-gun.

To the above were added a single .450 Express with telescope sight up to 300 yards for long shots when game was wild; a .44 Winchester carbine, a wonderfully accurate and first-rate little weapon for *Gazella Thomsoni* and such small game; a .295 rook rifle; and a 12-bore Paradox by Messrs. Holland. This is an admirable weapon, and cannot be too highly recommended for shooting in bush where game is generally to be seen within 100 yards, though it rarely offers more than a snap shot. A Paradox is particularly useful should the sportsman's dinner depend on a snap shot at an antelope, guinea-fowl, or francolin. In a country where transport is difficult to obtain and also expensive, and where every cartridge is important and has to be considered, it would be as well to take a 20-bore Paradox instead of a 12-bore.

Moreover, for a weapon that would rarely be out of the hand (except when stalking or following up a wounded beast), its lightness, especially on the march or when returning to camp dead beat after a good hard day, would be a great advantage. Many is the time I have longed for such a handy little weapon.

A very favourite battery amongst sportsmen, and one which many recommend, is as follows:—

A double 8-bore rifle.

A double .577 Express rifle.

A double .450 Express rifle.

A double 20-bore shot-gun.

If, however, I were asked to recommend a first-rate battery for East Africa, I should say:—

A single 4-bore rifle, as above, with only one sight—100 yards.

A double 8-bore, as above, with only one sight—100 yards.

A double .500 Express, as above.

A single .450 Express, as above, or .400 for long cartridge.

A 20-bore Paradox.

And a .295 rook rifle.

Hammerless rifles and guns are much safer in the hands of native gun-bearers than hammered guns, besides having other and most important advantages, which, however, it is needless for me to enter upon.

All guns, rifles, and ammunition should be taken out from England. The ammunition should be packed in tin-lined boxes with screw-down lids, and should not exceed 65 lbs. in weight. A strong solid leather cartridge magazine to hold 500

12-bore cartridges should be taken. It can be filled with an assortment of cartridges for immediate use, and can be replenished from the tin-lined boxes when necessary or convenient. To complete the shooting kit, a pair of powerful binoculars, which are much handier than a telescope, is indispensable. They should be made of aluminium (which is very light), and can be carried either in their leather case on the belt or inside the coat, which I think is by far the handiest place. A compass, though a good thing to have, is not altogether necessary; it can if wanted be carried either in a small pocket (which should be waterproof) between the brace buttons of the breeches, or let into the lid of the binocular case.

DRESS

In the matter of dress, which is a very important consideration in big game shooting, when everything has to be done on foot, regard should be had to the features of the surrounding country, and the stalker should endeavour to be as little conspicuous as possible. With this end in view, he cannot do better than have his clothes made of Kharki, and Indian Shikar cloth of mixed green and brown. In the dry weather, when the grass and bush are withered, Kharki is less conspicuous than Shikar cloth, as it assimilates better with the surroundings. Shikar cloth is excellent after the rains have fallen, and the grass and bush are green. Both are very strong, and wear well. I recommend the coat to be made Norfolk jacket fashion, loose and roomy about the chest and shoulders, but fitting fairly close at the waist. There should be one pocket *let in* on the left breast, but on no account should there be one of any kind on the right breast, as it would often interfere with getting the rifle or gun quickly up to the shoulder. The two pockets, one on each hip, should be fairly large and roomy, and should have a good deep flap to keep wet and dirt out. The flap should be made to button, to prevent cartridges, &c., from jumping out when running; it should, however, be made to button and unbutton very easily. It is a good thing to have six loops (made on the same principle as a cartridge belt, but of the same material as the coat), sewn to the left breast, and six or eight on to the right side, for the cartridges of the two Express rifles most in use. The loops on the left breast should be about on a level with the first button, if the coat is worn with an open V front, or the second button if worn tunic fashion, to button up at the throat; the loops on the right side should be just above the belt. They are a great convenience, as, if properly made, the cartridges never shake out, and are far handier than when carried in the pocket, and the stalker is much more independent of his gun-bearers who carry spare ammunition. The under part of the sleeve, from above the elbow to the wrist, should be covered with some kind of soft leather, as a protection against thorns, &c., when crawling up to game. The shoulders should also be protected by leather pads. Knickerbocker breeches made with plenty of room above the knees are perhaps more comfortable than anything else. They should be faced with soft leather, extending from the knee to half-way up the thigh, and from the inside to the outside seam, with an extra thickness just over the knee-cap. It is a good plan to have a small pocket between each pair of the front brace buttons to carry a watch and compass in. These should be made waterproof, to prevent perspiration injuring their contents. Excellent clothes can be had either at Mombasa or Zanzibar, and are far cheaper than at home. It is as well, however, to have one suit made in England, as a pattern, for the Goanese tailors are poor hands at making from measurements, though they can turn out first-rate work from a pattern. All under-garments should be of flannel, a mixture of flannel and cotton, or flannel and silk. Woollen stockings should be thick, as they not only protect the feet from the burning heat, but also prevent them from blistering. Merino socks are very pleasant for camp, but are too thin for marching, and soon wear out. Boots and shoes should be of brown leather, as it is much cooler than black, and I find that shoes worn with leggings with 'spat' feet are undoubtedly cooler than boots. Leggings of soft sheepskin, or so-called Sambur leather, are excellent, and as they can be made to fit close to the leg, they afford almost as much support as the Indian 'putti.' They have one disadvantage, however, as Sambur leather soaks up and holds water more than other leather. All boots and shoes should have the soles well studded with nails, of which an extra supply should be taken, as walking in dry grass very soon polishes the soles, and slipping about, disagreeable at any time, becomes very exhausting after a long day. In the matter of headgear, Ellwood's patent Shikar hat of felt and brown canvas is excellent when the sun is very powerful; it will stand any amount of rough usage, and has the advantage of being waterproof. A solar 'topee,' whether helmet or mushroom shape, is much too conspicuous; is apt to be dragged off the head when passing through thorny bush; tears and breaks very easily; and after a downpour of rain soon becomes reduced to a heavy shapeless pulp. A parson's felt wide-awake, covered with the same material as the shooting suit, is capital for stalking in, as the brim is just wide enough to protect the back of the neck when crawling up to game, and is not so large as to be conspicuous.

A waterproof of material specially made for the tropics is indispensable. A very convenient shape with kilt and cape, known as the 'Payne-Gallwey,' is made by Messrs. Cording, of Air Street; but for Africa I prefer a short coat with a cape sufficiently long to keep a rifle dry when tucked under the arm to a cape only. The kilt to protect the legs should reach well below the knees. The advantage of this combination is that after a heavy shower of rain the legs are still protected from the wet grass, while the coat can be dispensed with, as it is very hot and uncomfortable work walking in a waterproof in the tropics. An ulster, or warm dressing-gown, should also be taken for camp use, and a thick boating sweater is invaluable in cold or damp weather.

CAMP GEAR

In regard to camp gear, a thing of vital importance, a few hints may prove useful. Comfort in camp should be one of the first considerations. Some men incur risks unnecessarily, through ignorance of the dangers they are running, having probably read that men in South Africa sleep out in the open with impunity, or with nothing but a 'lean-to' of sticks and grass as a protection against dew, wind, or rain, and a bundle of grass and a blanket to lie upon; but men cannot do this in East Africa, and I recommend them not to try. The heavy dews and the sudden changes of temperature during the night are two of the chief things to be guarded against, and it is well never to disregard them. A tent is indispensable. A capital one, known as the 'Wissmann,' can be had from Edgington, of 2 Duke Street, London Bridge. His damp and insect proof canvas is excellent, and wet increases its weight very little. This tent, which is 7 ft. by 7 ft., is a very comfortable size for one man, and packs into two loads. The outside fly, however, should be 3 ft. longer on each side of the ridge-pole, and should nearly touch the ground. If this is done the tent is much more likely to stand firm in a gale of wind, and the space underneath affords plenty of room for private gear, and also a capital sleeping-place for the tent boy, provided he does not snore. The poles, excepting the ridge-poles, should be solid, and made of deal, which is fairly light; female bamboo cracks and breaks when the tent ropes shrink through getting wet, and male bamboo is heavy and difficult to obtain in England. Indian-made tents are not to be recommended for Africa; they are essentially for hot and dry weather. They absorb damp, and increase tremendously in weight in wet weather; tear more easily in transport through bush; rot sooner than English-made tents, and are not proof against the attacks of white ants. A floorcloth of the same canvas as the tent, but of a coarser and stronger material, cut to the exact size of the tent, is a great comfort. This can be packed with the body of the tent, without making it too heavy a load. A bathroom attached to the fly on the Indian principle is also a comfort, and affords extra room for private gear, &c. The bedstead should be of iron; a first-rate folding one, weighing about 20 lbs., can be had at the Army and Navy Stores. The bedding should consist of a cork mattress, three Austrian coloured blankets, a leather pillow stuffed with hair, with three linen cases for the same; all packed in a waterproof Wolseley valise, procurable at the Army and Navy Stores. Clothing, books, and all valuables should be carried in air-tight cases, the most convenient size being 27 in. × 12 in. × 9 in. Last, though not least, is a good bath, and this should be an ordinary oval one with lid. It is a great convenience to have a wicker-work lining, to lift in and out, in which clothing and suchlike light things can be packed to the regulation weight. When it is required for bathing, the lining, with everything in it, can be lifted out. This does away with constant packing and unpacking. It is certainly an awkward load for a porter, and one he dislikes very much, but it is well worth taking. Of course, india-rubber baths of different makes are very portable, but in case of a severe chill they are not deep enough for a really good hot bath, besides which the risk they run of being damaged and rendered quite useless by careless African 'boys' is considerable. The mosquito curtain is another important item. This should not be bell-shaped, but oblong, and a little longer and wider than the bedstead. The top should be of calico, and should be either sewn to the sloping roof of the tent or attached to it with tapes, to tie and untie. When not in use, it can be folded up and stowed away flat against the roof, where it is out of the way, and when wanted can be dropped down over the bed. I strongly recommend everyone at all times to sleep under curtains, as, even if there are no mosquitoes, sand-flies, or other noxious insects about, curtains help to keep off miasma to a very great extent. Before having the mosquito curtains removed in the morning, it is a good thing to take a cup of coffee or cocoa before getting out of bed, as I believe when so fortified a man is less liable to the influences of miasma, which, if floating about at all, is worse just when getting up, between 4 and 5 A.M., than at any other time.

A good, well-assorted medicine chest is a *sine qua non*. All medicines should be, if possible, in compressed tabloid form. Messrs. Burroughs & Wellcome, of Snow Hill, Holborn, supply every kind of chest suitable for African travel. For the porters, &c., an extra supply of certain medicines should be taken out, such as spirits of nitre, quinine, chlorodyne, ipecacuanha, Warburgh's tincture, castor oil, laudanum, extract of male fern for tapeworm (a common complaint amongst them), powdered sulphur (for itch, also a common and most disagreeable complaint), a few bottles of Elliman, iodoform (for ulcers and sores), and a good cough mixture in a concentrated form.

STORES, ETC.

Although European stores, wines, and spirits of every kind are obtainable at Mombasa, I should recommend everybody intending to go out on a sporting trip to take a certain amount of stores with them, particularly those which would come under the head of medical comforts, such as Brand's soups and extracts, arrowroot, champagne, brandy, and port wine. Other stores for ordinary use which can be purchased at Mombasa are not always fresh, and as there is very little difference between the price of those taken from England, including the freight out, and of those bought on the spot, I am in favour of taking everything from home. The quantity to be taken depends entirely on the length of the trip and the individual tastes of the sportsmen. The kinds usually taken are soups, erbswurst (a capital pea-soup in powder), a few tongues and tinned meats, potted meats in small tins, salt, mustard, pepper, Worcester sauce in small bottles, baking-powder, oatmeal, tapioca, sago, pearl barley, essence of lemon for puddings, tea in compressed form, coffee, cocoa, milk (Nestlé's), sugar, saccharine (Allen & Hanbury's), whisky, and candles (Ozokerits), &c., &c. No expedition should be undertaken without a few pint bottles of really good champagne, to be used medicinally, as few things are more efficacious in pulling a man together in cases of extreme prostration after fever, or when thoroughly exhausted and knocked out of time from long and violent exertion. A tumbler of champagne with a teaspoonful of brandy in it, I know from experience, has a marvellous effect in cases of over-exertion. Of course, although spirits should be taken, they should be used with extreme moderation in a climate like that of East Africa, and should not be taken until the sun is down. Provided a man can eat well—and most men can when in hard exercise—stimulants of any kind are not necessary; at the same time it is always advisable to have them in case of emergencies. There are times when a man after a long and hard day may be so tired that he is quite past the hungry stage, and does not feel inclined to eat. It is then that a whisky 'peg' with five grains of quinine in it on arrival in camp, and before having a bath, will be found a capital 'pick-me-up,' and will not only enable a man to eat, but render him far less liable to an attack of fever.

All stores and wines should be packed in boxes up to sixty-five pounds in weight. The boxes should be made with lock and key, and then screwed down with brass screws, and a careful invoice taken of the contents. To prevent the constant opening and re-opening of these boxes day after day, when any one particular thing is required, it is well to keep two or three for general use, stocked with such things as candles, tea, coffee, cocoa, sugar, milk, Worcester sauce, &c., and a bottle of whisky. As the stores diminish, these boxes can be re-filled from the general stock at convenient times.

All trade goods for barter with the natives can be bought at Mombasa, the starting-point. It is now of little use to go down to Zanzibar, since porters (for transport) are not allowed to engage themselves for up-country work. Everything can be done at and from Mombasa, where not only can all trade goods be purchased, packed into the regulation 65 lb. loads, each load numbered, and an invoice taken of it, but all the latest information about the most suitable quality and quantity of goods required for the countries about to be visited can be better obtained at Mombasa than elsewhere.

To obtain the latest information with regard to the different kinds and qualities of cloth and beads is most important. Fashions change even in East Central Africa, and beads of a certain colour or cloth of a certain quality, which were perhaps in great demand one year, will not even be looked at the following year. Should the wrong kind of goods be taken up by mistake, the natives, although they might be willing to exchange their products for them, would only do so at such exorbitant prices that a trip would have to be curtailed, and all sorts of annoyances and disappointments incurred on account of the unlooked-for and ruinous expenditure of goods, unless others of the right kind were sent for from the coast, or could be procured from one of the stations near at hand.

CHAPTER VII
GAME DISTRICTS AND ROUTES
BY F. J. JACKSON

At particular seasons of the year there is a considerable migration of game beasts, and though all the lines of their migration are not ascertained, it is quite certain that great numbers work their way towards the coast between April and July; instinct in all probability impelling them in that direction, where the grass and all other vegetation are abundant. It would consequently be advisable for the sportsman to choose the time for his contemplated trip to a certain district when game is most likely to be plentiful there. Regard should also be had to a place suitable and convenient for headquarters, where surplus baggage, trophies, &c., can be stored, and where food for the caravan is procurable. The Kilimanjaro district, with Taveta as a depôt, was at one time, and perhaps is still, one of the best game districts in East Africa. Here game of nearly every variety is to be found, with the exception of *Kobus defassus*, *Kobus Kob*, Jackson's hartebeest, sable antelope, *Damalis Senegalensis*, and the oribi. Elephants, though they are numerous in the wet weather, are confined almost entirely to German territory, at the base of the mountain below Mochi and Kiboso, and it would be necessary to get a permit to shoot them, either from the German Commissioner at Bagamoyo on the coast, or from the officer in charge of the district at Mochi. From about August to April the elephants are confined to the belts of dense forest on the mountain, at an elevation of from 7,000 to 10,000 feet, where it would be practically useless to attempt to follow them. About April they begin to leave this forest belt, and work their way down to the undulating country at the base of the mountain. This country is covered with bush, long grass (in places ten to twelve feet high), with plenty of mimosa and other trees scattered about, as well as with clumps of dense bush and large forest trees; and as it is well watered by numerous streams flowing from the mountain, which, lower down, form the Kikavo, Weri-weri, and other rivers, the elephants get plenty of food, and evidently find it altogether congenial to their habits, as very few of them wander into British territory. Within a few marches round Taveta the sportsman will come across every kind of country in which game is to be met with, from the bare, covertless, open plain, the haunt of the wildebeest, oryx, Grant's gazelle, Thomson's gazelle, &c., the ostrich, and the great bustard, besides the everlasting zebra and Coke's hartebeest, to the dense and almost impenetrable forest in which is found the elephant and a small duyker-like buck (*Cephalolophus Harveyi*). The district is varied by open bush, where the stalker can see game when three or four hundred yards off; dense bush, where it is impossible to see anything until pretty close up to it; and sparsely timbered country, quite park-like in appearance.

A Difficult Stalk

C. Whymper

Here every kind of stalking has to be practised. At one time the stalker must crawl painfully along, flat on his stomach, for long distances to get a shot at one of the wilder or scarcer antelopes; at another he must walk cautiously along in dense forest, with a thick covering of dead leaves on the ground, trying his utmost to tread lightly and noiselessly, and to avoid stepping on some fallen branch hidden away in the leaves, the snap of which would scare whatever he might be after, be it elephant or small duyker buck. In open bush—i.e. bush which is sufficiently open to enable the stalker to see the game when about a hundred yards off—stalking is generally easy work, as there are often plenty of ant-heaps, besides bushes, to be taken advantage of. In dense bush, stalking is often unsatisfactory and mere chance-work, as it is very difficult to avoid making a noise in getting through it, and disturbing the game before seeing it. Perhaps the prettiest, and often the easiest, stalking is done in park-like country, where there are both big trees, ant-heaps, and bushes dotted about, as well as grass some 18 inches high, to afford shelter to the stalker. In this district game is most abundant from September, when the young grass is just beginning to shoot after being burnt, to May, when it is long, coarse, and dry.

Easy Stalking Country

C. Whymper

The Kapite plains to the west and the Athi plains to the north-west of the Ukambani hills, with Machako's as headquarters, form another grand country with regard to the quantity of game in it, though it does not afford quite such a variety as the Kilimanjaro district; and as the game is almost entirely confined to the vast, undulating, open, grassy plains, stalking is often both difficult and laborious. Lions are very plentiful here, and are seen perhaps more often than elsewhere, owing to the open nature of the country. The cheetah is by no means uncommon. Rhinoceroses have here rather a bad reputation for charging, which may possibly be accounted for by the fact that they are so much harassed by the Wakamba, who, when out hunting, and unable to get within bow-shot of game by fair stalking, have to resort to driving, and wound far more rhinoceroses than they kill. In the river Athi hippopotami are very plentiful, and, I think, have finer teeth than those in the Nzoia river and Victoria Nyanza. September to April is the best time of the year for a trip to this country.

Further north, the district round Lake Baringo, with Njemps as a depôt, is very good. Here the natives are as trustworthy and civil as the Wa Taveta, and all surplus baggage, &c., can be left at headquarters in charge of a few men whilst the sportsman is away shooting in the surrounding country. A few marches to the north and north-east elephants are numerous. The waterbuck (*Kobus defassus*) takes the place of the common waterbuck (*Kobus elipsiprymnus*), and the lately described hartebeest (*Bubalis Jacksoni*) takes the place of *Bubalis Cokei*. The impala carry particularly fine horns here. As I have never made a prolonged stay in this district, I am unable to say which months of the year would be the best to visit it in; but from what I could judge, when up there in July, I should say November to May.

The Tana river is another excellent district, both on account of the variety of game and the quantity of certain species which elsewhere a sportsman might seek day after day and never come across, though he went out specially for them. These are Waller's gazelle, lesser kudu, oribi, 'tope' (*Damalis Senegalensis*) and Hunter's antelope (*Damalis Hunteri*), which has hitherto not been found excepting on the north bank of the river, some 150 miles from the mouth. There is also a small antelope found here which has been described as a distinct species under the name of *Gazella Petersi*, but it may possibly be nothing more than a local variety of *Gazella Grantii*. This trip is perhaps more easily undertaken from Lamu, as everything can be shipped by dhow as far as Kau, on the river Ozi, where canoes can be engaged with the help of the Arkida, the principal man in the town, and the whole caravan, baggage and all, transported through the Belazoni Canal into the Tana river and upwards. If the start is made direct from Mombasa, it would be necessary to either march the whole way to Golbanti, a mission station on the river, or, to save a good deal of time and trouble, a dhow could be chartered as far as Melindi, and the rest of the journey done overland. At Golbanti canoes can be hired and Wa Pokomo boatmen engaged to transport all goods and food up the river, whilst the porters can march along the bank empty-handed if sufficient canoes are not forthcoming for all. A trip up this river should be undertaken between September and April, as it is in flood, and a great part of the country under water, during the remaining months of the year.

There are also many other districts nearer the coast, which are well worth visiting, in which game is to be found, though in more limited quantities. These are—the district round Adda, on the main road from Vanga on the coast to Mount Kisagau in the Teita country; Mount Pika-pika; Ndara, and Kisagau in the Teita country; Merereni, north of Melindi on the coast, all of which are accessible from Mombasa. The mainland to the north of Lamu, and about opposite the small island of Tula, is another good place. The best time for any of these places would be from April to August. All these and the Tana district would, for the most part, come under the head of bush country, where stalking is comparatively easy.

So much has been written about the different routes into the interior that it is not necessary to enter upon them here. In the accounts that have been written, each writer's experience has differed so materially that it would be unadvisable to rely on the opinion, based on experience, of one writer more than another, particularly if taken from the records of expeditions of a few years back. One writer may have experienced no difficulties, as both food and water may have been plentiful when he passed. Another writer may have had plenty of food and no water, and another plenty of water but no food, &c. The rainfall in East Africa is uncertain, and the supply of food and water also uncertain in consequence. Therefore all the very latest information as to the food and water supply along the line of march should be obtained at Mombasa, before leaving. The information of a man who has traversed the route about to be taken only two months previously cannot be relied upon, although his veracity is not to be doubted. Only one month's dry weather will make an enormous difference in a water supply; but besides this there are other things to reckon against. Amongst these are the number of caravans which have subsequently passed up and down, and the number of natives from Teita and Ukambani, who are constantly going to and fro, often with herds of cattle, sheep, and goats, all of which very soon diminish even the largest supply.

But when once the game country is reached, all anxiety about food and water is virtually over. It is the getting to the game countries, when long tracts of foodless and often waterless wilderness have to be traversed before the sportsman's Eldorado is reached, that is such trying and often anxious work. The Teita route is the principal one into the interior, and is also the principal one from the sportsman's point of view, as it leads to all the best game countries. This route passes *via* Taru and Mount Maungu. The wilderness between Taru and Ndara is commonly known as the 'Maungu march,' and it is to this day more dreaded by both Europeans and natives alike than any other, and this more particularly when going up country, when the porters, not having recovered from their 'high old times' on the coast, are out of training and soft, and easily become disheartened. Coming down country with their faces to the coast, and the 'high times' before them, it is quite a different thing, and there is little or no anxiety, as the men will face almost anything. Unless there has been an exceptional drought or an unusual number of caravans upon the road, water is generally procurable at Taru and also at Mount Maungu, where, however, the men have to climb the hill 1,000 feet above the camping-ground to get it. Between these two points, a distance of some thirty-four miles (by the winding serpentine footpath, and not fifty-three, as some writers maintain), there is no water, excepting perhaps for a few days after heavy rain. This wearisome march can then be broken at a place called Ziwa Butzuma, and again at Ziwa-wa-tatu. The best way to get over this wilderness (and it is always best to rely on its being quite waterless) is to take a supply of kerosene oil tins from the coast, and engage extra men as far as Ndara in Teita to carry them from Taru, where they can be filled, to Maungu, where they can again be replenished if necessary.

If Taveta should be the sportsman's destination, I should strongly recommend him to take these tins with him as far as M'kameni, the last camp in Teita, before starting into the Siringeti plains. At this camp he can find out from the natives if there is any water between there and Lanjora, another long stretch of some thirty-five to forty miles. If there is no water, natives can be engaged to carry the water-tins for one march, which should be a good long one. As these Bura natives are a bad lot and great thieves, and as they are sure to demand payment in advance and will not stir till they get it, the askaris should be told to keep a sharp lookout to prevent any of them bolting. This Siringeti march, and the Maungu march, when coming down country, can be done best at night when it is cool; but it is not advisable to do any marching at night when going up country, as it is too near the coast, and night marching offers temptations to a porter to desert, which some of them could not resist. There are other ways of getting over these and other long marches without the aid of water-tins, but none of them are so comfortable. One way is to have the men called very early in the morning and told to cook their food for the day. They can then eat as much as they like and carry the rest with them; can quench their thirst and fill up their water calabashes before starting, and then march steadily on throughout the day, with a short rest every two hours to enable the stragglers to come up; they can sleep anywhere in the wilderness, and early next day arrive at the water before the sun becomes very powerful. Then, again, there is what is called a 'terageza,' which is a double march—one inconveniently short, say four miles, and the other inconveniently long, say sixteen to eighteen miles. This can be negotiated very much in the same manner as the above, but with this difference: Instead of beginning the day with a feed, which an African, as a rule, does not care to do, the men wait until they arrive at the water, at the end of the first short march, before cooking their food, and then go on and sleep in the wilderness without water, except what each man carries for himself.

The length of a march depends very much, if not entirely, on the distance between the places where water is procurable. As a rule, the water—excepting, of course, the running streams—is not good, and should be carefully filtered and boiled before being used, and it should be the special duty of one of the tent-boys to see that this is done. Before being filtered the water should be cleared of all extraneous matter by the use of alum. This can best be done by getting a bucket of water and stirring it round a few times with a lump of alum in the hand, which will soon precipitate all vegetable and mineral matter.

When on the march, it is a good plan to make a 'boma'[10] every night, even if only to keep the men together; but it is not really necessary to do so until nearing the outskirts of the Masai country or wherever the natives are of a thievish dispo-

---

[10] Zereba.

sition. In the game country a boma is always necessary, not only for protection and to keep the men together, but to keep out hyænas, &c., which might carry off or destroy a valuable trophy, if they did nothing worse.

The tent should be pitched in the shade, more particularly in a position to get the shade from the afternoon sun, when the sportsman is most likely to be in camp; but thick clumps of dense foliaged trees, under which the ground is thickly covered with dead and sodden leaves, should be avoided altogether. Such places are generally unhealthy, as the damp is pretty certain evidence that the wind does not get at them. It would be a mistake to have the leaves cleared away—in fact, care should be taken to avoid disturbing the ground as much as possible, and all grass, &c., should be cut instead of being pulled up by the roots. The chances of fever are increased by the proximity of freshly turned up earth. Rather than sleep in a place with such surroundings it is far better to camp in the open altogether, and to have a shed built, which the men can run up in a few hours, to sit under during the heat of the day.

Along the well-beaten caravan routes there is little chance of getting any sport when on the march, excepting with a shot-gun. By walking a short way in front of the leading men, a few shots at francolin, guinea-fowl, &c., can generally be had, and perhaps an occasional shot at a hartebeest or impala, but the chances are that, even if these beasts are seen, they will be so wild and on the alert, having seen or heard the caravan, that the sportsman will not feel inclined to leave the footpath to follow them. He need not therefore expect to see game in any quantities until he reaches the vicinity of his headquarters, excepting on the road to Kilimanjaro, after leaving M'kameni, the last camp before striking across the Siringeti plains, between Teita and Taveta, a stretch of some thirty-five to forty miles. These plains are often teeming with game, more particularly when the grass is beginning to shoot after being burnt. In September 1886 this place was literally crawling with hartebeest and zebra, besides impala, *G. Grantii, Oryx collotis*, and a few eland and giraffe, with an occasional steinbuck and wart-hog. But whatever quantity of game there may be, it is never advisable to go far from the footpath in pursuit of it when on the march. In places like this where there is little water, or more often none at all, it is as much as the porters can do to get through their long march, and when once they are on the move it is best to keep them going. The pleasure of bagging a couple of head of game or so, which will be found further on near headquarters, is hardly worth the risks of a long delay, which is sure to take place if a big beast is killed. Headquarters once reached, all the troubles and petty annoyances which are found so very trying on the march are at an end, and the sportsman, after he has overhauled all his gear, stores, &c., can leave them in perfect safety, as far as the natives are concerned, in charge of two or three of his men, and can sally forth into the surrounding district, changing his camp from time to time, with the pretty certain prospect of obtaining good trophies of all the game beasts seen on the road up.

'Teeming with Game'

C. Whymper

CHAPTER VIII

THE CARAVAN, HEADMAN, GUN-BEARERS, ETC.

BY F. J. JACKSON

The sportsman having decided on the districts which he intends to visit, and on the time to be spent approximately in each, and having obtained all the latest information as to the quantity and quality of goods required for barter purposes, presents, &c., the caravan ('safari') must be got together and organised. The first thing to be done is to engage a really good headman ('neapara'). Should the sportsman be fortunate enough to have such a one recommended to him who both knows the country and his work—the latter being far more important than the former—it would be advisable to engage him even though the pay he demands be high. So much depends on the headman that a really good one is worth a dozen who call themselves neapara, but who in reality are little better than porters. A good neapara not only knows his position in the caravan, but will take care to maintain his authority and command respect from those under him. One who hob-nobs and plays cards with the porters—and this is by no means an uncommon practice—soon loses all control over them, and will become wearisome with his complaints of their insubordination and indolence. The duties of a headman are not only to look after his master's property, but to see that everybody else does his duty, and he is responsible for the general working of the caravan. The headman superintends the buying of food and the issuing of 'posho' (daily allowance of food) to the men. In this matter, if he is dishonest, he has every opportunity of pilfering; but at the same time it is better to trust him, as should he find that his master is suspicious, and goes too much into details, it is quite certain that he will 'do' him in other ways. All orders should be given to him direct. Whatever his pay may be—and there is no fixed rule—he is only entitled by custom to double a porter's posho, whether it be rice, flour, beans, potatoes, or bananas, or cloth or beads to buy it with. Once a week, or every ten days, it is as well to give him a few strings of beads or a piece of cloth to buy 'kitiweo,' which may be anything he can get, such as a fowl, honey, &c., to make his meal of flour or beans more palatable, when there is no meat in camp. It is a recognised thing that each headman is allowed one porter to carry his tent (which he supplies and makes himself), bedding, &c., and if he thinks himself a great swell he may ask for two porters—if he does, and he is really a good man, it is as well to let him have them. Besides carrying his belongings, these porters will cook his food, collect firewood, and fetch water for him. One neapara is enough for every fifty 'pagazi' (porters) and 'askari' (soldiers).

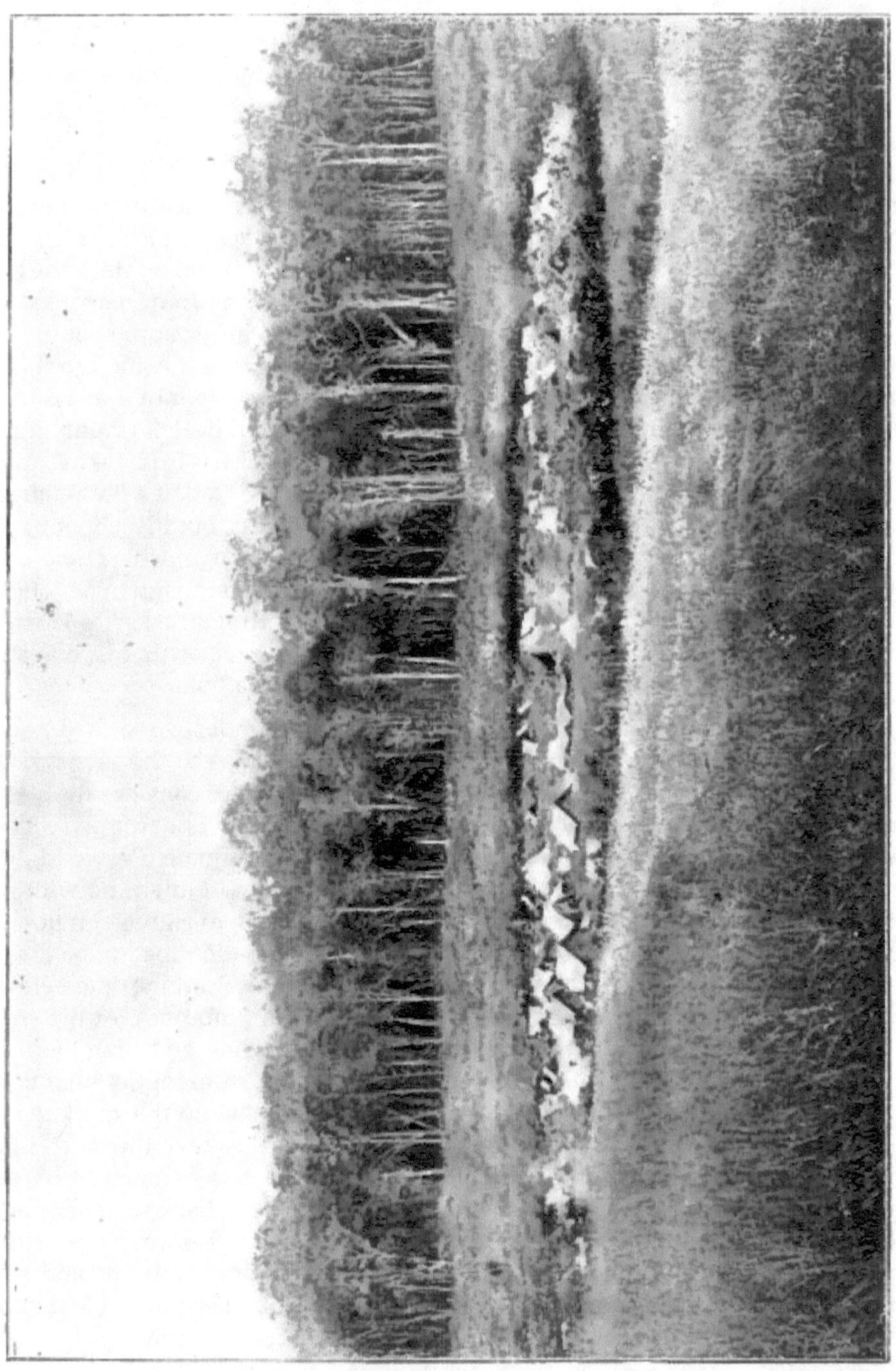

Camp with Boma at side, Kikunya Forest

From a photograph by E. Gedge

A caravan askari is in reality a spare man, and there should be one askari to every ten porters. When the porters have been divided into companies or messes of ten men, each of these messes is put in charge of an askari. This man receives into his care one 'sufria' (cooking pot), one 'senia' (plate to eat off), and two axes to cut firewood, &c. He also receives from the headman the whole of the posho for his company, and is also responsible for the loads his men carry, and for their general good behaviour. Apart from seeing that the men of their own companies do their work, the duties of the askaris are various. They keep watch at night, turn and turn about, superintend the men building the 'boma' (zereba); stack the loads in camp, and give their own men their proper loads in the morning; carry the load of a porter (not necessarily one of their own company) into camp, should he be taken ill or become lame on the march, and run messages, &c. Although it is not the custom, it is not a bad plan to allow one porter to every four or five askaris, to carry their food, sleeping mats, &c. This would save a good deal of grumbling and discontent amongst the porters, as it would prevent the askaris from taking advantage of them by piling their private kits and food on to the load of a porter already heavily laden. By right, askaris should carry their own kits, but in a shooting trip, when perhaps the sportsman wishes to get as far and do as much as he can in a given time, it is well to avoid all causes of friction amongst the men as much as possible by a little judicious leniency of this kind. The pay of an askari is 12 rupees per month, and his posho is half as much again as a porter's—that is, one and a half 'kibaba' or its equivalent. On the coast their posho is 12 pice.

The porters ('pagazi'), of whom there are several grades, good, bad and indifferent, although they often exasperate their master even to the verge of desperation, are, as a rule, first-rate fellows. A porter will do, considering his pay and food, what few other men, if any, will or can do. He is naturally cheerful and easily pleased, but no one can be more sulky and obstinate. Provided, however, that his stomach is kept full, it is possible to do almost anything with him. On the march—and a march varies considerably, from six to eighteen miles, and sometimes more—the porter will carry, besides his regulation load of 65 lbs., his sleeping-mat, with ten days' posho on the top of it, a Snider carbine, and belt with ten rounds of ammunition, and also his water calabash ('mbuyu'). At the end of the march it is his duty to cut down thorn-trees and bushes, and drag them into camp to make the boma, when his work for the day is over, excepting that he has to collect firewood and water for himself and his mess. Should the sportsman go out to shoot, he is ever ready to follow his master for the sake of the meat. I have known many porters, even at the end of a long, tiring, waterless march, who, after quenching their thirst, have filled their calabashes and gone back several miles, of their own accord, to help the stragglers into camp. A porter's wage is 10 rupees per month and his posho, one 'kibaba' (a measure holding about one and a half pound) of whatever can be bought from the natives—flour, beans, &c. On the coast his posho is 8 pice per diem. In a trip of six months' duration or more, all the men in the caravan, from headman to porter, will demand, and are entitled to, three months' pay in advance. Three months' wages in advance is the most ever paid, however long the trip may be. For trips of less than six months, a proportionate advance is made. The principle is a bad one from a European point of view, but it is the custom, and in this respect, as in many others in East Africa, custom is law.

We now come to the 'safari' (caravan) as a whole. After the headman has been engaged and an approximate list of loads made out, including everything—barter goods of beads, cloth, and wire, private kit, tents, stores, ammunition—both private and for defensive purposes, cooking gear, &c., the headman should be told how many porters and askaris will be required, and it is well to let him engage as many of them as he can himself in order that he may know something of their antecedents. As they are brought up by the headman to be engaged, they should be entered in the list in companies of ten men, each company under an askari. They then receive their advance pay, and can be either told off to do any work there may be for them to do, or they can have their posho given them at once and may be left to their own devices. As long as they are in Mombasa, or any coast town, they should be mustered every morning for any work there may be, and again in the evening to receive their posho. It is always advisable to engage two or three extra porters over and above the estimated number of loads, as even in the best organised caravans, and when all the porters are present at the last moment, something is sure to turn up that has been overlooked, such as a bundle of rope, a basket of potatoes and onions, or a crate of fowls. The two latter comestibles, although they have never been given a thought since the cook received the order to get them, are of much importance, and help considerably to save the tinned provisions and to reconcile a man to the miseries of the first few days in the wilderness, after the fleshpots of Mombasa. The first day of getting under way will perhaps be found the most trying of any to the patience and temper, unless some little trouble is taken to minimise the confusion generally attending the start of a caravan for 'up-country.' To effect this, the whole of the men should have at least two days' notice beforehand of their master's decision to start on a certain day, and the night before the start the whole caravan should be told, when they come for their posho, to muster and fall in in the morning at least a couple of hours before they are actually wanted. The whole of the loads should then be laid out in lots of ten. The porters having fallen in to their respective companies with their askari, and having answered to the roll-call, the rifles and cartridge-belts should be distributed amongst them. Their posho in rice should then be issued to them, and may vary in quantity according to the destination of the safari; but should it be anywhere along the Teita route, ten days' posho is usually given, which will last them well over the Maungu wilderness, till Teita is reached, where food of various kinds is procurable. Ten days' food is as much as a porter can be expected to carry on leaving the coast, when he is soft and out of training, though up country, in places like the Masai district, where no vegetable food is procurable, he will not only carry twelve to fifteen days' food, but also an extra heavy load into the bargain. Each company should then be told off to a lot of ten loads, and every man should be ordered to put some private mark of his own on his allotted load so as to recognise it again. This is important, as it not only prevents confusion, but a good deal of quarrelling amongst the men when moving camp each morning, sometimes in the dark, should there be a long waterless march ahead.

In the matter of food for the men when up country, this should, when feasible, be bought by the headman and collected in bulk, as it is much cheaper to buy it so; but when on the march and in a hurry to get on, cloth or beads should be issued to the men, who will buy whatever they like or can get. Cloth is given out in pieces of four hands, each of which is called a 'shuka', this being a measure from the elbow-joint to the tip of the middle finger. A porter's allowance is one shuka; an askari's, one and a half, or six hands; and a neapara's, two, or eight hands, which is called a 'doti.' As, however, the price of food varies in different places, and also according to the crops, information should be obtained on the coast as to the number of days one shuka will last in a certain district, as it will be a check to a certain extent on the headman, and will prevent him from taking advantage of his master. In order to curry favour with the porters—and some headmen do—he might say that one shuka will only buy four days' food, whereas it might buy six. Formerly, at Taveta, a shuka was equal to six days' food, but it will in all probability be more expensive now. Beads are given out in strings, and it is very necessary to ascertain before leaving the coast how many strings of each different kind of beads are equal to a shuka.

With regard to the arming of the men in a caravan for defensive purposes, and the number of rifles it would be necessary to take, it will entirely depend on the country in which the shooting trip is going to be made and the disposition of the natives of the country itself, as also of the natives of the countries or districts the caravan would have to pass through to get there. For a trip up to Taveta and the adjacent country, as far north as Kimangelia, a short way beyond Useri, twenty-five rifles would be quite enough; but for a more extended trip to the Njiri plains and beyond, it would perhaps be better to take fifty, or at the most eighty, armed men.

I have always considered the El Moran or Masai warrior a very much over-rated individual, neither do I think he ever could have been so awe-inspiring and terrifying as some writers have represented him. Still, as the porters have a very exaggerated idea of his fighting and bloodthirsty propensities, it is best to inspire them with confidence by arming them well, thus assuring them that in the event of an attack they are at least in a position to defend themselves.

For a trip to the Suk country, beyond Lake Baringo, it would be better to have at least 80 to 100 armed men, as the natives are not only very treacherous, but much more fearless of firearms than other tribes. For the Tana river twenty-five rifles would be ample, provided the caravan did not go more than one day's march from the river on the north bank. If the trip should be extended further north into the Somali country, it would not be worth while running the risks of entering the country of such grasping, treacherous, religious fanatics as the southern Somalis are with an escort of fewer than 150 rifles.

All arms should be breechloading. Carbines are much handier for the porters than long rifles, though the askari can be armed with the latter. It would add to the dignity of the headman (at all events in his own opinion) if he were allowed a Winchester repeater. Sniders are much safer in the hands of the men than rifles of any other make, and are also cheaper. Although it is more than probable that the weapons will never be called into requisition for defensive purposes, the moral effect of a well-armed party on the natives is good, and they are far less likely to try any bouncing or bullying if they see that the party is strong enough not only to defend itself but to turn the tables on them. If there is not a rifle, belt and pouch for every porter in the caravan after the headman and askaris have received theirs, the rest should be equally distributed amongst the companies. This should not be done, however, until the day of starting, and just before the loads are allotted. On no account issue ammunition to the porters until nearing the Masai country, as there is nothing to be feared from any other natives, excepting the Somalis, north of the Tana river; the Suks, north of Lake Baringo; and the Wa Nandi between Elgeyo and Kavirondo. It is then necessary to be prepared in the event of falling in with a roving band of warriors and cattle-lifters. Ten rounds per man is enough for porters; the headman and askaris can each have twenty rounds, and these can be issued to them before leaving the coast. A small fine, say half a rupee, should be levied for every cartridge lost, or supposed to be lost, as the men are much given to selling their cartridges to the natives for food and 'pombe' (native beer), the natives buying them for the sake of the powder and lead.

Gun-bearers are rather difficult to find; that is to say, good ones. Any number of men will come forward and offer their services, although they have never acted as gun-bearers before, and know absolutely nothing about their duties. They do this because they prefer to carry a rifle, waterbottle, and cartridge-bag (in all some 25 lbs.), rather than a full load of 65 lbs. to 75 lbs., and because they know that they will have altogether an easier time of it than a porter or askari. On the other hand, men who have been gun-bearers to Europeans whom they either know personally or by reputation, and whom they would follow into any kind of danger, will not volunteer their services as gun-bearers to men they do not know, and in whom they have no confidence.

Most Africans are gifted with not only long but very quick sight, are capital walkers at their own pace, are often extraordinarily keen about sport, and will wish to go on after game when their master is dead beat and wants to return to camp. They are wonderfully patient followers on a blood spoor, and if they have confidence in their master will follow him anywhere after wounded game, and can be relied upon not to run away at a critical moment. Europeans, however, often complain that their gun-bearers do not keep up with them when out shooting; but this is very often their own fault. East Africa is a land of thorns and prickly spikes of every description. Europeans who are booted and clothed cannot well expect an almost bare-footed and bare-legged man, with only a thin cotton shirt on and a pair of sandals, to follow close at their heels (the proper place for a good gun-bearer) through clumps of thorns and sharp spiky aloes. To enable the two principal gun-bearers to keep in their proper positions they should each be provided with a suit of clothes, of the same material and make as their master's, with leather knee-caps, &c., and either a pair of boots or, better still, leather socks and sandals. They should also be provided with any kind of old shooting cap, but not a red fez or white cap, the common headgear of the porters. In fact, a gun-bearer should be as little conspicuous and as thorn-proof as his master, and if this is seen to it will prevent disappointments, both from being sighted by game when stalking it or from losing wounded game through the gun-bearers being unable to keep in their proper position with either a spare rifle or ammunition. Gun-bearers should be provided with a good butcher's knife apiece, and care should be taken that these are kept sharp, as the African native is naturally cruel, and will cut and hack at the throat of a wounded beast with a knife no sharper than a piece of hoop iron. A good butcher's steel should be always taken out; it can be carried by one of the attendant porters, as it is rather an awkward thing for a gun-bearer to carry.

Besides the ordinary duty of gun-bearing when out shooting and when on the march, gun-bearers have other duties to perform. First, on arriving in camp they help to put up their master's tent, and see that a small trench is dug round it to carry off the water in case of a downpour of rain. They then clean all their master's rifles and guns, and, as a rule, do this well. It is also their duty to skin any heads and clean the skulls of the game shot, and attend generally to the trophies, though they always get friends to help them. When a beast has been killed, and their master has had the first choice of the meat, the perquisites to which gun-bearers are entitled, and which are now looked upon as theirs by 'dusturi' (custom), are the heart, liver, kidneys, &c., and any scraps of inside fat, and they take very good care to uphold their claims to these tit-bits. After a cold wet day or a first-rate day's sport, a little tobacco as 'backsheesh' will delight them, and can do no harm by causing jealousy amongst the other men, as gun-bearers are looked upon in a caravan as favoured individuals.

In the matter of pay, unless other arrangements are made when engaging them, their wages and food are the same as an askari's.

CHAPTER IX

HINTS ON EAST AFRICAN STALKING, DRIVING, ETC.

BY F. J. JACKSON

In East Africa, up to the present, all shooting has been done entirely on foot, as horses have not yet been introduced into the country, with the exception of two or three which have been sent up to Uganda. It is to be hoped that when horses are more generally employed (and there is no reason at present known why they should not be, provided the belts of 'fly' country are avoided), they will not be used in the pursuit of the herds of game, as they have been and still are in South Africa and the Somali country. There can be little doubt that it is owing to this almost universal custom in South Africa of riding down game that it has been exterminated or driven away from so many parts of the country; and it is not improbable that in the Somali country a similar result will follow from the same cause. When pursued on horseback, game is for the most part on the move when shot at, often at full gallop, and at much longer ranges than when stalked, and therefore many more beasts are wounded and lost when horses are used than when fairly outwitted by the stalker and shot at when standing still.

It is supposed by a good many people that the tsétsé fly only exists where game beasts, especially buffaloes, are most plentiful, and that the fly disappears as the game is killed off or driven away. This may be so in South Africa, but it is certainly not the case in East Africa, as the belts of fly country in East Africa are almost devoid of game, with the exception of the river Tana. As, however, the open, undulating, grassy plains of the Masai country, and other places of a like nature, are the headquarters of by far the greatest quantity and variety of game, and are entirely free from the tsétsé fly, and as they are also well adapted to hunting on horseback, the game would very soon be exterminated if pursuit on horseback were permitted, and I trust that when the game laws which will doubtless be drawn up for this, probably the finest game country in the world, are drafted, a clause will be introduced which will make the pursuit of game in this manner altogether illegal.

My first trip to East Africa was undertaken in the years 1884 to 1887, when that country was perhaps at its best with regard to the quantity of game. Within the last few years, however, since the country has been opened up, and the terrifying accounts of the dangers of entering the Masai country have proved to be absurdly exaggerated, various sporting expeditions have been undertaken, and large bags have been made. Some of the game is certainly reduced in quantity, especially rhinoceroses, owing to the ease with which these beasts can be stalked.

Buffaloes, too, have been almost destroyed by a kind of anthrax, the same disease which carried off nearly all the native cattle in 1891. This disease, I am told, was fatal to other species of game, including giraffe, eland, and lesser kudu, and even elephants; but as my informants could not speak from personal knowledge, but only from native reports, I am unable to vouch for their accuracy. However, game is still to be found in enormous quantities—indeed few countries, if any, can offer such a grand or varied field for sport. Within the limits of British East Africa there are forty-seven species, including no fewer than thirty-three species of antelopes and gazelles, which come under the head of big game. In addition to big game there are a great number and variety of game-birds, including ten species of francolin, four species of guinea-fowl, four of florican, five of sand-grouse, and two of quail, as well as enormous hosts of duck and geese of various kinds on the lakes and large lagoons, together with two species of snipe. All these add very considerably to the charm of a shooting trip, and afford a pleasant change from the rifle to the shot-gun, besides agreeably altering the monotonous menu of antelope venison or tough rhinoceros or buffalo steak.

As then, all the big game in British East Africa should be killed by honest stalking, without the aid of horses, and as the first principles of stalking have been dealt with elsewhere in these volumes, it only remains for me to call attention to a few points peculiar to stalking in East Africa.

To deal first with the wind, which here, as elsewhere, is the first matter for a stalker to consider, it may be said that in the plains and fairly open country the wind is generally steady in one quarter or another between the hours of eight or nine A.M. and sundown, except when the monsoons are beginning to change, and then it is constantly chopping and veering round from point to point throughout the day. In the early morning, between daylight and about eight o'clock, it is also steady and constant from one quarter, but between eight and nine it often chops about before settling into the quarter from which it will continue to blow for the rest of the day. That is to say, when the sportsman leaves camp at daylight the wind may be blowing from the south-east and will continue so up to any time between seven and nine o'clock, when, after chopping about for a short time, it will settle into another quarter, say north-east, for the rest of the day. In forest, thick bush, and long grass, it is often apt, at all times of the day, to be very changeable and uncertain, and may chop round in eddies when least expected, and this is what often makes shooting in these places so disappointing. It is therefore necessary to constantly test the wind. The most convenient and effectual way of doing this is to pick up and let fall from the hand a little sand, dust, or pulverised leaves. On a very still calm day, when there is not enough wind to affect dust or dry leaves, a puff of smoke from a pipe or from a match, will serve the same purpose if struck and blown out immediately. The smell of the tobacco smoke is in no way likely to frighten game, as, if a beast is able to detect it, it is equally certain that he will be able to wind the stalker. Personally, I use a pipe as a wind-finder more than anything else, and I have had a lighted pipe in my mouth at the time of firing at more than half of the game I have killed.

Before commencing a stalk up to dangerous game, the stalker should *always* put two or three cartridges for his big rifles into his pocket in order to have them handy and to render him perfectly independent of his gun-bearers. Even the best gun-bearers might fail him one day when in a critical position, and the want of a cartridge might be the cause of a very serious accident.

As elsewhere, so in Africa, one of the great secrets of success in big game shooting is to be up early and on the feeding grounds at daylight, when everything is in favour of the stalker. In the early morning most game will be found feeding, and will be more easily seen when so occupied than later on in the day when lying down in the shade of a tree or bush, with only one of the herd standing up. This beast, if it is the sentinel of a herd, will in all probability be a female, or a male with an inferior head, as the old bulls and bucks rarely act sentry; or it may be a solitary individual not worth stalking. The stalker, being possibly a long way off at the time of sighting it, and unable to see whether there is a herd lying concealed near it in the grass or not, may miss a good chance at a beast with a first-rate head through a pardonable dislike to going a long way out of his track on an off-chance. But when feeding the stalker has a good chance of examining with his binoculars each individual beast in the herd, he can compare one with another, and mark those with the best heads.

Then, again, in the early-morning the air is fresh and the ground cool, and a long stalk is not nearly so fatiguing then as later on; whilst in the cool hours of the early morning it is much easier to judge distances, as the air is clear and there is no haze. This haze, which only appears after the sun is well up, is caused by the moisture of the earth being evaporated by the sun. It is most noticeable after a heavy dew or a shower of rain, and is not only very apt to deceive even the most experienced in regard to distances, but as it makes everything appear to be in a perpetual quiver, it renders shooting very difficult. When taking a sight under such conditions the beast aimed at will often appear very indistinct, and will seem to move about in front of the muzzle of the rifle.

There is still another argument in favour of early morning stalks, and that is, that as all game beasts are thoroughly awake, and on the alert, even though engrossed in feeding, the stalker knows that he must exercise all his wits to the very utmost to keep out of sight, not only of the beast or beasts he may be stalking, but of other game which may be either to the right or left of him. This knowledge saves a man from carelessness, and makes him do his very utmost in that keen rivalry between animal instincts and human skill, in which lies the whole charm of big game shooting. But although the early morning has its advantages, a good many of which are of the nature of personal convenience and comfort to the stalker, and has also its many charms, which are not to be experienced later on in the day, it certainly has a fair amount of disadvantages. To begin with, as a rule, game is not so easy to approach when feeding as when standing about or lying down. When feeding beasts are constantly moving, and although they may be in a capital position when the stalker first tries to circumvent them, they very often move into an unapproachable one by the time he gets up to within range of where they had been; and of course, as before suggested, all beasts are very wide awake in the early hours of the morning, whilst, instead of being protected by only one sentinel as at other times, the whole herd is more or less on the *qui vive*, and the stalker may be detected at any moment by any beast which may happen to raise its head, or which may wander in his direction after some dainty morsel of grass and keep him waiting-in an awkward position.

The beast with the best head is not unfrequently in an awkward position for a shot, or out of range, and the stalker, being unable to improve his position or get nearer for fear of being seen by some of the other beasts, has either to risk a long shot at the best head or content himself with an easier and more certain shot at an inferior one. In this case, it is far better to give up the stalk for the time, and try your luck another day.

As an example of what can be done by a little patience and perseverance, I was successful in bagging the finest specimen of a bull eland ever shot by a European in East Africa, after a very long and tedious stalk on five consecutive days. This grand beast was accompanied by three cows, and each day they were found in the same locality, never more than a mile from the place at which I left them the previous day. This was a narrow strip of open plain, some two miles long by about a mile in width, which opened out at each end into a large open plain. The narrow strip was bordered on each side by thick bush and clumps of forest trees, and this appeared to be used by the enormous herds of game as a passage from one plain to the other. As I always found these four elands standing out well towards the middle of the strip, where there were only a few isolated mimosa-trees dotted about, the stalking was very tedious work, and as there was no covert but grass twelve to eighteen inches high, it was necessary to make a long crawl from the very outskirts of the bush. On each of the first three days I almost succeeded in getting within range, when the elands were alarmed by a shot fired in the distance and moved off, afterwards standing in such an exposed position that a stalk was quite impossible. On the fourth morning I was stalking them across the wind, which was blowing from my left, and was again nicely reducing the distance between myself and the bull, who was standing by himself under the shade of a thorn-tree, whilst the cows were quietly feeding some twenty yards beyond him.

As I lay under the shade of a small bush, which was within about 300 yards of the elands, taking a short rest, I noticed all four beasts suddenly raise their heads and stare hard up wind, evidently on the alert. At first I could not see anything to alarm them, and felt quite sure that they had not got a taint of my wind. On getting into a sitting position behind the bush, I saw a dark object in the grass dead to windward of the elands, and about the same distance from them as I was. My first idea was that it was a man, and I concluded that the fellow must be an idiot to attempt to stalk down wind, when I suddenly got a better view, and with the aid of my binoculars made out a lion and lioness, and saw that they were actually on the same business as myself. Wishing to see the result, I sat still and watched them, and could just manage to follow their movements, though I could only distinguish a small piece of the dark mane of the lion above the grass as he crawled slowly along. When the lions came to a tuft of rather longer grass they both raised their heads for a second, but the elands apparently took no notice of them, as they still stood perfectly motionless. As the lions crept on very slowly they came to another tuft of slightly taller grass, and the lion again raised his head, but this time he was seen by the elands, which all turned round and trotted off straight down wind. The lions then stood up, and after watching the elands a short time lay down in the grass; but before I could crawl up to them and get a shot, they went off for the bush on the other side of the plain. The elands were then thoroughly on the alert and in a bad position for a further stalk, and although I believe I could have got up to within a couple of hundred yards of them, rather than risk a long shot, and perhaps only frighten them away from the locality altogether, I left them in peace for the fourth time. Returning on the fifth morning very early, while skirting along outside the edge of the bush, keeping a sharp look-out, I found them in a grand position for a stalk, as they were not more than 400 yards from the edge of the bush on my side of the plain. The bull was lying down, one cow stood close by him, evidently on the look-out, whilst the other two were quietly feeding. Entering the bush, I skirted along inside the edge until I was just opposite to the elands. I then saw that between them and the bush in which I stood, with the wind blowing straight from them to me, there was a largish piece of bush some twenty yards long, though rather narrow and very thin, and not more than eighty yards from where the bull was lying. Between this patch and myself there was little or no covert of any kind, excepting grass which was about a foot high and very scanty, and one small skeleton bush within about twenty yards of the larger patch. I managed, however, by crawling flat on my stomach, followed by my pet gun-bearer, to get up to this scanty covert, and could just see through the larger patch that the bull was still lying down. At this moment, and before I could get any nearer, to my disgust I heard a shot fired in the distance. The bull stood up, and as he stared in the direction from which the shot had come I heard another report; but, as great good luck would have it, instead of bolting all four elands began to walk quietly towards where I lay. Exchanging my .500 Express for the 8-bore, as I wished to make certain of getting the bull, I waited, and thought they never would appear round the corner of the bush in front of me, as they kept stopping to look round every few paces.

In a short time a cow appeared round the corner within thirty yards of where I lay. I could still see the bull lagging behind, and was terribly afraid that this cow would detect me before he appeared; but she took no notice of me and walked straight on. Soon after this another cow appeared, and I could see the bull standing just on the other side of the bush, but would not risk a shot at him through it. At last his grand head appeared, but nothing more, and he again stopped. I shall never forget my feeling of intense excitement during those few seconds. I was in a most awkward position, lying flat on my face, and literally aching with suspense and suppressed excitement, and yet I dare not move to get into a better position for a shot, for fear of being seen by either of the two cows. At last the bull took a few steps forward, and I wriggled myself into a sitting position, gave him both barrels, one after the other, and after running about sixty yards he fell over dead. Never shall I forget my joy when I saw him drop. He was a grand beast with horns 31⅝ and 31 ins. respectively in length, and 25 ins. from tip to tip. His heart was encased in a solid piece of fat, which, after the heart had been cut out of it, and after it had been exposed to the sun for four hours, was found to weigh 18 lbs.

'At last the Bull took a few steps forward'

On the fourth day after the lions' visit I went up to where they had stood, and followed the well-marked track which they had made as they crept along, for a considerable distance. The track clearly showed what their intentions were. They had evidently seen the elands from the other side of the plain, and had attempted to cut them off by stalking across the wind as I was doing. Had the elands continued their course up wind and not stopped where they did they would have passed pretty close to where the lions lay in a thick patch of grass. On seeing that the elands had stopped, the lions had crept diagonally across and down the wind, until the elands detected them.

But to go back to the best time of day for shooting. Of course shooting in the heat of the day has its advantages and disadvantages, and some men advocate it in preference to the early morning. After feeding, which is always in the early morning, and again in the evening, as well as throughout the night (though some species of game, notably zebra and several antelopes, continue to feed at all hours of the day and night), game take up their quarters for the day either in the shade of a tree or bush or quite out in the open. When once they have found a place to suit them, they will lie down, or stand about ruminating, and enjoying their siesta, and are not likely to wander about and get into awkward positions.

Game, too, is less watchful in the hot hours, and even the sentinel has every appearance of being drowsy and off guard, as it stands at ease on three legs (nearly always with its back to the wind), with ears drooping or lying back, and a look of general contentment and repose about it, as if conscious that its feline enemies are not likely to disturb it, and that it has little else to fear. Even should the herd be lying rather scattered about, with their heads facing in all directions, they do not appear to be so keen at detecting the approach of the stalker as in the morning. Possibly they are either dozing or their senses are dulled from general lassitude, and they rely mostly on the sentinel; or it may be that the haze, which is thicker close to the ground, affects their vision in the same way as it does that of the stalker. Whether their senses are dulled from the effects of the heat, or whether they are less watchful because their natural enemies are unlikely to be abroad at that time, is difficult to conjecture. At all events, if several stalks were made under the same conditions with regard to the place, covert, and wind, some of them up to a herd feeding in the early morning, and the others when they were lying down and standing about in the heat of the day, I think that the stalker would find that he would have to exercise his wits against the game's instinct far less, and would also find the beasts much easier to circumvent during the heat of the day than in the cool of the morning. In the matter of physical exertion, however, the later stalks are much the most trying and fatiguing. Anyone who has done many long and tedious stalks will, I think, admit that being compelled to crawl two or three hundred yards, or more, flat on his stomach in the bare open plains (where game is generally most plentiful) is terribly trying work during the heat of the day. What with the sun pouring down on the back and nape of the neck, and the scorching heat of the ground striking upwards into the face, together with the burnt grass dust, &c., which get into the mouth and nostrils, and nearly choke him in his desperate efforts to prevent coughing or sneezing, such a stalk requires not only great physical endurance, but the most stoical patience on the part of the stalker. Moreover, stalks under such trying circumstances (and they are by no means uncommon), even though they may be successful, are apt to end in a splitting headache, which may develop into an attack of fever, and knock the sportsman out of time for several days.

And there is yet another argument in favour of early stalks, altogether apart from their advantages from a stalker's point of view, and this is that for a few hours after dawn Nature is at her very best. The air is deliciously cool, and as it is clear, excepting at certain seasons and at high altitudes, everything stands out sharp and well defined, and all the surrounding scenery is seen to the best advantage. If the sportsman is, as he ought to be, anything of a naturalist, he will see all nature under the most interesting aspects. Besides the various species of big game to be met with, he will observe many of the nocturnal animals still abroad after their night's peregrinations, and these he will see at no other time. He will see the ubiquitous hyæna, as he slinks along across the plain to his hiding-place, and will be able to form no other opinion of him than that he is a skulking, contemptible-looking brute, and will possibly feel a desire to have a shot at him, but will refrain from doing so, knowing that he is not worth a bullet, that the shot may disturb better game, and that, after all, the beast does little harm, but, as a scavenger, a vast deal of good. The cunning-looking little jackal, which by its howling during the night has disturbed the sportsman's well-earned rest, and called forth language more forcible than polite, may be seen at dawn trotting along to his earth, looking as unconcerned and innocent as possible, while various species of the larger ichneumons and that curious unwieldy creature, the ratel, will also be abroad. The ratel, by the way, with the porcupine (the latter, though plentiful, rarely seen) is responsible for the numerous shallow burrowings that may be observed so frequently, often in the middle of a well-beaten footpath which is as hard as a brickbat. These burrowings are made by the ratel and porcupine when searching for food. Perhaps, too, in the early morning the stalker will see a curious little ground squirrel, which is rarely found far from its retreat, and which on being disturbed scuttles away, and, if not too frightened, on arriving at its burrow, sits bolt upright to scrutinise the intruder like a marmot, before finally disappearing with a flick of its tail. He may see, too, that quaint and most interesting little beast, the brown mongoose, which is so common in East Africa, and goes about in large family parties. This jolly little creature, which is the personification of curiosity, makes a most amusing and intelligent pet. As they trot along, sticking their noses into or under everything that is at all likely to shelter or hide anything that is eatable, these mongooses keep up a constant low squeaking noise. I have often watched them, and have had them come close up to me, sitting up on their hind legs, trying to make out what I was. It is one of the funniest sights to see them scampering along in a desperate hurry on being frightened, and diving one after the other into the chimney-like holes of an ant-heap, in which they nearly always live. There are scores of other interesting little animals, too numerous to mention, all of which add consider ably to the pleasures of a day's shooting to anyone who is at all keen to observe the habits of little-known creatures.

Bird life is particularly in evidence in the early morning, and everything that has a voice seems to make use of it to the utmost, though with the exception of the yellow-vented bul-bul and one or two other small birds, few can lay claim to anything but a call note, which in most instances is neither melodious nor agreeable to the ears of ordinary people, though to a lover of nature there is something very pleasant even about these. The first bird to make itself heard is the bush cuckoo (*Centropus monachus*), whose curious guttural rolling note may often be heard on a moonlight night, and nearly always for a few minutes about 4 A.M., after which it becomes quiet again till dawn. The next to wake up is the small kingfisher (*Halcyon chelicutensis*), whose pleasant though plaintive voice is also the last to be heard in the evening, before the nightjar starts his monotonous sewing-machine-like chatter. No sooner is it daylight than all the game-birds in the vicinity begin to call and answer each other. There is the grating cackle of the guinea-fowl (*Numida coronata*) which is by far the most plentiful of the four species, excepting *N. ptilorhyncha*, which, however, is not found in any great numbers south of Lake Baringo, where it is very plentiful. There is the harsh and defiant scream of the bush francolin (*F. Grantii*); the less harsh and more pleasing call of the plain francolin (*F. coquei*); the strident guttural voice of the florican (*Otis canicollis*); the curious indescribable call of the yellow-throated spur fowl (*Pternestes infuscatus*); and later on, between eight and nine o'clock, the shrill scream of the small sand-grouse (*Pterocles decoratus*) and the guttural chuckle of the larger kind (*P. gutteralis*) as they fly high overhead on their way to their favourite drinking-place. Most of the above-mentioned game-birds, besides being heard, will probably be seen during a morning's tramp, together with innumerable small birds, which keep up a perpetual chatter. In fact, everything appears to be full of life and energy. Later on, in the middle of the day, everything is quiet and skulking in the shade; all nature seems dead or asleep, with the exception of the butterflies which flit about, and the myriads of other insects which keep up an incessant hum and 'sissing' noise.

The Bushman's Stratagem

C. Whymper

Having thus fairly considered all the pros and cons, I am decidedly of opinion that the stalker will get more pleasure and more game by stalking between daylight and 10 or 11 A.M., and again between 3.30 P.M. and sundown, than at any other time.

There are some places where game, although plentiful, is so wild, and the ground so absolutely devoid of any covert, that stalking is an impossibility. Under such circumstances, and more particularly if the game sought after is scarce, or carries a particularly fine head, there are ways of circumventing it which are admissible, and which cannot in any way be considered unsportsmanlike. These are driving, the Bushman's stratagem of the stalking ostrich, and sitting up at night near a drinking-place. The two former I have myself tried successfully.

It will be found that most antelopes are very partial to certain localities, where they are seen day after day in or quite near to the same place. They are also sure to have certain lines of retreat in case of danger; a habit very much in the sportsman's favour should he decide on a drive. To find this line of retreat is very necessary, and it can only be done by making one or two test drives without either the sportsman or 'stops' in position. Of course all game should be driven down or across the wind. The beaters, from ten to fifteen in number, should be formed into a long line, and should then slowly advance on the game. On no account should the beaters proceed too quickly, lest the game should become thoroughly scared, and (if in a herd) split up and driven in different directions. On the second day the same tactics may be tried again, and it will be found in all probability that the game will make off by exactly the same line of retreat. The third day the sportsman and the 'stops' can take up their positions in the line which the game seems likely to take, behind the most convenient shelter available, which may be artificial if there should be no natural covert, such as a bush, ant-heap, or tuft of grass large enough to conceal them. The 'stops,' who are generally gun-bearers, these being as a rule more intelligent than the ordinary porters, should be directed to take up their positions on either side of the sportsman, each at a distance of about 200 yards from him. They should be told to keep well out of sight, and not to show themselves unless they see that the game is coming too much in their direction, and is likely to pass out of range of the sportsman. In this case they must show themselves for about a second, as that will be quite enough to turn the game away from them. Most antelopes, if approached quietly, start off at a trot when they are first moved, sometimes even at a gallop, then settle down into a walk, and finally stop altogether. This they always do after going a short distance, to have a look round at the cause of their alarm. As the beaters draw up, the game will continue to advance in this manner, and may pull up just out of range of the sportsman to have another look round. The beaters should, therefore, be told beforehand to stop when they see that the game is approaching within range of the ambushes. Should they advance instead of stopping at this juncture, the game will start off again at a trot, possibly at a gallop, and may rush past the sportsman all huddled together, the best head in the middle of the herd, and well protected from a shot by several intervening females; whereas, if the beaters stop when they see the game getting near the ambushes, the game, after having a good look at the beaters, will continue to advance at a walk, and may stop altogether within range, and give a capital chance for a successful shot. To a man who is at all excitable this form of sport is perhaps more trying to the nerves than stalking. To see a fine bull eland or buck *G. Grantii* with a grand head slowly drawing nearer and nearer, at one time appearing likely to pass out of range, at another time coming straight for the ambush behind which the sportsman is concealed, is very exciting. There is the uncertainty as to whether the beast or beasts will pass him at a gallop, trot, or walk; as to whether they will stop altogether when within range: there is the absolute necessity of keeping still, however uncomfortable the position the sportsman may be in, combined with his eagerness to secure a grand trophy; and all these things tend to intensify the excitement. In stalking it is different, as the exertion of crawling and making himself as invisible as possible, a tax both on body and mind, helps to make the stalker forget his 'jumpiness.'

The second device for securing game otherwise unapproachable is that of the stalking ostrich, which can be made out of any kind of long thin pliable sticks formed into the shape and size of an ostrich's body, and covered with the common trade cloth (Americani), dyed the colour of a hen bird with mud from the nearest stream or puddle. The whole thing when complete will much resemble the shell of a large tortoise. The neck and head should be separate from the body, as, when in use, the actions of an ostrich while feeding should be imitated as nearly as possible. I only used this device twice, but each time with the greatest success, and on both occasions in the Rombo plains on the eastern side of Kilimanjaro, shortly after the grass had been burnt, and when there was absolutely no covert of any kind. The *G. Grantii* carry particularly fine heads on these plains, and would not allow me to approach nearer than 350 to 400 yards.

Although the construction of this ostrich excited much amusement amongst the men, and although I noticed a good deal of grinning and chuckling amongst them as I went out, they were very greatly astonished at the result. From the camp I could see two *G. Grantii* standing out in the open about a mile off. Within half a mile of them and on my left there was a slight rise in the ground, which I took advantage of, and thus got within about 600 yards of them before donning the ostrich. Directly I appeared over the top of the rise the gazelles saw me, but I soon allayed their suspicions by pretending to feed and pick about. I then went on, stopping every now and again 'to feed,' and without the least trouble walked up to within 90 yards of them, and got both with a right and left shot To show how successful the imitation was, I passed two wart-hogs within 60 yards on my right and a couple of greater bustards (*Otis kori*) within 40 yards on my left, and none of them showed the slightest signs of fear until after I had gone by them, when the wind exposed the deception.

The next day I approached a large herd of some thirty-five *G. Grantii*, got within 40 yards, and killed the best buck, a magnificent beast, in spite of three or four does which stood within 25 yards of me. After the shot, instead of revealing myself, I picked up the neck of the ostrich, which I had been obliged to drop in order to take the shot, and rushed after the retreating herd. When they stopped after going about 600 yards, the feigned alarm of the ostrich was apparently so real that they allowed me to run straight up to within 60 yards of them. However, I was so pumped from the run, and tired by the first long walk up to the herd in a cramped and stooping position, trying to assimilate my height to that of an ostrich's body, that I was very unsteady, and a shot at the next best buck missed him clean, and away went the herd.

I have only twice tried sitting over a water-hole or other drinking place, a method perhaps less sporting than any other, although a very favourite way of killing game in South Africa in former days; and my attempts at this form of sport met with such poor success that I know little or nothing about it. There can be no doubt but that the Kilimanjaro district and suchlike places are not favourable to this form of shooting, as there is so much water about, that game cannot be re-lied upon to drink at the same place two nights running. To be successful, water should be scarce, and there should certainly not be a running stream, with its numerous and well-used drinking-places, within at least eight or ten miles of the place to be watched. Although my two attempts were failures, this plan would no doubt be well worth trying, more especially when there were lions about. Other game, such as rhinoceroses, buffaloes, and various antelopes, if not to be found on their feeding grounds in the open at daylight, can be tracked into the bush, &c. The spoor of a lion, however, excepting in soft ground, is so difficult to see that it is almost useless to attempt to follow it.

If a well-used water-hole could be found where game was in sufficient quanti-ties to attract lions, it would be advisable to watch it on the chance of getting a shot at a lion—a chance which may not be offered for months by daylight, though lions may be heard roaring near the camp night after night.

And now to deal with the last feature of a stalk—the shot. It may be taken as a general rule that all big game should be shot behind the shoulder.

Roughly speaking, a bullet placed in the lateral centre of the body, or a trifle below the centre, and a few inches behind the shoulder in a perpendicular line with the back of the foreleg, will kill anything, provided, of course, the bullet has sufficient penetration; as, even if the heart is not touched, the lungs, which are a much larger mark, and almost equally vital, certainly will be. The chest shot when the beast is facing the sportsman is equally good. With elephants, however, when at close quarters, which would be either in long grass or thick bush, the head shot is preferable, as a bullet in the brain will be instantly fatal, and the risk of a charge under conditions unfavourable to the stalker will be avoided. The danger of a charge in such circumstances, more especially on a calm day, is greatly increased by the dense cloud of smoke caused by the explosion of ten or twelve drachms of powder, which hangs in the air and prevents the stalker from seeing the result of his shot.

With all one's care to avoid the infliction of needless pain, cases occur from time to time in every sportsman's experience in which it seems almost impossible to despatch a mortally wounded beast with anything except a shot in the brain or in the vertebræ of the neck. The wounded animal appears in these cases quite impervious to all sense of pain, being apparently in a state of semi-consciousness after the first shot, the shock of each subsequent shot seeming to have no further effect upon its nervous system, yet in nineteen cases out of twenty a beast hit in the same spot and at the same angle would die almost immediately.

Several cases of the kind have come under my own observation. At one time I thought that this extraordinary vitality was confined to the antelopes, but I have seen the same peculiarity displayed twice by buffaloes, once by an elephant, once by a rhinoceros, and once by a zebra. I used to be of opinion that a beast so wounded was reduced to a state of semi-paralysis, and was incapable of moving from the spot on which it was standing when hit, but I have proved that this is not always the case.

When first struck in such cases, the beast almost invariably drops its head, and sometimes stands with open mouth in the same manner that a beast stands after it has been shot through the stomach.

From my own observations, the shots which have thrown a beast into this curious condition have invariably struck it low down, through the lower edge of one or both lungs. The shot, however, has not necessarily been fired when the beast has been standing in one particular position, as I have known these shots fired when the beast was broadside on, stern on, and facing me.

If there is any doubt as to whether the animal is hit through the stomach or low down in the lungs, the sportsman should take advantage of the beast as it stands with its head down, and either give it another shot immediately or carefully approach nearer to make quite certain of placing his bullet in the right spot. Should he then be quite satisfied that his second bullet has struck the right spot behind the shoulder, and should the beast still continue to stand in the same position, or move on only a short distance, he can be pretty sure that the case is one of those I allude to, and he had better either finish with a shot in the brain or the vertebræ of the neck, or leave it to die quietly, as it very soon will do. Any more shoulder shots would be simply thrown away. Of course a beast shot in the stomach should be killed with the shoulder shot at once, as it is always likely to pull itself together for a while and travel for miles.

A Baby Elephant

C. W., after a photograph by E. Gedge

CHAPTER X

THE ELEPHANT

BY F. J. JACKSON

The African elephant (*E. Africanus*), known to the natives of Zanzibar as Tembo, to the natives of Mombasa and to the north as Ndovu, has, I venture to think, on account of its truly colossal size, majestic bearing, and sagacity, a much better claim to the position of king of beasts than the lion. It has disappeared from many parts of Africa since the introduction of firearms and the advance of civilisation, but in British East Africa, in certain localities, it is still to be found in enormous numbers. It may be hoped that whoever has the making of laws for that country will strenuously endeavour to preserve the elephants and protect them from professional hunters, who shoot everything—bulls, cows, and half-grown calves alike—utterly regardless of the size of the ivory, even though the tusks be little bigger than the lower incisor teeth of a bull hippo.

In the dry weather elephants take up their quarters in the thick forests at high altitudes—from 6,000 to 9,000 feet—such as Kikuyu, Mau, and Lykepia, and in the belts of forest on Kilimanjaro, Kenia, Elgon, and Ruwenzori, rather, perhaps, for the sake of food and water—both plentiful in such places—than for the sake of the shade. In the wet weather they leave the forests and roam out into the open, where food and water have again become abundant, and they are quite as likely as not to be found during the heat of the day standing in long grass with no shade of any kind. It is difficult for a man who has never hunted elephants, or seen places where they have stopped to feed, to realise the tremendous havoc they play in those places which are much frequented by them, and the amount of wilful damage they do for no apparent reason. When hunting them I have often come across places where the herd I was following had stopped and scattered about to feed, and the amount of wreckage created in the short time before they had again moved on was astounding. Trees of various kinds had been broken down and uprooted in all directions for the sake of a few twigs and young shoots which could have been plucked off equally well whilst the trees stood; bushes had been pulled up and thrown on one side with scarcely a leaf off; branches of larger trees had been torn off without a twig or piece of bark having been eaten; wisps of long grass lay all round, pulled up by the roots, but otherwise untouched, whilst the grass where the herd had stood was knocked down and trampled under foot by their huge feet. In fact, the whole place had more the appearance of a playground than of a feeding-place, and I am inclined to think that a good deal of the damage caused by elephants is done simply for amusement. I have come across other places where an equal amount of damage has befallen the same kind of trees and bushes, but with every proof that the elephants really have fed. The trees have been well cropped of their branches and twigs; bushes that have been torn up have been devoid of leaves, and their stems well chewed; the upper part of the wisps of grass have been missing, and the branches of large trees and the trees themselves have been stripped of their bark, which was left lying about in all directions after being chewed, &c. When in Uganda I once had an opportunity of watching a grand old bull elephant amusing himself. He was one of a large herd which I had no difficulty in getting within 150 yards of, but which I could not approach nearer, as they were standing quite out in the open. As I sat on the top of an ant-heap waiting for them to get into a better position, I watched this bull through my binoculars for about twenty minutes trying to destroy another ant-heap for no apparent cause, as he did not pick up the earth to dust himself, but simply dug his tusks into the heap, and with a sideways movement of the head sent the clods of earth flying away on each side of him. Had he thrown the earth upwards on to his back, or picked it up with his trunk to give himself a sand-bath, there would have been nothing strange about his proceedings. When the herd moved off, I went up to the ant-heap and found that the bull had knocked it about in a manner almost incredible even for such a huge and powerful beast. There can be little doubt that a great deal of the uprooted long grass which is found where elephants have stood is torn up simply for the purpose of dusting themselves, as I have twice had an excellent opportunity of watching them. On one occasion I got within 100 yards of five elephants standing in long grass in a hollow, and watched them for some time from the top of a rock whilst they had a dust-bath. This they did by simply twisting their trunks round wisps of grass, which they pulled up by the roots and threw up into the air over their backs. The weight of the earth in the roots caused these wisps of grass to descend roots downwards, and as they landed on the elephants' backs, a good shower of dry earth, sand, and dust was the result.

Tracking in East Africa is rather an unusual method of finding other kinds of game, excepting in very thick bush, or when the particular game sought after is scarce, as game can generally be found in the open, provided the sportsman is on the feeding grounds early enough in the morning. With elephants the case is different, as they are great wanderers, and tracking is the universal method of finding them, the nature of the country in which they are found (generally forest, bush, or tall cane-like grass) being very unfavourable for seeing them at any distance. It is therefore necessary to make an early start, as much time is often lost before finding spoor sufficiently fresh to follow. Even when found, and though it appears to indicate that the elephants have just passed, the sportsman may have to follow it for several hours before coming up with them. Perhaps few things will try perseverance and endurance more than elephant hunting, as even though the spoor seems not more than a few minutes old, and though there is apparently every hope of approaching the beasts very shortly, delays are often caused by having to pick out the spoor of particular animals from a number of other tracks, and the knowledge that the beasts are in all probability gaining on him during these delays is decidedly trying to a man's patience. After such delays the sportsman may manage to get on at a good pace, which, together with the rough going, soon tells on him, and after three or four hours (by no means an unusual time) he begins to feel a little down on his luck, and to despair of ever seeing the game again, when possibly he comes across the place where they have stood or stopped to feed. Here he may find fresh dung, into which some of his men will eagerly thrust their toes to try whether it is still warm or not. If it is, he starts off with renewed energy and buoyed up with fresh hope. Further on may be indications that the elephants have again stopped to feed, and the hunter's spirits go up with a bound at the knowledge that he must have gained on them, only to be damped a little later on when he finds that they have again moved on. Though feeling inclined to throw up the whole thing in despair, he decides to follow a little longer, realising by this time that a stern chase is a long one. At last, as he plods wearily along, he comes across dung that is actually smoking, a sure sign that he is now pretty close to his game. A little further on the welcome sound of a branch being snapped, or the rumbling noise peculiar to the elephant, catches his ear; then he realises that he may see the beasts themselves at any moment, and is therefore thoroughly on the alert. Taking one of his heavy rifles from a gun-bearer and putting two or three spare cartridges into his pocket, if he has not already done so, and telling his gun-bearer to keep close up, while the rest of the men remain behind until they either hear a shot or a signal to come on, he pushes forward with the greatest caution, a curious mixture of coolness and intense excitement.

Should the nature of the ground in which the sportsman finds them be open, so as to prevent his getting nearer than 40 yards, the shoulder shot is the best to take at elephants, and I believe is almost universally recommended by all old el-ephant hunters. Should the beasts, however, be found standing in dense bush or tall cane-like grass (and they are very partial to these places) where it is impossible to see them until within 20 yards or less, and where even then all but the head and outline of the back is hidden, the temple is the best shot, and a shot anywhere be-tween the eye and a little dark mark which indicates the orifice of the ear would be instantly fatal. When elephants are standing in thick bush and long grass, unless a sportsman has had a good deal of experience with them, the fact of seeing their huge backs towering above the covert is rather apt to deceive him in regard to the position of their heart and lungs. The great depth of their bodies would probably lead him to shoot too high, and a bullet placed too high, although it might eventu-ally prove fatal, would not prevent the beast getting clean away at the time.

The hunt after the first elephant I ever killed is a very fair example of many which I have had, though I regret to say a very large proportion have not been so successful as this was.

In May 1887 I was encamped on one of the numerous streams on the southern slopes of Kilimanjaro, below Kiboso, with my friend Mr. H. C. V. Hunter.

This country, as I have said elsewhere, is very undulating, and the covert on it very varied, brush and grass 10 to 12 ft. high alternating with open forest of ta-ble-topped mimosa or dense clumps of bush and large forest trees. It is, however, decidedly an unfavourable country for sport, as the wind is very uncertain and can never be relied upon to keep steady, owing probably to the proximity of the mountain, which causes the cross currents and eddies that constantly betray the sportsman's presence. Mr. Hunter and I were three weeks in this country, and I think we each came up with elephants nearly every day we were out; but one of these cross currents or eddies in the wind betrayed us before we could see the beasts in the dense covert. When we did see them, they were nearly always in the densest bush or long grass, and we got very few good shots compared with the number of times we were actually within shooting range. On the morning of the 29th I left camp with thirteen men, very early, with the intention of following up the spoor of a grand bull which I had severely wounded the day before. This beast I had followed up until he brought me round in a circle to within a couple of miles of camp, and as it was late in the afternoon and I was pretty well knocked up at the time, I gave up the hunt for the day, intending to take up the spoor again on the following morning. Unfortunately, there was heavy rain during the night, which, however, stopped just about an hour before we started from camp, and when we picked up the spoor we found that all traces of blood, which had been very con-spicuous the day before, had been completely washed away. However, there was no mistaking the spoor of this beast on account of its size; we managed to get along at a good pace, and had gone about three miles when we found that a big herd had subsequently got on to the same track, and had completely obliterated the spoor of the wounded bull. As this herd had passed since the rain had stopped, evidently within about two hours, I decided to follow them, but had not gone more than half a mile before we found that they had split up, five big fellows going off to the left, up wind, whilst the rest of the herd kept straight on, across the wind. After a short consultation, we decided to follow these five big ones, and we went off at a killing pace through the long grass, in spite of the ploughed-up condition of the path, and at the end of an hour and a half came to a small deep stream which the elephants had crossed. As I was already wet through from the grass, and as my boots were worn out and full of holes, which prevented them holding water and making a 'squishing' noise, I waded across this stream, and ascended the steep bank on the other side, which was covered with dense bush and thick forest trees. Here we came across a small mud-hole where the elephants had rolled, whilst a little further on they had stopped to rub themselves against the trees. They had then left this belt of bush and forest, and gone on across undulating country covered with long cane-like grass and a few small trees, one or two of which they had torn down, and had loitered to feed on the young shoots and twigs. We also found fresh dung which was still warm inside when I kicked off the outer surface and tested it with the back of my hand. This was decidedly encouraging, and we pushed on as fast as we could plod through the heavy ground. A little further on we received a check, as another small herd had got on to the track, but fortunately had turned off in a different direction after going a few hundred yards, and we were once more able to get along and make up for lost time. About eleven o'clock I sat down to have a short rest, but on starting again and arriving at the top of a big rise, from which I had a good view of the surrounding country, I felt inclined to give in, as I could see no covert in which the elephants were likely to take up their quarters for the day.

We went on, however, and shortly afterwards came to a patch of dense bush down in a hollow, which I had been unable to see before, where they had again waited for a time. At 12.30 we came to the top of another rise, and I saw a large bit of forest and dense bush lying in the hollow below us. My spirits began to rise, but before entering it I sat down for another short rest, feeling quite sure that the elephants were inside, as we had just found some dung that was quite warm. As I sat smoking a pipe I heard the crack of a branch being broken ring through the forest. Jumping up and putting two or three cartridges both for the 4-bore and 8-bore into my pockets, we entered the dense bush, which was some 15 to 20 ft. high, and soon afterwards heard the crack of another branch right ahead of us. Thinking the elephants might be scattered about feeding, and not wishing to run the risk of any of them getting our wind, I sent one of my gun-bearers up a tall thin tree to see if he could make out their whereabouts. He soon spotted them, well to windward of us, about 150 yards off, and on coming down from the tree reported that they were all together, moving along slowly and feeding as they went. Taking the 4-bore from the second gun-bearer, I crept forward with my head gun-bearer carrying the 8-bore, and on coming to a place where the covert was rather more open, I saw a large dark bush violently shaken some 70 yards ahead of us, and at the same time heard another branch being torn off a tree more to my right.

Resting the 4-bore on the fallen Tree

C. Whymper

I then sent my gun-bearer through a small gap in the bush on my right to see if he could sight the beast that had broken the branch, and in a very few seconds he signalled to me by snapping his fingers (the usual method of attracting attention). As I crept through the gap I saw two elephants about 70 yards off in a small open hollow, one standing stern end on, the other, a grand beast, broadside on, but with only his head showing from behind a big bush. As 70 yards is too far for a head shot, T crept forward to within 40 yards of him; but at that moment he stepped out clear of the bush, giving me a grand chance, of which I immediately availed myself, and before he knew where he was he had received a 4-bore bullet behind the shoulder, but a trifle too high. The dense cloud of smoke hanging in the damp heavy atmosphere prevented me from getting a shot at the other one before he disappeared in the bush. On going up to where the one I shot at had stood there was no difficulty in finding blood, and on following up his spoor we came across him in about 200 yards, standing in dense bush, evidently very sick and unable to move, and another couple of shots killed him. He was a splendid beast, the finest I have ever killed, but as I only had a small steel yard measure with me I was unable to measure him properly. His tusks were 7 ft. and 6 ft. 9 in. long respectively, and weighed about 60 lbs. apiece; his forefeet measured 54 in. in circumference, and the length of his ear was 5 ft. 4 in.

Dead Elephant

From a photograph by E. Gedge

Although the hunting of elephants is as a rule very hard and trying work, there is always the possibility of getting them without much trouble, as happened to myself one day in Turkwel, a district in the Suk country east of Mount Elgon.

While the camp was being pitched a porter came up to say that when collecting firewood in the bush he had seen elephants close by, and had left them quietly feeding and standing about. Though it seemed very improbable that I should find them after all the noise that had been and still was going on amongst the men, I went out and found a herd of some twenty-five elephants, standing within 600 yards of camp. The country was undulating and very open, and as the grass had lately been burnt there was no covert excepting table-topped mimosa trees, while to make matters worse the elephants were much scattered and standing on the other side of a swampy hollow, with the exception of one bull, which was standing in it. With great difficulty I managed to crawl up to a fallen tree on the edge of the swamp, and within about 80 yards of where the bull was standing. Resting the 4-bore on the fallen tree, I took a steady shot at him as he was in the act of drinking, and gave him another bullet from the 8-bore far back in the ribs, which, as he turned, raked forward into his vitals. Running forward into the swamp, I gave a fine cow a good shot behind the shoulder with the left barrel, and again getting hold of the 4-bore gave another cow a shot, but too far back and low down, and before I could get through the swamp the herd went off. The bull after going less than 100 yards fell over dead, and another couple of shots finished the first cow; then followed a long chase after the other cow, which I finally got with a shot almost in the ear-hole, after giving her a great number of ineffectual body shots.

CHAPTER XI
THE AFRICAN BUFFALO
BY F. J. JACKSON

The African buffalo (*B. caffa*), known to the natives as 'Mboga' or 'Nyati,' is, I consider, on account of its enormous strength and vitality, combined with great pluck and natural cunning, the most dangerous beast in East Africa, and I believe this opinion is shared by the majority of men who have hunted it to any extent. As it rarely happens that a beast of any kind charges without provocation, excepting the rhinoceros, to which I shall come later on, I use the word 'dangerous' as applied to a beast after it has been wounded. Compared with an elephant, a buffalo is of course inferior both in size and strength; as compared with a lion, in activity only. When wounded all these three beasts will endeavour to get into thick covert to hide themselves. This is greatly in their favour when they are being tracked by the sportsman, more particularly so in the case of a buffalo or a lion. All 'dangerous' beasts, such as elephants, buffaloes, lions, rhinoceroses, &c., are more likely to charge when taken unawares and at close quarters, and under these circumstances a charge by a buffalo is not only the most dangerous of all, but more probable for the following reasons. Thick bush 5½ ft. high (whether in large belts or small patches and clumps) will hide a buffalo when it is standing up, even if only a few feet away from the sportsman, and should it be lying down, thick covert only 3 ft. to 3 ft. 6 in. high will conceal it quite as effectually.

With an elephant, which would never lie down, the bush or long grass must be exceptionally high and thick to render it invisible at 15 to 20 yards distance. A lion would of course be more difficult to see than either. A buffalo, whether it is standing up or lying down, will never give the sportsman the slightest indication of its proximity, and to detect it he has to trust almost entirely to his own or gun-bearer's eyesight, unless perhaps the beast's lungs are badly injured by the shot, when it may breathe heavily enough to be heard at some little distance. The same may be said of an elephant, but there is a greater chance of seeing it on account of its enormous size. A lion, on the other hand, will very often, if not always, warn the sportsman of its presence by a low growl when at a distance of some 15 to 20 yards.

A buffalo has a better chance of seeing the sportsman than the sportsman has of seeing it, as bush is usually thinner a foot or two from the ground than higher up, and a buffalo, standing with his head much lower than a man's, can therefore see under it. A sportsman will generally see an elephant first, and can dodge and creep about in the bush, which, if only 5 feet high or even less, will enable him to keep out of sight. A lion has a still better chance than either, as his head is much nearer to the ground, whether the beast is standing or lying down, and he has both a better chance of seeing and of hearing the sportsman's approach.

A buffalo, if it sees or hears the sportsman approaching at a distance, is as likely to stop to fight it out as to bolt away. The same with an elephant. A lion will generally give a low growl and slink off. Therefore a sportsman, taking it all round, is more likely to come unexpectedly to very close quarters with a buffalo than with a lion or an elephant.

In the event of a charge by one of these three beasts, covert that would stop a lion would stop neither a buffalo nor an elephant.

A buffalo may not at all improbably be within a few feet before a shot can be fired, owing to the sportsman's inability to see it sooner. The chances are against this with an elephant. A lion is not likely to wait until the sportsman is quite close up, but will come on, if it comes on at all, from a greater distance, and the greater distance a beast comes from the better chance the sportsman has of pulling himself together and taking a steady shot.

Bull Buffalo

When hit, the difficulties of killing, stopping, or even turning a buffalo are greater than with an elephant or lion. A buffalo holds its head up, with its forehead almost horizontal, too high to enable one to get a shot at the brain, and there is a great chance of the bullet ricochetting off the horns. A shot at the chest when at close quarters is almost an impossibility, as the beast is so very low on its legs. In the open this is the best shot to take, as by kneeling down the sportsman is more on a level with the animal, and the head is not so much in the way. An elephant also holds its head up, and the chances of a shot at the head proving fatal as the beast charges are so remote as to be almost infinitesimal. An elephant's head, however, is a large mark, and a bullet striking it in the centre of the base of the trunk, if it does not penetrate to the brain, will knock it down, or at all events turn it. The chest is a better mark in the open, but when in thick covert cannot often be taken advantage of. Even if this shot should not be fatal, it would nine times out of ten stop or turn the beast. A lion being a much smaller beast than either, and being more active, is naturally more difficult to hit, but when hit is more easily disabled, and not so tenacious of life.

Should a buffalo charge and miss the sportsman, it will hunt him as a terrier does a rabbit, and will rarely leave him as long as it can see or smell him. An elephant has poorer eyesight than a buffalo, and there is a better chance of escaping observation in covert after being missed, as an elephant, being less active, cannot turn so quickly and would overrun itself. It will, however, also hunt him and beat about the covert to try and catch sight of him or scent him. A lion would be less easy to dodge than either, but, as it is possessed of less pluck, would be more easily cowed and less likely to renew the attack.

Buffaloes were at one time exceedingly plentiful throughout British East Africa, and in some districts, where the country was best suited to their habits, were to be found in enormous herds. Towards the end of the year 1890, and in the early part of 1891, they unfortunately contracted a kind of anthrax, the same disease which carried off nearly all the native cattle, and they were almost destroyed by it. On my way down from Uganda in July 1890, between Lakes Baringo and Naivasha, I saw in one day's march as many as six herds of buffaloes, varying in number from 100 to 600 head in a herd. In this same district in the following March, my friend Mr. Gedge, on his way down to the coast, saw nothing but carcases, and in one day counted as many as fifteen lying rotting in the grass, close to the footpath. In 1892 the officers of the Mombasa and Victoria Nyanza Railway Survey only saw on two different occasions the spoor of a single beast, although they traversed a great part of the country where buffaloes were once so plentiful. Amongst other places where this grand beast was particularly abundant was the Arusha-wa-Chini district, now in German territory, to the south of Kilimanjaro, and the Njiri plains to the north of the mountain; Turkwel, in the Suk country to the east of Mount Elgon; the extensive undulating plains on the top of the Mau and Elgeyo escarpments; Lykepia, to the west of Mount Kenia; the banks of the river Tana, and the thick bush country on the mainland near Lamu. There can be little doubt that it will take many years for them to recover to any extent, if they ever do so. A sportsman intending to visit this country must therefore not be disappointed at being unable to add one of these beasts to his bag, though of course he may have the luck to meet with an odd one here and there. It is to be hoped, however, that everyone who goes out to shoot will endeavour to give them a fair chance of increasing by scrupulously refraining from shooting at any cow that may be met with. Buffaloes feed out in the open during the night and early morning, and retire to the bush or other covert where they lie up during the heat of the day. In places where they were unlikely to be disturbed I have seen them lying out in the open in the middle of the day, although there was plenty of thick bush within a mile or less. This may be accounted for, partly by the fact that these particular countries were uninhabited, and therefore undisturbed, but more probably by a desire on the part of the buffaloes to escape from the incessant torments of the various species of noxious horse-flies.

Blissful Ignorance

C. Whymper

Old bulls, whether solitary or when in parties of two or three, as is so often the case, have the reputation of being more savage and dangerous to approach than when in a herd, but I am quite sure that this is not so. An old solitary bull when wounded is no more dangerous than a wounded one that has been picked out of a herd, which will then nearly always turn out and go off by itself. Solitary bulls are much more easily approached than others, as the cows in a herd, more especially if they have calves with them, are very watchful, and when feeding are often scattered about in all directions. But whether in herds or solitary, the sportsman must never forget that he is dealing with a most formidable beast, and should always endeavour to get up to it close enough to insure his putting a bullet as near as possible to the spot aimed at, in order to kill or render it helpless at once. The greatest caution should be exercised in the approach, and the stalker should endeavour to keep out of sight not only before but *after* taking a shot, as a beast is far less likely to charge if it is quite ignorant of the stalker's whereabouts before it is fired at and wounded than when aware of his presence beforehand, and though perhaps unable quite to decide what he is, is given his exact whereabouts by the dense cloud of smoke. Personally I have never been charged at close quarters by buffaloes, although I have had many encounters with them quite exciting enough to assure me that a wounded buffalo is a beast that is not to be trifled with. I owe this immunity primarily to the fact of my having used very heavy rifles—a single 4-bore for the first shot, with a double 8-bore in reserve, and I have generally succeeded in getting within 80 yards, far more often indeed within 50 yards of them before firing. Then again, when a beast has been wounded, I have always endeavoured to keep it in sight, in order to save myself from being taken at a disadvantage, and also to avoid the loss of time spent in following up the blood-spoor. Whenever a beast has got into thick covert where it was quite impossible to watch its movements, I have nearly always waited a short time before taking up the spoor to give it time to lie down, become stiff, and partly forget its fear and trouble. But perhaps I owe my safety principally to my having had the good luck always to see the beast before or at the same time that it saw me, when I have at once saluted it with a 4-bore or 8-bore bullet, which has knocked out of it, whatever inclination it may have had to charge.

In buffalo shooting it is perhaps more important to be up early and on the feeding grounds by daylight than in any other kind of big game shooting, as it can be taken as a general rule that buffaloes, after feeding in the open plains and glades during the night and early morning, enter and lie up in bush or other thick covert during the day. In the first place, when they are in the open they are easier to see, a herd of buffaloes, or even a single one, being a very conspicuous object at a long distance. In the very early morning they are generally to be found, when in a herd, moving along in a fairly compact body (nearly always led by a cow), and not wasting much time in feeding on their way from their drinking-place, but heading in the direction of the covert they intend to lie up in during the day; or they may be found on the outskirts of the bush, still feeding, before turning in for the day. This is the best time to come across them, as the stalker, when he finds them pretty close together, has a good opportunity of examining them and marking the best bulls. When found feeding in the open close to the bush, or in open bush, they are, with an ordinary amount of care and trouble, easy enough to stalk. It is, however, very often aggravating work to follow on the outskirts of a herd, waiting for a favourable opportunity to crawl on to get a shot at the best bull, but unable to do so from the fact that several cows are feeding between the stalker and the bull. Should they, however, be quite out on the open, and unapproachable, the only thing to be done is to wait patiently inside the cover of the bush they are likely to make for to lie up in, keeping as near to them as possible as they move along, and attempt to cut them off as they enter the bush. I have tried sending men round to move them, but only once succeeded in cutting them off after a long run, and found it much better to wait patiently, as they will generally give the stalker a fair idea of the place at which they will enter the bush. A large herd of buffaloes filing slowly past at a steady walk, within a range of 30 or 40 yards of you, is a grand sight, and it is decidedly exciting, after waiting for the bull you have marked, to take your shot and listen to the tremendous commotion and crashing of the bush which follows it as the herd stampedes.

Shooting buffaloes in thick bush, when the only means of finding them is by tracking, is not only intensely exciting works but most dangerous, and as a rule most unsatisfactory. It is exciting because in thick covert the stalker must make up his mind that there will be little chance of his seeing a beast until he is pretty close up to it, and if he is at all 'jumpy,' as he steals carefully along, avoiding sticks and dry crackling leaves and loose stones, or brushing up against the bush, he has ample time to think about and realise the dangers he is possibly running. Most men will agree that the deep guttural grunts of buffaloes, as they stand and lie about, which can be heard at long distances in the stillness of the bush, are not calculated to soothe the nerves of even the coolest and most experienced, while doubtless a good many have felt their hearts thumping against their ribs to an extent which is not conducive to good shooting. Again, as the herd is probably scattered about, there is a possibility that some of them may be on either side of the tracks you are following, and there is also some uncertainty as to whether in their first stampede on detecting danger some of the buffaloes which have neither seen nor smelt you may not be coming towards you instead of rushing away from you. This kind of sport is dangerous, as the chances are for the most part in favour of the buffalo, should it turn vicious. The stalker may not see it until at close quarters, when it has probably already seen or heard him, and a beast which has become aware of the enemy is far more likely to charge on being fired at and wounded (unless of course it is disabled) than it would be if it was altogether unaware of his presence. As it is quite impossible to tell where beasts may or may not be when the herd is scattered, there is the possibility that some of them are on either side of the tracks which the stalker is following, and should one of these be a bad-tempered old bull, or a cow with a calf, he or she might, on being taken by surprise at close quarters, charge in self-defence from a quarter from which the stalker least expects attack. As I have said before, the charge of an infuriated buffalo is very difficult to stop, owing to the position in which it carries its head, and if the stalker fails to stop or turn it, and has to bolt, he may be so hampered in his movements by the bush, a single creeper, like so much packthread to a buffalo and yet quite strong enough to hold the stalker fast or trip him up, that he may be unable to get out of the way. Following buffaloes into bush sufficiently open to enable the stalker to see and get a shot at them at a range of 30 or 40 yards is not attended with nearly so much danger as following them into dense bush, where, owing to the dark shadows, it is almost impossible to distinguish a beast from its surroundings. Although the spoor of a beast may be seen leading directly up to a bush, which looks a likely spot for a buffalo to lie down in, the stalker may not be able to discover whether the beast is there or not, and if it is there, he may be quite sure that the buffalo, as it is standing or lying down in the shade, has a far better chance of seeing him, as he stands more or less in the open, than he has of seeing it. As the chances are so much against the stalker seeing the beast until he gets within a few yards of it; as the difficulties of stopping it should it charge are so great; and as, if it misses him in the first charge, it will hunt him, I repeat, as a terrier does a rabbit, it remains for the sportsman, however keen he may be, to consider whether these risks are worth running, even on the chance of being rewarded by an exceptionally fine trophy. In any case he should not attempt to follow up a buffalo unless he is properly armed with a heavy rifle.

Again, such sport is unsatisfactory, because in thick covert the wind is very changeable, and is apt to chop round when least expected. Such a change in the wind, even though quite imperceptible to the stalker, is quite enough to reveal his presence to the buffaloes, and away they will crash without giving him a chance, just at the critical moment when he is close up and expecting to see one of them at any moment. As a buffalo is a very difficult beast to see when standing or lying in the dark shade, the stalker has in most cases to fire as soon as he sees it, and even though he kills it, it may as often as not turn out that the beast is only a cow or a young bull, with a head not worth keeping as a trophy.

I think there can be little doubt that very old bulls, which are almost invariably solitary, become nearly if not quite deaf, and it is partly owing to this infirmity that many accidents have happened to unarmed natives, and occasionally to caravan porters prowling in the bush in search of firewood, &c. The buffalo, being deaf, is not aware of the approach of an enemy, and when he perceives one close to him is so startled that he charges in self-defence, his onslaught being so quick and furious that the man (equally taken by surprise) is unable to get out of the way. In support of this theory as to deafness I remember when in Turkwel, in the Suk country, on December 14, 1889, the camp had been pitched at least two hours, and some 400 porters had been roaming about collecting firewood and water, shouting and yelling, as their custom is, when a man came into camp to say that a buffalo was lying under a tree within 200 yards of us. The man's story appeared so im- probable, although he pointed out the exact tree, which I could see as I sat in my tent, that I did not credit it in spite of his earnest protestations of 'Queli, bwana, queli' (True, master, true), so I sent my head gun-bearer to verify it. In a few min- utes he returned and reported that a bull buffalo was certainly there apparently lying asleep at the foot of an ant-heap under the tree. I immediately went out, and walked straight up to the ant-heap, on the top of which there was a large leafless bush, and on crawling up the side of the heap I saw the buffalo within five yards of me. Just at that moment he turned his head, and, seeing me, stood up, had a look at me, and turned to bolt, but before he had got many yards I knocked him over all in a heap with an 8-bore bullet which raked him from stern to stem. On another occasion, in the Kidong Valley (July 30, 1890), when camp was being pitched with its attendant turmoil, a porter came in to say that a buffalo was lying asleep close at hand. Accompanied by Dr. Mackinnon, medical officer to the expedition, I went out, and we were led by the man direct to the beast, which was lying evidently asleep under a small bush, and so close to camp that we could distinctly hear the orders being given to the men. We were within 20 yards of him before we could see him, and at first thought that he was dead, he lay so still, and I could detect no movement of his side even with the aid of binoculars; but a bullet from an 8-bore brought him to his feet with a plunge, and two more killed him. Both these beasts were very old, judging from the smoothness of the frontlet or palm of their horns, the usual ruggedness being quite worn away.

Buffaloes, like rhinoceroses, are very often attended by birds (*Buphaga erythrorhyncha*), when they are much more difficult to stalk than at other times. Besides the rhinoceros bird, buffaloes, particularly when in herds, are often attended by a flock of little egrets (*Herodias garzetta*), which, like the former, are attracted by the great numbers of ticks on these animals. They do not, however, render the stalking more difficult, as they do not warn the game of the stalker's presence like the rhinoceros bird, but are rather a source of danger to the herd than otherwise, more particularly in bush country, their habit of rising and circling round in the air before again settling being often a means of indicating the position of a herd, which would otherwise have been passed unnoticed; whilst, should they rise on detecting the sportsman, the buffaloes are so used to these sudden and short flights that the occurrence causes them little or no alarm.

When single, or in twos and threes, buffaloes are quite as easy to approach as a rhinoceros.

To kill a buffalo the shoulder shot is the best. This should be rather low down, if anything, below the central lateral line on the body, as the enormously thick neck and the high dorsal ridge are rather apt to deceive the sportsman as to the actual depth of the beast's body, more especially when standing in grass or low bush, so that the legs and lower outline of the body cannot be discerned. Should a beast be standing behind a thick tree or bush, so as to present only its head and neck, a shot in the neck, rather far back to avoid the backward curve of the horns, and about half-way down, would be almost instantly fatal; but this shot should not be attempted if the beast, although standing broadside on, has its head facing the sportsman, as the near horn will probably be in the way. This reminds me of a curious shot which I once made at a buffalo standing in this position behind a small thorn-tree, which, when I came to measure it, I found to be 11 ins. in circumference, and which just covered the best spot for a shot at the shoulder. On getting up to a small bush within seventy yards of it, I decided to take the neck shot; but just as I was getting into position to fire the beast saw me. Fearing it would bolt on discovering me, I took a quick aim at the shoulder, rather than risk the neck shot, knowing that if the bullet did not hit the tree it would be pretty sure to go somewhere near the lungs. Directly the smoke cleared, my gun-bearer told me that he had seen the tree fall, and on going up to it I found the bullet, an 8-bore, had caught it exactly in the centre and so shattered it that the heavy table-top had caused it to break off where the bullet entered. Whilst measuring it I heard a deep groan in the direction the buffalo had taken, and on taking up the spoor found my beast quite dead, lying in the grass about 150 yards off, shot through the shoulder. On cutting it open I found the bullet had gone through both lungs, and was sticking in the ribs on the other side. A shot at the head, even with an 8-bore, with hardened bullet and twelve drachms of powder, would in most cases have little effect on a buffalo, unless, of course, the beast should be sufficiently near to enable the sportsman to make sure of putting his bullet just under the frontlet of the horns into the brain; but I think that most men who have shot buffaloes would say that such a range would be far too near to be pleasant. As the chances that a head shot at a buffalo will prove fatal are so very small, this shot should be avoided altogether except in the case of a charge, where it may be the only one offered.

'Often attended by Birds'

C. Whymper

Although I have killed a good many buffaloes, and under all sorts of conditions, I have only once had recourse to the head shot. This was in the district lying between Kahe and Taveta, where I was shooting in February 1887. The country was here fairly open, with numerous patches of bush dotted about, and a few small isolated rocky hills, appropriately called by one writer 'earth boils.' On climbing up one of these to get a better view of the surrounding country, I spied an old bull buffalo about a mile off, quietly feeding close to a patch of bush, which was about 150 yards long and about 50 yards wide, and, as the wind was favourable, I felt pretty sure of getting him without much difficulty. On arriving at the bush, I found a small low ant-heap just opposite the place where I had last seen the buffalo, and I stepped on to it to try and see exactly where he was on the other side of the bush, but could see nothing of him. As I stood on the ant-heap consulting with my gun-bearer in a low whisper, I heard the well-known hissing cry of a rhinoceros bird, and saw it fly up out of the bush on the farther side of it, a little to the left of me. The buffalo, though disturbed by the warning cry of the bird, was evidently not much alarmed, as he began to move across my front at a slow walk, and I could follow his movements by the shaking of the bush as he passed through it, but could not see him. When he was just about opposite to where I stood, he changed his course and came straight towards me, still at a slow walk, and when he arrived within a few yards of the edge immediately opposite to me, I slipped out of sight behind the ant-heap and waited for him to appear. He came to the very edge of the bush, stopped for about half a minute, and I then began to fear that he had either seen me, as I was quite out in the open, or had heard a slight noise I made in exchanging the .500 Express (always loaded on such occasions with solid bullets) for the 8-bore, when the barrels struck together. Whilst I lay on the side of the ant-heap, peeping over the top, he moved forward, and I covered the place where I saw the bush move, in readiness to fire, as he was then only 16 yards from me. At last I saw his grand head, which he held high, come through the bush, but was unable to get a good view of his chest, as directly his head was clear of the bush he lowered it, and my only chance was at his head. Drawing a bead on his forehead, I pulled the trigger, but the cartridge missed fire. He, however, did not hear the click of the hammer, and before he was clear of the bush I dropped him dead in his tracks with the left barrel at a distance of exactly 14 yards, the bullet entering the centre of his forehead about an inch below the frontlet of the horns.

As I have said before, a buffalo when it charges does not come on with its head down, but always with its nose held straight out, and its forehead almost horizontal; and it does not even lower its head when at striking distance, but turns it to one side, and, with a rapid sidelong sweep of the horns, impales or knocks down its foe as it passes. The fact that it does not lower its head when about to strike not only makes the charge difficult to stop or turn, but also lessens the stalker's chance of getting out of its way, as the beast is able to see where it is going, and see also any movement on the sportsman's part. As buffaloes stand very low on their legs, a shot at the throat or chest is very difficult, unless there is time for the stalker to kneel or sit down, when he would be more on a level with and better able to get a shot at either of these spots.

After a stalk and a successful shot every sportsman should avoid firing at the retreating herd, on the chance of bagging another by a fluke, unless he is prepared to follow up all the beasts that are wounded. Apart from the cruelty of this practice, the fact of several wounded buffaloes being in the vicinity of a shooting ground, and the uncertainty of their whereabouts, is a source of great danger not only to the sportsman himself and his men, but to other men, sportsmen or otherwise, who come after him. When a buffalo is down, it should always be approached with the utmost caution, and on no account should the stalker go up to it without a heavy rifle in his hand, as there is no knowing what a buffalo is capable of, however far gone he may appear to be—so long as its side heaves, or it gives any other indication that life is not quite extinct.

Should a buffalo after being wounded enter thick bush or other covert, it is a good plan (and one I always adopt myself) to wait for a quarter or half an hour before taking up the spoor, as the beast will be almost certain to lie down, and will not only become weak and stiff from the effects of the wound, more especially if a leg is damaged or broken, but its suspicions will be to a certain extent allayed.

The African natives, whether professional hunters or only porters, &c., with their extraordinarily sharp sight, are, as a rule, so much quicker in detecting the slightest sign of a beast having passed, be it a minute speck of blood, a bruised blade of grass, or a fragment of freshly turned up earth, that I must advise the sportsman to let his gun-bearers take up the spoor, whilst he, a yard or so in advance, with rifle at full cock and ready for instant use, keeps a sharp look-out ahead of him.

A buffalo very often—but not always, as some writers maintain—gives a deep bellowing groan when just on the point of dying, and the sportsman should always be on the alert for such an indication, as much time can be saved by walking straight up to it without fear, instead of cautiously poking and peering about in the bush, as is generally done when following up a wounded buffalo.

The following account of a hunt I once had in the Arusha-wa-Chini district in March 1887 will serve as an illustration of a buffalo's cunning, ferocity, and vitality.

I was encamped on the river Weri-weri, a short distance above the native villages, but as the people were afraid to prowl far from their homes on account of the Masai and other enemies, game was not only very plentiful but less wild than elsewhere. Buffaloes were very numerous, in large herds, besides a good many old bulls, either solitary or in small bands of two or three. This country was also one of the best I was ever in, from a stalker's point of view, as the alluvial plains on both banks of the river, though open, were dotted about with trees of various kinds and sizes, and were in places quite park-like in appearance. There were also numerous ant-heaps, and occasionally small bushes dotted about, besides the grass, about 18 inches high, all of which afforded capital covert. The plain on the left or eastern bank of the river varied from a mile to a mile and a half in width, and was bordered on its eastern side by a belt of thick bush and clumps of forest trees, in which the buffaloes took up their quarters during the heat of the day, coming out again in the evening to feed in the open during the night and early morning. The bush, like most African bush which borders on open plain, was fairly thin on the outskirts, and was what is commonly known as open bush. Here was a very favourite feeding-ground for waterbuck, impala, and other bush-loving antelopes, besides buffaloes, which were generally found feeding in the early morning before the sun became too hot.

As I walked over the plain on the left bank of the river I passed great quantities of game—including eland, waterbuck, impala, and a troop of thirteen ostriches (which I had tried many times to circumvent, but always unsuccessfully until I drove them, when I got a fine old cock bird), besides the everlasting zebra and 'kongoni' (hartebeest). After going about three miles up the river, I at last saw two old bull buffaloes on the opposite side of the plain, quietly feeding close to an isolated patch of bush which stood some little distance from the main belt out in the plain. As buffaloes have rather poor sight, and as there were two or three big trees between the beasts and myself, about 400 yards from them, I told my men, some twenty-five in number, to follow me in single file, and we all got up to a tree without the least trouble. At that moment a herd of zebras, which had hitherto taken no notice of us, suddenly took fright on getting our wind, and galloped round between us and the buffaloes. The latter, being thus disturbed, lumbered off into the isolated clump of thick bush close by. After giving them time to settle down and forget their fears, I proceeded more cautiously with my two gun-bearers, leaving the rest of the men under the tree with orders to come on when they heard a shot or other signal. The buffaloes, however, were evidently on the alert, and as they were standing in the shade, they discovered us when we were still 100 yards off as we crossed the open, and bolted out on the opposite side, making for the main bush. Running round the clump to try and keep them in sight, I was just in time to see them enter the open bush and disappear from view.

This made it necessary for us to take up their spoor, and while the gun-bearers were so engaged I kept a look-out ahead. After going a short distance, I suddenly saw one of the brutes trotting back towards us, and when about 100 yards off it dived into a small dense clump of bush some 20 yards square, followed almost immediately afterwards by the other one. This proceeding on the part of buffaloes I have read of, though it was the first and only instance in my own experience, and as my suspicions were aroused, instead of making straight for them along their spoor, I made a détour through the low straggling bush and stalked up to a small tree within 60 yards of the clump they were in. At first I could see nothing of them, the clump being too thick, but with the aid of binoculars I made out part of the head and the outline of the neck of one of them as it stood broadside on. Taking the 8-bore, I fired at the place where I thought his shoulder ought to be, and he fell with a deep groan, which at first led me to believe that he was either dead or dying. The other one promptly floundered out of the bush and stood broadside on, looking in my direction sufficiently long to enable me to change rifles and plant a 4-bore bullet in his shoulder; but it was too high and too far back, and off he went. In the meantime the other one in the clump, after kicking and plunging about, picked himself up and went after his companion, and as I saw that he was very lame, I made so certain that he would not go far that I did not fire at him again. Before following them I took a hasty survey of the ground and found my suspicions confirmed. They had returned on their own spoor when I first saw them trotting back, and had I not seen them, I should have followed up their spoor, which I found led close past the bush they were in, and they might have made themselves disagreeable and taken me at a disadvantage. I then hurried after them with the 8-bore, and, outrunning my gun-bearers, soon overtook them, as they were both lame, getting within 70 yards, when the one which had received the 4-bore bullet, and was a trifle behind the other, evidently heard me coming along behind him, as he whisked round and stood staring at me, broadside on, whilst the other continued to retreat. Sitting down (my favourite shooting position, and as I was much blown after my run with a heavy rifle), I took a steady shot at his shoulder, and distinctly heard the bullet strike, but it had absolutely no effect, and the beast never even flinched. Hastily jamming in another cartridge in order to have one in reserve in case he should charge, I again fired at his shoulder, and he dropped as if struck by lightning; he fell so quickly that I did not see him fall. He was, however, not dead, as I could see his side heaving above the top of the grass as he lay. By this time the gun-bearers had come up, followed shortly afterwards by the rest of the men, who had come on when they had heard the first two shots, and who, on seeing that the beast was down, ran up like a pack of wolves to 'chinja' it—i.e. to cut its throat. Knowing, however, that it was not dead, I ran forward and shouted to them not to go near; but they were too excited to pay heed to my warning, and were standing all round it, when, after a desperate effort to regain its legs, it jumped up, the men flying in all directions. Catching sight of my second gun-bearer, who had also gone up to it, and who at the time was carrying my 4-bore rifle, it went straight for him. The man bolted, and, finding that the buffalo was close upon him, dropped the rifle—the stock of which was snapped short off at the grip by the buffalo treading on it—and ran for dear life, the beast being within a few inches of him, and giving vent to a furious grunt at each step. For some little time I was unable to shoot, as the rest of the men were scattered and dodging about between myself and the buffalo, so I shouted to the gun-bearer to run round towards me, which he did, and I was able to fire, but the 8-bore bullet had apparently no effect on the infuriated beast. At the same moment the man doubled and ran straight away from me, making for a small tree about 100 yards off, twisting and turning as he ran, but the buffalo still stuck close to him and doubled as quickly as the man did. All this time I was tearing along in pursuit, hoping to get a shot, but dared not fire for fear of hitting the man, who was dodging about from side to side, and I was some 60 yards behind when they reached the tree. This the man endeavoured to catch hold of so as to swing himself round, but he was going so fast that the impetus caused his hand to slip, and he tripped up and fell forward flat on his face into the grass, which was some 2½ feet high under the shade of the tree. The buffalo, being so close to him at the time, overshot him, but whipped round, and I twice saw it give a vicious dig at him with its head and then kneel down two or three times, when I could only see its stern above the grass. By the time I got close up the buffalo was in a kneeling position; and, thinking the man was probably dead, I raised my rifle to fire, when the man, whom I could not see in the longish grass, raised his head and shoulders from underneath the beast's stomach directly in the line of fire, obliging me to divert the muzzle until he wriggled himself out of line, when a couple of bullets at close quarters settled this cunning, savage, yet plucky beast. The man's back and the calves of his legs were covered with blood from the buffalo's mouth and nostrils during the run, showing how very close it had been to him all the time. He told me afterwards that when he fell he turned over on to his back, and the buffalo made a bad shot each time it lunged at him with its head, or tried to kneel on him, owing perhaps to the fact that it was weak and dazed from the loss of blood, and he was therefore able to twist himself out of the way. It, however, caught him a very severe blow on the knee, which nearly dislocated it, and made it necessary to carry him into camp on a litter; but after a little careful doctoring and complete rest he was able to take the field again in three weeks.

The Buffalo was close upon him

C. Whymper

On cutting up the beast, I found the 4-bore bullet was too far back, and also too high. The first 8-bore bullet had caught the beast fair behind the shoulder, and had gone through both lungs rather low down, and I think, if the beast had been left alone after it had been knocked down by the next shot, it would very soon have died quietly; but, as it was, the men rushing up and standing round it seemed to inspire it with a final desire for revenge. The second 8-bore bullet was, as I expected, too high, and had passed through the dorsal ridge just above the vertebræ. The shot fired at it as it ran past me caught it in the proper place, went through both lungs and just grazed the heart, and it is more than probable that it was this shot which prevented what might have been a serious accident.

The other old bull, although we followed him for a long way, eager for revenge, got clean away.

CHAPTER XII

THE LION

BY F. J. JACKSON

The lion (*F. leo*), known to the natives as 'Simba,' when described as 'King of the African forests,' is, I venture to say, altogether misnamed, as he has neither the awe-inspiring and majestic bearing of the elephant, nor the viciousness and indomitable pluck of the buffalo. His roar when heard pretty close to camp on a still night is certainly very grand, more particularly when two or more lions are together, and this must be heard to be thoroughly appreciated. I have twice heard a troop of lions roaring inside thick forest, close to my camp, which was pitched just outside in the open. The continuous chorus of roars they emitted was quite extraordinary, as it vibrated and rolled along through the trees, the foliage of which appeared to confine and intensify the volume of sound.

When seen out in the open there is absolutely nothing majestic in the bearing of lions; their heads are carried low down below the line of their backs, as they slouch along their hind-quarters have an appearance of weakness, and when seen from behind sway and wobble from side to side, while the up-and-down movement of their shoulder-blades at each step, and their general appearance of looseness, do not add to their dignity. Certainly a maned lion, when standing broadside on or facing, with head erect, is a grand-looking beast; but when galloping or trotting away on being disturbed, with head held low down, there is nothing of the majestic about him—indeed he even compares unfavourably with a rhinoceros, which, as it trots away with tail held erect, has the merit of looking defiant, if not altogether dignified. Perhaps lions are seen at their worst after being wounded and brought to bay, when as they lie crouching flat to the earth, with head slightly raised, ears held back, and mouth open, giving vent to low snarling growls, they by no means present a noble or awe-inspiring appearance. In East Africa the lion is essentially a game-killer. There are, however, a few cases on record of lions having turned cattle-killers; but I am inclined to think that in most instances they have been driven to it by force of circumstances, on account of the scarcity and wildness of the game. As I have said elsewhere, nearly all the game-beasts migrate from their favourite haunts where they have been concentrated in large herds as long as food was plentiful. Between March and the end of July they disperse, many of them work their way towards the coast, become scattered over a much larger area, and are found in smaller herds. These herds of game are naturally followed by the lions, some of which doubtless stray away occasionally from where the game is to be found, and are driven to killing cattle, or donkeys, or whatever else they come across. Within the last ten years several lions have strayed as far as Mombasa, and have even crossed over from the mainland to the island, where they have done considerable damage amongst the cattle, &c. In 1887 a large lion which had been on the island for several months was killed within 200 yards of the town by Count E. de Kegl, who tied up a bullock as a bait and shot the lion from a tree at night. Another one was killed early in the year 1893. In Ukambani and the Masai country a few cattle are occasionally carried off by lions, but I do not think this is a common occurrence. I have never heard of any well-authenticated instance of lions becoming man-eaters, though I know of two cases in which a porter has disappeared on the march, and on men being sent back next morning to look for him, they only found his remains, and reported the spoor of a lion close by; but native report is not to be relied on in cases like this.

Lions when in the game country rarely go a night without something to eat, and I venture to think that in most instances of attacks on camps the reason is not so much their reputed natural boldness and daring, but that they are driven to it by the pangs of hunger. But even the cowardly skulking hyæna will enter a camp within the ring of fires under such circumstances. Although there is, as a rule, plenty of game in the districts in which lions are found, they no doubt, for reasons stated above, occasionally and of necessity retire foodless and hungry. This may also be accounted for by old age and inability to catch and kill game. But whatever the cause of their hunger, they will always make for the nearest water, not only to quench their thirst, but also as being a likely place to find their prey; and in the event of a camp being pitched close by, in which there may be cattle, donkeys, or something equally attractive, they are prompted to attack it.

I only know of one instance of a camp being attacked at night by a lion, and this was within my own experience. It occurred in the waterless and also *gameless* wilderness between Mount Kisigao and Mitati in the Teita country, when on my way to Kilimanjaro. The night before the attack the lion was seen close to camp by some porters who were lying under a tree rather outside the ring of fires, and it was evidently intent on a white donkey tied to a tree close by, which belonged to a missionary who was travelling up with me for the sake of protection. The donkey was therefore brought into the centre of the camp, and the lion was only heard at intervals during the night as it prowled around. The following night when we encamped without a 'boma,' the men being too tired to make one, we merely formed a circle of fires, round which the members of each mess were for the most part lying asleep. About midnight I was awakened by a tremendous commotion with cries of 'Simba! Simba!' (lion!), and on rushing out of my tent to investigate was told that a lion had attempted to carry off one of my men. It appeared that this man was outside the ring of fires, when the lion came up and grabbed him by the head as he was lying on his back with his feet to the fire. Fortunately for him his head was enveloped in several pieces of cloth, which he used during the day as a pad, to protect his head when carrying a load. This cloth evidently slipped and prevented the beast from getting a good grip of the man's head, and probably killing him on the spot. As it was, he received a nasty gash just above the eyebrow, beginning at the temple and extending to above the bridge of his nose, with another long gash across the top of his head, corresponding to the large canine teeth, and other smaller scratches between these two gashes. There were also cuts, though less serious, on the other side of his head, which had been done by the teeth of the lower jaw. Curious to say, the lion carried off the pieces of cloth, and we never succeeded in finding them when following the spoor for a considerable way next morning.

I also know of two cases of attacks being made on man in open daylight, both quite unprovoked. The first was also an experience of my own.

At the time I was in command of a large caravan, and was accompanied by Dr. A. D. Mackinnon, who was walking ahead with me on the march through dense bush, the men straggling along in single file, doing what is called a 'teregeza.' As we walked along, we noticed the spoor of a lion on the footpath for a considerable distance, and saw where he had left the track, and entered the bush just before coming to a small opening, but we thought nothing of it. Some quarter of a mile or so further on we were startled by a terrific yell and continued screaming in the rear, and thinking that a prowling band of Masai warriors had attacked the caravan, I snatched a Winchester repeating carbine from my boy in exchange for a shot-gun I was carrying, and ran back followed by the doctor with a Snider. As we ran, we met the cook and my small tent-boy, who had been carrying my .500 Express in its waterproof case, as I did not expect to meet with any big game in such dense bush, which extended for miles ahead of us, and my gun-bearers had somehow lagged behind and given the boy my rifle to carry. Both the cook and boy were in a most abject state of speechless terror, and could only gasp out 'Simba!' but when they were able to speak, they told us that a lion had bounded out of the bush across the small open space we had shortly before passed and had chased them. With the yell we had heard the cook dropped the kettle with our precious supply of water, and the boy the rifle, and both ran after us screaming all the time, too afraid to look behind them to see whether the lion was following them or not. Hurrying back to the scene of their adventure, we found the kettle on the footpath, but the rifle was nowhere to be seen. However, one of the men soon found the lion lying in the shade of a bush within 15 yards of us, though for some little time I was unable to see it, until I looked along the man's arm as he pointed at it. When I made it out, I saw it was crouching flat on the ground facing us, but could not get a good view of its head, as there was a thick aloe sticking up just in front of it, and I could see little else but its eyes on either side of the stem. As my gun-bearers had not come up, I had nothing more powerful than a .44 Winchester 12-shot carbine, so I asked the Doctor to stand ready, told my boy to keep behind me with the shot-gun in case of a charge, and risked a shot at its head, when away it floundered out of the bush. As it leapt over a clump of aloes to the left I again fired, and it answered to the shot with a growl, and disappeared from sight. When I went up to see the effect of my first shot, which I found had gone through the aloe, one of the men discovered my rifle lying close to where the lion had been, having been carried thither by the lion from the place where it was dropped by the boy, a distance of 15 yards, and I had the mortification of finding that the brute had not only destroyed the cover, but had broken both triggers short off, twisted and broken the trigger-guard, and severely mauled the stock, from which it had taken a piece out.

As this happened late in the afternoon, there was no prospect of reaching water that night, so I gave orders to pitch camp, and not wishing to build a 'boma,' which was hardly necessary, was anxious to satisfy myself as to whether the lion was wounded, since a beast that dared to attack in daylight might prove an unpleasant neighbour during the night if not already wounded, more especially as we had several donkeys with us. When the gun-bearers came up I took my 12-bore Paradox, and, followed by the Doctor, entered the bush, and was flicking the sharp points off the aloes with a knife, never thinking for a moment that 'John Bounder' was close at hand. After going a few yards we found a thick drop of blood on a leaf, and I felt fairly satisfied that he would give us no further trouble during the night. However, as there was still an hour or so of daylight we decided to go on a little further, and I was still flicking off the aloe points and talking to the Doctor, when we came to a small green bush, which I took the precaution of peeping round before advancing. There lay the lion crouched flat on the ground, within seven feet of me, with his head between his paws.

The lion was unfortunately on my right, so that I could not fire except from my left shoulder, a shot which I did not care to risk, any more than I cared to walk backwards and expose the whole of my body at such close quarters before I could get a sufficiently good view to enable me to shoot from my right shoulder. Stepping back, I whispered to the Doctor that the lion was quite close, and asked him to stand ready, whilst I crept back to try and get a better view of it from another point, but by the time I had struggled through a dense clump of aloes the beast had slunk away under the shade of a black bush two or three yards off, and I could only see the tip of its tail twitching from side to side. It was quite impossible to make out which way the lion's body lay, even with binoculars, and a shot fired at the place where I thought and hoped it might be had no effect. This made the beast move off to more favourable ground, and after a short hunt one of my gun-bearers saw it lying under a tree in a small opening. At the same moment that I saw the lion it saw me, and stood up with a growl broadside on, and I sent a Paradox bullet clean through both shoulders, which dropped it dead on the spot. It was a fine full-grown beast, with first-rate teeth and claws, but was remarkably thin. As the country for many miles round was absolutely devoid of game, excepting a few *Neotragus Kirkii*, this lion had in all probability wandered about for several days without food, and was goaded on by hunger to make the attack on the boy. On examination, I found my second shot with the Winchester had only caught it in the hind foot as it leapt over the aloe clump. The first shot which had gone through the aloe had missed it clean, or had lost all power of penetration—at all events, there was no mark of a bullet about its face or head.

The other instance of men being attacked in open daylight occurred near Machako's, in Ukambani, when a small caravan of some twenty porters was attacked by a troop of twelve or thirteen lions, which they came upon when on the march. When the lions charged out of the grass the men dropped their loads and bolted, though, after the men had fired about 150 rounds of ammunition at them from a respectful distance, the lions retired. After waiting an hour or two, the men plucked up courage and returned for their loads. My friend, Captain J. W. Pringle, R. E., saw the loads when they were brought into the station, and found that several of them had been severely mauled by the lions. In this instance I am unable to account for such an unprovoked attack, unless the lions, whilst lying asleep in the grass close to the footpath, were taken by surprise and charged in self-defence, it being very improbable that they were prompted by hunger, as game was very plentiful at the time.

Only two cases of lions charging after being wounded and followed up have come under my notice. The first happened to Sir Robert Harvey when following up a wounded lioness. This beast, which he failed to stop as it came at him, jumped clean over him as he bobbed down to see the result of his shot under the smoke, but fortunately missed him, and he killed it with his second barrel.

The above instances of lions proving at all aggressive are, I think, quite exceptional, and at all events form a very small percentage, considering the great number of lions in the country, the fair number that have been killed, and the still greater number that have been wounded and got away, and I am inclined to think that both the boldness and pluck of East African lions compare very poorly with those of South Africa and the Somali country. Even when wounded, I have found them anything but plucky or savage beasts. Three out of the four lions I have myself bagged, and three others which got away wounded, never attempted to charge, although they were all followed up into bush where it was impossible to see them until fairly close, and in each instance they could see me some time before I could see them, but they merely lay and snarled, or slunk away altogether.

Lions in East Africa, when found near the coast, which is mostly thick bush country, are for the most part maneless, or nearly so. I have heard it suggested that the thick bush has something to do with this, as the long hairs of the mane get pulled out and worn away, and it is quite possible that this may be so, for the buffaloes on the coast are also very scantily covered with hair, and are of a dull slate colour from the skin showing through. In the Masai country lions have very often splendid manes, and the buffaloes, even the old bulls, are well covered with hair. This, however, may be accounted for more reasonably by the great difference in the temperature than by the more open nature of the country, the air of the higher altitudes being bracing and cool, not to say cold, whilst that on the coast is moist and muggy. Lions with both dark and light coloured manes are found in East Africa, those found north of Machako's being darker as a rule than those further south.

Buffaloes and zebras are the two species of game on which lions mostly prey. In my own experience I have come across the remains of more buffaloes which have been killed by lions than anything else. The zebra comes next, and then the hartebeest. Since, however, the buffaloes have been decimated by disease, the zebra, of which there are still countless herds, will probably stand first. Although I have carefully examined the carcases of several buffaloes and zebras, I have never been able to discover anything about them to warrant my expressing an opinion as to how they had actually been killed by the lions. The most noticeable thing about two freshly killed buffaloes and one zebra was the terrible way in which they were lacerated about the hind-quarters, evidently by the lions at their first spring and during the subsequent desperate struggle before they actually killed them. In every case when I found a fresh kill the stomach had been torn open, and the liver, heart, and entrails had formed the first meal. On one occasion I was attracted by vultures to the spot where a lion and two lionesses had shortly before killed a cow buffalo, and I had a good opportunity of watching them before I fired, as I was well concealed. The lion was devouring the entrails, &c., and one lioness was tearing at the throat, whilst the other, which I did not see at the time, was lying under a bush close by, eating a fœtus calf which she had dragged out of the cow. After shooting the lion and severely wounding a lioness, which unfortunately got away, I carefully examined the buffalo, which was lying on its right side, with its head twisted round until the back of its head, and the curved points of both horns were resting on the ground, with its nose upwards. The soft part of the nose had been eaten off, the tongue torn out by the gullet underneath the lower jaw, and the flesh under the uppermost foreleg was also eaten away; the tail had been bitten short off at the root and was lying on the ground, and a small piece of each hind-quarter just below the tail had also gone. The stomach was torn open, the liver, heart, and part of the entrails eaten, and the fœtus calf was also half eaten. When my men had cut the remainder of the beast up to sell to the natives for flour, &c., I examined the vertebræ of the neck, but could find no signs of dislocation. When I shot the lion he disgorged in his dying struggles large pieces of buffalo skin, pieces of liver, entrails, and clots of blood, and his stomach was blown out to almost bursting point with a further accumulation of entrails, liver, blood, and pieces of flesh and skin, besides a piece of heart so large that it is a wonder that he managed to get it down. The zebra that I found about two hours after it had been killed by a lion and lioness, which latter I shot after a long hunt, had absolutely no marks on it to show how it had been killed. One ear had been bitten off, and its hind-quarters and hocks were torn and lacerated as if gashed by a knife, the cuts being so clean, but there were no marks on the throat or back of the neck. With the exception of a small piece of entrail lying on the ground, which had the appearance of having been chewed, the whole of the inside and the soft flesh and skin of the stomach were gone; the rest was untouched.

Good Guides

C. Whymper

In the extensive game countries of Masailand and Turkwel, a district in the Suk country, lions are very plentiful, and may be heard at night; but though undoubtedly numerous it is quite by chance that they are met with. The greatest number seen at one time by myself and Dr. Mackinnon was twenty-three. This troop was seen near Machako's, in Ukambani, on August 7, 1890. It consisted of three lions with splendid dark manes, five or six lionesses and the rest cubs from three parts grown down to the size of a fox terrier. Another large troop of eleven was seen near Rombo, to the east of Kilimanjaro, by Mr. T. W. H. Greenfield in 1888. Perhaps the best guides to the whereabouts of a lion are vultures. Should these birds be seen soaring high up in the air, gradually getting lower and lower, and finally going off in a bee line, the sportsman should certainly follow them, as it is a sure sign that they have detected the carcase of a dead beast. If, however, as he proceeds in the direction they have taken, sees the vultures, marabou storks, &c., sitting in trees, or circling round a few hundred feet up in the air, in the event of there being no trees, it is a pretty certain sign that a beast of prey is still at the carcase, and although it may turn out to be only a hyæna or a lot of jackals, it is always advisable to go up and have a look on the chance of there being lions. I was myself attracted by vultures to three out of the four lions which I killed, and on other occasions when I was less successful vultures were my guides. Sitting up at night near a water-hole, provided there is no other water nearer than 8 or 10 miles, might be well worth trying, also sitting up a tree near a bullock or donkey tied up as a bait; but as I have never tried either way I cannot speak from experience. For lions I prefer a hollow Express bullet with copper tube, as they are soft beasts, and the smashing power and shock to the system of a bullet that flies to pieces *inside* a beast is tremendous. The bullet should, however, be much longer and heavier, with longer solid base, than Eley's ordinary Express bullet, which often flies to pieces before it can penetrate to the vitals of even a soft beast like a lion, as I have found to my cost on more than one occasion.

In support of my contention that the lion of East Africa is by no means plucky or savage when wounded, I will give two examples. On both occasions I was attracted to the lions by vultures. On the first I found that a lion and lioness had killed a zebra in the open, and had dragged it into a large belt of dense bush. Leaving the men outside, and being closely followed by two gun-bearers, I got within 15 yards of the lions before I could make out the form of the dead zebra in the dark shade, but could see no lions. The lioness, which had been lying down behind the kill, at that moment stood up, but as I only saw a small patch of tawny colour through the dense foliage, I could not tell whether it was a lion or lioness, still less whether it was a chest, shoulder, or hind-quarter in the gloom. As, however, the lions were evidently aware of my presence, there was no time to be lost, so, kneeling down, I took a deliberate shot at the tawny patch. The result was fairly satisfactory, though decidedly alarming, as she—for it was the lioness—reared up on her hind legs with a terrific roar, fell backwards, and disappeared from view behind the carcase of the zebra. Not knowing whether she was dead or not, or whether she was still behind the zebra, I listened for some time, but could hear nothing on account of the buzzing of swarms of large red-headed bluebottle flies, and then crawled forward very cautiously to the carcase, but found she had gone.

As there was a considerable amount of blood about, I lost no time in following her. For a long time the lion stuck to his mate, but finally left her, and went off by himself, after being harassed and kept constantly on the move, which was in all probability distasteful to him after his feed. From 12.30 to 5.30, most of the time on my hands and knees owing to the denseness of the bush, I followed the lioness, and kept putting her up with a low growl every 100 yards or so; but I only once saw her—a mere glimpse when she was on the move and about 20 yards off—as she kept down wind nearly the whole time, and never allowed me to come near enough to see her well, but slunk away with a low growl. Finally it became too dark to see anything, so I had to abandon the hunt for that day.

Next morning I was back at daylight, and visited a small water-hole just outside the bush, close to where I had left her, and found from her spoor and faint traces of blood that she had been there to drink during the night. She had afterwards re-entered the bush and was lying down just inside, but was disturbed by our talking, as we heard her growl and move off. She must then have skirted along just inside the edge of the bush, for whilst we were consulting as to the best means of following her up, or whether we should attempt to drive her out, she left the covert some 300 yards off on our side, and went limping away across a small tongue of open ground towards a narrow strip of bush, which she entered. Hurrying round with my gun-bearers in a wide circuit to the other side, I was just in time to see her come to the edge of the bush, but at the same time she saw me, and lay down facing me, with her head well raised. This gave me a capital chance; a shot in the chest rendered her *hors de combat*, and another at close quarters finished her off. The Express bullet of the day before had caught her on the point of the shoulder as she faced me, smashing the blade-bone into fragments and tearing the flesh to a frightful extent. This wound may have knocked all inclination to charge out of her, if she ever had any; otherwise, considering the way she was harassed and the reputation lions have for charging under such circumstances, she might have done so, more especially as the nature of the covert in many places was decidedly favourable for such a demonstration on her part.

The second time I was attracted to where a lion and two lionesses had killed a cow buffalo, mentioned above. As the vultures and marabou storks were sitting patiently waiting in a large leafless tree, I felt pretty sure that lions were still at the kill, and I also knew before I actually saw them that they had killed a buffalo, as the ground was cut up in all directions by the fresh spoor of a large herd of these beasts as they stampeded. On crawling up to a bush and looking through it, I saw the head of the lion, as he stood on the far side of the dead buffalo. As there was nothing but the lion's head showing, and as I could only get an indistinct view of one lioness as she lay, I sat and watched them with the aid of binoculars for a considerable time, until the lion stepped clear of the carcase and stood broadside on, offering me a splendid shot. Aiming at his shoulder, I fired at a range of a trifle over 100 yards, and he answered to the shot with a growl, bounded forward a few yards, and stood behind a small skeleton bush. At the shot the lioness stood up and looked hard in my direction, but could not see me, and I then noticed for the first time that there was another lioness standing under a small bush close by; but as I could only make out the head of either of them, and could not see the effect of my shot on the lion, I reloaded and waited. In a short time I had the satisfaction of seeing the lion limp back to the buffalo, dead lame, and feeling pretty confident that he would not go far (in which I was greatly mistaken), I took a shot at the nearest lioness, as she stood facing me. She also answered to the shot with a grand roar, reared up in the air and fell backwards, but picked herself up and bolted in one direction, whilst the lion and the other lioness went off in another. These two I followed, and after a sharp run got up to within about 80 yards of them, when the lioness turned round, having evidently heard me. A shot at her head, which was all I could see of her over the grass, missed her clean, and off she went, leaving her lord and master to take care of himself. As, however, I had lost sight of him in the grass, my gun-bearers took up the spoor, whilst I kept a look-out ahead, and after going a short way I saw him get up from under a bush about 120 yards off and bound away across my front, evidently very angry, judging from the noise he made. With the right barrel I missed him clean, and with the left merely broke his tail, but he only went a short way and lay down. As I approached within 80 yards he stood up and growled, but dropped down again so quickly that I could not get a shot, and as he did this several times I told two of my gun-bearers to stand still, so as to divert his attention from my own movements, whilst I and my head gun-bearer crept round to a small ant-heap on the right, which was also a little nearer to him, from which position I hoped to get a shot at his shoulder. He, however, saw me all the time, as there was very little covert, and as I peeped over the top of the ant-heap, some 60 yards from him, he again stood up and growled, but nothing more, and as he had turned and was still facing me, I took a shot at his head with a solid bullet, not wishing to smash his skull more than I could help. This shot, which knocked him down, hit him a little under the right eye, broke off two of his upper molar teeth, and lodged in the flesh of the neck, but he picked himself up, bolted to another bush and again lay down. As he lay facing me, and crouching close to the ground, I walked up, this time to within 40 yards of him, and sat down to get another shot at his head; but just as I did so he raised his head, and not wishing to damage his skin more than possible with a .500 Express bullet, I took my .360 double Express from the gun-bearer and fired at the centre of his throat, when the poor beast dropped his head and lay still. On going up to him I found he was not quite dead, but choking fast from my last shot, and as I stood over him his side gave two or three mighty heaves, like a dog's when in the act of disgorging something, and out gushed part of his last meal, an accumulation of buffalo skin, flesh, entrails, and clots of blood. This was his last effort, and he never moved again. Leaving some of the men to skin him, I went back to the buffalo and took up the blood-spoor of the wounded lioness, and came across the place where she had been lying down. She had evidently just left as I came up, as the blood leading to the spot was quite dry from the heat of the sun, whereas that leading away was fresh and wet.

She unfortunately kept down wind, and although desperately wounded, she eventually managed, after going about two miles, to get into some hard stony ground, where, as her wound had almost stopped bleeding, I had most reluctantly to give her up. Several times I came across places where she had rested and bled profusely, and in one small pool of blood I picked up a piece of flat bone, about half an inch square, with a ridge down the centre, evidently part of her shoul-der-blade, which had worked out of the bullet hole; but she never allowed me to approach near enough to see her in the thick covert.

CHAPTER XIII
THE RHINOCEROS
BY F. J. JACKSON

Mr. F. C. Selous has proved beyond a doubt that there is only one species of the so-called black rhinoceros (*R. bicornis*) in South Africa, and his arguments apply equally to the East African beast. There can be no doubt that the range of this beast extends from the Soudan to South Africa, and that there is only one distinct species of prehensile-lipped rhinoceros known throughout Africa. If the classification of the black rhinoceros depended on the comparative size of the horns (and this appears to have been the principal basis of former arguments), then there would certainly be no difficulty in making two or even more species. Adult rhinoceroses are to be found in East Africa (and perhaps there is no place where they exist in greater numbers at the present day), varying in size, temperament, and in the length and shape of their horns. I have myself shot them with almost every variety of horns, from a beast with front horn 27 ins. and second horn only 9 ins. in length, to one with front horn 21 ins. and the other horn 22 ins. in length. The latter specimen, together with the one in the illustration, answers to the *so-called species R. Keitloa.*

Few beasts, if any, vary so much in temperament as rhinoceroses, and no rule can be laid down as to their general behaviour, though in most cases they will retreat before the presence of man. Personally, I consider the 'kifaru' (Swahili for rhinoceros) to be by nature an extremely stupid beast, and were it not for the birds (*Buphaga erythrorhyncha*) which nearly always accompany it, and act as sentinels for it, the rhinoceros would be quite the easiest of all game to stalk, and would, in consequence, be far less plentiful than it is. If not accompanied by these birds, there would be no difficulty in approaching sleeping rhinoceroses to within a few yards; in fact, if so inclined, I believe one might kick them up. I have often got to within 30 or 40 yards of one, have then failed to rouse it by whistling and shouting, and have had to throw sticks, stones, or bits of earth at it before it would get up. Should the birds detect the stalker, however, they will fly up in the air and give vent to a curious and prolonged shrill hissing note, not unlike the call of our missel-thrush, and away the rhinoceros will go before the stalker can get within range. These birds follow the rhinoceroses for the sake of the ticks which are always plentiful on them.

Dead Rhinoceros and Gun-bearer

From a photograph by F. J. Jackson

When alarmed, the rhinoceros becomes easily flurried, appears to do things on impulse which other animals endowed with more sagacity would not do, and is by no means the vicious and vindictive brute which some writers have found him to be in South Africa and the Soudan. In the majority of cases, where a rhinoceros is said, by men who perhaps have not been very well acquainted with his peculiarities, to have charged in a most determined and vicious manner, I believe this so-called charge to have been nothing more than the first headlong and impetuous rush of the beast in a semi-dazed state, endeavouring to avoid an encounter rather than court one.

In spite of the fact that buffaloes are generally considered the most dangerous of all big game, rhinoceroses will test the nerve of a beginner more perhaps than any other big beast. In the first place, 'rhinos' are generally found standing or lying down quite out in the open plain, often under the shade of a small thorn tree, where there is very little covert of any kind, except, perhaps, a few scanty bushes and low ant-heaps (the majority of which would afford little or no protection in the event of a charge), and grass from 12 to 18 inches in height. Again, there is no knowing what 'rhinos' will do when shot at and wounded, and their behaviour is sometimes decidedly embarrassing, as they will often spin round and round, and these gyrations, accompanied by violent snorting, are rather alarming until one gets used to them. Rhinoceroses, when at rest, almost invariably stand and lie with their sterns to the wind — i.e. the beasts face more or less in the direction from which the stalker approaches them.

They also nearly always retreat up wind when alarmed, as, being gifted with very poor sight, they depend almost entirely on their extraordinary sense of smell for any warning of the presence of danger.

I have on several occasions passed to leeward within 100 yards of one, even in the open, and, though followed by several men, it was evidently quite unable to make us out, though it saw us, and showed no signs of fear by running away or of curiosity by advancing towards us for a closer inspection, the latter a common feature in the behaviour of some game. On one occasion, however, I walked close past to leeward of a rhino which haunted a certain plain in the Arusha-wa-Chini district, and which I knew well by sight, as he had a very short stumpy horn. I was after a herd of buffaloes at the time I passed him; on my return I saw him standing in almost the same position, and, wishing to see what he would do on getting my wind, I walked past to windward of him within 300 yards.

As I had only a double .360 Express in my hand, with no gun-bearer nearer than 100 yards, every man being engaged in carrying the meat of a buffalo I had shot, I was not quite prepared for the change in his demeanour as he came straight for me. When about 80 yards off, a shot at his head only had the effect of increasing his pace, and when within 20 yards the second barrel failed to turn him, as I had hoped. I was forced to make a bolt for it, but he never attempted to follow me. After this experience I did not try any more experiments on the different temperaments of rhinoceroses under varying circumstances, nor would I recommend others to try any, unless they have an 8-bore rifle in their hands and a trustworthy gun-bearer at their heels.

This habit of retreating up wind is one of the reasons, if not the principal one, that rhinoceroses have gained for themselves the reputation for charging more often than other beasts, not only from the natives, but from many European sportsmen. To begin with, a rhinoceros rarely drops on the spot to the shoulder-shot, even when hit with a 4-bore bullet, but will dash forward whichever way his head may be pointing in at the time of being fired at, which, as I have said before, may be in the direction of the sportsman. If they should spin round and round, which they very often do, particularly when shot through the lungs, they will rush off in the direction their heads are in when they cease their gyrations. Should they, however, start off down wind in their first rush, they will very quickly turn up into the wind, and either in so doing, or in rushing straight forward, they are quite as likely as not to come in the sportsman's direction, who, as he will probably be within 80 to 90 yards of the beast before firing, might be led to mistake this headlong rush for a charge.

I have many times experienced this myself, and have had a rhinoceros come tearing along, snorting like a steam-engine, to within 10 or 15 yards of me; but with three exceptions, when I was unable for want of covert to keep out of sight, they always turned off to the right or left of me, and did not charge.

Although I do not consider rhinoceroses very dangerous beasts, I have always had a certain amount of respect for them, and have been careful to use heavy rifles; still I have had more really exciting encounters with these beasts than with any other of the larger game, and have three times been charged in a determined manner. I account for two of these charges by the fact that I was very close up before firing, failed to knock the beasts down, and was unable to keep out of sight. The third charge, which is the only one worth recording here, occurred in Turkwel on January 25, 1890. I had shot three antelopes on the march, some distance from the footpath, and as there were a great number of vultures about I left a gun-bearer with each beast to keep them off. The last one—a *G. Grantii*—had given me a long run, so I left my Winchester carbine with the gun-bearer in charge, as the natives were a treacherous lot and had caused us much trouble. When I was returning to the caravan track to call men to carry the meat, having only a 12-bore shot-gun in my hand, loaded with No. 8 shot, there being a good many sand-grouse about, out floundered a cow rhino and calf from behind a bush 25 yards off. To slip behind two small mimosa saplings, within a few feet of me, was the work of a second, but I was not quick enough to prevent the rhino catching sight of me, when she came straight at me with her head down. When within 15 yards, which I thought quite close enough, I fired at her head with splendid effect, as she lunged forward and stumbled on to her knees, ploughing up the ground with her chin; but quickly recovering herself swung round on her hind legs and bolted, followed by the calf. Stopping a charging rhino with No. 8 shot is perhaps unique.

Rhinoceroses will often charge through a caravan without any apparent provocation, but in most cases, if not in all, I believe the cause to be stupidity rather than viciousness, and also their almost invariable habit of retreating up wind. I have never known of a case in which a rhinoceros has charged a caravan down the wind, except once, when the beast was in such close proximity to the footpath that, being suddenly aroused from sleep by the noise of the men, and seeing them, it charged in self-defence. I know, however, of several cases of a rhinoceros charging through caravans from a considerable distance, but always up wind, and, from what I observed, can only account for it in one way. The rhinoceros is generally lying asleep, perhaps several yards off, when the caravan passes to windward of it, and as the countries where these beasts are found are for the most part uninhabited, the caravans on the march are often of considerable length, as the men straggle along much more when there is little fear of trouble from natives.

The beast on being aroused will start up, stare about, sniff the wind with head raised, and trot off to the right or left, by which time the caravan, moving on, is extended in a long line well across the wind, and the rhinoceros, finding that whichever way he turns he is unable to get clear of the men's scent, and possibly imagining himself surrounded, becomes more and more confused, and rushes up wind rather than down. Should the beast, however, happen to get clear of the scent of the foremost men in the caravan as it first starts off on being disturbed, it will circle round in front of them and make off with tail erect in its usual grotesque manner rather than go out of its way to charge.

It is a curious fact that natives are, as a rule, more afraid of a rhinoceros than of either an elephant or buffalo. They also find him more difficult to kill, but this is entirely owing to his tough hide, and the primitive nature of their weapons. The people of Turkwel, in the Suk country, who live by hunting, and who kill large quantities of game, including elephants, all of which they kill at close quarters with spears, told me that they feared a rhinoceros more than anything else, and rarely cared to attack him. This I can understand, as he is a much more active beast, and, owing to his tougher hide, is more difficult to kill than a buffalo. I may mention that these people first of all snare all their game in the manner described by Sir Samuel Baker in his 'Wild Beasts and their Ways,' vol. ii. p. 94; otherwise, having only the most primitive of spears (made out of iron found in or near their country, and not out of trade iron wire), they could not hope to kill anything, as they use neither pitfalls nor bows and arrows. With the exception of the elephant, the rhinoceros has fewer enemies, except man, than any other game, as it is very doubtful whether lions, were they to attack him, could do any harm beyond giving him a severe clawing, and I think they can scarcely be counted as enemies.

The facts that he is generally found in the open, that he stands stern to the wind when at rest, and that he is usually attended by bird sentinels, obviously prevent him from being taken at a disadvantage. This security from surprise, together with his immunity from enemies (the natives rarely attacking him in the open), may account to a certain extent for his indolent and sleepy nature.

Rhinoceroses (*R. bicornis*) are exclusively bush-feeders. The various species of mimosa form their favourite and principal food. During the day, from about 9 A.M. till about 5 P.M., they rest and sleep, and are then generally found in the open, though I have come across them quite unexpectedly in thick bush, enjoying their midday siesta, even though an open plain was close by. About 5 P.M. they begin to wend their way in the direction of their drinking place, feeding here and there as they go on any tempting-looking mimosa bush, but they do not drink until after sundown. They then make for their feeding grounds, browse throughout the night, drink again just before sunrise, often have a roll in a mud-hole, and then make their way to the place where they intend to lie up for the day. It is when on their way to or on their arrival at their quarters for the day that the sportsman will generally see them.

The Rhino raised herself like a huge Pig

C. Whymper

Should a rhinoceros be found standing in open country where there is but little covert, and should it be accompanied by birds, which are easily seen with the aid of binoculars, the sportsman should wait at a distance until it lies down before beginning to crawl in. He will then have to stalk the birds rather than the rhinoceros. This reminds me of an incident which occurred to me before I had had much experience with these beasts, when I stalked a rhino unattended by birds, and got up to it rather closer than I should otherwise have done, but was betrayed at the last moment by the sudden appearance of birds. This happened in December 1886, when encamped on the river Lumi, one march above Taveta to the east of Kilimanjaro, in a delightful spot, which is now known as 'Kampi ya Simba' (lion camp) from my having shot two lions there. On the 29th I went out, and was making for the foot of the mountain when I saw two rhinos under a tree about a mile and a half off. I was on my way to circumvent them when another one, which I had not seen, appeared from the left, and walked across my front, about 300 yards off. By the length and thinness of its front horn I knew it to be a cow, so I sat down in the grass, as there was no other covert, and waited until she walked under a small thorn-tree about half a mile off. Under the shade of this tree the grass was considerably longer; she soon lay down, and I walked straight up to within about 200 yards, when she got up, obliging me and my gun-bearer to drop down into the grass and lie still till she again lay down.

Although she had no birds on her back, she appeared restless, and kept raising her head, which I attributed to the fact that she was dead to leeward of the other two rhinos, some quarter of a mile off, and as she was almost facing us, we lay still to give her time to settle down and go to sleep. I was particularly anxious to make sure of her, as she had the best horn I had seen up to that time. As the grass was some 18 ins. long, though there was not a particle of other covert, we crawled forward on hands and knees and had little difficulty in getting within 100 yards of her, when we took a short rest, as grovelling through the grass was hot work. We then crawled on, flat on our stomachs, and when within about 50 yards I raised my head, saw that some 20 yards further on there was a tuft of slightly longer grass, and determined to get up to this before firing. However, just before we reached it, some half-dozen birds came from the direction of the other two rhinos, and settled on our cow's back, but we eventually succeeded in reaching the tuft. The difficulty now was to get into a sitting position and ready to shoot without being seen by the birds. To do this I worked my legs towards the rhino as I lay on my side, and gradually raised myself into a sitting position, but at that instant the birds saw me, and flew up with their usual cry of alarm. At the same moment the rhino raised herself on her forelegs like a huge pig, and I then realised that I was nearer than I intended to get, only about 20 yards separating us, but she did not appear to see me. As she remained sitting in this position, without moving my body, which I knew might attract attention, I stretched out my arm behind me for the 4-bore, but did not feel it at first, and thought that for once my faithful Ramazan had received rather a shock to his nerves on finding himself at such close quarters. However, he put it into my hand at last, after a delay of perhaps two seconds, which appeared to me much longer, and I quickly planted a bullet on the point of her left shoulder which knocked her over. Reloading before I moved, I saw she was still down, but making desperate efforts to get up; but as she was lying on her left side with her broken shoulder under her, she was unable to do so, and I ran up and despatched her with a shot in the neck. This was the only time I ever knocked a rhino down on the spot with the shoulder shot, but I took it here because she was too much end on for the neck shot, which I always prefer for these beasts when within a range of 35 yards, as when struck in the right spot they drop dead, and the chances of a charge are removed.

A rhinoceros when once started is a difficult beast to stop, though a shot from a heavy rifle will generally turn it. Their most determined charge is less to be feared than that of a buffalo or elephant, as they rarely if ever hunt a man, but rush straight on, whether they miss him or knock him down. The only instance I have ever heard of in which a rhinoceros renewed the attack under any circumstances (i.e. wounded or unwounded) after it had dispersed or knocked down its enemy, happened to Captain Pringle, R.E., when returning from Uganda in 1892. This occurred between Machako's and Kibwezi, in Ukambani. The beast—which, by the way, was not wounded—repeatedly charged the men, who were, however, too nimble for it, and it finally amused itself by tossing Pringle's load of bedding about, ventilating it in some half-dozen places with its horn before being driven off.

When within range, which may be any distance between 80 and 30 yards, unless safely ensconced behind a small tree or ant-heap, the stalker should cast a look round immediately to leeward of his position, to see that there is no wart-hog hole or other obstruction, in which he might come to grief, should it be necessary to dodge in case of a charge. The stalker should always endeavour to get within a range of 80 yards, to ensure a vital shot at the shoulder. If the country is favourable and the beast can be approached within 35 yards or less, a shot in the neck, a trifle below and a few inches behind the base of the ear, would be instantly fatal. Although the object of this shot is to break the vertebræ of the neck, it is better to aim rather low than too high, as there is always a chance of the bullet severing the main arteries of the neck or jugular vein should the vertebræ be missed, whereas a shot above the vertebræ might go clean through the neck and the beast be none the worse.

Every sportsman will probably have his own ideas as to shooting positions, and as most shooting (except elephant shooting) in East Africa is done in fairly open country, he can please himself, and will in most cases be able to adopt the position most convenient, whether it be standing, kneeling, sitting, or lying. Personally I prefer to sit down, and always fire even a 4- or 8-bore in this position, provided the grass is not too high to obscure my view of the beast. The recoil of such rifles—a push, rather than a kick—is too much for any man, except a Hercules, in this position, and always pushes me back and causes my legs to go up in the air, if it does not send me actually on to my back. When 80 yards from a beast I do not mind it, but when within 40 yards or less it is better not to have one's equilibrium upset in this manner, and I therefore make my gun-bearer sit behind me with his hands within an inch or so of my back to hold me up. This is a capital plan, but on no account must the gun-bearer touch the sportsman's back, as he might give a slight push just as the trigger is being pressed. I remember once coming rather to grief, and being in a ludicrous though not critical position, owing to my gun-bearer being unable to get behind me. I was out shooting with Dr. Mackinnon at Machako's on March 30, 1889, and as he had not then killed a rhino and was anxious to do so, we kept together and came across two of them in a capital position. Followed by our gun-bearers we got up to a bush within 60 yards of them, when the Doctor gave the larger one, a cow, a good shot behind the shoulder and another one as she ran away. The second rhino I missed clean with both barrels. After running about a quarter of a mile, they both pulled up close to a bush, and, swaying about two or three times, the wounded one sat down and subsided, looking just as if she was asleep, while the other one stood close by her. Within about 20 yards of them there was a large ant-heap with very steep sides, and as the wind was fair I went round and got up to this heap without the least trouble. After crawling up and peeping over the top, I could only see the nose and front horn of the one standing, to the left of the bush, but I saw that the other one was quite dead. As I did not wish to risk a shot through the bush, I crept round to the left side of the ant-heap, and could then see the head and quite enough neck to afford a good shot; but the difficulty was to get into a steady shooting position, as I could neither stand up nor sit down. I at last managed to squat down on my right heel, with my left leg also tucked up under me, and in this awkward position fired at the beast's neck. The result was rather more startling than I expected with regard to myself, as I was knocked over by the recoil of the rifle, and sent flying backwards to the bottom of the ant-heap, where I nearly turned a complete somersault, but quickly recovering myself I had the satisfaction of seeing that the rhino was still more completely knocked over than myself.

'I was knocked over'

C. Whymper

Among many and varied experiences with East African big game, two rhinoceros fights, of which I was a witness, were perhaps not the least interesting. The first I saw on a short trip from Taveta, with my friend Sir Robert Harvey, to the Rombo and Useri plains early in January 1887. On New Year's Day we were changing camps from Kampi ya Simba to Rombo, both on the Lumi river, and we each took different beats, Harvey keeping to the plains on the right bank, whilst I took the left bank. Shortly after separating, I managed by great good luck, rather than by good management, to get within about 70 yards of three ostriches, all of which I succeeded in bagging. After skinning them and taking their thighs, the only meat there is on an ostrich, I went on keeping close to the river, and came across a rhino standing in the open; but the ground was so devoid of covert that I could not get nearer than 100 yards, and a shot with the 4-bore struck her too low, as I foolishly forgot to raise the back sight, and only wounded her high up in the forelegs, which, however, soon caused her to settle down into a walk. As she headed for a patch of grass that had not been burnt, with several bushes and ant-heaps dotted about, I kept within 150 yards of her, intending to get nearer when she entered this covert. After she had entered it, I took advantage of a bush and drew up to within 100 yards of her, when another rhino jumped out of the grass where it had been lying to leeward of her, and made straight for her. She, however, heard him (for it was a bull), and whipped round to face him; and so they stood about three yards apart, giving vent to a succession of squeals and low guttural roars, the latter not unlike the roars of a lion. For quite twenty minutes I watched them, and a most interesting sight it was. At first they did not close, but alternately rushed at each other; as each in turn charged, the other backed away, and I observed that neither of them ever raised its head, but held its snout close to the ground, keeping up a continuous roar and squealing the whole time. At last they closed; but not for long, for after a few most violent and vicious digs at each other, they separated and again stood facing. As this sort of thing went on for about a quarter of an hour, their bouts becoming more and more vicious and prolonged, and as they were entirely engrossed in themselves, I exchanged my Express for the 8-bore, and, followed by Ramazan with the 4-bore, crept up to a large ant-heap within 40 yards of them, and lay watching them for another five minutes. How long they would have kept up this fight there is no knowing, but, as it was becoming somewhat monotonous, I whispered to Ramazan that I was going to shoot, and, following his advice, fired at the wounded one, planting a bullet behind her shoulder. The result was rather curious: she dashed at her opponent and attacked him with great fury, this being quite their best 'round,' lasting more than a minute, until my shot began to take effect on her, and she had to give way to the now superior strength of the bull. As the cow stood this time with her head held high, snorting blood from her nostrils, she swayed from side to side and then dropped over dead.

The bull went up and stood over her, prodding her in the stomach with his horn, offering me a good broadside shot, which I took, placing a bullet in his shoulder. From his subsequent behaviour one might have imagined that he thought that the defunct cow was the cause of his discomfort, for nothing could have exceeded the furious way in which he attacked her. He dashed at her as she lay on her side, and dug with extraordinary rapidity at her between the forelegs, when I put an end to his ferocity with a bullet in his neck, which dropped him. On going up I found him lying with his head under the uppermost foreleg of the cow, but with the exception of a small jagged wound in her arm-pit, neither of them bore traces of their combat, beyond innumerable white-looking surface scratches on their heads, the sides of their necks, and front of their shoulders. It is quite evident that they held their heads low throughout the encounter on purpose to protect their throats, the softest, and perhaps most vulnerable, parts of their bodies. In this case, as also in the other fight I witnessed, one beast was wounded, and was attacked by an unwounded one.

I think there can be little doubt that when rhinoceroses do fight, it is in a most determined and dogged manner, though it is highly improbable that they ever kill each other. I once shot a rhino which was terribly scored about the face and neck, with several of the abrasions still bleeding. As the grass had been quite lately burnt I followed back on its spoor, which was very distinct, and came to the spot where it had fought with another rhino. The ground for a space of 30 yards showed unmistakable signs of the severe and evidently prolonged combat. It was cut up, and loose stones a foot or more in diameter displaced and scattered in all directions. One large boulder, some 3½ ft. high, near which the encounter seemed to have been most severe, was smeared and splashed with blood. Two or three times I have shot rhinoceroses with only one ear, the other one most probably having been bitten off in a fight.

The following experience with a rhinoceros has the merit of being a curious one, though attended by absolutely no danger to myself.

Having successfully stalked three rhinoceroses—a bull, a cow, and a three-parts-grown calf—all standing together, I gave the bull a shot behind the shoulder, which knocked him down. I was so certain he was shot through the lungs, and would not go far, that I did not fire again when he picked himself up and galloped off. In this I was mistaken, as he went away across the open plain apparently unhurt, the other two going off in another direction. As I sat down on an ant-heap, feeling by no means pleased with myself, I watched the bull for a long time, and saw him pull up about two miles off and walk under the shade of what I took at the distance to be a low bush, close to the bank of a dry watercourse. On following him up, keeping along the watercourse, I got within about 500 yards of him, and made out that he was in reality standing in the shade cast by a table-topped mimosa-tree which was growing in the bed of the watercourse, and that he was within a few feet of the edge of the bank, which was quite precipitous and some ten feet high.

'In this awkward position'

C. Whymper

I immediately saw from the open nature of the ground that my only chance of getting near him was to cross the watercourse where I stood, and make a détour on the opposite bank until I got the top of the mimosa-tree between myself and the rhino. On arriving back at the edge of the bank, and being now immediately opposite the beast, which was quite hidden by the top of the tree, I found that the watercourse, which was just here very wide—as the banks had given way when the stream was in flood—was full of tall dry cane-grass. Climbing down into this grass, which was about eight feet high, I crept along very slowly, and as noiselessly as I could, the grass being very brittle, until I came to a narrow strip of sand, the actual watercourse; but on raising myself I found that I had come too near, and was unable to see the rhino, as he was standing a little back from the edge of the bank. Retracing my steps a short way, I was still unable to see him, this time on account of the tall grass; but being determined, if possible, not to be done, I again went forward and got up to the foot of the tree, which stood within four feet of the precipitous bank. At that moment the beast must have heard me, as I could hear him give two or three snorts, and stamps with his feet, which sounded unpleasantly near. Feeling, however, that I was perfectly safe, I very quietly swarmed a few feet up the tree, and saw the rhino was standing facing me, with head up, about eight feet from the edge of the bank. At the same moment he saw me and came forward to the extreme edge. Slipping down the tree, I gave Ramazan, my gun-bearer, to understand by signs what to do, and again swarmed up the tree, caught hold of a small branch with my left hand, and hung on to the trunk with my legs; Ramazan, after handing up the 8-bore, supporting me from behind with both hands. As I only had one hand available for the rifle in this awkward position, I rested it in the bend of my left elbow, and with an effort raised myself until I had brought the rifle to bear on the beast's throat, which was not more than seven feet from the muzzle; but both barrels missed fire, and before I could reload, owing to my position, the beast bolted and went clean away. Although disappointed[11] at the result after all my trouble and excitement, it was perhaps as well for me—as likewise for the rhinoceros—that the rifle did not go off, as the heavy recoil might have had very unpleasant results to myself.

---

[11] This was one of many disappointments from the same cause, as at the time I was using a consignment of cartridges lately received from England, out of which 45 per cent. missed fire; and after I had had rather a disagreeable encounter with an old bull-buffalo, and had twice failed to stop a charging rhinoceros, my nerve was so shaken that I gave up using the 8-bore until I had sent to the coast for and received another lot (Messrs. Eley's) which I had left behind, and which never once failed me, although they had been in the country, and in a moist atmosphere, over two years.

Dead Hippos

From a photograph by E. Gedge

CHAPTER XIV

THE HIPPOPOTAMUS

BY F. J. JACKSON

The hippopotamus (*H. amphibius*), known to the Swahili people as 'Kiboko,' is found nearly everywhere in East Africa where there is a sufficiency of water.

In 1885 hippos were very plentiful in the river Tana, at the mouth, and for a few miles further up, but I am told that they have since then been either killed off by the Wapokomo, or been driven away, and have taken up their quarters either in the Ozi river or the salt-water creeks. They are still, however, very plentiful in the upper waters of this river beyond Koro-Koro, where the Wapokomo dare not go to hunt them for fear of other natives more warlike than themselves. In the Ozi, near Kipini, at the mouth of the river, they are to be found in fair numbers, and again further up beyond Kau, as also in the Sabaki river. There would, however, be little chance of getting a shot at one in any of these places, except in the upper reaches of the Tana, without the aid of a boat or canoe. In the small lakes at Jipi, on the mainland opposite the island of Lamu, they are found, at Mpecatoni near Kipini, and also at Jilori near Melindi, besides in several of the salt-water creeks.

Further inland there are a good many in Lake Jipi near Taveta, and also in a large 'Ziwa' (swamp) to the east of Kilimanjaro and in Lakes Naivasha and Baringo. They are, however, far more plentiful in the river Nzoia in Northern Kavirondo than in any other place that I know of. In the Nile, both above and below the Ripon Falls, they are also numerous. The river Athi, to the north of Machako's, is another good place. I have shot them there with finer teeth than anywhere else, and this is the experience of others besides myself.

The food of the hippo consists of coarse grass, reeds, and other plants growing in damp and wet places. In places like Kavirondo, where the natives cultivate the ground to a large extent and where hippos abound, they are a source of great annoyance, as during the night they do much damage to the crops. With the exception of a few caught in pitfalls, these beasts are rarely killed by natives, except by the Wapokomo of the river Tana.

At night when in search of food hippos will wander long distances, and I have seen their spoor as much as three miles away from the nearest water. On one occasion, at Merereni, on the coast, I followed the spoor of an old bull hippo for over eight miles and then gave it up, as I found it was leading in the direction of a salt-water creek, which I knew to be some two miles ahead. I did not follow up the spoor with any idea of coming across the beast on land, but simply to see where he was going. As I often saw him for three or four days running in the creek close to my camp, then saw nothing at all of him for the next few days, and afterwards noticed his fresh spoor leading away from the creek, but could find no signs showing that he had returned, I thought he might have gone off to some fresh-water pool he knew of in the bush, and this I was anxious to find, as being a likely spot to attract other game.

As it was, I came to the conclusion that he was merely changing his quarters, and this supposition was confirmed by his reappearance in the creek a day or two afterwards.

Hippo-shooting, compared with other sport, is poor. In the first place it depends more on accuracy of aim and proficiency in quick shooting than on stalking. To crawl up to the edge of a high bank, probably several feet above the surface of the water, in which a school of these huge beasts is lying basking in the sun on the shallows, requires little skill provided the wind is fair. Neither is a steady pot shot at a range of 25 yards, at a well-defined mark such as the beast's eye and ear, or in a line between the two, as he lies perfectly still, half out of the water and possibly asleep, or floating quite motionless on the top of the water, a great test of prowess in shooting. When once scared, however, the conditions are changed, as hippos then become very cunning and take a great deal of circumventing, and will test the sportsman's patience as well as the accuracy and quickness of his aim to the utmost. If they have not been much shot at or disturbed, they will show up again in a few minutes after the first shot. After this first shot the sportsman should not be in a hurry to fire at the first head that appears above water, but should wait patiently, concealed from their view if possible, and let them settle down again, as they soon will do, when they will keep their heads above water for some considerable time, gazing round to try and detect the cause of their fright.

It is reckless firing, utterly regardless of the position of the beast's head, that is the cause of so many of these poor brutes being wounded and lost, when by the exercise of a little patience the sportsman would be able to pick out a good head, get another steady shot, and kill his beast clean.

My friend, Mr. A. H. Newmann, who is well known both in South and East Africa, not only as a splendid shot, but also a most careful one, when on his way to Uganda with a large caravan shot four hippos in four consecutive shots, and, what is perhaps still better, with the next seven shots, fired a little further on, he killed five elephants. In the same river Nzoia, in 1889, when 500 men depended on our rifles for food, on November 10 I killed nine hippos in ten consecutive shots, only one of them requiring a second bullet. Should hippos, however, detect the sportsman or get a whiff of his wind, they display the most extraordinary cunning, rarely rising twice in the same place, and then only showing for so short a time that he, not knowing where a head will next appear, has no time to bring his rifle to bear on a vital spot and fire before the head again disappears. More often than not, they pop up the top of their snouts, the two nostrils only appearing above the surface, when it is useless to fire at them. If the water is deep enough to allow of it, they will often swim up to the bank and put up their nostrils under an overhanging ledge, or anything floating on the surface of the water, such as reeds, &c., and as they will breathe very silently under such circumstances, and do not make the slightest disturbance in the water, it is often quite impossible to tell where they have gone to. I once had a first-rate opportunity of watching a hippo, and observing how he managed to raise his nostrils above water without showing the rest of his head. As I came round a bend of the river in sight of the pool he was in, I saw him floating on the surface, but, having got my wind, he never afterwards showed more than his nostrils. The water being quite clear and the surface like a sheet of glass, I sat down on the bank opposite to and within 15 yards of him and watched him for a long time. Each time he rose I could see him some little time before he came slowly to the surface, and saw that he raised his body at an angle until his two nostrils only appeared above water and almost instantly disappeared again, as I could distinctly see his head, the fore part of his body and forelegs, but not his hind-quarters. In fact, he reared up, but whether his hind-legs were resting on the bottom or not I was unable to make out, as I had no means of testing the depth of the water.

The spots at which to aim in order to penetrate the brain are various, and depend entirely on the position of the beast's head when fired at. If it should be facing the sportsman, he should aim between the eyes or at the eye; if broadside on, in a line between the eye and the ear; if diagonally towards him, at the eye; if diagonally away from him, behind the ear; and if straight away from him, at the base of the big lump of flesh that shows up at the back of the head between the ears. Either an accurate Martini or a .450 Express with a solid bullet is a first-rate weapon for this sport. When killed, hippos always sink, and the time that elapses before they rise may vary considerably from one to as much as six hours, depending both on the temperature and depth of the water and also on the condition of the animal. Hippos, when shot in the head and not killed outright, often behave in an extraordinary way. They will rear up out of the water, fall backwards, and float, belly upwards, on the surface, lashing out with their short stumpy legs, or rolling over and over, churning up the water in a marvellous manner, and will drown through being unable to raise their heads, in this stunned condition, above water. Their movements are, however, so rapid that it is seldom they offer a chance for a shot at the head, though they often expose the greater part of the body. The sportsman should therefore always have a heavy rifle with him to enable him to dispatch them with a shot through the lungs, as the beasts, being only stunned by the bullet passing close to the brain, will often recover sufficiently to enable them to escape for the time, though they will probably die in the end.

I have only once had a wounded hippo attempt to get out of the water at me, but as I was on the river bank, a foot or two above it, it never had a chance, and dropped dead to a shot between the eyes. My friend Mr. Gedge was once charged in a most determined manner by a wounded cow. As it was only stunned by the first shot, and went floundering and plunging down stream, he ran along the bank, a little below the beast, and got on to a rock, in order to have a better shot with his 8-bore as it passed him. It, however, recovered itself before it got to him, and seeing him so close to the water's edge, came straight at him, but he dropped it dead with a bullet in the head when within a few feet of him. The only case I know of a man being killed by a hippo was at Mumia's, in Kavirondo. This man was an envoy, sent by Mwanga of Uganda to meet us, and he was so severely hurt that he died next day. He had gone out with other men, one of whom managed to wound a hippo, and, as it kicked and plunged about, he waded out into the water waist deep, when, having recovered, it charged him with open mouth, catching him by the face in its jaws, and crushing it to such a frightful extent that he was quite unrecognisable.

I do not think that a hippo would ever attempt to follow a man on dry land, though I once read of a case where one of a school, living in a small lake near Mombasa, and having a very bad reputation for viciousness, actually left the water before being shot at and chased the man *three hundred yards*. As this sporting scribe also stated that he shot buffaloes, lions, giraffes, elands, &c. &c. within ten miles of Mombasa town so late as 1890, and that he used to send the meat into the town to sell, I think that this, with other startling facts (!) mentioned by him, may be taken *cum grano salis*.

CHAPTER XV

OSTRICHES AND GIRAFFES

BY F. J. JACKSON

The two species of game most difficult to approach are the giraffe and the ostrich. Their watchfulness and powers of scent equal those of other game, and if anything their sight is even more extraordinary. Besides these wonderfully developed senses, they possess a tremendous advantage over other game in their great height, being able to easily see over covert amply sufficient to conceal the approach of the stalker from the view of other animals.

Giraffes (*Giraffa camelopardalis*) were a few years ago fairly numerous in places suited to their habits, but I am told that a good many of them have fallen victims to the same disease which has destroyed the buffaloes. Still there are plenty left. Giraffes are very partial to the table-topped mimosas, on which they principally feed, and should be sought for in places where these trees abound. As a rule, they are found in small herds of six or eight, sometimes up to twenty or more, but solitary individuals are occasionally met with.

Giraffes kept in confinement give very little idea of the adult beast in a wild state. The wild one is not only much taller, but very much more bulky, and would weigh at least half as much again as any beast that was until lately to be seen in the Zoological Gardens. They are also very much darker in colour. The meat of the giraffe is not, as a rule, much appreciated by the Zanzibari porters, and some of them will not touch it. This is not from any religious or superstitious scruples, but on account of its causing a rash, a kind of herpes, of a most irritating nature to break out upon them. My head gun-bearer, Ramazan, and some of the porters once suffered for a fortnight after eating the meat of the first giraffe I shot, when there had been no other meat in camp for three or four days previously. He assured me that it is a well-known fact that it affects some men and not others.

The meat of the lesser kudu also affects certain constitutions only, but in a different way, as it acts as a salivant, and causes great pain in the mouth and gums. Several times my tent-boy, Sadala, was unable to eat anything but a little rice for some days after eating the meat of this beast. I mention these facts solely to induce sportsmen to avoid shooting these beautiful beasts (except as trophies) when meat is required for the men and other game is to be obtained. The marrow-bones of a giraffe, which are considered by some epicure sportsmen to be the greatest delicacy in Africa, not excepting elephant's heart, I have always found very inferior to those of the eland, or even the buffalo.

A Family Group

C. Whymper

Amongst the places where I have seen the giraffe in fair numbers are the caravan routes between Vanga and Teita, especially at Adda and Kisagao, and between Ndara in Teita, and Nzoi in Ukambani, particularly near Ndi, Mto Ndai, and Mto Chumvi. In 1887 the open bush and sparsely mimosa-wooded country just outside Taveta forest, on the road to Langora, was a sure find for these stately beasts.

Unless giraffes are found in ground fairly well wooded with mimosa and other trees, with also a fair undergrowth of bush, there is little chance of approaching to within range of them; but if found in such covert, and not too much scattered, the stalker, by dodging from bush to bush and by being careful to keep the thickly foliaged crown of a mimosa or other tree between the beast and himself, ought with ordinary care to have little difficulty in getting a shot. If an Express rifle is used on these beasts, it must only be with solid bullets, as their hide is very thick and tough. Personally I prefer an 8-bore.

I once watched a small herd of giraffes from the top of an 'earth boil,' and from my elevated position got a splendid view of them. They were standing about 500 yards off, in fairly open bush of uniform dark green, which in the distance appeared to be pretty thick, and formed a good background to the numerous mimosa-trees with their table-tops of a much brighter green, on which the giraffes were feeding. The strongly marked colouring of these gigantic and stately creatures towering above the bush made them stand out in clear contrast to their surroundings, as they slowly moved from tree to tree, gracefully twisting and turning their long necks to enable them to nibble the tender shoots of the mimosas in their usual delicate manner, giving me the impression that they might indeed be 'monarchs of all they surveyed.'

The ostrich (*Struthio molybdophanes*) of East and Central Africa is distinguished from the South African bird by its greater size, and by the cock bird having a blue neck. The feathers at any time are inferior and of little or no market value. The only two birds that I have ever seen with feathers that were at all good were killed by Mr. H. C. V. Hunter at Kilimanjaro in 1887, when he had the good fortune to bag them shortly after they had moulted, and before they had rubbed and damaged their wing-feathers when dusting themselves. The ostrich is plentiful in many parts of the country, and goes about in small troops, generally three or four together, though I have twice seen a troop of thirteen, once in the Arusha-wa-Chini country, and once at Machako's. An adult cock ostrich, when standing upright, would measure quite 10 ft. to the crown of his head, the hen being rather smaller. How far this bird ranges to the south I am unable to say, but to the north I have seen it near Lake Baringo. The Swahili and Arab traders, who now go up to Lake Rudolph, occasionally bring down small bunches of feathers, which, however, are probably of another species. Throughout the Masai country and east of it to the coast ostriches are to be found in most of the plains and open bush country, where they find plenty of green herbage to feed on, whether grass or the leaves of various bushes. At Merereni, on the coast, in 1886, where I bagged three, two cocks and a hen, the hen bird was feeding on the young shoots of a small-leaved mangrove bush by the side of a creek. Each of these birds when cut open was found to have about 3 lbs. weight of pebbles inside its gizzard.

Ostriches are even more difficult to stalk than giraffes, as they are mostly found out in the open, and unless the sportsman can get a bush sufficiently tall to prevent their seeing him over it, or can take advantage of the dry bed of a water-course, should there be one near, it is almost hopeless to try to stalk them. They are, however, not difficult to drive, and I have twice succeeded in circumventing them in this way, once with Sir Robert Harvey, and another time when alone. Once I tried to approach a troop of five by using my imitation ostrich, the Bushman's stratagem (with which I was so successful with *G. Grantii*), but failed so hopelessly—the birds at once detecting the fraud and never allowing me to get within 500 yards of them—that I never tried it again. The best day I ever had with these birds was when I came across three, which I saw from a long way off, feeding amongst some small scattered bushes on a slope in undulating ground. By taking advantage of the low ground on the other side of the undulation, I succeeded, after a long and painful crawl, in getting up to a bush near the top. Here I could see the long neck and head of one of them over the brow, and was pleased to notice that they had altered their position and were feeding in my direction. Sitting quite still, I waited until they were within seventy yards of me, and got two of them with a right and left shot. The other one bolted down the slope of the hill away from me and disappeared for a few seconds, but apparently lost its head; for on standing up I saw it coming back; as it had not seen me, I stooped down behind the bush, and when it raced past about seventy or eighty yards off, with head held back and wings extended, I knocked it over.

C. Harveyi, G. Petersi, N. Montanus, and C. Bohor
1 C. Harveyi. 2 G. Petersi. 3 N. Montanus. 4 C. Bohor.

C. Whymper

CHAPTER XVI

ANTELOPES

BY F. J. JACKSON

Antelope shooting is unattended with danger, and yet antelopes afford if anything better sport than any of the dangerous game-beasts found in Africa. Creatures such as rhinos, buffaloes, and elephants have not so many enemies as the antelopes, and can therefore afford to be far less watchful than these beasts, whose natural shyness and marvellously developed senses test the stalker's skill to the very utmost. If, as it seems to me, sport should be measured not so much by the amount of danger incurred as by the degree of skill required, there is more sport to be had in outwitting the ever-watchful oryx or wildebeest or eland than in killing either a rhinoceros or buffalo—beasts peculiarly easy to stalk unless accompanied by birds, as already described. In antelope stalking, from the beginning to the end of the business the greatest care has to be exercised, lest an incautious movement, either of the stalker or the gun-bearer who crawls behind him, should alarm the watchful game; and the anxiety lest something of this kind should occur, coupled with the physical strain in crawling on the hands and knees or flat upon the stomach during a long stalk, intensifies the satisfaction when the hunter does succeed in outwitting them.

At certain seasons of the year, when the grass has grown 18 ins. or 2 ft. high, stalking is comparatively easy even in the open plains, and requires then nothing but endurance on the stalker's part to enable him to succeed. But stalking is a very different business when the grass has been burnt and there is no covert except a few skeleton bushes and small ant-heaps, or a few patches of grass which have escaped the fire.

But perhaps the accompanying diagrams of three stalks which I made myself will give a better idea of the way to take advantage of very scanty covert than any written advice.

In the alluvial plains, which extend for a considerable distance on each side of the banks of a perennial river, the country is often interspersed with large shady trees which give it a park-like appearance. In such places, among scattered mimosa-trees, occasional bushes, and a few ant-heaps, stalking is not difficult, and it is in such places that elands, waterbucks, impalas, and buffaloes are often found. In open bush, where game is frequently seen by the sportsman within a couple of hundred yards, a stalk, though sometimes rather difficult, is generally short. To approach within range of antelopes in thick bush is not nearly so much a test of skill in stalking as of quick sight and ability to walk quietly and to pass through bush without making a noise. Quick shooting is also necessary, and the rest depends a good deal on whether one's lucky star happens to be in the ascendent or otherwise. Provided the sportsman keeps up wind and walks quietly, and is always thoroughly on the alert and prepared for a snap shot, a good day's work may be done; but if he does not exercise these precautions, although he may come across any amount of fresh spoor, and may now and again catch sight of an antelope, he may go out day after day only to be disappointed, and will possibly blame everything and everybody but himself. Antelopes when in thick bush have often great difficulty in making out the direction whence a shot is fired, and I know of many instances when out shooting for the 'pot,' when, shortly after having fired at partridges or guinea-fowl, I have suddenly come across an antelope, standing intently listening, evidently on the *qui vive*, but apparently unable to make out from where my last shot was fired. Remembering this, the sportsman should never throw away a chance of shooting an antelope not already added to ascendan- through fancying that a shot or two will lessen his chance of procuring a particular and perhaps rarer species which he may be in quest of at the time.

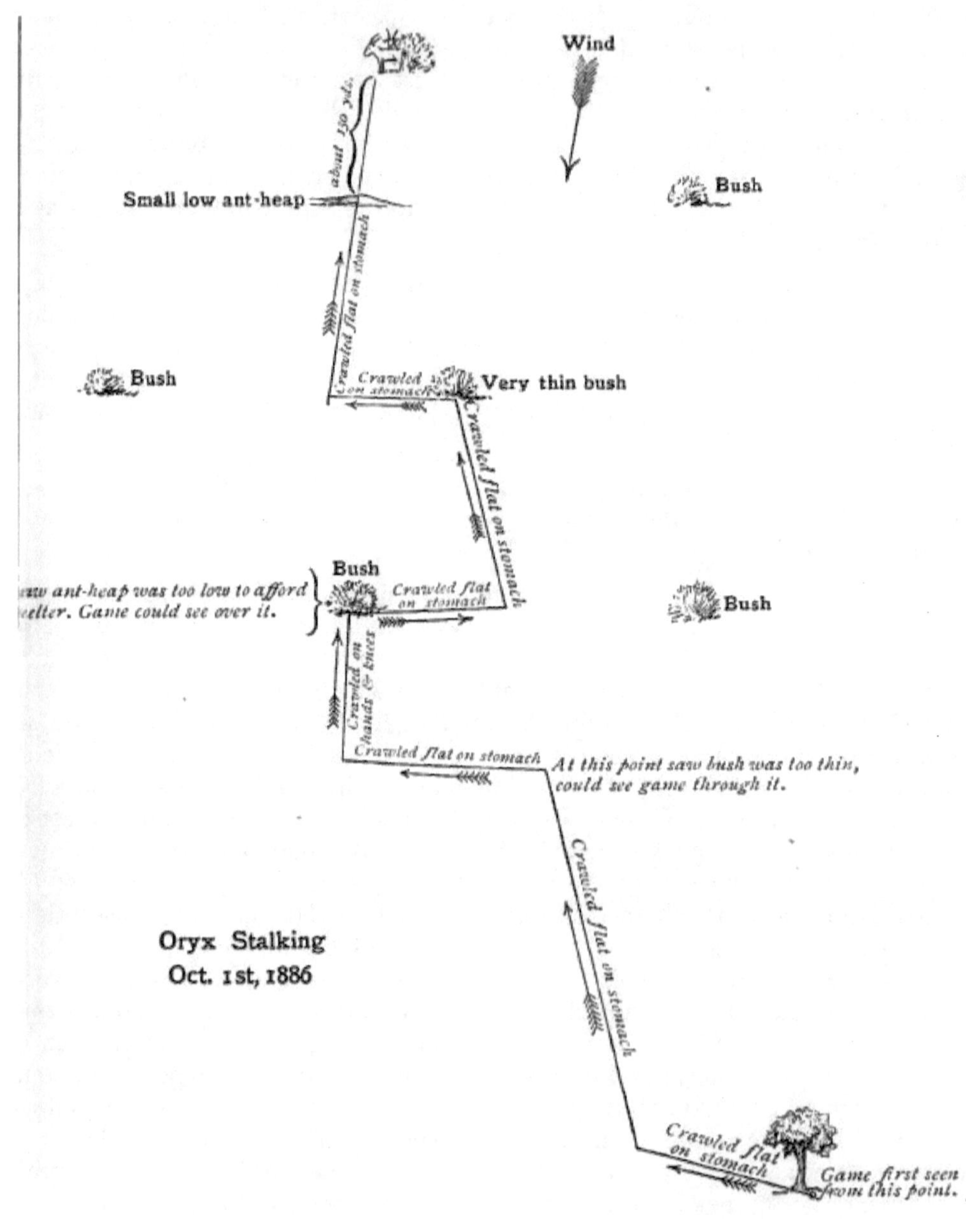

Plan of an Oryx Stalk

F. J. Jackson

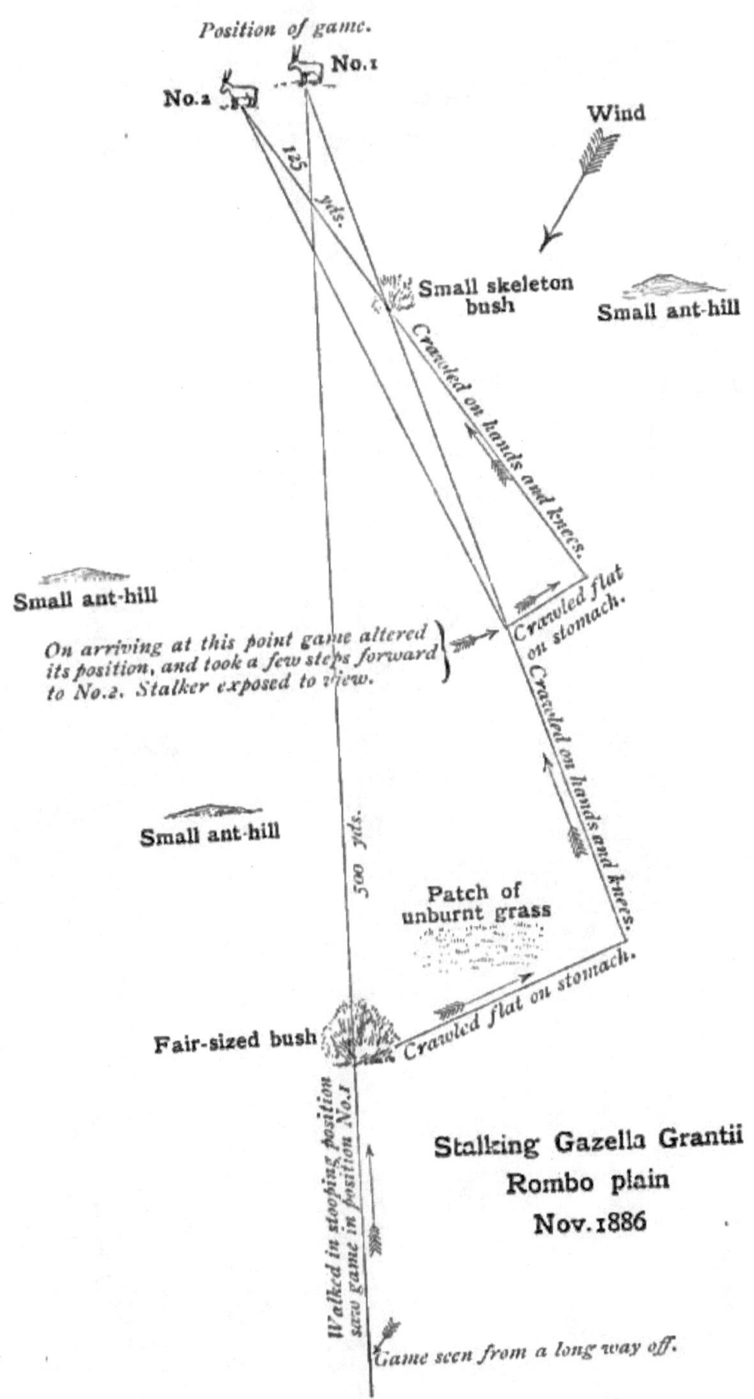

Plan of a Gazella Grantii Stalk on Rombo Plain

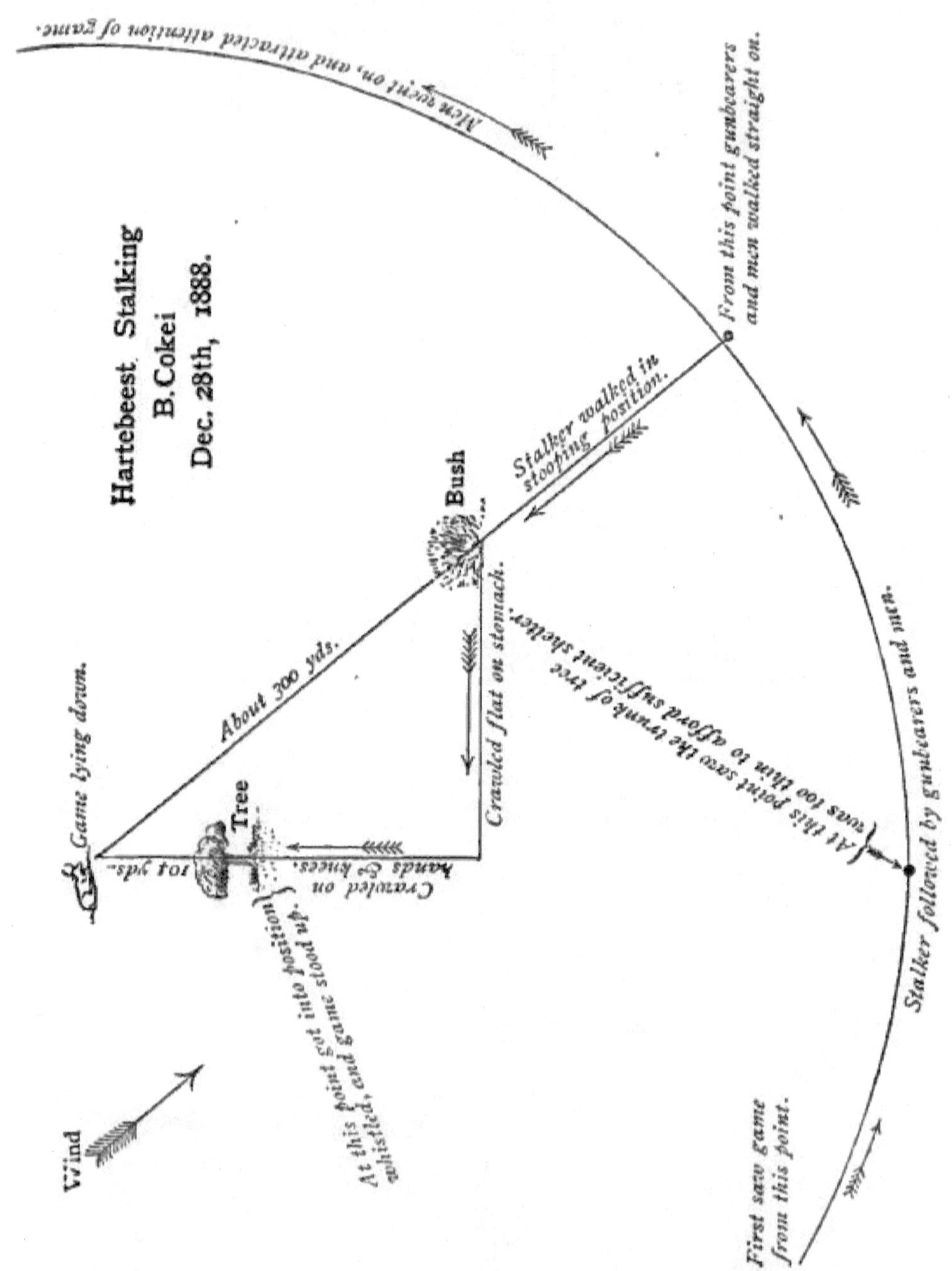

Plan of an Hartebeest Stalk

If the sportsman should come across the spoor of an antelope he is particularly anxious to get, and sees that the beast has been disturbed by his last shot,

he should wait a quarter of an hour or so before following it, to allow it to settle down and forget its fear; and as antelopes rarely go far away, he will have a very good chance of eventually getting a shot. For this sort of shooting one of Messrs. Holland & Holland's Paradox guns will be found invaluable, as one barrel can be loaded with a bullet and the other with a charge of shot, when the sportsman is prepared for anything from a kudu or waterbuck to a duyker or 'paa' (*N. Kirkii*).

Zebras, wart-hogs, &c. may be stalked in the same manner as antelopes.

The following is a complete list of the antelopes at present known to exist in British East Africa:—

Antelopes, from the sportsman's point of view, can be divided into two kinds: those which frequent the open plains, and those which are found in the bush. The antelopes coming under the first head would include the

1. Eland (*Oreas canna Livingstonei*).

2. Wildebeest, white-throated (*Connochætes taurinus albajubatus*).

3. Hartebeest, Coke's (*Bubalis Cokei*).

4. Hartebeest, Lichtenstein's (*Bubalis Lichtensteini*). The *B. leucoprymnus* of Dr. Matschi.

5. Hartebeest, Jackson's (*Bubalis Jacksoni*).

6. 'Topi' (*Damalis senegalensis*). The *D. jimela* of Dr. Matschi.

7. *Damalis Hunteri.*

8. Roan antelope (?) (*Hippotragus equinus*). Seen north of Mount Elgon.

9. Sable antelope (*Hippotragus niger*).

10. Oryx, East African (*Oryx collotis*).

11. *Kobus kob.*

12. Lesser Reedbuck (*Cervicapra bohor*).

13. *Gazella Grantii.*

14. *Gazella Thomsoni.*

15. *Gazella Petersi.*

16. Oribi, Abyssinian (*Nanotragus montanus*).

17. Oribi, East African (*Nanotragus hastatus*).

18. Steinbuck (*Nanotragus campestris*).

Those found in thick bush, open bush, or on the outskirts of the bush, and which take to the bush when disturbed, include:

1. Waterbuck (*Kobus elipsiprymnus*).

2. Sing-Sing (*Kobus defassus*).

3. Kudu (*Strepsiceros kudu*).

4. Lesser Kudu (*Strepsiceros imberbis*).

5. Bush-buck (*Tragelaphus sylvaticus Roualeyni*).

6. Impala (*Æpyceros melampus*).

7. Gerenook (*Lithocranius Walleri*).

8. Duyker (*Cephalolophus Grimmii*).

9. Red Duyker (*Cephalolophus Harveyi*).

10. Mountain Duyker (*Cephalolophus spadix*). This duyker is found on Kilimanjaro at high altitudes.

11. *Cephalolophus melanorheus*.

12. Klipspringer (*Oreotragus saltator*).

13. *Neotragus Kirkii*.

14. *Nanotragus moschatus*.

15. The Sitatunga (*Tragelaphus Spekei*).

ELAND

The striped variety of the eland is the only one found in East Africa. It is known to the Swahilis as 'Mpofu,' and is decidedly a local beast. It is seen more often in open bush and country thinly wooded with mimosa-trees than quite out in the open. In 1887 it was plentiful round Taveta, where I have seen as many as sixty to seventy in one herd. In the open bush country west of Mount Kisigao elands are fairly numerous. Other places in which they are found are the park-like country below Ndi in Teita; the open country east of Ndara and north of Mount Maungu; and the Siringeti plains. I have also seen them between Lakes Nakuro and Baringo, and again in Turkwel, in the Suk country. As a rule they go about in herds of four or five up to fifteen or twenty. Sometimes two or three bulls will be found together, and very often an old bull quite by himself.

Very old beasts, both bulls and cows, are of a dark slatey-blue colour, owing to the skin showing through their scanty covering of hair, and these old fellows lose all trace of the white stripes. The bulls grow to a huge size and become enormously fat. Elands are decidedly difficult to stalk, both on account of the watchfulness of the cows and the nature of the ground they generally frequent. They are, however, fairly easy to drive. I remember having one eland drive which was one of the grandest sights I ever witnessed, on account of the enormous number of game which passed close to me.

I had gone up to the top of a large 'earth boil' to reconnoitre the country, and from it saw a large herd of some fifty elands, a herd of about 120 buffaloes, besides innumerable hartebeests and zebras, two rhinos, and a small herd of five giraffes. Although they were all well to windward, a stalk was out of the question, as the grass had lately been burnt and the zebras and hartebeests were scattered in all directions.

As I had not yet shot a good eland, and was particularly anxious to get one, I decided on a drive, for which the country was well adapted. About 300 yards from the foot of the earth boil there was a deep, dry watercourse, and it was through the passage between the two that I decided to drive everything if possible. About half-way across there were several thorn-trees and a few low ant-heaps which commanded the whole of the passage.

After directing the beaters to work round in a circuit, to get well to windward of the game, and telling off two other men to act as 'stops' on the other side of the 'boil,' I took up my position on one of the ant-heaps, and lay flat on the sloping side, sufficiently near the top to enable me to look over it. Ramazan, my gun-bearer, lay at the foot of it. The first beasts to appear were the five giraffes, which had seen the beaters long before any of the other game could do so, and came striding along in their stately fashion, stopping every now and again to have a look round. The old bull was an enormous beast, and one of the darkest in colour I have ever seen. When just level with me, and about eighty yards off, as there was still no other game in sight, I could not resist the temptation of startling them, as they seemed to be taking things so easily, and therefore jumped up and showed myself, shouting as I did so, 'Hi! Yambo!' (a Swahili salutation), after which they went off at a gallop, with their tails screwed up, their long necks swaying backwards and forwards at each stride, and were soon lost to view in a cloud of black dust. Shortly after this little interlude I saw a dense cloud of dust rising in the distance to windward of me, heard a low rumbling noise from the same direction, and knew at once that the beaters had begun their work. Several zebras which stood out well against the dark background came cantering along, together with a few hartebeests, but I soon lost sight of these, as they shortly afterwards pulled up, and the clouds of dust drifting before the wind obscured them from my view. I began to fear I should be unable to see anything, but as the game approached, I could distinguish several zebras and hartebeests, and could see them fairly well when about 100 yards off, some of them even walking and trotting past within thirty yards of me. As I had not the remotest idea where the elands were, on account of the dust, I whispered to Ramazan to keep a sharp look-out on the right, whilst I kept watch on the left, the side towards the watercourse. Suddenly I was rather taken aback by hearing the buffaloes advancing apparently straight towards me, as I could distinctly hear them grunting, some of the cows, probably those with calves, being particularly noisy. Thinking it better to be well prepared for them, and on the safe side, I turned round and beckoned to Ramazan to crawl up nearer to me with the 4-bore, although I already had the 8-bore and .500 Express by my side. Shortly afterwards I felt him grip me by the leg, but on turning my head saw, not the elands, but several cow buffaloes, the leaders of the herd, advancing towards us, a little to the right of our position, and I confess I breathed more freely; not that I think there was much danger, but I was so anxious if possible to avoid firing at anything but eland, as it would have lessened my chance of getting one of these beasts. As it was, the buffaloes all passed at a quick shambling walk within sixty yards of me, and I was at one time sorely tempted to have a shot at a grand bull with beautiful wide spreading horns, which passed within forty yards. I may mention that I believe I got this identical bull a day or two afterwards—if so, my forbearance was rewarded.

When the buffaloes had gone past, the air became a little clearer, and I had the satisfaction of seeing the elands bringing up the rearguard at a gentle trot, still some 200 yards off, coming in such a direction that they would pass between myself and the watercourse. On they came, quite unconscious of my presence, and stopped just about 100 yards from my left front, although all the other game had stampeded after passing us and getting our wind. There were two good bulls in the herd, but the best one had lagged behind with two cows, which provokingly stood between him and myself and prevented my taking a shot as they stood, so that I had to wait until they moved on again. This they did at a walk, as my men were fairly good at driving, and had stopped directly they saw the elands were close to my position. As the three last beasts came just level with me and within seventy yards, one of the cows was still between the bull and myself, and fearing that if I waited longer I might not get a shot at him at all, I gave the cow a bullet behind the shoulder with the Express to make her get out of the way, and before the bull had gone many yards gave him both barrels of the 8-bore—the first shot a good one behind the shoulder which went clean through him; the other a poor one, which, however, knocked him over. The cow went on about a quarter of a mile, and was found dead behind a bush. The two rhinos I never saw at all, although the beaters told me they had passed. They must have escaped my observation owing to the clouds of dust. Several other zebras and hartebeests broke past the two stops, but everything else passed within 150 yards of me, and had there been a little grass, which would have prevented the dust rising, I should have had a still better view of this grand sight.

BRINDLED WILDEBEEST

The Brindled or Blue Wildebeest (Swahili name, 'Nyumbo') is essentially an antelope of the plains, though it is occasionally seen in thin open bush. It is more plentiful in the Useri district to the north-east of Kilimanjaro, and the Athi plains to the north and west of Machako's, than anywhere else. In the latter place on August 5, 1890, Dr. Mackinnon and I saw an enormous herd of 1,500, but this is quite unusual, as they are rarely found in herds of more than from twenty to sixty.

A single bull is often seen either by himself or with other antelopes and zebras. Wildebeests are amongst the most difficult beasts to stalk, owing to the open nature of the country in which they are found, and will probably try the sportsman's patience more than any other antelope. They will stand gazing at him, and will sometimes allow him to get within a range of 200 yards, if he pretends to walk past them, though in reality closing in upon them in a semicircle; but directly he stops to take a shot they will shake their heads in the most defiant way, and, with a few snorts and flicks of their mule-like tails, kick up their heels and caper off jauntily. As they will, as a rule, pull up a short way off, the sportsman will have the annoyance of again adopting the same tactics, with probably like results, until he might almost believe that the wildebeest is enjoying itself at his expense. He should, however, avoid risking a long shot (the wildebeest is an extremely tough brute, and will go for miles when wounded in such a way as would soon bring other game to a standstill), since after two or three fruitless attempts if no shot is fired its suspicions will become allayed, and it will probably stand sufficiently long to give him a good chance.

COKE'S HARTEBEEST

Coke's Hartebeest (Swahili, 'Kongoni')is by far the commonest antelope in East Africa, and is found almost everywhere in fairly open country, excepting in the Galla country and north of Lake Baringo. It may be met with from April to August as near the coast as Maji Chumvi, three marches from Mombasa, and ranges throughout the year as far north as Doreta, a little to the south of Njemps, where Jackson's hartebeest takes its place. Mr. Gedge obtained a hybrid between the two species somewhere near Doreta, on his way down from Uganda in 1892.

LICHTENSTEIN'S HARTEBEEST

Lichtenstein's Hartebeest, also known to the Swahilis as 'Kongoni,' though they do not confound the two species, I include as a British East African antelope on the authority of General Lloyd Mathews, who told me that he had shot some of these beasts (one skull of which he showed me) on his way down from Kilimanjaro to Pangani, but whether actually in British territory I am unable to say. It is a common beast south of the Pangani river, and in the beautiful undulating parklike country on the banks of the river Wami, where I shot several in February 1887. It is, therefore, quite possible that a few range as far north as the river Umba, the boundary line between German and British territory.

This beast has lately been described as a new species by Dr. Matschi under the name of *B. leucoprymnus*.

JACKSON'S HARTEBEEST

Jackson's Hartebeest, also called 'Kongoni' by the Zanzibar porters, is first met with near Lake Baringo, and on Mau escarpment west of Lake Naivasha, which is, perhaps, its most southern limit. It is quite the commonest antelope in Turkwel, and also in the undulating country west of Elgeyo, where it is found in the plains, open bush, and thin mimosa-wooded country.

THE TOPI

The 'Topi' is, I believe, not found south of the Sabaki river. It is, however, the commonest antelope in the Galla country, and it ranges from the coast right away N.E. to Uganda, passing round to the north of Mount Kenia, but I do not think it is known either in Lykepia or south of Lake Baringo.

The topi found in Uganda has been lately described as a distinct species (*Damalis jimela*) by Dr. Matschi, but whether it is really so or is only a local and somewhat larger variety of *D. senegalensis* I am unable to say. It is found both in plains and open bush, and is plentiful at Merereni and on the mainland near Lamu, where I have shot it within a quarter of a mile of the sea. I believe the topi to be capable of greater pace than any other East African antelope. One of the peculiarities of this beast is the way it varies in colour when seen standing at different angles in bright sunlight, at one time appearing quite black and at others a slatey-blue or stone-grey.

Bubalis Jacksoni

C. Whymper

DAMALIS HUNTERI

D. Hunteri, first obtained by my friend Mr. H. C. V. Hunter in 1888, is only found north of the Tana river, but how far north it ranges into the Somali country is at present unknown. In habits it resembles the topi.

ROAN ANTELOPE

The Roan Antelope I have added to the list with a query after its name. I do not believe that it exists anywhere in British East Africa south of Turkwel.[12] On the northern slopes of Mount Elgon I saw two beasts which, as they stood facing me some 400 yards off, I took to be waterbucks, but on being alarmed at my firing at a hartebeest which crossed the footpath just in front of me, I at once perceived, as they cantered off, that they were animals which I had never seen before. As they appeared to tally at that distance with the roan, in respect of size, colour, shape of the horns, and length of ears, I have put them down as the roan, though I think it is more than probable that they may some day prove to be quite a different species, possibly *Hippotragus Bakeri.*

SABLE ANTELOPE

The Sable Antelope, known to the Swahilis as 'Pala-hala,' is very rare, and up to the present has not been bagged in British East Africa by a European. Sir John Willoughby, in his book 'East Africa and its Big Game,' mentions that he saw a small herd of five near Maji Chumvi. Mr. Gedge and I also saw a herd of about ten or twelve near Gulu Gulu in November 1888. Both of these places were open bush and thinly-wooded country. The sable antelope is fairly plentiful in the undulating park-like country on the banks of the river Wami, near Kidudwe, in German territory.

EAST AFRICAN ORYX

The East African Oryx is known to the Swahilis as 'Cheroa.' This oryx was for a long time confounded with the *Oryx beisa* of the Somali country, which, however, does not range south of the Tana river. The cheroa is easily distinguished from the other by the presence of a tuft of long black hair on the ears. It is found in the Kilimanjaro district in greater numbers (particularly near Useri) than elsewhere. It is also plentiful in the Galla country, between the Sabaki and Tana rivers, and I have myself seen it within a mile of the sea at Merereni.

It is found more often in open bush country than in the bare arid plains. It is not only a beautiful beast, but is very shy, difficult to approach, and exceedingly tough, and for these reasons many sportsmen covet its head more than the trophies of any other kind of antelope. The skin of its neck is extraordinarily thick, and *à propos* of this, all head-skins preserved as trophies should have the skin of the neck shaved down to at least half its thickness to ensure its being properly cured. The oryx is found in herds varying in number from six or eight up to thirty or forty. A bull oryx is very often found entirely by himself, and occasionally with a herd of *G. Grantii* or other antelopes.

It is perhaps as well to warn sportsmen to approach oryx, when lying wounded, with caution, as on one occasion my gun-bearer, on going up to cut the throat of an oryx, received a severe blow on the thigh from the side of one of the wound-

---

[12] Since this was written the roan antelope has been killed near the coast by Mr. Jenner. It is evidently very local.

ed beast's horns. The blow might have been very serious had the oryx caught him with the point of his horns instead of with the flat.

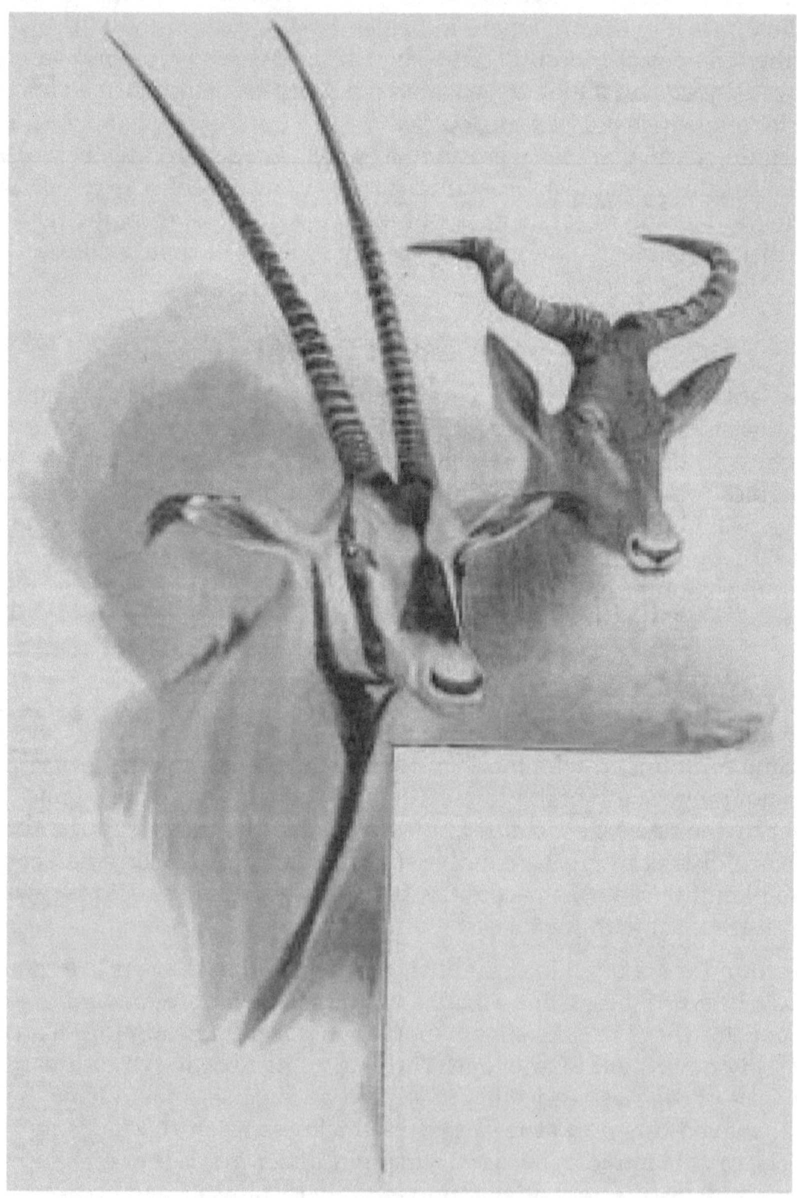

Oryx Collotis and Bubalis Cokei

C. Whymper

One of my most memorable stalks was up to a herd of some twenty-five of these grand beasts near the Useri river, in May 1887. The country was for the most part undulating and covered with open thorn bush, the ground in many places was very rough and stony, and, to add to the discomforts of the stalk, carpeted with a creeping plant, the long tendrils of which were covered with large and very hard seeds with sharp spikes on them. These seeds, whichever way they lay on the ground, always had a spike uppermost which went completely through coat-sleeves and breeches when crawling up to game. I was returning to camp about midday, feeling rather disappointed at having wounded and lost a fine bull oryx, when I saw the herd standing in an open space surrounded by thin bush. As there was an 'earth boil' close by, I walked partly up it to reconnoitre the country, and saw that immediately to leeward of the herd, about 100 yards off, there was a clump of table-topped mimosa-trees; but between the edge of the bush and this clump, a distance of 200 yards, there was absolutely no covert with the exception of one or two stunted shrubs and a few large stones. Seeing that a long and very hot crawl was my only chance, I went round, keeping out of sight in the bush, and got the clump between myself and the oryx, when I began quite the most painful and trying stalk I have ever made. I started by crawling on hands and knees from bush to bush until I arrived at the last outlying one, and was rejoiced on looking round it to find that the greater part of the herd had lain down. I then knew that I had plenty of time before me. The ground between myself and the clump, with the exception of one small bush some twenty yards on my side of it, was so bare that it seemed almost hopeless to attempt to get over it without being seen. However, I decided to try, and, leaving my gun-bearer behind the bush, began crawling slowly forward flat on my stomach. At every movement several of the sharp-spiked seeds penetrated through my breeches and coat-sleeves, causing me considerable pain; moreover, as they stuck to the cloth, it was necessary to brush them off every two or three yards—no easy matter in my position. To make things still more discomforting, the heat reflected from the hard stony ground was almost unbearable. On reaching a large stone I was tempted to risk a shot, at about 200 yards, at a bull with a fair head that was standing up, and should have done so had I not at that moment caught sight of a grand cow lying down just behind him. Still creeping, in time I succeeded in reaching the bush, lay with my head in the shade of it, glad of a few minutes' rest, and had a good look at the herd through my binoculars.

There was no doubt that the cow I had noticed had quite the best head of the whole herd, and as I was not more than 125 yards off, I decided to take a shot from where I was and not run the risk of being seen in attempting to creep nearer.

After waiting about ten minutes in the hope that the cow would get up, I could no longer stand the heat of the sun pouring down on my back, and so carefully sat up and worked myself round to the right of the bush. Aiming at her as she lay I gave a whistle, which brought all the oryx to their feet, and as she stood up pressed the trigger and heard the welcome 'phut' of the bullet as it struck her; but I could not see the result of the shot, as the recoil of the rifle caused several beads of perspiration to run down my spectacles, and I was unable to see anything. My gun-bearer now came running up, and in answer to my question if the beast was down or not, said, 'Umianguka' (It has fallen), and my joy was unbounded. It was a splendid beast, the best I have ever shot, and well worth the trouble I had taken to get it.

KOBUS KOB

Kobus Kob

The Kobus Kob is first met with in British East Africa near Mumia's, in Upper Kavirondo. Here I saw a small herd on three consecutive days on the banks of the Nzoia quite near to the same place. As I was after hippos at the time, and never got near the antelopes, I mistook them for impalas, and paid no further attention to them, until one day Mr. Gedge brought in the head of one he had shot, and I at once recognised my mistake. On going out specially to get one or two I found them fairly plentiful. This beast is rarely seen more than 300 or 400 yards from water. It is very shy, and unless found in long grass (about the only covert there is, excepting ant-heaps, in the places it haunts) is very difficult to stalk. It is extraordinarily tough, and requires a great deal of killing. When wounded it will take to the reeds along the river banks and in swampy hollows; but when only alarmed prefers to keep to the open for safety. This antelope is evidently plentiful near the shores of Victoria Nyanza, as nearly all the Waganda canoes are ornamented on their high projecting prow with its frontlet and its horns. These beasts are usually found in small herds, consisting of a buck and three or four does. I have also seen one herd of some twenty-five, consisting entirely of bucks.

LESSER REEDBUCK

The Lesser Reedbuck (Swahili, 'Toi' or 'Tohi') is very local, and as a rule only frequents the vicinity of rivers and swamps which are never dry. These bucks are found on the shores of Lake Jipi and the Ziwa to the east of Kilimanjaro, and in a few other places. I also saw several small herds of them, out of which I shot two bucks, on the top of the hills to the north-west of Machako's station. These had evidently been driven up into the hills by the grass fires in the plains, which had destroyed every particle of covert. The reed-bucks give a shrill whistle when disturbed, and are very shy and difficult to stalk. They, however, lie close when in long grass, and will sometimes allow the sportsman to approach within twenty or thirty yards of them, when they rush off at such a pace that, as their colour very closely resembles the dry grass, they are difficult to hit. They go about in small herds of three or four, but more often in couples or quite alone.

GRANT'S GAZELLE

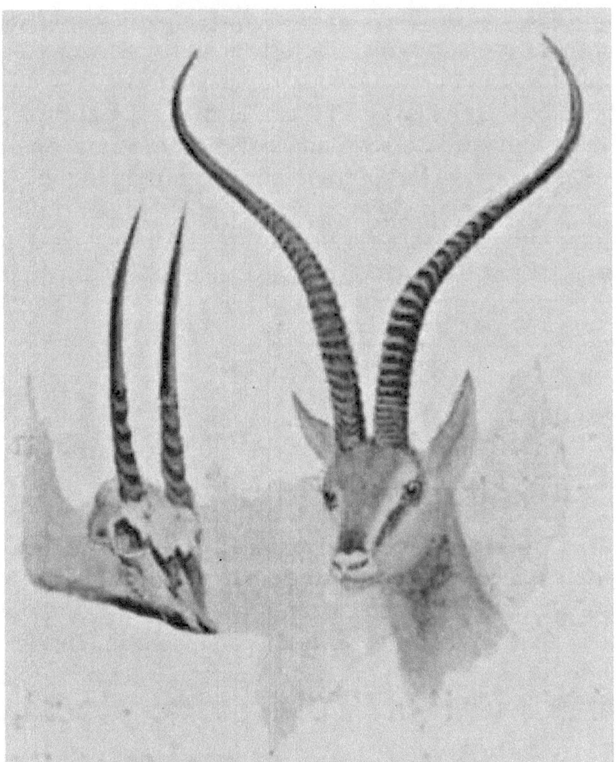

Adult and Immature Gazella Grantii

The *Grantii* (Swahili name, 'Sala,' or 'Swara') is met with almost everywhere in the plains and open bush country. It and the impala are perhaps the most beautiful of all the smaller antelopes, and both are among the most coveted trophies of the sportsman.

In the Rombo and Useri plains the horns of this antelope grow to a much greater length than anywhere else that I know of. Thirty inches along the curve is the length of the record head, but horns of 26 ins. in length are by no means unusual in this locality. In other parts of the country a buck with horns 24 ins. in length would be considered to carry a first-rate head.

These antelopes are found in herds of from three or four up to fifteen or twenty, though I have seen as many as sixty in one herd at Machako's.

THOMSON'S GAZELLE

The '*Thomsoni*' in habits is very like the *G. Grantii*, but as a rule is found in rather larger herds. Single bucks of this species are, however, more often seen than single *Grantii* bucks. At Lake Naivasha, in July 1890, I saw a large herd of some sixty head, composed entirely of does, and in the same place, in September of the previous year, I saw a herd of some thirty or forty beasts, every one of which was a buck; but I do not think that this can be taken as evidence that the bucks and does separate at certain seasons of the year, as on the same days on which I saw these two herds I also saw others in which the bucks and does were together. A *Thomsoni* is a confiding little beast, and, except in places close to a well-beaten caravan route, where it has been constantly shot at, can be easily approached within 120 yards with ordinary care and perseverance, even in the most open and covertless places. These beasts appear to be confined almost entirely to the Masai country, as I have not heard of their having been seen east of the Sigarari plains to the south of Kilimanjaro, or south of the Useri river and the head-waters of the Tsavo. I saw none at Njemps near Lake Baringo, or in Turkwel and Ngaboto in the Suk country, though *G. Grantii* was plentiful in all these places.

PETERS' GAZELLE

Gazella Petersi (known to the Swahilis also as 'Sala') may be a local variety of *G. Grantii* rather than a distinct species. It used to be plentiful at Merereni on the coast, and is still found further inland in the Galla country. It is certainly a smaller beast than *G. Grantii* from Kilimanjaro or Machako's, but in other respects is almost identical, excepting in the shape and size of the horns, which I have never known to exceed 22 ins. in length measured along the curve. Their horns are also straighter, and have not nearly such a pronounced backward curve as those of the *Grantii*, neither do they diverge towards the points so much, being rarely more than seven or eight inches apart at the widest parts. *G. Petersi* is found in the small open plains and open scrub.

ABYSSINIAN ORIBI

The Abyssinian Oribi (Swahili, 'Taya') is, I believe, not found to the south of Upper Kavirondo. Between the river Nzoia and the base of Mount Elgon it is fairly plentiful, as also in Turkwel. In habits it differs from its East African congener in one respect only, not appearing to be so partial to long grass, but being confined more to rough stony ground and short scrubby bush. This gives the sportsman a chance of seeing it at a distance, and an opportunity of stalking it which the oribi of the coast very rarely affords, unless the grass in which they usually lie has lately been burnt.

EAST AFRICAN ORIBI

The East African Oribi (also known to the Swahilis as 'Taya') I have found more plentiful on the mainland near Lamu than anywhere else. Sir Robert Harvey and Mr. Hunter, in October and November 1888, also found it in fair numbers up the Tana river. I have never seen it myself south of the Sabaki, though doubtless it is to be met in suitable places. At Merereni where the country seems admirably suited to its habits, although I was shooting there for some time in 1885 and 1886, I never saw one, though some fifteen miles further south, near Mambrui, I observed its spoor. This confirmed me in my theory that the oribi is very partial to the vicinity of cultivated tracts, and I do not remember having seen one in an uninhabited district. At Taka, a small village on the mainland opposite Patta island, I saw great numbers in 1885.

In the vicinity of this village there was a great deal of land which at one time had been under cultivation, but was then lying fallow and covered with coarse dry grass, about two feet high. This afforded excellent covert, and, as the colour of these little antelopes closely resembles that of dry grass, it was very difficult to see them. Except in one way, stalking them was quite hopeless. I found that the only plan to get them was to walk them up with one or two beaters on each side of me, and shoot them with a gun loaded with S.S.G. shot. They lie so close that they will let the sportsman get within ten or fifteen yards of them before they will move, but they rarely give him a chance of a shot under forty to fifty yards. When they first get up it is only possible to follow their movements by the waving of the grass. It is necessary, however, always to be prepared for a snap-shot, as after going some twenty to thirty yards they will bound up into the air, offering a capital chance, which may be the only one, as they will be out of range before they again appear in a like manner. This bounding into the air is, I believe, to enable them to see where they are going to, and it is a curious fact that when they alight they invariably do so on their hind legs, not unlike a kangaroo.

An oribi, even when only slightly wounded, will, as a rule, go a very short distance before lying down, and the sportsman should, therefore, be careful to follow up all those that he thinks he may have touched.

STEINBUCK

The Steinbuck (Swahili name, 'Ishah') is better known to some sportsmen as the 'grass antelope.' It is more plentiful at Kilimanjaro than elsewhere, though I have seen a good many all along the caravan route, wherever it passes through open grass country, between Mombasa and Nzoi in Ukambani. This little antelope is the smallest found in the open plain. It is a stupid little beast, and requires very little stalking to outwit it. It will often stand gazing at anyone who approaches, and allow him to walk up to within 100 yards of it. I once witnessed a most interesting sight in which one of these little bucks played an important part. It was being hunted by two cheetahs (hunting leopards). This occurred on the low hills west of Machako's. As I was walking along the side of a steep hill, I saw four cheetahs cross a dry watercourse at the bottom and ascend half-way up the side of the opposite hill, when they lay down and began gambolling like kittens. About half-way between the top of the hill and the cheetahs was a pile of huge rocky boulders, and thinking that they would in all probability make for these, and lie up in the shade of them during the heat of the day, I hurried round, making a wide circuit, to the back of the hill. On looking down from the top I had the satisfaction of seeing the cheetahs still in the same place, and gained the boulders without any difficulty. My gun-bearer and I then took up our position under a small thorn-tree, which was growing in a crevice of the largest boulder. As this afforded us a certain amount of shade, we awaited events there, hoping that the cheetahs would come in our direction when it became too hot for them in the open. In about half an hour, during which time they still continued to play and roll about, I noticed that their attitude suddenly changed. All four stood up and gazed fixedly in my direction, and I feared that an eddy in the wind had caused them to scent us; but on having a look at them with my binoculars I was delighted to see that they were not looking directly at me, but rather to the left of me, and on turning my head I saw a steinbuck quietly feeding some 150 yards off to my left, on the same level as myself. I then turned my attention to the cheetahs, which for a short time stood all together, and I concluded, from the difference in their size, that there was one male and three females. Only two of them, however, took up the hunt, the male and a female. These advanced by short rushes, and not by a stealthy crawl like a couple of lions which I saw stalking some elands, described elsewhere, neither did they both advance at the same time; the male always took the lead, and after each rush, in a crouching position, squatted down and waited until the female saw her opportunity to get up level with him. In this manner they approached within 160 yards of the steinbuck (it struck me they could have easily got considerably nearer) when they both ran in, and were within 100 yards before the little buck looked up, and, seeing them coming, without the slightest hesitation bolted straight uphill as hard as it could go. The cheetahs, however, were more than a match for it in pace. As they laid themselves out flat to the ground they gained at each stride, and I expected every second to see the male, which was leading by some few yards, run into the buck; but when only about ten yards off the plucky little buck doubled sharp to the left, throwing off its pursuer, which immediately gave up the chase. The female, however, then took up the running, but had not the pace of her companion, and the little antelope, which now kept a diagonal course up the hillside, gained the top, still followed by the cheetah, which was only a few yards behind, and they both disappeared from view on the other side. As the male lay where he had given up the running, the other two females which had remained behind joined him, and the ground being far too open to attempt a stalk I waited, still in the hope that they would make for the boulders. In this I was disappointed, for in a few minutes I saw the female reappear over the top of the hill, about 300 yards off, and was delighted to see that she had failed to catch the steinbuck; but, instead of coming down to the others, she took up a position on the top of an ant-heap, sitting up like a huge cat, when her companions saw her and went up to her; they all disappeared over the top of the hill, and I eventually lost them in the bush and long grass on the other side.

WATERBUCK

The Waterbuck (Swahili name, 'Kuru') is common everywhere south of Lake Baringo, near fresh water, and is also found in the vicinity of a good many of the salt-water creeks on the coast. It is particularly plentiful on the banks of the Tana river, and in the Kilimanjaro district on the banks of the Weri Weri. Like most bush-loving antelopes, it is fairly easy to stalk, but is a very tough beast and takes a good deal of killing if not hit in the right place. Its flesh, though much relished by the natives, is coarse and exceedingly rank—indeed that of an old bull is almost uneatable. Near the coast it is generally found in thick bush, unless the sportsman is up very early and out by daylight, when he may find it on its feeding-ground in the open. Up country, where it is less hunted, it is more partial to park-like and open bush country. On the banks of the Weri Weri herds of fifteen to twenty were not uncommon, but the ordinary herd consists of a bull and three or four cows. Single bulls are also constantly met with. The waterbuck is a grass feeder.

THE SING-SING

The Sing-Sing (also known to the natives as 'Kuru') resembles the waterbuck in habits, but is easily distinguished from it by its darker colour, and by a considerable amount of rufous hair on the top of the head, as well as by an entirely white rump in place of the elliptical white band of the other. The horns are also as a rule longer and more massive than those of the waterbuck, the horns of the latter never growing to the size they do in South Africa. It is not met with until near Lake Baringo, and extends west to Uganda, where it was first obtained by Captains Speke and Grant. It is fairly plentiful in the open bush country of Turkwel; but it does not appear to go about in such large herds as the waterbuck. I have never seen more than five or six together, and more often a bull and two or three cows.

THE GREATER KUDU

The Greater Kudu is a rare beast in East Africa, and is only found in certain places. There are always a few in the Teita country west of Ndara and Kisigao and on the banks of the Tsavo river, down which it ranges from the head-waters to the Sabaki, and then north up the Athi river. All these places are more or less undulating, very rough, dry, and stony, and covered with thick bush.

LESSER KUDU

The Lesser Kudu (Swahili, 'Kungu') is very plentiful on the banks of the Tana river. In 1885-86 it was also numerous at Merereni, on the coast. A few are found in suitable places near Taveta, and as far west as the Sogonoi hills in German territory. They appear, however, to be confined principally to the belt of dry bush country extending from the coast for about 100 miles inland, and I think that very few of them range west of the Masai country. I was told by Messrs. Hobley and Bird-Thompson, on their return from a trip up the Tana river in 1891, that many of these antelopes had fallen victims to the cattle disease (anthrax), and that they found several dead in the bush between the river and the northern boundaries of Ukambani. These beautiful beasts are bush feeders. They should be sought for in the early morning, and again in the evening in the open bush which usually fringes thick bush, in which they take up their quarters for the day. They are generally found in small parties of two or three does and a buck, though, like the bush-buck, both single bucks and does are often seen by themselves. At Merereni, in 1886, I witnessed a fight between two bucks. On emerging from the bush I suddenly came across them, and watched them for about a quarter of an hour as they fought with great fury, in spite of my being to windward of them, and not more than 400 yards off at the time. They fought so furiously, and kept their heads together so long, that I thought they had got their horns locked together, and I attempted to take advantage of them whilst in this position, and ran across the sandy open space intervening between us, but before I got within range they separated and bolted. The jumping powers of the lesser kudu are simply marvellous. When I first went to Africa, I kept a record of the length of the strides of the various game-beasts when at full gallop, but unfortunately lost it, and never took it up again. I remember, however, measuring the jump of one of these beasts, which struck me at the time as being very wonderful. She had been chased by a hyæna along a narrow footpath in dense bush. In the middle of the path there was a thick green bush about 5 ft. high, round which the path took a turn, and then went straight on again. The kudu had taken a flying leap over this bush, and the distance between the spoor of her hind feet where she took off and the edge of the bush was 15 ft. The diameter of the bush was 6 ft., and the distance from the edge of the bush on the further side to where she landed—i.e. to the spoor marks of her hind feet—another 10 ft., in all 31 ft. The hyæna had given up the chase some thirty yards further on, where the kudu had entered the bush. The note of alarm of this beast is a distinct and loud bark, much resembling that of an 'old man' baboon. Lesser kudu appear to bark only when they scent danger but are unable to see it. As I have said before, many natives will not touch the flesh of this beast, as it causes them great pain in the mouth and gums.

BUSH-BUCK

The Bush-buck (Swahili, 'Mbawara') is common everywhere on the coast, and I have seen it as far west as the edge of Mau forest. In habits it much resembles the lesser kudu, but, as a rule, is found in much thicker bush, and where all vegetation is more luxuriant. Although I have seen great numbers of bush-bucks, I have never noticed more than two together, except on one occasion when I saw a male and two females; but animals of either sex are more usually found by themselves. They are rarely seen out in the open or far from thick covert. They are often found day after day in, or quite near to, the same spot.

IMPALA

The Impala (Swahili name, 'Nswala') is not, I believe, known on the coast, though some sixty miles inland it is met with in small herds. At Adda and in the Teita country it is plentiful, and is found as far north as Turkwel, in suitable localities. It is never seen very far from water, and is partial to park-like, open bush and thinly-wooded country. The best heads I have ever seen have been obtained between Lakes Naivasha and Baringo, particularly in the vicinity of the small salt lake Elmateita, where these beautiful beasts inhabit the open woods of juniper-trees.

Impalas congregate in herds varying from eight or ten up to 150 in number. In the small herds there is usually only one adult buck, but in the larger herds there are several. I have seen herds composed entirely of bucks. On account of the nature of the ground which they usually frequent they are fairly easy to stalk. When alarmed they have a curious habit of bounding up into the air, and present an amusing sight when many of them are jumping about at the same time. In common with many other bush-loving antelopes, they often have difficulty in making out the direction whence a shot comes, and if the sportsman takes care to keep out of sight he may get several shots before they finally make off. The impala is a grass feeder.

The Walleri

LITHOCRANIUS WALLERI

The Walleri is plentiful on the banks of the Tana river, and there are a fair number at Merereni. It is also found in the Kilimanjaro district. The East African walleri is very much smaller than the one found in the Somali country. There is no mistaking this antelope for any other, on account of its extraordinarily long and thin neck, which in a fully adult buck, killed by myself at Merereni, was only 10 ins. in circumference; two females measured 7 ins. each round the neck. When walking and seen at a distance they look not unlike pigmy giraffes, as they carry their long necks stretched out at an angle. They frequent the open bush fringing the outskirts of dense thickets, into which they at once retreat on being disturbed. Their note of alarm is a low short 'buzz!' The Walleri is essentially a bush feeder. At Merereni I once watched a doe feeding on a small-leaved bush, not unlike the privet in appearance, and several times saw her rear up on her hind-legs, bend down a branch with her forelegs, and feed on the leaves in this upright position like a goat. This quaint-looking little antelope, like the bush-buck, will haunt one particular spot, and may be seen in or quite near to it for weeks together. The sportsman, if encamped near a place where he has seen one of them in the morning, but has been unable to get a shot at it, may have a very fair chance of finding it feeding about the same place if he goes out again in the evening between five o'clock and sundown, keeping close to the edge of thick bush. These bucks are very shy, and by no means easy to stalk; and as they have a happy knack of hiding behind bushes in the most effective manner, they are very difficult to see.

THE DUYKER

The Duyker (Swahili name, 'Ngruvu') is found throughout British East Africa, and I have shot it as far west as Tunga's in Upper Kavirondo. At Taveta it frequents the low stony hills covered with long grass and short scrub. On the coast it is found in open bush country, and also in low scrub and grass some eighteen inches high. Unless this covert has been lately burnt, the duyker rarely gives the sportsman the chance of stalking it. All the duyker I have myself got have been killed with a shotgun and B.B. shot; but as a duyker is very tough I should recommend sportsmen to use S.S.G., which would lessen the chance of their getting away wounded. A duyker when in covert lies very close, and will almost allow itself to be trodden on, when it will go off with such a rush and noise through the long grass that the sportsman might be led to believe that it was a bush-pig or something equally large until he caught a glimpse of it thirty to forty yards off. This glimpse will probably be his only chance of a shot at it.

The Red Duyker, or 'bush-buck,' as it is more commonly called by the few sportsmen who have shot it, was first obtained by Sir Robert Harvey in 1887 on the forest-clad banks of the river Lumi. He unfortunately blew its head off with the .577 Express bullet and did not keep the skin. Later on I devoted ten days exclusively to hunting this rare and very local little beast in Kahe forest west of Taveta, and had the good fortune to bag two good bucks, from which this new species was described. This buck is entirely confined to dense forests or forest-clad watercourses. It is very shy, and owing to the nature of the ground it frequents is very difficult to approach, as the sportsman has great difficulty in moving along silently on account of the ground being thickly covered with dead leaves. Added to this it is very hard to see, as its colour, in the shade, assimilates so closely to its surroundings. It is very solitary in its habits, and I have never come across more than one at a time.

The Mountain Duyker has so far only been obtained by Dr. Abbot, the American naturalist, who secured one specimen on Kilimanjaro at an elevation of 9,000 to 10,000 ft. It is highly probable that it may also be found at high altitudes on Mounts Kenia, Elgon, and Ruwenzori, and on this supposition I include it as a British East African species.

BLUE BUCK

The Blue Buck is a little beast which I have only found in one place—in the dense undergrowth of bush in the Witu forest near Lamu. I believe it is also met with in the small forest belts in Uganda.[13] In habits it much resembles the paa (*Neotragus Kirkii* and *Nanotragus moschatus*), and is known to the natives of Lamu and Witu by that name.

THE KLIPSPRINGER

The Klipspringer is only found in rocky broken ground on the slopes of some of the hills and large 'earth boils' from Teita to Turkwel. It would probably have to be specially sought for, as there is little or no other game to attract the sportsman to its rocky strongholds.

THE PAA

The Paa (*N. Kirkii*) is found throughout East Africa in thick and open bush on dry sandy soil. It is exceedingly plentiful on Manda island opposite Lamu, Merereni, the thick bush east of Taveta, and again in Ngaboto in the Suk country. It is the smallest of the East African antelopes, and is usually bagged with a shotgun and No. 5 shot, as it darts about among the bush and scrub like a rabbit. The flesh of this little beast has a strong flavour of musk and is very disagreeable to eat at all times, but in the rutting season is altogether uneatable; the natives, however, revel in it. Its note of alarm is between a shrill whistle and a scream. It feeds on the leaves of various shrubs, and doubtless its curious little prehensile nose is admirably adapted to securing its food. The paa is found throughout the year in the driest and most arid wildernesses, where for several months there is neither rain nor even a drop of standing water for many miles round. It is therefore quite evident that the juices of the vegetation on which it feeds and the dews at night are sufficient for its requirements. The best way to obtain this little beast is to take three or four men to act as beaters, and they must thoroughly beat every bush at all likely to hold a buck, as it is in the habit of lying very close and takes a good deal to move it, but when once started affords capital snap-shots.

---

[13] The small *Celalolophus* from Uganda has lately been described as a new species of *C. equatorialis*.

GRAVE ISLAND GAZELLE

The *N. moschatus*, commonly known as 'Grave Island gazelle,' derives this name from being for a long time only obtained on a small island in Zanzibar harbour on which the English cemetery is situated. How this little antelope got on to this and another small island no one knows, as it is not at present known to exist on the islands of Zanzibar or Pemba. It is, however, found in the thick bush behind Frere Town, the Church Mission station at Mombasa, and also in the Duruma country. It is, like the paa, a bush-feeder, and requires little or no water.

THE SITATUNGA

I might add another species to the already long list of British East African antelopes—the Sitatunga (*Tragelaphus Spekei*). My friend Mr. Gedge, in a letter to the 'Times' from Uganda, mentions that he shot several antelopes of a species which he concludes to be the sitatunga on an island in Victoria Nyanza, but until he returns to England with a specimen his inference cannot be verified.[14]

B. senegalensis

C. Whymper

In conclusion, a few remarks on the climate of British East Africa and the expenses of a shooting trip may be of use.

[14] It has now been verified from specimens obtained by Captain W. H. Williams, R.A.

The climate, taking it all round, is good. On the coast, where the temperature in the shade ranges between 82° and 86° (Fahr.) throughout the year, the climate is, on account of the moist atmosphere, rather relaxing. In the vicinity of mangrove swamps it is malarious, more especially if there are large expanses of reeking mud-flats exposed at low tide, alive with thousands of small crabs, which bore into the mud and let out the poisonous gases. When an elevation of 1,200 to 3,000 ft. is reached the climate is delightful, as between eight and nine o'clock A.M., if not before, a cool breeze generally springs up, and the heat is rarely excessive, excepting in such places as are sheltered from the wind. The nights are cool and refreshing, often quite chilly, when an ulster or warm dressing-gown is almost a necessity. Higher up still, from 5,000 to 6,000 ft. (the altitudes of the Athi plains and vicinity of Lake Naivasha), and up to 8,000 and 9,000 ft. (the altitudes of Lykepia and Mau), it is quite cold at night. At Mianzini in September 1889 the thermometer registered 6° of frost.

In the matter of health the amount of exercise that the sportsman will have to take will do far more to keep him fit and well than anything else. Care should, however, be taken to avoid chills, and any unnecessary exposure to the sun, as fever contracted up country is more often to be attributed to one of these causes than to malaria. The complaints to which Europeans are most liable are fever, dysentery, diarrhœa, sun headache (which often develops into fever), for which Anti-pyrine is an excellent remedy, and ulcerated sores from scratches and abrasions.

With regard to snakes and other noxious creatures, there are many of them, and of many varieties. Most of the snakes are non-poisonous, but there are several, including a species of green whip-snake, a large black water-snake, a cobra, a small viper, and the puff-adder, which are very poisonous. The last of these, and perhaps the most deadly, is also the most common, and is often met with both when out shooting and when the ground is being cleared for camping. These little 'disagreeables,' however, are rarely, if ever, thought about, otherwise life in East Africa would be intolerable. It is very rarely that one hears of anyone being bitten, and I only know of three instances, all the victims being porters, who are of course more liable to such misfortunes owing to their going about bare-legged. In case of an accident a bottle of ammonia should always be included in the medicine-chest, and permanganate of potash used hypodermically is also said to be an excellent remedy. A syringe and glass cylinder to hold a solution of the latter, fitted into a handy little pocket-case, can always be carried.

The expense of an expedition entirely depends on the number of sportsmen forming the party, and on their individual requirements, some men being more luxurious than others. Roughly speaking a caravan of fifty porters, five askaris, and a headman will cost 65*l.* a month, and this will include cost of trade-goods to buy food. It does not, however, include interpreters, cook, tent-boy, or gun-bearers, whose wages vary according to their qualifications; neither does it include arms and ammunition for the men. Interpreters receive the same food allowance ('posho') as headmen; cooks and tent-boys the same as askaris. If two or more sportsmen go out together, their individual expenses would be a little less than if they had gone alone. There are very few places, however, where four men can comfortably shoot from the same camp without interfering with each other's sport, although it can be managed by three. If a party is made up of four guns, I should recommend them to divide, on arriving at their headquarters, and shoot in different localities from two camps.

CHAPTER XVII

THE LION IN SOUTH AFRICA

BY F. C. SELOUS

In those districts of Southern Africa made historic by the stirring narratives of Sir Cornwallis Harris and Gordon Cumming, where but half a century ago every species of wild game native to that part of the world, from the ponderous elephant to the graceful springbuck, was to be met with in such surprising numbers that vast tracts of country assumed the appearance of huge zoological gardens, one may now travel for days without seeing a single wild animal. In British Bechuanaland the elephant and the rhinoceros are as extinct as the mammoth in England, and the myriads of zebras and antelopes which Sir Cornwallis Harris saw daily scouring the plains in commingled herds are now only represented by a few scattered hartebeests, blesbucks, and gemsbucks, which still exist in the country bordering on the Kalahari desert. The high veldt of the Transvaal too, once black with innumerable herds of wildebeests, blesbucks, and springbucks, is at the present day for the sportsman or the naturalist a dreary waste, more devoid of animal life probably than any other sparsely populated country in the world. With the antelopes and buffaloes the beasts of prey have disappeared too, and in many districts where fifty years ago the magnificent music of the lion's roar was the traveller's constant lullaby, no sound now disturbs the silence of the night, except indeed the ceaseless rattle of the quartz-crushing machinery in the mining districts.

Yet, in spite of the total disappearance of the game in certain districts, it would be a great mistake to say that there is no more big game in Southern Africa; for if we take, as I think one fairly may, South Africa to mean all the country south of the great Zambesi river, then with the single exception of the true quagga (*Equus quagga*), which is undoubtedly extinct, every wild animal encountered by travellers in the early part of this century may still be met with; for the great square-mouthed rhinoceros (*R. Simus*) yet lingers in northern Mashonaland; elephants and black rhinoceros (*R. bicornis*) are still numerous in certain districts; whilst as for buffaloes, zebras, and various species of antelopes, it is difficult to believe that these animals ever existed in greater numbers in Bechuanaland than may still be seen in South-Eastern Africa, in the neighbourhood of the Pungwe river. Here, too, lions are still numerous; so much so that during a period of six weeks spent by the writer in this district last year, 1892, not one single night passed that they were not heard roaring, whilst upon several occasions three or four different troops of them roared round the camp at the same time.

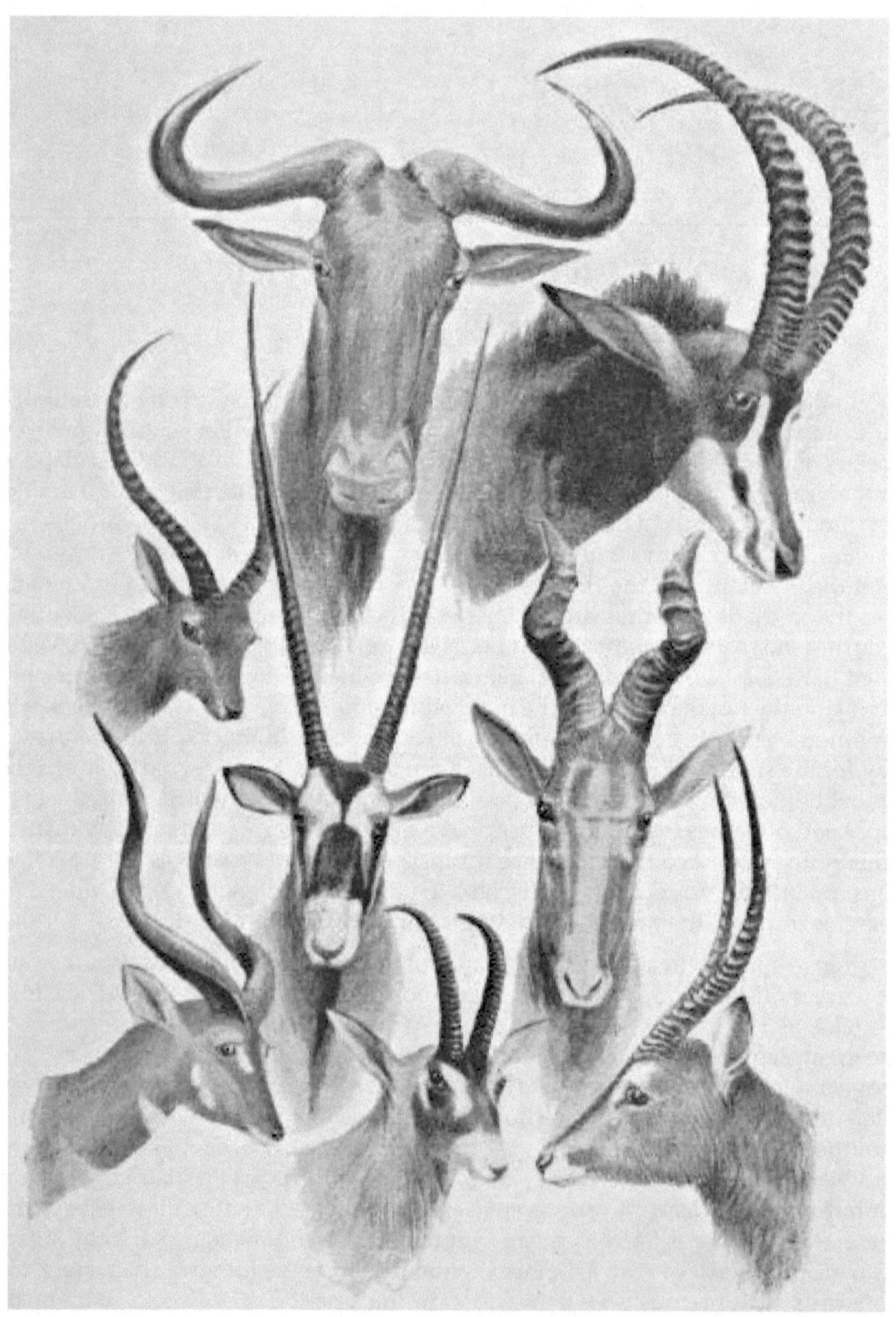

A Group of South African Antelopes

C. Whymper

As it is impossible within the limits of a single chapter to give a detailed account of all the rich and varied fauna of South Africa, I will now proceed to say a few words concerning the animal to which I have twice referred, and whose skin is the trophy most coveted by sportsmen. I am often asked, 'Is the lion a dangerous beast, or is he a cur?' This is a difficult question to answer, for not only do lions differ much individually in character—one when encountered showing himself to be an animal of a very cowardly nature, whilst another may prove to be very bold and savage—but it would even seem that the disposition of lions, in general, varies in the different large areas of country over which they range. Nothing has struck me more than the different behaviour exhibited by lions encountered in Eastern Africa during several years of travel by a friend of my own and those which I have myself met with in South Africa. My friend is a careful naturalist, an experienced hunter, and a man of absolute reliability, and what he has told me concerning the lions he has met with in Eastern Africa is so different from my own experience that I can only conclude that, speaking generally, those animals differ, as I say, in character in different portions of the continent; and if that is the case, my remarks will only apply to lions in Southern Africa.

I ought first to say, however, that though my experience of lions is considerable, it is not as great as many people might suppose. I have never missed an opportunity of shooting them when it presented itself, but I have never systematically hunted these animals. Thus, although I have spent twenty years in the wilds of Africa, I have only shot twenty-five lions when entirely by myself, though besides these I have assisted at the shooting of eleven others, and helped to skin eight more in which there were no bullets of mine. The greatest number of lions I have shot in one season is only seven. Altogether this is a very poor record compared to the prodigious bags of lions made of late years in Somaliland by Colonel Arthur Paget, Lord Delamere, Colonel Curtis, Lord Wolverton and other English sportsmen; though I think that there are portions of South-Eastern Africa where equally large bags might be made, if one devoted oneself systematically to lion hunting. Such as my experience has been, however, I will give it.

When lions are encountered in the daytime, they will almost invariably give way before the presence of man, even when several are together feeding upon the carcase of an animal they have just killed, and at a time when they are presumably hungry. In parts of the country where firearms have been much used, lions will sometimes retreat so rapidly when they are disturbed that it is next to an impossibility to get a shot at one. I remember one cold cloudy winter's morning in Mashonaland coming suddenly upon a male lion, as he was chasing a small herd of koodoo cows. When he observed me, he at once stopped and gazed fixedly at me for just one instant of time, and then, wheeling round, went off through the forest at such a pace that, had I not been well mounted, I should never have seen him again. As it was I galloped after him, and when he found that my horse was gaining on him, he stopped and stood at bay, when I shot him. In parts of the country where they have been but little disturbed, lions will only walk slowly away when unexpectedly encountered in the daytime, often turning round and gazing fixedly at the intruder, and sometimes growling savagely and twitching their tails angrily the while. A lioness with cubs, or a savage lion feeding at a carcase, will occasionally come rushing forwards when disturbed, with every demonstration of anger, and an apparent determination to charge home. But in the great majority of even these exceptional cases such a demeanour would be nothing more than a demonstration, only made in order to frighten the intruder away; and if the man were to stand his ground, the lion would retreat. I remember an instance of this. Two friends of mine having shot some elephants on a Saturday, resolved to take a rest on the following day. Early on the Sunday morning some of their Kafirs having gone up to cut some meat from the carcase of one of the elephants, returned with the news that there was a lion there that would not let them come near it. Wood and Clarkson thereupon at once took their heavy old muzzle-loading elephant guns, the only weapons they possessed, and went to investigate. As they approached the carcase, Clarkson told me they could see nothing of the intruder and thought he had decamped, but when they were still some hundred and fifty yards distant, a magnificent dark-maned lion suddenly appeared from behind the dead elephant, and came rushing towards them, holding his head low between his shoulders, twitching his tail from side to side and growling savagely, and looking as if he meant to charge home. He only came on for about fifty yards however, and then stood growling, and, as my friends said, looked grand in his fury.

Clarkson had dropped on his knee to get a steadier shot with his heavy elephant gun, but Wood, who was an old and very experienced hunter, said, 'Don't fire, Matt; let him come nearer.' Clarkson thereupon took his gun from his shoulder and waited. Suddenly he told me the lion, after having stood for some seconds looking the picture of rage and determination not to give way, stopped growling, and turning quickly round, made a bolt through the forest, past the carcase of the elephant, just as hard as he could go. No one fired at him, as heavy elephant guns were not suitable weapons for shooting quickly at a comparatively small animal moving rapidly amongst the stems of trees, and so this lion got off scot free. He had only tried to frighten my friends away from the carcase at which he was feeding, but whether if a single unarmed man had come near him he might not have bitten him it is hard to say. During the second year of the occupation of Mashonaland, a prospector named Jones, having lost a donkey, walked out from Salisbury along the main road to look for it. Before he had proceeded far, and when he was still in sight of the huts and houses of the township, he came upon a dead donkey lying near the roadside, and thinking it might be the animal he was in search of, went to examine it, when a lioness by whom the ass had been killed, and who was lying near the carcase, sprang upon him, and seizing him by the shoulder, with her teeth dragged him to the ground, and stood over him growling. Fortunately for Mr. Jones, a young colonist named Swanapool, a lad only fourteen years of age, was at that moment coming along the road with a rifle in his hands, and he at once fired at and killed the lioness before she had inflicted any further injuries on her victim. Mr. Jones, however, had been badly bitten in the shoulder, and was an inmate of the hospital at Salisbury for some considerable time in consequence. The two anecdotes I have just related will serve to show that in Southern Africa lions do not invariably at once beat a retreat when brought face to face with man in the daytime. These cases are, however, exceptional, and it may fairly be said that, speaking generally, these great cats have a most wholesome dread of the human biped, and avoid him as much as possible by daylight, but when once the sun has set and the darkness of night has come on, lions become bold and fearless, and often, when urged on by hunger, incredibly reckless and daring. It is by no means unusual for oxen to be seized at the yokes or horses to be killed inside a stable, or when tied to the wheel of a waggon; whilst in Mashonaland alone four men were carried off and eaten by lions during the first two years of the occupation of that country. One of these unfortunates was a young man who was about to start a market-garden in the neighbourhood of Umtali settlement. He had gone away with a cart and four oxen to buy some native meal at one of the Kafir kraals, and had outspanned for the night at a spot about six miles distant from the little township. The oxen were tied up to the yokes, and Mr. Teale was lying asleep under the cart, alongside of a native, when a lion walked up, and, seizing him by the shoulder, carried him off and killed and ate him. This lion, be it noted, showed a refined taste in disregarding the oxen and the Kafir, and seizing the European. It is supposed that a lion and a lioness took part in the feast. The lioness was subsequently shot, and the head and one of the feet of the unfortunate market-gardener recovered, but the lion escaped.

As an example of much greater boldness, let me relate the following anecdote. In August 1892, Captain Graham, the resident magistrate of Umtali, visited Marauka's kraal with a patrol of twelve mounted white men and a small native contingent. A large camp was formed at the foot of the hill on which Marauka's village was situated, the horses were tied on a picket-line, and several large fires were lighted in different parts of the camp. In the middle of the night a lioness walked right past the outside fires, passed close by two white men who were covered by their blankets, and seized a native who was lying alongside of a fire in the centre of the camp. She caught him by the shoulder, dragged him past the outside fires, and then dropping him, gave him some terrible bites about the head and arm. The man had, of course, shouted out when he was seized, and he retained his presence of mind in a marvellous manner, for when some of the white men approached with a lantern, he called out, 'Don't shoot now, the lion is lying on me'; this was translated by the interpreter, and presently the plucky fellow again spoke and said, 'Now fire, she's standing up over me.' Three shots were then fired into the lioness, which was very badly wounded, and ultimately killed the next morning. The wounded native was then pulled back into the camp, but, though conscious, he was so terribly mutilated that he died early the next day. The lioness was now *hors de combat*, but two young lions that were with her soon afterwards invaded the camp and attacked the horses tied on the picket-line. Five of these broke away all tied together, and all five were more or less scratched and bitten, two of them very severely. None were killed, however, and ultimately all of them recovered. Later on one of the young lions came back to the camp, and carried off a saddle, which it tore all to pieces. When day broke, the wounded lioness was shot, but the young lions had made off, and were not seen. I have given this anecdote because I was in Umtali shortly after the return of the patrol and spoke with all the men who had taken part in it, and saw the horses with their wounds still unhealed, and the remnants of the saddle that had been torn all to pieces. However, although in the interior of South Africa a certain number of natives are killed annually by hungry lions, I do not think that these animals are so destructive to human life as are tigers in India. Although cases do occur, I think it very exceptional for a lion to kill human beings for food except when driven to it by hunger. In the neighbourhood of the Pungwe river, where game of all kinds abounds, and where lions are also very numerous, the natives assured me that the lions never troubled them; but in Northern Mashonaland, where game is comparatively scarce, the lions in 1886 became so dangerous, and carried off so many women whilst they were working in their cornfields, that the few scattered families of Mashunas living in the district to the north of Lo Magondi's deserted the country. Old lions, whose bodily powers are on the wane, are probably the most dangerous. When they can no longer catch and pull down wild animals, they approach the native villages and prey on the goats and dogs, and if they are not destroyed soon take to killing women and children. In countries where both game and lions abound, I presume that the old and weakly lions can always get a living, like the hyænas, on the remains of the carcases of animals killed by younger and more vigorous animals. As man is not the lion's usual food, most lions would probably give way before a human being even on a dark night and allow him to pass unmolested, provided they were not hungry; but were a man to come within the ken of a hungry lion under such circumstances I should look upon him as a dead man whether he were armed or not, for the lion would probably spring upon him suddenly from behind and give him no time to make use of his weapon. Therefore I look upon it as foolhardy in the extreme to walk along a road or a native footpath, on a dark night, in countries which are infested by lions, if you can avoid doing so. You may walk twenty times at night before meeting a lion at all; and you may meet twenty lions before encountering a really hungry animal; but when you do at last meet him, he will, most assuredly, be the last lion that you will have any knowledge of in this world.

There is an old fable, still believed in more or less, that the lion is a very clean feeder, and that he will eat nothing but the flesh of an animal that he has killed himself. That has not been my experience. On the contrary, I have found that, even where game abounds, lions will seldom pass the carcase of an animal killed by a hunter, but will almost invariably feed on it, even though the flesh be quite putrid. Sometimes when several elephants have been shot, lions will feast on the stinking carcases as long as there is any soft meat left, and I have known this to happen in a country where game of various kinds was plentiful, especially zebras, which are always a favourite food of lions. However, although the lion is not a clean feeder in the sense that he will only eat fresh meat, he is wonderfully dexterous in disembowelling a carcase, without messing the meat. When Kafirs kill an animal and cut it up, they almost invariably tear open the paunch and intestines and spill the contents over the meat, making everything in such a filthy mess that some people would lose all appetite at the very sight of it; but lions invariably remove the interior economy of their victims with a surprising neatness, and without defiling the meat in any way. When they have killed an animal, they will sometimes commence feeding on the soft meat of the inside of the buttocks, tearing the carcase open at the anus; but in nine cases out of ten they work through the thin skin of the flank, at the inside of the hind leg, and then remove the paunch and entrails.

After this they eat the heart, liver, lungs, and kidneys; next, as a rule, they attack the buttocks and tear off the soft meat in mouthfuls, swallowing it in great lumps, often with the skin attached. If the animal they have killed is fat, they will eat the whole brisket, bones and all, and also chew off all the ends of the ribs, but they never swallow any of the larger and harder bones. The paunch and entrails are almost invariably left untouched, and are often covered over with earth and grass. But there are exceptions to every rule, and I think it is indisputable that in some cases lions will eat both the entrails and the paunch of an animal they have killed.

In March 1892, whilst examining the country between Manica and the East coast, in company with Mr. Jesser Coope, with a view to laying out a new waggon road between Umtali township and the railway terminus, we came suddenly upon the remains of a buffalo which had been killed only a few hours previously by a number of lions. These animals must have heard us approaching, and only retreated into the long grass just as we rode up, and as the whole country was covered with grass eight feet high all pursuit was hopeless. Judging by the number of distinct 'lay places' round the carcase of the buffalo, which were ten in number, there must either have been ten lions, or five, each of which had lain down in two different places. The latter number, I think, is the true estimate, and the party probably consisted of an old lion and four lionesses, as there were no cub spoors. The carcase of the buffalo, from which almost all the meat had been eaten, had been disembowelled in the usual neat and cleanly manner, and at a distance of some ten yards off it stood two mounds, apparently of earth and grass. I pointed these out to my young friend, and said, 'The lions have buried the paunch and entrails of the buffalo beneath those mounds.' This work had been done most effectually, a space of several yards square having been cleared of grass, all of which, together with a great deal of earth, had been piled up on the two mounds. Wishing to sit up that night and watch over the carcase, we did not at the moment disturb the earth and grass-covered heaps or do anything which might have aroused the suspicions of the lions, but rode back to our waggon, and returning at once with some Kafirs built a shelter at the foot of a tree, a few yards from the carcase of the buffalo, in which Mr. Jesser Coope and myself took up our positions for the night, the Kafirs returning to the waggon. However, strange to say, the lions never put in an appearance, and so our watch was in vain and we neither saw nor heard anything more of them. On the following morning I commenced to turn over the heaps in which I thought the paunch and entrails were hidden, in order to get some of the large horned dung beetles which are common in this part of Africa, and I very soon found to my surprise that, though the vegetable contents of the paunch and entrails had been hidden from view, there was no animal matter there whatever, so that I cannot but conclude that in this instance, at any rate, the lions had eaten all the animal portions of the paunch and entrails of a recently killed animal.

Two instances have come under my notice of lions eating the remains of one of their own species, and I think that when hungry they would never be above such acts of cannibalism, but they would probably prefer something else, just as a shipwrecked sailor would prefer Polar bear to a steak off the comrade who had drawn the fatal lot. But with lions, as with shipwrecked sailors, necessity knows no law, and I don't think any the worse of them because they are occasionally driven to cannibalism.

There has been much discussion as to the manner in which lions kill their prey. In 'Wild Beasts and their Ways,' the last of the many interesting works on travel, sport and natural history for which Englishmen are indebted to Sir Samuel Baker, that great authority says that the lion uses his paw in attack with which to deal a crushing blow in contradistinction to the tiger, which only makes use of its claws to hold its prey. Now it is always possible that in a vast continent like Africa animals of one species may develop different habits in widely separated portions of the country; but, however that may be, all my experience goes to show that, in Southern Africa, lions kill their prey very much in the same way as Sir Samuel Baker tells us tigers do in India; that is, they use their claws to hold their victim, and do the killing with their teeth. A single large male lion will sometimes kill a heavy ox or a buffalo cow, without using his teeth at all, by breaking its neck, or rather causing the frightened beast to break its own neck. Almost invariably when an ox or a buffalo has been killed by a single lion, deep claw marks will be found on the muzzle of the animal, and when that is the case, it will usually be found that the neck has been dislocated. Such animals have been killed in the following manner. We will suppose that a large heavy ox weighing 1,000 lbs. is seized by a lion, whilst grazing or walking, the attack being made from the left side. In that case the lion seizes the ox by the muzzle with its left paw, pulling its head in under it. At the same time with the extended claws of the right paw it holds its victim by the top of the shoulder, its hind feet being firmly planted on the ground. The ox plunges madly forward, and from the position in which its head is held not seeing where it is going, and hampered by the weight of the lion, soon falls, and rolling over, as often as not breaks its neck by the weight of its own body.

When several lions attack an ox in concert, they do not kill the animal as quickly and artistically as a single old male lion would have done, but bite it and claw it all over, especially on the back of the neck, the tops of the shoulder-blades, and on the elbow-joint and the insides of the thighs. This inartistic work may possibly be owing to the fact that when a family of lions is together the old lions leave the younger animals to do the killing, in order to allow them to learn their trade, or else because as soon as an old lion has seized an ox, or a buffalo, or whatever animal it may be, the young ones, being unable to restrain themselves, spring on to it, and bite it all over, with the result that the unfortunate animal is not so cleanly killed as he would have been had he been left to one old lion. Horses, donkeys and zebras are killed by lions by being bitten at the back of the neck, just behind the ears, or else in the throat; but always just round the head. As far as my memory serves me, it is not usual for them to hold a horse by the nose with one paw as they do an ox, and this ruse is, I think, employed by them with horned animals in order to prevent them making use of their horns. Full-grown giraffes are sometimes killed by lions, though not very often. When they do fall victims they are probably seized, and bitten high up in the neck near the head, whilst lying down. Human beings when carried off by lions are usually seized by the head, and in that case are killed instantaneously, the canine teeth being driven through the skull at the first bite. If the head is not the part first bitten it will be the shoulder, and in that case the man will probably have been lying on his side with the one shoulder exposed.

As far as my experience goes, I have never known an instance of a lion carrying its prey raised from the ground. Even such small and light animals as goats, impala antelopes, and young wart-hogs are always held by the head or neck, and dragged along the ground at the side of the lion. When a heavy animal like a horse or an ox is dragged, it is always held by the neck. I simply cannot believe in the possibility of a lion's springing over a palisade and carrying the carcase of an ox with him. When lions break into cattle kraals at night, they never or very seldom spring over the fence even when it is a low one, but work their way through the bottom of the fence. They will sometimes walk round and round a stockaded kraal, that one would have expected them to leap over at once without difficulty, and finally effect an entrance by forcing two poles apart and squeezing through. If suddenly disturbed or fired at at night whilst inside a kraal, they will often spring over the fence in their hurry to get out.

My best Lion

The wild lion of Southern Africa seldom presents the majestic appearance of the picture-book animal, because as a rule he does not carry a long shaggy mane, like the lions one often sees in menageries. Occasionally, however, one sees a wild lion with a fine full dark mane, and then he is a magnificent animal, and one of the noblest prizes that can fall to the sportsman's rifle. I have been much struck by the beauty of the manes of many of the lions shot by Colonel Arthur Paget, Lord Wolverton, Lord Delamere and other sportsmen in Somaliland, and I think there can be no doubt that in that part of Africa the lions grow better manes on an average than in South Africa. The dark parts are, too, of a deeper black. But I have not yet seen a lion's skin from Somaliland with so full a mane as in the three best skins I have seen from South Africa. None of these three splendid animals were, alas! shot by myself. One was killed by the natives in Matabeleland and its skin given me by Lo Bengula, and I still have it in my possession; the second was killed at the Umfuli river in Mashonaland by my friend Cornelis van Rooyen, and the third two years ago within a few miles of the same spot by Hans Lee, the young Boer hunter who accompanied Lord Randolph Churchill on his recent expedition to South Africa.

Although I have seen a very large number of skins of wild lions, I have never yet seen one with long hair growing on the belly as is so common in menagerie lions and invariable in the picture-book animal. A wild lion with a very fine mane will have a tuft of long hair in the arm-pit, another on the elbow, and in some cases a tuft in the flank, but the hair of the belly is always short and close, as on the rest of the body. In the great majority of cases the mane of the wild lion is simply a ruff round the neck with an extension down the back between the shoulders. In very rare and exceptional cases the angle formed between the end of this extension and the point of the shoulder is covered with mane, as it is very commonly in the menagerie lion; but, as a rule, the whole shoulder of the wild lion is devoid of mane. Very often a large heavy full-grown male lion, a splendid animal in strength and symmetry, will have scarcely any mane at all, and his skin is not then a handsome trophy.

There are very few authentic statistics regarding the weight of lions, and I am unfortunately not able to cast much light on this subject. Sir Samuel Baker, in 'Wild Beasts and their Ways,' gives no actual statistics regarding the weight of any particular lions, but appears to think that full-grown well-fed males of this species would on an average weigh from five to six hundred pounds. Not long ago a question was asked at my suggestion through the columns of the 'Field' newspaper on this very subject, but with one exception no satisfactory information was elicited. The exception to which I refer was a communication from Mr. William Yellowly, of South Shields, and ran as follows:—

> In reply to the query in last week's issue of the 'Field' anent the weight of lions, I beg to state that a fine black-maned lion, which died in the late Mrs. Edmond's menagerie at Warrington on February 18, 1875, was sent to me the next day. The following measurements before skinning will give an idea of its magnificent proportions: Length from nose to root of tail, 6 ft. 10 ins.; from

nose to tip of tail, 10 ft.; girth behind shoulder, 4 ft. 9 ins.; girth of upper arm, 1 ft. 10 ins.; height at shoulder 3 ft. 6 ins.; and its dead weight was 31 stone or 434 lbs.

These statistics appear to me to be perfectly reliable, and I regard them as the carefully taken weight and measurements of a large well-fed menagerie lion. How the measurement for length was taken from nose to tip of tail I do not know, but I should fancy along the curves of the head and back, which would make it an inch or two more than if it had been taken in a perfectly straight line between two pegs, one driven into the ground at the nose, and the other at the extremity of the tail of the dead animal. I will now give the few statistics regarding the weight and measurements of wild lions which I can vouch for as being authentic.

Many years ago a lion was shot one night at Kati in Western Matabeleland inside the cattle kraal, where it had killed an ox, and the next morning early the carcase was placed on the large scale used for weighing ivory, which stood under the verandah of one of the traders' houses at only a few yards distance from the cattle kraal. This lion weighed 376 lbs.; it was a large full-grown animal, but in low condition.

In 1887 a lion, shot by myself and friends close to our waggon, was carried into camp and carefully weighed, and was found to turn the scale at 385 lbs. This was a fine animal in good condition but with no fat about him, and my impression at the time was that he would have grown bigger and heavier, as his mane was short, and did not appear to have reached its full length and beauty.

In the end of 1891 I shot a very large lion at Hartley Hills in Mashonaland, and weighed and measured it carefully, as it was killed within three hundred yards of the settlement. This animal, which was a remarkably fine specimen of a wild lion, was in excellent condition, its whole belly being covered with a layer of fat quite half an inch in thickness; it was also a very large animal, as its measurements will show, and I was much surprised to find that its weight was not greater than it proved to be. As the scale on which I weighed it only registered a weight of 220 lbs., I had to skin and cut the lion up, and weigh him by instalments, and the aggregate of the weights was 408 lbs. As a good deal of blood was lost when his head was cut off, I will add two pounds to this figure, and say that this lion's dead weight was not less than 410 lbs. I was much disappointed with this lion, as I expected him to weigh 500 lbs. He was an old animal, and might have weighed more when he was a few years younger, as in spite of being fat and well fed, I don't think his quarters were so rounded and muscular as they might have been. The measurements of his skull—which is now in the collection of the Natural History Museum at South Kensington—are identical with those of the skull of the largest lion shot by Colonel Arthur Paget in Somaliland, as given in Mr. Ward's book of game measurements; the weight of the skull is 5½ lbs., or ½ lb. in excess of the weight of the very large skull of a lion shot by Mr. Geddes in Eastern Africa, the measurements of which are recorded in the same book. I took the extreme length and the standing height of this lion very carefully; taking the distance with a tape line between pegs driven in firstly at the point of the nose and the tip of the tail, and secondly at the top of the shoulder-blade and the ball of the forefoot, the limb being held straight the while. These measurements give his extreme length in a straight line as he lay dead as 9 ft. 11 ins., and his vertical standing height to the top of the shoulder-blade as 3 ft. 8 ins. The height to the top of the mane, however, with which his shoulders were thickly covered and which was his apparent standing height, was exactly 4 ft. When the skin of this lion was pegged out on the ground it measured 11 ft. 9 ins. in extreme length from nose to tip of tail.

The last lion which I shot, on October 3, 1892, near the Pungwe river in South-Eastern Africa, was a very thick-set, massive animal, and enormously fat. He would, I think, have weighed very heavy, but unfortunately I had no scale with me. I took a few careful measurements, however, which are as follows: Length as he lay in a straight line between pegs driven into the ground at the nose and tip of the tail, 9 ft. 1 in.; vertical standing height at shoulder, 3 ft. 4 ins.; girth of body behind the shoulders, 4 ft. 0½ ins.; girth of forearm, 17 ins.; length of pegged-out skin exactly 11 ft. If any conclusion can be drawn from these few statistics, it is I think that a lion which weighs much over 400 lbs. is an exceptionally heavy animal.

One of the most striking characteristics of the lion is his roar, for there is no more magnificent sound in Nature than the volume of sound produced by a party of lions roaring in unison, that is, if one is fortunate enough to be very near to them. It is, however, a rare occurrence to hear lions roar loudly within a short distance of one's camp, and in all my experience, though I have heard these animals roaring upon hundreds of different occasions, I can count the nights on the fingers of one hand when, all unconscious of my near vicinity, a party of several lions has roared freely within 100 yards of where I was lying. Last year, whilst hunting with two companions in the neighbourhood of the Pungwe river, I don't think a single night passed during the six weeks we remained in that part of the country that we did not hear lions, and sometimes three different parties of these animals were roaring round our camp at the same time. But on no single occasion were they ever within a mile of where we were sleeping, and as there are probably few parts of Africa where lions are more plentiful than in this particular district, I think it is quite possible to have had a very considerable experience of African travel and yet never to have heard lions roaring freely at very close quarters. If ever experienced, such a serenade can never be forgotten, for it is at once magnificent yet calculated to fill the soul with awe.

It is a fact I think which admits of no dispute that lions only roar freely in countries where they have not been much disturbed, and where they are practically the masters of the situation, and as soon as a district in which these animals exist is much hunted over, they become comparatively silent. Thus, although lions are still fairly numerous in the neighbourhood of the outlying mining camps in Mashonaland, where they continually make their presence disagreeably felt by killing the donkeys, oxen and horses of the prospectors, they are seldom heard to roar at nights, and I have noticed this same peculiarity in other newly settled districts. Loud roaring is usually, I think, a sign of happiness and contentment, and is indulged in very often when on the way down to drink, after a good meal. Naturally, when hungry and on the look out for their prey, lions do not roar, but remain perfectly silent, and when they attack one's camp at night, the first intimation received of their presence will be given by the cries and struggles of the animal they seize. When standing at bay lions do not roar, but keep up a continuous loud hoarse growling, which can be heard at a considerable distance.

It has always appeared to me that lions succumb more quickly to wounds in the front part of the body, in the neighbourhood of the heart and lungs, than do any of the antelopes living in the same country; but, as with all other animals, shots through the stomach, intestines, or hind-quarters do them little immediate harm, unless indeed the back or leg bones are injured, when they are at once disabled. Although, as I have said earlier in this chapter, lions almost always retreat before the presence of man, they become very savage when wounded, and it is undoubtedly highly dangerous work following them into long grass or thick cover without dogs. My experience in Southern Africa has shown me that wounded lions are far more likely to charge than wounded buffaloes, and although they may be more easily stopped, they are much quicker and more difficult to hit than those animals.

I have only shot lions with two kinds of rifles, a single 10-bore carrying a spherical bullet and six drachms of powder, and a .450-bore Metford rifle by George Gibbs of Bristol, carrying either a 360-grain expanding bullet and ninety grains of powder, or a 540-grain solid bullet and seventy-five grains of powder; and in my opinion the .450-bore with the heavy 360-grain expanding bullet was the more deadly weapon. These expanding bullets, having but a very small hole at the point and a good solid base, possess great penetrating power, as may be believed when I say that they will reach the brain of a hippopotamus, should they enter at the side of the head between the ear and the eye. They will go clean through a lion behind the shoulders, after first making a very large hole through his lungs; and if the animal be struck in the shoulder, the bones will be smashed and the solid end of the bullet will go right through the cavity of the chest, probably piercing the heart, and lodge in the further shoulder. I think that the effectiveness of a rifle depends more on the bullet it carries than on its bore, and should consider a .450-bore rifle such as I have described carrying a 360-grain expanding bullet, with only a small hollow and a good solid end, a more trustworthy weapon than a rifle of a much larger bore carrying a short light bullet with a very large hollow. Doubtless a good .577-bore rifle is a much more powerful weapon than any .450; but the latter if carrying a good heavy bullet will be found very effective for lion shooting, and is not only lighter and handier than the larger rifle, but has no recoil, as the charge of powder is comparatively small.

I will now conclude this chapter by giving an account of the death of the largest lion that it has been my fortune to bag—the same animal whose weight and dimensions I have given on p. 329.

Towards the end of the second year of the occupation of Mashonaland by the British South Africa Company, I was sent to some of the mining camps to the north and west of Salisbury, in order to make a report upon the roads in those districts. On December 8, 1891, I reached Hartley Hills, one of the outlying stations of the British South Africa Company, where, at the time of my visit, there were about twenty Europeans living, most of whom were employed in mining work. Among the company's officials were Mr. Woodthorpe Graham, the gold commissioner and chief magistrate of the district, and Dr. Edgelow, the district surgeon. For some days previous to my arrival at the station, the weather had been very rainy, and the sky dull and cloudy. Hartley Hills are, I may here say, two small 'kopjes,' formed of granite boulders piled up one upon another to a height of perhaps 100 feet above the surrounding country. On one of these hills stood the stores and dwelling houses of Frank Johnson & Co., while the Gold Commissioner and the Doctor occupied the other; and it was at the foot of the latter hill that I outspanned my waggon at a distance of not more than twenty yards from Mr. Graham's compound. As I knew that a great deal of damage had been done lately by one particular lion, which had been seen on several occasions, and which was always described as a very large animal with a fine mane, I was in hopes that he might still be about, and thought that if he would only be good enough to pay a visit to the settlement whilst I was there, I might get a good chance of shooting him, as the wet weather, I imagined, would make the ground sufficiently soft to enable me to track him. Not content with killing oxen and donkeys at some little distance from the settlement, this lion had one night so frightened two valuable horses belonging to Mr. Frank Johnson that they had rushed at the door of their stable, and breaking the thongs with which it was secured, broken out, and run up the hill, where they were both killed within a few yards of a dwelling hut usually occupied by Mr. Johnson, who was, however, absent at the time. The carcase of the one horse was left entirely untouched, I was informed, the animal having been killed by a bite at the back of the head, the lion making his meal off his other victim, which was possibly in better condition.

My first question after my arrival at Hartley Hills was as to whether this lion was still in the district, and I was much disappointed to learn that nothing had been heard of him lately. I found my old friend Mr. Graham just packing up for a three days' trip into the country to the west of the Umfuli river, where some rich gold reefs had been discovered, on which he was anxious to report. That evening I had dinner with Dr. Edgelow, and a long chat afterwards, and as, when it was time to turn in, a drizzly rain was falling, I resolved to take possession of Mr. Graham's hut for the night, instead of going down to my waggon. As it wanted about three days to full moon, it would have been a bright moonlight night had the weather been fine, but as it was the sky was thickly overcast with clouds. Before quitting Dr. Edgelow I remarked to him what a beautiful night it was for a lion, regarded, of course, from a lion's point of view, as these animals are always most dangerous on dark, rainy nights. My waggon, as I have said before, was standing just at the foot of the rocks, the oxen being tied two and two in the yokes; but besides the working cattle I had a spare animal that always lay loose at no great distance from the others. My old shooting horse was tied to the forewheel of the waggon, on the side nearest to the hill, whilst my old servant and waggon-driver, John, and two Kafirs, were sleeping under a shelter which they had made on the other side of the waggon.

I had sat up till a late hour talking with Dr. Edgelow, and when I at last went to bed in Mr. Graham's hut the camp was perfectly quiet, everyone being fast asleep, an example which I was not long in following. I must have slept for some hours when I was suddenly awakened by the discharge of a rifle. Being inside the hut I awoke without any distinct idea of the direction in which the shot had been fired; but the first report was quickly followed by a second which I knew must have been fired from my waggon. Jumping up I at once made for the door of the hut and opened it just as a third shot was fired. 'What's the matter?'I called out in Dutch to John. 'It's a lion, sir; he has killed the loose ox,' he answered, and again fired. This time the shot was answered by a low hoarse growl, the bullet, I suppose, having passed very close to the marauder. I was soon down at the waggon alongside of John, but nothing was to be either seen or heard. The rain had ceased, but as the moon was now down, and it was very cloudy, the darkness was intense, and it was evident that nothing could be done till daylight. John felt sure the ox was dead, as he had heard it make a short rush and fall heavily twice, after which all was still, and as we could now hear nothing, we both thought the lion had been scared away from the carcase by the last shot. It is worthy of remark that, although this ox was seized and killed by a lion within thirty yards of fourteen other oxen that were tied to the yokes, not one of them evinced the slightest alarm, and the greater part of them lay quietly chewing the cud till daylight, undisturbed either by the near proximity of the lion or by the shots fired by John. I suppose the lion had come up below the wind, and never having scented him, they did not realise what had happened. My old horse, however, which was always very nervous and fidgetty in the presence of lions, seemed fully aware of what had occurred, as with ears pricked forwards, and looking in the direction whence the low hoarse growl of the lion had proceeded, he kept shifting his feet uneasily, every now and again snorting loudly.

It did not want more than an hour to daylight, so I had a kettle of coffee made, and then sat over the fire talking with John, and discussing the probabilities of getting a shot at the lion in the morning. As the ground was so wet from the heavy rain that had been falling during the last few days, we both thought we should be able to follow the lion's tracks and come up with him without the aid of dogs, and I was in great hopes that our visitor would prove to be a fine male with a good mane whose skin would fully compensate me for the loss of the ox.

When at last the morning broke dull and misty I went and examined the carcase of the ox, which, as soon as there was a little light, we could see lying just on the edge of the waggon-road coming from Salisbury, at a distance of about thirty yards from the waggon. The ground being so soft from the recent rains we had an excellent opportunity of seeing exactly how this ox had been seized and killed. The lion had evidently approached the unsuspecting animal very quietly whilst it was lying asleep within twenty yards of the other oxen, and seized it unawares, or just as it was rising to its feet after becoming conscious of the unwelcome presence. Then springing upon his victim, with his left paw he had seized it by the muzzle, holding it by the top of the shoulder-blade with the claws of the right paw, and at the same time keeping his hind feet on the ground. Thus held, the ox—a large heavy animal weighing as he stood 900 or 1,000 lbs.—had plunged madly forwards for a few yards, rolled over, regained his feet, and after another plunge again fallen, apparently breaking his neck by his own weight. The lion seemed never to have relaxed the first hold he had taken of the muzzle and shoulder of the ox, and the marks of his hind feet, stamped deep into the muddy ground with outstretched claws, were plainly discernible alongside the tracks of the ox. The ox was ultimately killed by having his neck broken, and lay with his head doubled in under him, there being no mark of a wound upon him but the claw marks on the muzzle and shoulder. Except that one ear had been bitten off, the carcase was untouched, the lion having been scared away by John's bullets, which must have whizzed unpleasantly near him, and caused him to beat a hasty retreat.

'Springing upon his Victim'

C. Whymper

As soon as it was fairly light I saddled my horse, and John and I took up the spoor, which led us down to the little river Simbo, a small stream, about three hundred yards from my waggon, which runs into the Umfuli River, just below Hartley Hills. For about a mile beyond the Simbo we were able to follow without difficulty the tracks of what was evidently a large male lion, as the ground was low-lying and soft from the recent heavy rains; but after this the spoor got into soil of a different nature, thickly covered with short grass, where the footprints left but little trace. Suffice it to say that we followed the tracks for over three hours, and finally lost them in stony ground, and could not manage to pick them up again. For another hour I rode about examining all the patches of bush in the neighbourhood, as I felt sure the lion was somewhere near at hand, waiting for night, to return to the carcase of the ox he had killed. However, as I could not discover his whereabouts or find any further trace of him, I was obliged to give up the pursuit and returned to camp, resolved to sit up and watch the carcase that night.

On again reaching the settlement, Mr. Somerville, who was in charge of Mr. Johnson's compound, informed me that the lion had walked past his cattle kraal, in which there were a few goats, sheep, and calves, and had killed one of the goats by putting his paw between the poles of which the enclosure was made. Seizing the animal by the throat, which he had torn open, the lion had severed the jugular vein, so that the beast bled to death. This had evidently been done before my ox was killed, and apparently out of sheer exuberance of spirits, as no attempt had been made to pull the carcase out of the kraal by forcing two of the poles forming the palisade apart from one another.

After breakfast, I went and examined the ground round the dead ox, with a view to choosing a position from which to watch for the lion. The carcase was lying with its back on the edge of the waggon-road, the hind quarters being nearest to my camp. A small tree was growing close to the extended legs of the dead ox, and actually within six feet of either the fore or hind feet. This tree branched into two main stems at about two feet from the ground, and as a rifle protruded between them would be within three yards of any part of the carcase, I resolved to make a small shelter behind its trunk. I wished to be as near as possible to the carcase, because, on a former occasion, I had lain for several hours one night within ten yards of a dead ox at which lions were feeding without being able to see anything of them, and as they left before daylight I never got a shot at them at all. This time, as I thought it possible that the lion might not come back until after the moon had set, when it would be intensely dark, I was determined to be as close to him as possible. There being only one lion to deal with, I was not much afraid of his interfering with me, at any rate before he was fired at, and so made my shelter as small as possible in order that it should not attract his attention. We first chopped a few straight poles, and leant them together at the back of the tree, and then covered them with some leafy branches.

That evening I had dinner with Dr. Edgelow, and about half-past seven, just as night was closing in, took my rifle and blankets and crawled into my shelter, in which I had only just room to sit upright. John then closed the entrance behind me, and I prepared for a long vigil. As the moon was now within two nights of the full, it would have been a lovely moonlight night had it not been that the sky was overcast with clouds; but these clouds were light and fleecy, so that the moon gave a strong light through them. Looking through the side of my leafy shelter, I could very distinctly see John and the two Kafir boys sitting by their fire at the side of the waggon, as well as the head of my old horse, which was tied to the forewheel on the further side; my oxen, too, I could clearly distinguish, so clearly indeed, that I could make out their colours, and see the raw-hide thongs with which they were tied to the yokes. Some were standing up, and every now and again one of these would move about and rattle the iron trek-chain as he did so, but the greater part of them were lying down chewing the cud contentedly, after a good day's feed. Besides my waggon, I could see, too, all the huts on the hillside within Mr. Graham's compound, and hear the Kafir workboys talking and laughing noisily, as is their wont while sitting round the camp fire of an evening.

As the shooting-hole between the diverging branches of the tree behind which I sat only allowed me to get a view directly over the carcase of the ox, I arranged another opening to the right which gave me a good view up the waggon road along which I thought the lion would most likely come, and I placed the muzzle of my rifle in this opening when I entered my shelter. As the night was so light, I thought it very likely that my vigil might be a long one; for even if he did not wait until the moon had set, I never imagined that the lion would put in an appearance until after midnight when the camp would be quite quiet. Under this impression, I had just finished the arrangement of my blankets, placing some behind me and the rest beneath me, so as to make myself as comfortable as possible in so confined a space, and was just leaning back, and dreamily wondering whether I could keep awake all night, when, still as in a dream, I saw the form of a magnificent lion pass rapidly and noiselessly as a phantom of the night across the moonlit disc of the shooting-hole I had made to the right of the tree stem. In another instant he had passed and was hidden by the tree, but a moment later his shaggy head again appeared before the opening formed by the diverging stems. Momentary as had been the glimpse I had of him as he passed the right-hand opening, I had marked him as a magnificent black-maned lion with neck and shoulders well covered with long shaggy hair. He now stood with his forelegs right against the breast of the dead ox, and with his head held high, gazed fixedly towards my waggon and oxen, every one of which he could of course see very distinctly, as well as my boy John and the Kafirs beside him. I heard my horse snort, and knew he had seen the lion, but the oxen, although they must have seen him too, showed no sign of fear. The Kafirs were still laughing and talking noisily not fifty yards away, and, bold as he was, the lion must have felt a little anxious as he stood silently gazing in the direction from which he thought danger might be apprehended.

All this time, but without ever taking my eyes off the lion, I was noiselessly moving the muzzle of my little rifle from the right-hand side opening to the space that commanded a view of his head. This I was obliged to do very cautiously, for fear of touching a branch behind me and making a noise. I could see the black crest of mane between his ears move lightly in the wind, for he was so near that had I held my rifle by the small of the stock I could have touched him with the muzzle by holding it at arm's length. Once only he turned his head and looked round right into my eyes, but of course without seeing me, as I was in the dark, and apparently without taking the slightest alarm, as he again turned his head and stood looking at the waggon as before. I could only see his head, his shoulder being hidden by the right-hand stem of the tree, and I had made up my mind to try and blow his brains out, thinking I was so near that I could not fail to do so even without being able to see the sight of my rifle. I had just got the muzzle of my rifle into the fork of the tree, and was about to raise it quite leisurely, the lion having hitherto showed no signs of uneasiness. I was working as cautiously as possible, when without the slightest warning he suddenly gave a low grating growl, and turned round, his head disappearing instantly from view. With a jerk, I pulled the muzzle of my rifle from the one opening and pushed it through the other, just as the lion walked rapidly past in the direction from which he had come. He was not more than four or five yards from me, and I should certainly have given him a mortal wound, had not my rifle missed fire at this most critical juncture, the hammer giving a loud click in the stillness of the night. At the sound the lion broke into a gallop, and was almost instantly out of sight.

For a moment I was almost paralysed by the magnitude of the misfortune that had befallen me. That a magnificent black-maned lion should have been within six feet of the muzzle of my rifle, and should yet have escaped, owing to a miss-fire, seemed the very irony of fate. I could scarcely believe that the whole scene was not an illusion or a vivid dream; but when I called out in Dutch, 'Myn Gott, John, myn roer het dopje afgeklap' ('My God, John, my gun has missed fire'), and heard him answer, 'Ik hor em, Sir' ('I heard it, Sir'), then I knew that I had really experienced a most extraordinary piece of ill-luck. It was not yet half-past eight, and the first thing I did was to go up to Dr. Edgelow's hut, and take my rifle to pieces. The cap had been untouched by the striker, and I thought at first that the point of the latter was broken, but I found it in perfect order. Finally I discovered that the miss-fire was owing to the safety-bolt having got so loose that it must have shifted up a little when I jerked the rifle rapidly from one opening to another, and thus prevented the striker from coming down on the cap. After fixing the safety-bolt down to full cock I went to my waggon. I felt sure the lion would not now return, if he came back at all, till just before daybreak, when the moon would have set and it would be very dark.

I was so upset and exasperated by the cruel experience I had met with that I could not lie still or sleep, and so spent the greater part of the night in walking about round my waggon. At last the moon went down, and I then turned in and lay listening, hoping to hear the lion at the carcase, but he did not return, and presently, just as the day was breaking, John brought me the usual early cup of coffee. As I had not slept at all, I told him to see if he could follow the lion's spoor and see in which direction he had gone, and then tried to doze a bit. Presently I got up, when John came up with a broad grin on his face, and said, 'Sir, after the lion went off when your rifle missed fire, he went up to Mr. Johnson's kraal and killed a lot of sheep and goats. One of these he ate in the kraal, and he has taken another away with him. I can see the spoor plainly where he has dragged it along towards the little stream running below Hartley Hills.'

I felt there was yet a chance, and a good one, of retrieving my evil fortune of the previous evening, and at once had my horse saddled up. The spoor of the lion himself was easy enough to follow in the soft ground at the foot of the hill, and the tracking was made all the easier by the fact that he had dragged the goat alongside of him, holding it, I suppose, by the back of the neck, and trailing its hind-quarters on the ground. In less than five minutes after I had put the saddle on my horse we were down at the little stream across which we had followed the lion on the preceding day. Here the ground became stony, and we lost the spoor. John was looking about near the edge of the shallow water, and I had turned my horse's head to look along the bank higher up, when the unmistakable growl of a lion issued from the bushes beyond the rivulet, and at the same time John said 'Daar's hij' ('There he is'). I was off my horse in an instant to be ready for a shot, when he turned round and trotted away, and John ran to try and catch him. I thought the luck was all against me, as I expected the lion would make off and get clean away; but I ran forward, trying to get a sight of him, when he suddenly made his appearance in the bush about fifty yards away, and catching sight of me, came straight towards me at a rapid pace, holding his head low and growling savagely. I suppose he wanted to frighten me, but he could not have done a kinder thing. He came right on to the further bank of the little stream just where it formed a pool of water, and stood there amongst some rocks growling and whisking his tail about, and always keeping his eyes fixed upon me. Of course he gave me a splendid shot, and in another instant I hit him, between the neck and the shoulder in the side of his chest, with a 360-grain expanding bullet. As I pulled the trigger I felt pretty sure he was mine. With a loud roar he reared right up, and coming over sideways fell off the rock on which he had been standing into the pool of water below him. The water was over three feet deep, and for an instant he disappeared entirely from view, but the next instant regaining his feet, stood on the bottom with his head and shoulders above the surface. I now came towards him, when again seeing me he came plunging through the water towards me growling angrily. But his strength was fast failing him, and I saw it was all he could do to reach the bank, so I did not fire, as I was anxious not to make holes in his skin. He just managed to get up the bank, when I finished him with a shot through the lungs, to which he instantly succumbed. He proved to be a splendid specimen of a wild lion, an old animal, but in good condition, with an excellent coat and a full, long, and silky black mane.

This is the largest lion it has yet been my good fortune to kill, and I have given his weight and dimensions in a former part of this chapter. After leaving the carcase of the ox he had killed, which I suppose he considered to be too near to my waggon to be altogether safe, he had gone up to Mr. Johnson's kraal, and, forcing his way in by separating two of the poles that formed the palisade, had deliberately killed seven sheep, seven goats, and one calf. These poor animals had evidently all huddled into a corner, where they had stood paralysed by terror. I examined all the carcases carefully, and found that every one had been killed by a single bite in the head. In every case the long fang-teeth had been driven deep into the brains, which in several cases protruded from the fractured skulls. One sheep had been eaten in the kraal, and a goat had been dragged away to be devoured at leisure; and the assurance of this lion may be imagined when I say that the spot where he had taken up his quarters for the day was within three hundred yards of the compound on the top of the hill.

My best Koodoo

CHAPTER XVIII
BIG GAME OF NORTH AMERICA
BY CLIVE PHILLIPPS-WOLLEY

Many statements to the contrary notwithstanding, I venture to assert that, in spite of the evil doings of the 'scallawag' and the meat-hunter, there is still quite enough big game in many parts of the American continent to amply satisfy the desires of any reasonable big game hunter, meaning by that term one who is content to work moderately hard in an exquisite climate, free from fever and other Oriental troubles, for a few good trophies every season, and enough meat to keep his camp supplied.

It is undoubtedly true that you cannot any longer kill hundreds of head of big game to your own rifle in one season; it is also true that the game laws of Canada and the United States have somewhat curtailed the liberty of the sportsman; but it is true too that amongst English sportsmen the number of those who would care to shoot down hundreds of stags, &c. in one season is limited, and that not a few of them realise that the game laws of America, though often ill-framed and always badly enforced, are still in the best interests of those whom they control. There are, of course, mistakes in every code of laws. For instance, it is a mistake I think to protect sheep absolutely in Colorado, while wapiti are not similarly protected; for sheep are now more numerous there than wapiti, are much less easily obtained by the meat-hunter, and are less profitable to him when he has obtained them.

Still, if the Americans would enforce their own laws as rigidly against the native meat-hunter who makes a profit out of shooting as against the alien who pays for his sport, I think no one could justly complain.

Of course the buffalo has disappeared, and the antelope is not as plentiful as he was, while some of the old shooting grounds dear to the memories of the fortunate hunters of twenty years ago have been very much shot out. This is true; but it is also true that if the successors of the Williamsons, Buxtons, Jamiesons, and others of an earlier day would display as much enterprise as those gentlemen did before them, they would probably find fairly good sport still.

The man who follows another to an old shooting ground, getting there by a well-cut trail, or even by railway, to find camps made and the country thoroughly surveyed, naturally does not get as good sport as the 'first man in,' and does not deserve it.

An old friend, whose reputation as an Indian sportsman stands as high as any man's, told me that, though the old grounds were certainly a good deal shot out in India, he knew that close to them were other grounds unvisited which were almost as good (if not quite as good) as the old ones, and this he proved by sending a subaltern nephew off an old route for a very short distance into a country usually passed by, with the result that he got almost as good sport in the nineties as his uncle had had in the sixties.

So it is in America to-day. One man follows another, as sheep follow their leader, and if you trust to guides they will, of course, take you to the places they know from experience, an experience which has been obtained at considerable cost to the game of the district.

As I write I am reminded of an excellent example of that of which I am writing. There is in British Columbia a certain Irish baronet, a most excellent sportsman, who has probably had better sport with cariboo and grizzly than anyone else in the country. His two favourite grounds are now overrun by his followers, but in the year that *he cut the trail to his* cariboo ground (it took him several days) he had excellent sport, and in Alaska he did so well with bear that next year a friend and myself found that all the skin-hunters in the country were on Sir Richard's tracks. Of course we went elsewhere. So it is always. On the grounds which you find for yourself you may get excellent sport: on the grounds found for you by other people you have hardly a right to expect it.

Before dealing then with the game list of North America in detail, let me say to the intending sportsman, Don't be discouraged by every evil report: go and see for yourself: if possible get a hint as to where game is likely to be and then look for a country yourself, not slavishly following your predecessors or entirely depending upon men whom perhaps you don't know very well to present a stranger with an accurate chart of the best hunting grounds they are acquainted with, the way to which they have discovered by their own hard work.

As in everything else in life, so it is in sport: if you want to get anything worth having, you have got to earn it yourself in one way or another.

There is no royal road to success in the mountains, but there is the old road still for the self-reliant and adventurous who don't stick to old trails and the railroad, and there is still plenty of game, for those who know how to seek it, in Colorado, British Columbia, Washington Territory, Ontario, Alaska, and even in parts of the province of Quebec. So much I dare personally guarantee.

I. PANTHER (FELIS CONCOLOR)

The American Panther (*Felis concolor*) is a beast of many *aliases* but of few virtues. He is the 'painter,' 'catamount,' 'mountain lion,' 'cougar,' 'Californian lion,' or 'puma' of early American legends; but, in spite of his many high-sounding titles, he is a mean, sneaking beast, hiding in dense timber by day, stealing or destroying more sheep in one night than he can eat in six months, affording no sport to anyone, and very little profit even to the fur dealer. Those who hunt the panther generally hunt him with dogs, and no dog is too small for the work, for the American lion will tree before a terrier and let himself be shot by a boy with 'bird-shot.' I am not traducing the beast, for I have myself hunted him with terriers in the States. But let an American authority be heard upon the question. A book was published in 1890 called 'Big Game of North America,' to which several well-known authorities contributed, such as Caton, Van Dyke, and Fannin. The authority referred to, however, is not one of these three, but a Mr. Perry, who maintains that the American lion is not a cowardly animal, and cites in support of his contention six or seven instances in which panthers attacked human beings unprovoked. In the first instance (p. 413) the ferocious animal was defeated and driven off by an heroic boy of twelve armed with an empty brandy-bottle. In the second case a blue-jacket who had deserted from Esquimault and 'found his way through the woods until he rested under the domain of the starry flag,' killed the panther which attacked him there by a 'gladiatorial thrust' with a spade (p. 415). The third and fourth of Mr. Perry's pugnacious panthers behaved somewhat differently—one followed a gentleman, the other followed a lady, and in both cases showed the human beings somewhat marked attentions, licking their hands, gazing 'intently' into their eyes, and tearing off most of their clothes, but nothing more. The fifth panther was caned by a gentleman from Snohomish, and the sixth was stared out of countenance and put to flight by someone from Brownsville, whom the panther had knocked off his horse; but it was reserved for another hero from Snohomish to perform the marvellous feat of catching a panther on the wing ('as it was passing in the air') with 'his left arm round its body just behind the forelegs.' Of course, having got his grip, the gentleman from Snohomish thumped the head of that poor panther with his gun-barrels till it died. In this Homeric struggle the victor lost nothing but the tail of his night-shirt.

Now, no doubt all these stories are quite true, and they undoubtedly prove great courage in someone, but not, it seems, in the panther; so that in spite of Mr. Perry I am obliged to accept the general opinion upon this subject as the correct one, backed as it is by a statement just made to me by Mr. John Fannin, the curator of the British Columbian Museum—an accepted authority in the American press upon such matters, and an 'old timer' who has had many opportunities of observing this beast—that he had never come across a well-authenticated story of a panther showing fight to (much less attacking) a man. From Mr. Fannin I obtained the measurements of the largest panthers out of the twenty-five or so which have been sent to him in late years to be skinned. The longest of these was a male from the mainland of British Columbia, killed on the Frazer river, which measured 8 ft. 2 ins. from the tip of the nose to the tip of the tail. The largest killed upon the island and sent to my friend was also a male which measured 7 ft. 3 ins. One hundred and fifty pounds is the weight of a large panther as given by Mr. J. E. Harting, in some notes published by him upon American mammalia, and I have no doubt that this is about what an average male would weigh, but I am only judging by my eye, and not from any accepted record of the actual weight of any particular beast.

The panther's food consists of small game of all kinds, deer, and more especially sheep and pigs, and other farm produce. In nine cases out of ten the panthers which are killed are found near a sheep ranch, and it is notorious that the men who get panthers are not hunters, explorers, or men on a survey party where only wild game is likely to be found, but rather farmers and others who have stock to look after near a settlement.

Puma (Felis concolor)

C. Whymper

It may be that in Montana and Wyoming the panther grows larger and is more courageous than he is on the Pacific coast; but even there he is held in some contempt by the mountain-men who know him. He has a habit, it is said, of following a belated hunter to camp howling in the most diabolical manner, but he never proceeds to extremities.

Some idea of the number of these beasts upon Vancouver Island and in British Columbia generally may be derived from the fact that the British Columbian Government paid bounties for the scalps of seventy-two in 1892, all but two, I believe, having been killed upon the island.

II. THE GRIZZLY (URSUS HORRIBILIS)

Mr. Sclater, the Secretary of the Zoological Society of London, writes me that the best naturalists only recognise three species of bears in North America, namely: the Grizzly (*Ursus horribilis*), the Black Bear (*Ursus americanus*), and the Polar

Bear (*Ursus maritimus*). My correspondent adds that 'a lot of varieties and sub-species have been made, but not upon any certain characters.' Among these varieties and sub-species may, I suppose, be reckoned *Ursus Richardsonii*, the Alaskan grizzly, as well as a whole host of bears, best known to Western trappers as cinnamon bears, silver-tips, roach-backs, bald-faces, and range bears.

Luckily for me, the question of species is one for naturalists rather than for sportsmen to decide; the claim to rank as a distinct species appearing to rest rather upon a beast's anatomy than upon his outward appearance and manner of life.

Dead Grizzly

From a photograph by A. Williamson, Esq

Having studied bears with some care and under favourable circumstances in more than one portion of the globe, I incline to the belief that the different species cross almost as freely as do different breeds of dogs; and certainly it seems probable that upon the North American continent all the different varieties owe their origin to the grizzly or the black, or to a union between the two. In this view I am supported by such a practical field naturalist and sportsman as Dr. Rainsford, as well as by a number of the best hunters and trappers whom I have met, and by certain very significant facts. Dr. Rainsford alludes to the first of these facts in his admirable article upon the Grizzly Bear in 'The Big Game of North America.' He says: 'I myself have shot three young bears going with one sow, one almost yellow, one almost black, and another nearly grey. I have seen ordinary black bears, with year-old grizzly cubs, shaped differently from the mother, unmistakably owing both their shape and colour to the parentage of the male grizzly.' This is the evidence of Dr. Rainsford, and I have heard similar statements as to the occurrence of different coloured cubs in the same litter, not once but a score of times, from Indians and white men who had passed their lives in the mountains; and I have round me in my house at the present moment a number of skins of bears killed by myself, which, if colour be any criterion as to species, represent almost as many species as there are skins.

But if anyone wishes to judge of the futility of trying to 'place' a bear by his colour, he should visit the drying-yard of our principal merchant in furs, here in Victoria. In that yard on a sunny day, when the bear skins are laid out to air, he will see skins of every shade between black, white, and red, all collected from a comparatively limited district, and all shading so gradually into one another, that you cannot yourself decide where the smoky grey of the true grizzly has changed into the reddish brown of the cinnamon, or where that has become dark enough to be considered a rather brownish black.

As it is with the colour so it is with the shape of the beasts, and with the shape and colour of their claws. The typical grizzly should be higher at the shoulder, somewhat shorter in the back, and generally more massive than the black bear. He should be so high at the shoulder as to appear almost humpbacked, whilst his head should be heavy and massive, broad between the ears, short in proportion to its size as compared to the head of the black bear, sharp at the snout, and somewhat flat behind the eyes; the whole expression of the head being as unmistakably pugnacious and dangerous as the expression of the long shallow head of the black bear is weak and inoffensive. As most people are aware, naturalists rely for purposes of identification more upon the shape of a bear's skull than upon any external characteristics, and for that reason I have inserted here an engraving from a photograph of two skulls placed side by side, the larger one being that of a medium-sized grizzly bitch (or sow) from Alaska, the other that of a very large black bear (male) from British Columbia.

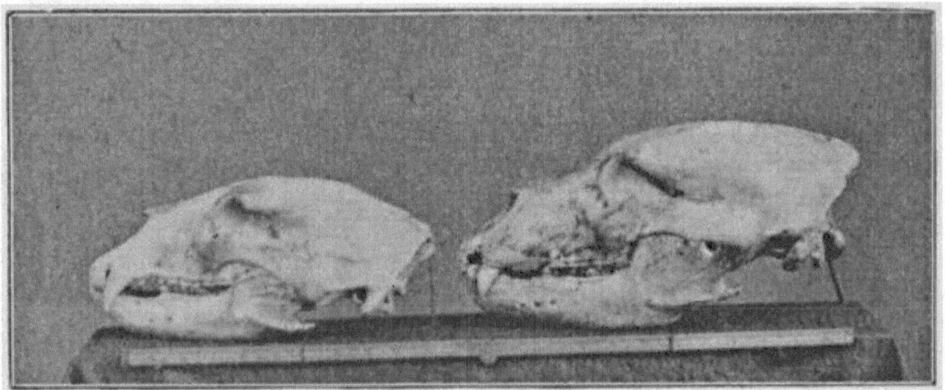

Specimen Skull of Black Bear, Grizzly Bear

From a photograph

As far as the general expression of the beast goes, it seems to me that that is no better guide than his colour, for even amongst grizzlies I have in one trip come across one specimen with a head as full of vice as a viper's, and another as mild as a Chinese cook's. It is true that the sexes differed; the mild face naturally belonging to the lady.

As to the claws again, the typical Californian grizzly should have extremely long flat claws of a bony whiteness—claws obviously meant for digging and not for climbing; while the genuine black bear should have claws to climb and fish with, sharply curved, small and dark coloured.

But here again the characteristics are not constant. The Alaskan grizzly (if it is a true grizzly) has claws far too arched or curved to be typical; whilst in colour, all those which I have seen were a light brown or slate colour growing white towards the tips. A bear shot by me in the Hope Mountains is a good illustration of the strange varieties which sometimes arise from crosses between black bear and grizzly. This little fellow would have weighed about 350 lbs. live weight, and was a full-grown bear when killed. His head was a typical black bear's as far as shape went, and he had not a distinctly marked 'lift' or hump at the shoulder; his claws were very light coloured (almost white); his face and shoulders were a rich straw colour, fading into a very light grey towards the rump, whilst his arms, belly, cheeks and ears were a deep rich brown, almost black in places.

The Indians said he was a grizzly; the trapper who was with me called him a cinnamon; a friend who wished to belittle my bear said he was only 'a rum-coloured black and a little one at that.' I only venture to suggest that he was 'very much mixed.'

But perhaps I have already said too much upon this point, and I will therefore only pause to add this significant fact. No cinnamon or other similar variety seems to be found where both black and grizzly do not exist together. For example, upon Vancouver Island, no grizzly has ever been heard of, no cinnamon has ever been reported, but black bears swarm. The same, I believe, may be said of the island of Anticosti, and elsewhere. In habits bears differ, of course, considerably, and yet even here the points in which they resemble one another are more numerous than those in which they differ.

All bears appear to be omnivorous, but the grizzly is said to be more of a flesh-eater than *Ursus americanus*. Perhaps he is. No doubt he dearly loves to gorge himself upon a carcase, and he does occasionally kill a weak beast or a young one for himself; but like his cousin he is a great vegetarian, grubbing up roots and devouring berries by the gallon. But a black bear is not by any means a total abstainer from meat diet, more especially if that meat be pork; indeed, if the pig needs killing, and the farmer neglects to play the butcher, the mild-mannered gentleman in black will not be slow to do the killing and help himself.

To furnish an exhaustive or even adequate list of the things upon which bears feed is by no means an easy task, but it is so essential to success that a man should know where to look for his game (game always being where its food is) that this must be attempted.

Let me begin at the beginning of the bear's year. As most men know, all bears on this continent (except, perhaps, the Polar) lie dormant during the winter. The den, as a rule, is at the head of one of the hundred gulches which seem to radiate from a common source amongst the snow peaks, the grizzly and the cinnamon choosing their lairs at a higher altitude than the black bear.

The road to a grizzly's den, as I remember it, is generally up a snow-slide, through a dense belt of noisy brush, which the weight of the winter's snow has laid as a thunderstorm lays ripe wheat; and above this belt, under a sheer bluff, sheltered from the wind and hidden by the snow, lies the den itself.

Up here, mist and snow, a few stunted pines, and the sleeping bear have the world to themselves from November to April, the exact date of the bear's retirement to winter quarters, as well as of his reappearance above ground, depending somewhat upon the seasons. This much, at any rate, seems to be generally admitted amongst mountain men—that, some time in November bears begin to 'hole up,' the black bears being first and the grizzlies following a week or two later; whilst in spring the grizzlies are up and out before their 'softer' cousins.

When they first come out of their dens both bears feed entirely upon vegetable matter, even the grizzly being too weak to wander round to look for the carcases of beasts which have perished during the past winter. This he becomes strong enough to do a week or so later, but at first he is every bit as sorry a spectacle as *Ursus americanus* under similar conditions, being almost too weak to stand, and sitting down to groan and wag his old head from sheer exhaustion after every few yards he walks. If at this time the weather looks unpropitious, both bears not infrequently come to the conclusion that it is not yet time to get up, and therefore turn in for one more nap.

In early April (that is, on first leaving their dens) both *Ursus americanus* and *Ursus horribilis* frequent the river bottoms to feed upon the rank herbage which grows there; and a little later find food very much to their taste in the young mountain grass which springs wherever the snow leaves the hill-sides bare.

It is in April that the hunter gets some of his best chances at bear, for if he be lucky enough to find one of the earliest of these mountain pastures, and patient enough to watch it for a few days, he is almost certain of his reward.

At this time, too, a bear is worth killing, for his hide is at its very best when he leaves his winter quarters, though it deteriorates very rapidly as summer advances.

Towards the end of April (in an average year) when the bear has purged his system with a diet of mountain grasses, Nature provides him with somewhat stronger food, in the buds of the olali bushes (service berry, &c.), in the roots of the wild parsnip, and a little later in the catkins which come upon the willows. Later still (in May), when the woods begin to swarm with ticks and other insects, the bears follow the snow in its retreat to the high places, finding at its very edge great patches of golden lilies (*Erythronium giganteum*) and the small pinkish blossom of *Claytonia carolineana* (Indian potato), both blossoms springing from bulbs of which bears are as fond as the Indians, with whose women folk the former not seldom clash in their morning operations in these wild potato fields.

But to find the bear feeding either upon bulbs or grasses, or any stronger meat, the hunter must be out early and up late, for bears are reasonable beings, rarely if ever feeding grossly at midday, but breakfasting at dawn and dining after dark.

Indeed, bears are more or less nocturnal in their habits, and this is especially true of grizzlies, who, when much hunted, become purely nocturnal in their feeding and in their wanderings.

I know a country (the name of it I prefer to keep to myself for a year or two yet) which appears to be a high tableland, densely timbered and full of caribou, and from this innumerable gullies and clefts lead down to lower levels, where, at the bottom of steep canyons, are piled rock and stone slide, and débris of dead pine wood. There are opens among the pines at the top, and here in snow-time, if you leave a caribou carcase for a couple of days, you will find plenty of bear-tracks going to and fro. Every day the number of them increases, until it seems to you that the place must be alive with grizzlies; but you will never see one of the track-makers by day. The bears here have been a good deal hunted, and have become as cunning as monkeys, coming up from the gullies at night but vanishing like spectres at the first peep of day. It was here that a friend of mine killed and left a mule deer, hanging its head up in a tree hard by, to be called for on some future occasion. When that occasion came, the head was missing, and was found a little further on, laid with the carcase and carefully covered up with moss and sticks and snow.

This, of course, is a common trick of the grizzly's, but it was quaint of this particular beast to gather up the fragments so carefully. By the way, whilst I am on the subject of 'carcases,' I may as well say that it is not my own experience that grizzlies are very gluttonous feeders, upon flesh at any rate. Indeed, it seemed to me that a deer's carcase lasted some bears whom I have known almost as long as it would have lasted an ordinary camp Indian. I knew, for instance, of a mule's carcase in the spring of 1892 which served as an attraction to four bears (two black and two grizzlies) for at least a fortnight in the Kootenay country.

But to come back to the bear's menu. About the same time that the *Erythronium* is in bloom, black bears feed freely upon a plant called 'arpa' by our British Columbian Indians (*Heracleum lanatum*) upon skunk cabbage, and upon a plant which Professor Macoun has kindly identified for me as *Peucedanum triternatum*.

What the black bear eats from choice, the grizzly will eat from necessity; so that if there are no carcases about, and few or no bulbs in the country, the hunter may expect to find *U. horribilis* making the best of 'arpa' and skunk cabbage. As the season advances, the bear changes his diet somewhat, and before his great autumn harvests of fish, fruits and nuts, we find him tearing up rotten logs for ants and beetles, turning over boulders for the larvæ which lie below them, digging up yellow jackets'(wasps, &c.) nests for the sake of the grubs inside, and occasionally burrowing in the hill-sides for marmots or ground hogs.

The bear's season of plenty begins with the ripening of the first fruits on the flats by the river bottoms, when those who care to shoot game out of season may find some sport in killing both varieties of bear as they wander over the sand bars of Alaskan rivers, looking for fruit and a cold bath to allay the irritation of their bald and mangy-looking hides.

The berry season in British Columbia begins at midsummer, and from that time until late in the fall there is always plenty of bear food in the woods: raspberries (which bears love beyond all things), currants, gooseberries, soapberries, service, wine, salmon, bil- and black-berries, strawberries, choke-cherries, and a score of others, whose flavour I can remember but whose names I never knew.

I have never seen, except in the Caucasus, such a land for wild fruit as British Columbia. Compared with it, Colorado, for instance, is a most unfruitful country; but, to make amends, Colorado abounds in acorns and pine nuts, of which there are few, if any, in British Columbia. Where the acorns are, there will the bears be also, but acorns are an uncertain crop, failing utterly one year and abounding another.

By the way, just before the acorn crop comes in, the silver-tips of Colorado seem to devote a good deal of their time to digging in woodland bogs, but whether they dig for roots or insects I am not sure. In Alaska, in British Columbia, and all along the Pacific Coast the bear's *bonne bouche* is kept until nearly the end of the year. In spring the 'tyhee' salmon (*O. chouicha*) turns up the streams, and a few of this 'run' stay all through the season; later on come the humpies (*Onchorhynchus gorbuscha*), and of these, the Indians say, none return to the sea. In October, then, in Alaska and elsewhere, the glacial streams, tributary to the main rivers, are full of these misshapen salmon, crimson and purple, and patched with all manner of vivid leprous patches, their dorsal fins frayed and rotting as they swim. The streams stink of them; your paddle strikes one which is already broken up and drifting seaward; others, swollen with decay, are standing, tail upwards, on the river bottom; whilst others, driven by some strange madness, diseased and dying, still struggle up the shallows towards the glacier.

At this time of year, the dense woods of grey and mildewed pines and prickly devil's club, which crowd down to the river's edge, are full of bears; the mud flats between forest and stream are pitted with huge tracks (I have measured many 12 ins. by 9 ins.), and the filthy gorged American eagle sits puking and moping with ruffled feathers among cleaned back bones and rejected heads and tails of humpies, left over from the grizzlies' last meal.

And here, at the end of their year's feeding, it seems appropriate to say something of the weight to which grizzlies attain, and the size to which they grow. Like human beings, they seem to fatten most in a civilised or domestic state, the great grizzly of San Francisco having really attained to the enormous weight of 1,500 lbs.,[15] presumably upon hog food. It is said that the Californian grizzly grows larger than any other, but I doubt whether he much exceeds the Alaskan in size, and I am absolutely certain that all the largest grizzlies have grown to their fabulous proportions in the whisky-scented atmosphere of Western saloons. 'If you

[15] Tradition puts this bear at 1,900 lbs., but Mr. John Coles writes me that he saw the bear exhibited by a man named Adams in San Francisco; it was then said to weigh 1,500 lbs., and Mr. Coles adds, 'I never heard any doubt expressed as to its weight.'—C. P.-W.

will hear them,' as the 'boys' say, 2,000-lb. grizzlies are quite common, and 'as big as a bull' is but a mild way of describing nine bears out of ten shot by them.

As a matter of fact, I am by no means prepared to doubt all their stories. There are unquestionably some exceptional monsters met with now and again, but too many of those instanced have been described merely from the impression made on the hunter's mind by the sight of a gigantic track which has spread in soft snow or mud. The largest grizzly of which I have had anything like trustworthy information in my own wanderings was shot in Alaska, at English Bay, Kodak Island, by Mr. J. C. Tolman, now Customs officer at Wrangel. As Mr. Tolman allows his name to appear, and as he enjoyed an enviable reputation for veracity among men who had known him for years, I give the dimensions of his big bear as he gave them to me, extracted from notes made in his diary at the time at which he killed him. The bear was killed only a few miles from a settlement, and was actually weighed, turning the scales at 1,656 lbs. dead weight not cleaned; his hide when freshly skinned measured 13 ft. 6 ins. from nose to anus; from ear to ear he measured 13 ins.; from poll to nose, 20 ins.; the length of the hind-foot was 18 ins., and the breadth of the forefoot 12 ins. He was killed by a single shot in the head from a Winchester rifle.

The largest bear which I have myself shot was also an Alaskan, but infinitely smaller than the above; still, even this bear gave four strong men all they could do, with a rope round her neck, to drag her, when dead, down a sloping mud bank into a canoe laid over on its side to receive her. Her forearm, when skinned, measured 23 ins., fair measurement, the tape being stretched as tight as it would go. The Indians put this bear at from 1,000 to 1,500 lbs., and I dare say she really weighed nearly 800 or possibly 900 lbs., but I am no judge of an animal's weight, and had no means of weighing her. I have myself measured skins in Mr. Boscowitz's store at Victoria (also brought down from Alaska) which measured 9 ft. 10 ins. from end to end, but then some 6 ins. must be allowed for on all American skins, as they are skinned up the hind legs in such a way as to give quite that length of hide beyond the anus. Of course, too, a skin may be so laced and strained upon its frame in skinning as to stretch it a good deal beyond its natural dimensions.

In Colorado the bears appear to be mostly silver-tips, and if you can rely upon the verdict of the local hunters whom I met (and I have no reason to doubt their word) a Colorado silver-tip weighing 600 lbs. would be a big bear.

The stories of the ferocity of *U. horribilis* owe something to the vivid imaginations of hunters and the sombre surroundings in which they meet their prey; but there can be no doubt that on occasion this bear will face a man (or men), and fight with intense ferocity. As a rule, like all bears, the grizzly will run rather than fight, and very rarely attacks without provocation, but when surprised near a carcase, when cornered, when wounded, or with cubs, *U. horribilis* is apt to be dangerous. I know of a good many deaths due to bears under such circumstances, and only last year (1891) a very well-known meat-hunter in Colorado was attacked in green timber by a silver-tip and regularly worried by him, although the man had a companion with him, and had not even seen the bear until he was charged. I have myself seen the marks of this bear's teeth in the leg and forearm of my old guide, who explained the unprovoked attack by saying that the bear had supped on a carcase poisoned for coyotes, and was 'feelin' pretty mean from belly-ache' when found. The Alaskan grizzly has a peculiarly bad reputation among the Indians in that country, who upon dry land can hardly be induced to face 'Hoots' or 'Noon,' as they call the grizzly and cinnamon. Most of the skins sent to Wrangel are those of bears strangled in nooses, like big rabbit-snares, which are set in their paths, or else of bears shot down by men on snow-shoes in the deep snow of early spring, or shot on the river banks from a canoe. Here it is as well to say that I know of two instances in which grizzly bitches have, when hunted, deserted their cubs, and left them up a tree at the mercy of the hunters; but this is, of course, unusual. As a rule, grizzlies are distinctly 'ugly' when they have young with them, and will defend them to the last. However, *with* cubs or without, a man with a good rifle and a steady nerve need never let a bear go in the open. In thick brush there are times when caution is better than courage. As I write, a picture comes before my eyes of a willow swamp, high up on the head-waters of a mountain stream in the States. An old guide of mine is on the edge of the timber watching, whilst the brush swings and rattles, and an unseen form shakes down the yellow leaves and fills the gulch with her growls. It is only a bitch silver-tip, who has got the man's wind and is trying to collect her cubs; but, although it is exasperating to stand while the old lady makes her escape up the gully, there is nothing else to be done. If she does not mean to face the open, none but a greenhorn would attempt to go to her when she was 'fighting mad,' in bush too thick to walk through, and in places over six feet high. All the old authorities talk of grizzlies rising to an upright position on closing with a man, but I have never met a man who had seen anything of this habit, although I have known more than one man who has been struck down by a bear. I have myself come suddenly upon a grizzly, and seen him rise and face me in the position I refer to, but he did not stop in that position long enough for me to dismount and fire, and I am convinced that his only object in rising upon his hind legs was to get a better view of the intruder, not to attack him.

There is no doubt that a bear's sight is his weak point. In bright moonlight I have had one walk past myself and another man in the open at forty yards without seeing us; but if his sight is indifferent, he has the ears of a hare and the nose of a caribou, and this is especially the case with the black bear, whose timidity has possibly somewhat sharpened his senses.

That grizzlies do not climb, except as cubs, appears to be true; not that it matters much to the hunter, as anyone will allow who gets his friend to give him 100 or 150 yards' start and then tries to 'tree' in time to escape him. The right tree never grows in the right place, and climbing in a hurry sounds easier than it is. It will be found that most men can run 100 yards in less time than they can choose their tree and climb it to such a height that their *feet* are ten feet above the ground. A bear, too, travels faster even than a frightened man on the flat. If you are charged, the best thing you can do is to stand fast and go on shooting; and if there are two of you, and both of one mind, and *not standing too close together*, there should not be much danger; but better than that is to take pains about your first shot: or go close to your bear and shoot him in the head or neck, as the natives do. If you hit him in either of these places, you can kill him at once with an ordinary Winchester (45·90); whilst if you are using a Paradox or a big English Express, a shot ranging forward from behind the shoulder or (with a solid bullet) through the shoulder is good enough.

Don't shoot at a bear above you unless you are sure of killing him; a wounded beast will almost always come down hill and may take you on the way; and don't shoot at a bear in the brush as if you were 'browning' a covey of partridges; nor follow a wounded bear into thick covert unless you are well insured, about to be married, or at the end of your ordinary resources for supporting your family.

Opinions vary as to the comparative ferocity and vitality of the different species, but perhaps individuals vary at least as much as species. I have known a black bear take a bullet from an English rifle fired by me point blank into her chest at ten paces, and then turn and *gallop* uphill for 200 yards before dying; and I have known a two-year-old black bear take three bullets, scattered indiscriminately over his back by my friend's Paradox (12-bore), and then turn and charge like a hero. He charged the wrong man, though, and got shot in the head for his impudence.

To finish these remarks, and convey, if possible, some idea of hunting the grizzly, let me take a leaf from my note-book, kept in Alaska in the autumn of 1891, whilst hunting with my friend Mr. Arnold Pike.

Nature has a way of always suiting her creatures to their environments, but none of her creatures are more exactly suited to their surroundings than *U. horribilis*. Savage and silent and grey as the grizzly is, the forests and waters amongst which he chooses to dwell are more grim, more savage, and more forbidding than himself. The part of Alaska in which we were hunting in 1891 appears to have escaped from that process described in Genesis by which the waters which were above the firmament were divided from the waters which were under the firmament. On the Stickeen river there is no firmament. As a rule, a damp darkness broods upon the face of the deep, and the waters which should be above touch and mingle with the waters which should be below. There is no dry belt between the bottom of the sea and the roof of heaven, at least in that district which lies between Wrangel and Telegraph Creek, in the month of October. We were out for forty days and forty nights, and I cannot swear to more than three and a half moderately fine days in that time: a fine day in Alaska being one in which you wear oilskins and gum boots, and go to bed in a dry shirt; whilst on a wet one you wear gum boots and oilskins, and go to bed to dry your shirt. The river Stickeen runs its rapid course between dank forests, grey at the top with mildew, and hung with dark mosses, in which the devil's club forms an impenetrable undergrowth, and even the pines are thorny. The pace of the river is such that you make as much in one day, drifting down it, as you made in five pulling and poling up it; and your camping-grounds are of necessity upon barren sandspits, for nothing but a bear could force its way into this timber. In this land no gentle things live: there are no deer, no small birds, no squirrels, no sunlight—nothing but a few wolves, a stray seal, which comes whistling up on the tide in the grey of the morning, great flights of Canada geese, and dying salmon. All along the course of the main river are the mouths of its ice-fed tributaries, little streams of greenish-blue water, rising in a glacier and fringed with narrow strips of glacial mud, upon which a rank growth of *Equisetum* (horse-tail) flourishes. These banks are the hunting grounds, and the number of huge tracks upon them, as well as the *débris* of half-eaten salmon, proclaim that there is no scarcity of game; but if the hunter would get a shot he must haunt them at all unseasonable hours, when winds are most chill, and nature is at her gloomiest: for 'Hoots' only creeps out upon the creek's edges with the first shadows of the night, and vanishes from them with the earliest rising mists of morning.

In this land it was that one evening we pitched our tents upon a sandspit, cut wet brush in the rain to make our bedding for the night, and then, tired with a hard day and dispirited by weeks of failure, stepped once more into the canoe and paddled for all we were worth up and across the stream to the mouth of a salmon creek.

Once in the green water, pipes were put out, conversation ceased, Pike and I laid down our paddles and took up our rifles, and only the Indian worked, the canoe gliding up the still waters without a sound.

At the mouth of the stream, a few flashing shadows beneath the water attracted our Indian's attention, and a few quick thrusts with his spear provided us with enough fresh salmon to last us for a day or two. A blow or two with the axe silenced them, and again the canoe stole up stream, the men in it noting fresh tracks upon the banks, and peering into the shadowy woods, which grew darker and more impenetrable every minute.

Once or twice on our way up stream the canoe ran aground, and all hands had to get out to push their craft through the sands (quicksands as often as not) into which we sank over the tops of our waders.

But these are small matters. Pike sitting with one leg dangling over the side, always ready to jump out, seemed rather to like it—it reminded him of days among the ice near Spitzbergen—and all of us had long since become amphibious.

At last the stream ceased to be navigable even for our shallow craft, which we beached upon certain muddy shallows, among stunted bushes and dead equisetum, and our watch began. All round us stretched the swamp, and above it rose the densely timbered hills, while far above them again towered the triple peaks of snowy Sacoclè. For an hour and a half no one stirred, though our fingers were numb, and we were too cold to feel cold. A good Siwash (Indian) won't move a muscle for hours, nor sneeze, nor cough, nor do any of the hundred and one things which no one ever wants to do except upon such a vigil as this. For an hour and a half the rain went on, the darkness deepened, and the silence became intense, broken only by the occasional splash of a 'humpy' who had run himself aground, and could not get off again into deep water.

At last Jim came to the conclusion that no bears would come that night, and as a glance at our sights proved to us that we should probably miss them even if they came, we signalled him to push off, and in a minute the canoe was again fleeting over the waters in breathless silence, the thin line of forest seeming to glide by us while we stood still. An Indian in the bows was looking out for 'snags ahead' or shallows, and for my part I had played this game so often before that I had given up hope, and was dreaming of other things. All at once the canoe was violently shaken from stem to stern. 'D— — the fellow,' I muttered, 'I suppose he has run aground,' and I went on dreaming. Again the canoe trembled under me, and this time I remembered that this was to be the signal for game ahead. At the same moment I noticed that the Siwash's face was working, and his hands were drawing his Winchester from its case, when my friend crept up to him, and made him understand that if he fired it would hurt him more than the bears, and then at last I saw *them*. Until then the Indian's body had been in my way, but now they were in full view, standing almost up to their shoulders in the stream, still as stone images in the dark shadow of the overhanging bank, their heads turned over their shoulders looking in our direction, and the long silvery ripples running from their legs down stream. It was lucky for me that night that I carried a Paradox, with which a man can shoot at short ranges as if he were snap-shooting at rabbits in covert, for I had to stand up to get a clean shot, I had not a second to lose, and the canoe rocked horribly under my feet. The big beast of the two fell to my first barrel, sinking where she stood, while her mate got my second barrel in the back as he scrambled up the bank, making good his escape for the moment into the dense scrub.

I don't suppose that the whole incident, from the find until we began to fish up my bear, took a minute, and yet into that minute was crowded a third of the reward for forty days of hard work, short commons and general misery. Is the game worth the candle? I think it is, but I don't want to persuade any man to be of my way of thinking, nor do I want to convey the impression that all bear hunting is necessarily as grim and miserable as it is in Alaska. But in places where bear hunting is easy, bears are getting scarce (at least, grizzlies are), for their hides bring a good price and there is a bounty upon their scalps as well. The result is that more bears are trapped in one year than would be shot in five under ordinary circumstances. For instance, two brothers whom I know killed thirty-five bears in 1890 within a radius of eighty miles of their cabin. Of course, this sort of thing cannot last.

It seems a pity, as, whether you hunt him among the mists and storms of an Alaskan autumn, or watch for him by a hill at the edge of some dark canyon, until even the bird *chiquetta* stops her noisy little song, and the outlines of all objects become indistinct and moving, *Ursus horribilis* is better worth hunting than any other beast, except perhaps the bighorn, in all America.

P.S.—Since writing this, Sir George Lampson has kindly furnished me with the length of eleven American grizzly skins in his warehouse at one time—87, 89, 90, 93, 94, 95, 96, 97, 98, 101 and 103 ins. respectively. On the day these particulars were furnished I myself put the tape over a grizzly skin in Sir George Lampson's possession which measured 9 ft. from the eyes to the tail.

Standing still as Stone Images

C. Whymper

III. BLACK BEAR (URSUS AMERICANUS)

I have said so much incidentally about the black bear while writing of his congener the grizzly, that I have very little left to say of him in the proper place. A recent American authority describes this bear's habitat as being confined nowadays 'to some portions of the various ranges of mountains south of the St. Lawrence river, the Great Lakes, and (east of the Mississippi river) to parts of those portions of the Mississippi river and its tributaries which are yet unsettled,' and to 'the dense thickets of the Colorado, Trinity, and Brayos rivers.' Colonel G. D. Alexander should have bethought him of those countries west of the Rockies (Alaska, British Columbia, Washington Territory, Vancouver Island, and Oregon) which are at present the principal stronghold of *Ursus americanus*; and as I am informed the chief source from which the fur-traders draw their supplies of black bear skins. Unfortunately for the black bear, the price of his hide has gone up lately in the fur market. Ten years ago $15 was a long price to pay for a bear's skin; this year a trader out here paid as much as $35 for one. Whatever the ultimate result of this rise in value may be, the immediate consequence of it has been to show the world what a vast number of bears can be killed in America if they are wanted.

Here are some statistics of recent crops of bear in America which speak for themselves.

The Hudson Bay Company, of course, draws *all* its supply of hides from this continent, and I am assured that the same maybe said (with scarcely any allowance for Russian, Norwegian, Indian, or other skins) of the great firm of C. M. Lampson & Co. These two firms collected in 1891 and offered for sale in 1892 no fewer than 29,081 bear hides, to which enormous total the Hudson Bay Company contributed 11,027 hides.

Some idea of the proportion of black to other skins at these sales may be obtained by looking at the Hudson Bay Company's lists for 1891, in which we find 11,414 black, 1,875 brown, 253 grey, and 130 white bear skins offered for sale.

There can be little doubt, then, that there were plenty of black bear in America in 1890 and 1891; and, in spite of the immense harvest of hides which is annually gathered in, I venture to prophesy that until Alaskan river bottoms and the dense timber districts of Vancouver Island, Oregon, and Washington Territory are cleared and ready for the plough, there will be plenty of bear left for those who care to look for them. Here on Vancouver Island and on the north-west coast of British Columbia black bears are especially plentiful, one of our great fur-dealers (Mr. Boscowitz) having taken in over 1,000 hides last year, whilst I see by a newspaper ('Colonist,' Dec. 6, 1892) that at Sumas in the New Westminster District (one of our best farming districts) seven bears have lately fallen to one rifle and three to another; and I am well convinced that a salmon-canning friend of mine told me the truth when he asserted that about dawn, one day during the great annual salmon run, he saw seventeen black bears at one *coup d'œil*, feeding along the bank of one of the northern rivers of British Columbia.

'When Spring in the Woods'

C. Whymper

But it must not be inferred from these facts that every tenderfoot who comes along will run up against bears the first time he goes in search of them. On the contrary, an old friend of mine (every inch an English sportsman) has been out in this country for twenty-five years, travelling from time to time all over the province, and has never yet seen a bear alive in the woods. The reason is simply that my friend uses a shot-gun, and doesn't look for bears; and if you want to see these beasts you must look for them at the right time and in the right place, and even then be thankful if you see more than their fresh tracks, for Nature has given them noses as keen as the nose of a caribou, and ears which are always on the alert, as well as an impregnable sanctuary in the dense timber and tangled woodfall of their native forests. To those who live upon the Pacific coast the black bear is an animal to be thankful for, affording as he does an excuse for carrying a rifle when spring is in the woods; when the cedar swamps smell heavy with the musk of the skunk cabbage, and are lit in their green darkness by stray beams of May sunshine; when *Cormus Nuttalli* is white with blooms as big as the palm of a man's hand, and underfoot all is bright with the red and orange of columbine and 'Indian pink,' or white with the delicate petals of the dog violet. To me the black glossy hide beneath my feet always brings back memories of spring-time, either here on the island, or on the mainland by the Frazer, where the beautiful olalis are smothered in white blossom, and where the great yellow swallow-tails and plum-coloured Camberwell Beauties sail and sun themselves upon the stone slides round the lake.

But though the black bear affords an excellent excuse for bolting out of town in spring-time, it cannot be said that he is a very sporting beast. He hasn't got an ounce of 'fight' in him, and stalking is of course impossible in such districts as those which he frequents. Even 'still hunting' is very nearly useless in such timber as exists on this coast; so that unless you use hounds to hunt him with, your best chance of meeting *Ursus americanus* is to take a canoe and paddle quietly up untravelled streams, where fish are plentiful, or where in autumn the berry bushes grow thickly. In spring you may get a shot by watching woodland swamps where the skunk cabbage grows, or hill-sides when the Indian potato is ripe, but you are nearly as likely to have your chance if you are out early upon the best trail in the country, which runs near such feeding places, for the black bear appreciates a good road as much as a man does, and always uses one when he can.

In Eastern America the black bear is principally hunted with hounds, and even here a good dog which will tree a bear is useful; but my own experience of such sport has been, that in nine cases out of ten the hounds' music ceased just as I had done the hardest mile on record up hill and over fallen timber, and the hounds themselves turned up ten minutes later, meek and dejected, their muzzles full of porcupine quills, which they evidently expected me to pull out for them.

Most of the skins sent in to Victoria from Alaska are taken by trapping (by noose, gin, or deadfall), or by hunting with dogs, between the time the bears leave their dens and the time the snow leaves the river bottoms. It is a short season and an uncertain one, but I am assured by those who have tried it, that for a man who is a good goer upon snow-shoes, it is excellent fun whilst it lasts. The dogs used for bears are of every breed and combination of breeds, but perhaps the best are collies. It does not require a big dog or a powerful dog for the work, for no dog is big enough to close with, whilst any dog is big enough to frighten, a black bear. I remember upon one occasion seeing three dogs, two small Pomeranians and a cross-bred setter, run a two-year-old black bear to bay on the ford of a river. The dogs had to swim, but by standing up the bear could rest upon firm ground, and keep his arms and jaws free for fighting above water.

The bear had already received a shot in the stomach before the dogs tackled him, but when they ran him to bay he seemed strong and well. Neither dogs nor bear took any notice of me, though I was standing up to my knees in the water of the ford within a few paces of them; and in five minutes the fight was over without interference on my part. At first the bear cuffed the dogs as they swam up to him, as a man might cuff who knew nothing of hitting out from the shoulder, and once he took the big dog in his jaws and went right under with him. However, the setter came up smiling, and shortly afterwards poor old Bruin was floating down stream, his head under water, and the dogs tugging with impunity at his flanks. I suppose that this bear weighed less than 200 lbs.

Captain Baldwin in his excellent book on the game of Bengal describes two kinds of bears: *U. labiatus* and *U. tibetanus*; and almost everything that he says of the Indian black bear would apply equally well to *U. americanus* (even to his weakness for yellow raspberries), except that *U. labiatus* appears to fight upon occasion, whereas *U. americanus* is hardly ever known to fight even in self-defence, and has never, as far as I know, been accused of making an unprovoked assault upon a human being.

Baldwin seems to have been somewhat surprised when he discovered that the Indian black bear fed upon carrion. No one in America would be surprised at anything which *U. americanus* considered good for him. I have seen a cub take rotten melon, a piece of meat, a cake of chocolate, a plug of T. & B. tobacco, and the end of a half-smoked cigar for breakfast. Being a true American, the cub naturally showed a preference for the plug of T. & B., but none of the other things came amiss to him. In a wild state a black bear will eat any garbage, putrid fish, dead animals, or anything else which comes in his way. In fact, the poor black bear is in all his tastes and habits a thorough hog: a pig without a pig's pugnacity.

As a rule he is a lowland beast, living in swamps and river-bottoms, but I have seen him once or twice even in a mountain sheep country, probably crossing over the divide from one river-bed to another. It is well for him that he generally eschews the open, for once out of the timber everything which has eyes must see him. A man may mistake a burnt log for a bear, but no man could mistake a bear for a burnt log. The intense blackness and gloss of a bear's coat is not thoroughly appreciated until you see it contrasted with other objects which you are accustomed to call black.

Where the sportsman runs any chance of seeing tracks of both black and grizzly in one and the same piece of country, it is as well to be able to distinguish the one from the other.

It is not easy to do this, but, as a general rule, if the ground on which the track is made is soft, you should be able to see the long *cuts* made by the grizzly's claws, as contrasted with the little holes made by the points of the black bears. I am talking now of the forepaws, and it will be remembered that the claws of the black are much arched, and therefore only touch at the tip, whereas the grizzly's claw is flat and should touch almost along its whole length.

Again, there is no doubt that the heel of the grizzly is much broader and squarer than that of the black bear, which makes a very narrow impression, even upon soft clay.

Like the grizzly, the black bear varies greatly in size and weight. On Vancouver Island I am inclined to think that the average black bear would not weigh 300 lbs.; but no doubt there are many exceptional bears, even upon the island, which greatly exceed that weight; and I have myself seen an old male upon the mainland which, if I am any judge of weight, was not an ounce less than 500 lbs., and probably weighed more; while there are from time to time black bear skins in the warehouses of Mr. Boscowitz, the principal fur-dealer in Victoria, which would measure nearly 9 ft. from end to end (if allowance were made for the mask beyond the eyes), and 6 ft. from side to side below the arms.

In 1891 I measured in this store a black bear's skin which did not seem unduly stretched, the length of which was, to the best of my recollection, 8 ft. 6 ins. from eyes to tail, or 8 ft. 10 ins. as measured.

Amongst the skins for sale by Messrs. C. M. Lampson & Co., at their small summer sale, June 12, 1893, at which I was told that the black bear skins were small, I measured one skin 93 ins. from eyes to tail, and one of the employés of the house assured me that a black bear skin measuring 8 ft. 6 ins. was not uncommon.

Before leaving the subject of bears altogether, I should like to refer to an extraordinary skin which I saw among Mr. Boscowitz's consignments from the upper country last year. In size this skin is considerably larger than the average bear hide; the colour of it is white, with a few straw-coloured patches (little more than a few hairs in each) on the head and about the rump. The paws and claws of the animal were attached to the skin, and from the jaws and skin of the head I should imagine that the beast had a long shallow head like a black bear's, though the skin is more like the skin of a Polar in summer season, *except that* whereas other bear hides are of hair, this is distinctly woolly, more like the fleece of a sheep than the hide of a bear.

I am informed that this skin was sent to Mr. Rowland Ward's. The bear was killed on one of the inlets of the north-west coast, and is the only one of the kind ever seen in our British Columbia fur market.

IV. BISON OR BUFFALO (BISON AMERICANUS)

In writing of big game in North America, it is impossible to write for more than the immediate present. That which was ten years ago has already ceased to be, and it is probable that the conditions, both of game and country, will change almost as much in the coming decade as they have done in that which has just passed.

Ten years ago, as I travelled along the Northern Pacific Railway line, the skin-hunters were at work in the neighbourhood of Glendive and Little Missouri, and I had an opportunity of killing my buffalo like my predecessors. Unfortunately for me, I agreed with Colonel Dodge's plainsmen in 'scarcely considering the buffalo game.' Now the herds are gone, and neither I nor any other man will see the prairies again 'all one vast robe.' All that remains of the vast herds which used to roam 'over the whole of the Eastern United States to the Atlantic Ocean, and southward into Florida,' are two or three half-domesticated herds (one which was Colonel Bedson's and one in the Kootenay country among the Flat-head Indians), and a small band of wild beasts, protected by the United States, in the Yellowstone Park. 'Forest and Stream,' January 29, 1892, puts this last herd at about 400 head, with an increase of 100 head per annum. West of Winnipeg the buffalo paths are still visible, worn deep in the grey prairies by millions of passing feet; but the herds have gone, and the men and beasts who lived upon them. All that is left are a few piles of bleaching bones and a few weather-worn skulls, and even these have almost all been gathered and turned into dollars by the manure manufacturer and the trophy-monger. In this practical money-grubbing age it does not do to lament the good old days, unless you want to be laughed at; but it is hard, nevertheless, to look on the ocean of grassland when the spring flowers are coming, and not regret the great waves of animal life which used to sweep over it. Such evidence as I can offer as to the mode in which the buffalo was hunted must of necessity be hearsay evidence, collected, however, at first hand, principally from an Indian confined, at the time I saw him, at the Stony Mountain Penitentiary, and from a white skin-hunter, whose last hunts were conducted in 1880, 1881 and 1882, in Montana and North Dacota.

A white skin-hunter's 'outfit' of the most modest kind consisted in those days of one hunter carrying a Sharp's rifle (with bullets weighing 500 grains), two skinners, and an extra man for camp work and odd jobs.

During the rutting season (from July 20 to September 16) the buffaloes all ran together, but during the rest of the year the old bulls kept together, apart from the cows and young bulls. Except during the rutting season, the bands were comparatively small—from 20 to 200—led, if consisting of cows and young beasts, by an old cow. In hot weather the bands would lie quiet during the heat of the day, but in windy weather they would keep travelling all day against the wind, feeding as they went. As soon as the herds had been found the hunter would begin operations, shooting at long ranges, and keeping out of sight as much as possible. The first beast shot was the leader of the band, and as often as the band seemed to have selected another leader he, too, had to be dropped in his tracks. Without a leader, and with no enemy in sight, the remainder of the herd would generally become confused, and allow the hunter to shoot down a large number 'at a stand,' as he called it. Having killed as many as he could, the hunter left the carcases where they lay, his assistants coming to skin them the next day. Fifteen head a day was, so my informant stated, a fair average for one man to kill and two to skin, although in the fall of 1880 and spring of 1881 he and his party averaged twenty-four heads per diem.

The best shot was low down behind the shoulder, about ten inches from the brisket. A ball placed there would penetrate the lungs, and, after a few plunges, the beast would drop and die.

The price of all the blood shed by the skin-hunters may be summed up briefly as 2 dollars 75 cents each for 'leather hides'—i.e. hides of old bulls all the year round and young beasts during the summer season—and 3.50 cents for 'robe hides.'

My informant told me that if it would pay him he thought that he could still find buffalo on the northern tributaries of the Saskatchewan, east of the Rockies, as some friends of his, trapping 'away back' in 1886, had seen plenty of them, though the difficulty of bringing the robes out had prevented their shooting any.

The last buffalo killed by a white man to my own certain knowledge was shot by Mr. Warburton Pike far away to the North, near the Great Slave Lake, when out after musk ox.[16]

---

[16] Cf. W. Pike's *Barren Grounds of Northern Canada.*

Colonel Bedson's herd of Buffaloes

C. W., from a photograph

Some idea of the number of the buffaloes in early days may be gathered from the well-attested fact that the pioneer settlers often drove through the herds for days and days with buffalo in sight all round them all day long, as well as from the statistics collected by Colonel Dodge, in his 'Plains of the Great West.' That author states that, from information furnished to him by the Atcheson, Topeka and Santa Fé Railway Company, he concludes that not less than a million and a half were killed in the States from 1872 to 1874.

Colonel Dodge mentions a mountain buffalo as a variety of the common buffalo, and Mr. J. E. Harting, in some remarks published originally in the 'Field,' alludes to a beast of the same class, which he calls 'Zacateca.'

The Zacatecas, of which specimens were exhibited at the American Exhibition of 1887, inhabit the mountainous regions of Northern Mexico; they are smaller than the buffalo, are hornless, and have tails more like the tails of yaks than like those of the common buffalo, who by the way is, properly speaking, a bison (*Bos americanus*). I have taken the liberty of calling him a buffalo because in his native haunts he has been so called, and as such he will go down to posterity in the legends of those great plains which know him no longer.

The Wood Buffalo and the Mountain Buffalo appear to be almost, if not quite, identical with the common type of *B. americanus*, from which they differ only in habitat, in the quality of their coat, and in that they are of somewhat smaller size than their kinsmen of the plains.

A better idea of the appearance of the subject of these remarks may be obtained by a glance at the illustrations than could possibly be given by any amount of descriptive writing, the illustrations having been drawn by Mr. Whymper from photographs of the pure-bred beasts in Colonel Bedson's herd, taken by Lady Alice Stanley, and by a photographer at Winnipeg, Manitoba.

An idea of the size of a buffalo bull may be conveyed by the fact that, in 1889, one of the bulls in Colonel Bedson's herd was estimated at 2,000 lbs., and a much smaller beast, a half-bred bull, was killed, which dressed without the head 1,100 lbs. This was a four-year-old, by a buffalo bull out of a Durham cow.

P.S.—Since writing the above, I have spent a season with an old-time buffalo hunter, who confirmed all the statements made to me by others; and added that, as an instance of the numbers killed by individuals, he himself accounted for 3,500 head in four years, whilst a friend of his, A. C. Myers, killed 4,200 buffaloes in the Pan Handle Country, in Texas, in one year, 'about the time Hayes was President.'

My old friend S. W. explained to me why men used such a gigantic weapon as the 'old reliable' Sharp, which used to weigh 16 lbs. and upwards, although the bullet was but a small one.

In buffalo shooting, he said, you had often to fire a deuce of a lot of shots one after another; the weather was hotter than 'the hottest part of the hot place,' and as you were shooting at long ranges, if the barrel got hot, a sort of mist would get between your eye and the sights, which helped the buffalo somewhat. Besides, where shooting was your trade, you didn't want to get your shoulder 'kicked' at every shot; and as for the weight of your rifle, that didn't matter to you, for your pony packed it.

'A Pile of Buffalo Bones'

C. Whymper

V. THE BIGHORN (OVIS MONTANA)

To a man who loves the hill-tops, where the winds blow keen and pure over the red gold of sun-dried grass and the deep blue of snow-fed tarns, there is no game in America to compare with the bighorn of the Rocky Mountains. Other beasts may hide away in the dense timber of Oregon, Washington Territory, and Vancouver Island; other beasts may sneak out only at dusk and dawn, but the gallant bighorn still lives out in the open, trusting for safety to the grey-faced ewes who watch over him, or to his own marvellously keen sight and scent. In spite of this, the man who kills a 16-in. ram generally deserves his good luck, for there is no beast better able to take care of himself than an old bighorn, nor any more difficult to stalk. Where he lives the wind seems never still, and never constant in any given direction; at night it strains at the hunter's tent-rope and makes his fire roar and blaze like a mad thing, and in the morning it curls round the hill-tops and heralds the stalker's coming from every quarter. It is the fashion in books of sport to describe the haunts of *Ovis montana* as being 'the highest, raggedest, and most forbidding mountain ranges.' Nothing could be further from the truth than this, if the statement is intended to be general. Sheep are undoubtedly sometimes found in difficult and even dangerous places, but to describe sheep shooting as anything like ibex or chamois hunting is pure folly. The first sheep it was ever my good fortune to see was in the Bad Lands, on an eminence not 200 ft. above the level of the Northern Pacific Railway line, and the last I shot in 1892 was not 1,000 ft. above the level of the Frazer. As a rule, sheep in early autumn keep to the bald knolls above the timber-line (where patches of snow still linger), seeking refuge when disturbed in the abrupt rock faces with which the hills abound. When the snow comes they retire to the edge of the timber, sheltering among the juniper bushes and stunted balsams from the early winter storms. Later on, when the deep snows have covered all their upland pastures, the sheep come down to the benches immediately above the river, retiring at midday to the canyons which lead to the first ridges. On the Frazer river in late November and early December all the sheep of the district are down by the river; indeed, one ram which I shot in 1892 was first sighted feeding in the middle of a small band of cattle on the flat. But winter is not the time for sheep hunting, nor the flats above the river the proper places to hunt them in. To enjoy sheep shooting to perfection a man should leave the Pacific coast in September, pass through the belt of water meadows and pine forests, where the pink fireweed contrasts vividly with the grey stems of the pines and the soft green of the ferns, and through the country of sage brush and rolling yellow bluffs. From this point his road will lie steadily upwards, over the rolling prairie, through belts of green timber where the deer swarm in winter, and then by thread-like trails over side-hills and stone-slides along the course of some tributary of the Frazer, until at last a great yellow cone, patched here and there with snow, rises clear above the timber-line in front of him. This is sheep-land, the land of the roaring wind (Skulloptin), but it will take him a good long day to reach it, and both he and his horses will be dead tired by the time they stop to camp. At first a sheer rock wall rises from the river; on the top of the rock is a bench of golden grass, and then again there is a sharp ascent and another bench of grass. Finally the ladder of benches is lost in the forest, which goes climbing away uphill in resolute fashion until towards nightfall the hunter reaches the land of stone-slides and burnt timber, and passing through that comes out upon the edge of the sheep downs, where the stream becomes no more than a succession of small pools amongst the moss, and the only trees still left are dwarfed, stunted, and twisted into all manner of forms by the violence of the mountain winds. If the sun has left the landscape when the hunter first sees it, the effect is weird and cheerless. The great brown wastes above, the soft silent mosses underfoot, the trees huddled together in little groups as if for mutual support, the hanging fringes of blackened beard moss, all help to accentuate the bleakness of the land over which the mountain wind sobs or shrieks. But in the morning all changes as if at a magician's word. The skies are cloudless, the sunlight dances on snowfield and streamlet, and even the grey stems of the trees are beautiful when contrasted with the ruddy orange of the Indian pinks at their feet—better than all, the hunter's lungs are filled with air which acts on him like champagne, and on the skyline, as likely as not, he sees the great white sterns of half a dozen sheep feeding quietly on their way back to their sleeping ground. By ten o'clock at latest those sheep will lie down, and then where they lie down they will stay, motionless as the grey rocks they lie amongst, until nearly four o'clock, their eyes apparently open the whole time and fixed steadily upon the *nearest skyline*. Generally, sheep will choose a little sheltered meadow at the foot of a small glacier, lying down in the very middle of it, each old ram with his head turned in a different direction, and each with his eyes fixed on a different skyline. When sheep have chosen such a position as this, the only thing to be done is to lie and watch them until they move away to some more accessible country. Many a time have I lain like this waiting until first one old ram and then another rose, stretched himself, and then lay down again for another forty winks. It is very exasperating, but when at last the whole band gets upon its legs and feeds slowly over a ridge from behind which it is possible to stalk them, verily you have your reward.

A Group of Bighorn

As illustrative of the nature of the country in which sheep west of the Rockies are killed, I have seen a well-known British Columbian rancher ride up to a band of ewes in the highlands of the Ashnola country, *galloping* after them until within range, then dismounting and killing two out of the band. This was in early autumn, and in what I consider the easiest country I have ever seen; in winter, of course, when the snows are heavy on the mountains, the sheep come right down on to the flat, by the edge of the Frazer river. Indeed, in the winter (end of November 1890) I found a fair-sized ram feeding amongst a band of cattle, and killed him before he had put a hundred yards between himself and them. Another recent statement to which I must take exception is that 'a man who can find a band of ten or fifteen (sheep) after a week's riding and climbing is a fortunate man.' Sheep extend from the Missouri to Alaska, and whatever their numbers may be east of the Rockies, they are certainly plentiful enough west of that range. In Cassiar they are very numerous, and along the banks of the Frazer I have in one season (1889) seen one band of seventy, one of sixty, and on another occasion, late in the fall, a friend of mine and myself came upon an immense band feeding in little bunches of fifteen and twenty, aggregating, I should think, at least 150. I did not and could not count them, but should imagine my estimate was absurdly within the limit. M. D. and I took them at first sight for strayed cattle from a neighbouring ranch. Later on we met a portion of this band going uphill, and watched them file past us, within twenty yards of us, each beast coming up on to a little mound immediately below our ambush, pausing for a moment to look downhill, and then making place for the next. In this procession the barren ewes led, the ewes and lambs came next, and the rams brought up the rear, with the biggest ram, for whom we were waiting, last of all. But though the Frazer River country contains plenty of sheep, neither this country nor Alaska seems to produce such fine heads as are found east of the Rockies. A 16-inch head (honest measurement) is an exceptionally good head for British Columbia. Let those who doubt this statement tape their trophies and judge for themselves. East of the Rockies larger heads are not uncommon; the largest of which I have any accurate information having been bought at Morley by my friend Mr. Arnold Pike. This head measured 17.25 ins. round the base of the horn, being, therefore, considerably bigger than the fine heads exhibited by Messrs. F. Cooper and H. Seton Karr in the American Exhibition. The record sheep head, according to Ward's excellent book, is 41 ins. in length and 17¼ in circumference.

Of course, there are stories of heads which measure far more than this—of giant heads with two twists to the horns; but they are never seen, although, like most sportsmen, I have myself once seen a head, which I did not secure, that will haunt me until my shooting days are done.

There is a tiny sheep district very far up in the mountains at the head of one of the Frazer's tributaries to which my Indian guide alone knew the trail. He had blazed it three years before, and burnt some timber whilst he was up there, in order that another year the sweet grasses which would spring in the *brulé* might attract plenty of deer to this his private hunting ground. From the bald top of Siyah, as I prefer to call this ground, we could see the great hills round the Frazer rolling down fold upon fold into their river-beds, their sides red-brown in the sunlight, a rich dark purple in the shadows. We were lying on the very highest ground, spying into a hollow below us in which a solitary sheep was feeding. 'Yoharlequin,' muttered the Siwash, 'it is a ewe.' Just as he spoke we both crouched close to the ground, though we were safe enough even from a bighorn's marvellously all-seeing eyes, for at that moment five more sheep walked slowly into sight. There was no doubt as to the new-comers. We were looking upon the finest bit of sheep ground I had ever seen, and the five were worthy of it. There was one enormous ram, two which would have satisfied any man, a fourth such as I had often killed before, and a small fellow.

Mr. Arnold Pike's great Ram

From a photograph

Everything seemed to favour us at first. The little glacier at the head of the dark gulch had sent a snow-stream tearing through the hollow, and this had cut a deep course up which we could sneak unseen. I suppose the water must have been bitterly cold, but we crawled through it for ten minutes without so much as noticing that when we had to come down to our knees the icy current ran into our trousers pockets, and though the wind blew off the glacier it was welcome, because for once it was right in our teeth. In the middle of the gulch was a big mound, and 240 yards from this (I measured the distance afterwards) stood the glorious three. Unless we could have burrowed, no man could have crept closer unseen, so that from this point I had to fire. But why tell the story, and what is the good of trying to instruct others when I so often break every rule myself? Three things I did on that day which I ought not to have done, and I paid the penalty for my folly. First, I took my Indian with me on the stalk, and, of course, at the critical moment he flurried me with his accursed 'Shoot, shoot!' He knew what the ram was like upon which I was trying slowly to draw a bead. Then I took two rifles with me upon that trip, and shot sometimes with one, sometimes with another. The result was that I shot badly with both, and knew nothing of either of them. Lastly, when I had missed or only wounded the big ram, I lost my head, and instead of waiting until the beasts should pause for a moment to look back, I fired three fluky shots at them 'on the run.' Not until the big beasts were behind a piece of rolling ground did I realise what a fool I had made of myself, and then, as we wanted meat badly, I took a quiet steady shot at the little ram which had hung behind, and killed him neatly at a good 400 yards—a shot which under ordinary circumstances I should never dream of attempting.

After waiting for awhile we followed the wounded beast, hoping that as we had given him time he would lie down and afford us a chance of another stalk. But, as the Indian said, 'there was no lie down in that ram.' He could only go very slowly (at a walk), but he could keep going, and over the ground to which he took us we could do no more.

We tried everything that we could think of to circumvent him, but it was no good. When the dusk was falling I got my last view of his great white quarters, lurching slowly over yet another ridge. He was evidently bound for a far country, and had no intention of stopping until he reached it; I was limping almost as badly as he was, and was far more 'done.' I had left a nasty piece of rock and ice behind me to recross on my way to camp, I had not a notion how far I had come, where my Indian was, or which was the nearest way to my camp, so with a heart full of bitterness I turned back, vowing to track him on the morrow and stay with him as long as he stayed in British Columbia.

But then I knew only that he was a very big ram. When I stood beside the beast which the Indian and myself had taken for a two-year-old at most, and taped his horns at 14½ ins., I had a better idea what the beast must have been like beside which this fair ram had seemed a pigmy. Of course, that night enough snow fell to hide the tracks of a mammoth! I try sometimes to console myself with the reflection that after all he was probably only a 16- or, at most, 17-in. ram, but it won't do. I know better. From blood-stains upon the rocks (my Indian had my glass) I am pretty sure that I shot through the withers the first time, and probably hit him very far back with one of the others.

It is an extraordinary thing that though sheep so often turn and bolt *downhill* when merely frightened, a wounded ram, especially a big one, will struggle on higher and higher as long as life and the possibility of ascending lasts.

I have noticed the same habit in Caucasian *tûr*; but, of course, my experience may be exceptional.

Sheep rut in October, but the season varies somewhat in different localities, being a little later in some than in others. However, in a good sheep country the hunter may be pretty sure of hearing the hollow clang of the horns of fighting rams some time in October, and, at least, he may be sure that in that month he has the best chance of coming across the really big beasts, which, his Indian will tell him, retire during the rest of the year to the very highest peaks. This I doubt myself, as I have always tried the highest ground, and never done any better there with the big rams than elsewhere. My own belief is that all the sheep frequent the open tops in July and August, when the grass is fresh where the snow has but recently disappeared; that in September they come down nearer the timber, and even into it, in search of sweeter feed than that which the sunburnt tops afford; that during this time the old rams are away by themselves hiding in the bush; and that in October, when the uplands have been revived by the late autumn rains, the ewes seek the hill-tops again, and the amorous rams follow the ewes.

But at whatever season you seek the bighorn, remember that he is very easily driven away, that all his senses are exceptionally keen, and that from his vantage ground above he incessantly watches the valley beneath. Therefore, if you are changing camp, do not arrange matters so as to arrive in a new country, which you intend to hunt, about nightfall, or if you do, reduce the chopping which has to be done to a minimum; don't light big fires, and let those you light be as much hidden as possible from the ridges upon which you expect to find game. If possible, it is better to get to a fresh shooting ground so early that you can do a day's hunting before there is any necessity for cutting timber or lighting a fire.

As it is not easy to weigh large game in camp, and as I am no believer in guess-weights, I shall not attempt to estimate the weight of a bighorn ram; but, bearing in mind that the *O. montana* is one of the most compactly built animals in the world, the curious in such matters may form an approximate idea of the beast's weight from the following measurements of a 16-in. ram, which I took myself within an hour of his death. Measuring him as he lay, this ram was 3 ft. 6 ins. from the root of his tail to where the neck is set on to the shoulder; his girth under his forelegs was 3 ft. 9 ins.; and his height, as nearly as I could get it, 3 ft. 2 ins. at the shoulder.

VI. THE ROCKY MOUNTAIN GOAT
(HAPLOCEROS MONTANUS)

The Rocky Mountain Goat may, like other animals, vary in its habits a good deal in different localities. In British Columbia, which appears to be peculiarly its home, I am bound to say that it appears to be the biggest fool that walks on four legs. I am aware that some authorities upon sport, whose opinions deserve consideration, differ from me upon this point, but living as I do at present amongst British Columbians, I am not afraid of being contradicted by local sportsmen when I aver that there is no wild animal easier to stalk than *Haploceros*. There are many men out here who, after having killed their first few heads, will have nothing more to do with goat hunting, regarding it as unworthy the name of sport. I remember well one old goat which I stalked in the Bridge River country. The beast was a very big one, and was first seen feeding upon a bare hillside. He was on one side of an amphitheatre, we were on the other. Between us lay over half a mile of rattling shale and moraine, and there was no cover for a mouse. However, there was nothing else to hunt, and the goat was the largest I had ever seen, so with my Indian behind me I began the stalk. I am confident that any other beast would have seen us before we had gone a hundred yards; we slipped and fell, we rattled the stones about, and the whole thing was so ludicrous that I had to sit down and laugh more than once; but in spite of all this I got within forty yards of the poor stupid brute, who had been looking in our direction in a puzzled way for the last ten minutes, and felt thoroughly ashamed of myself when I put an end to his doubts with a bullet. To give an idea of the tameness of these brutes, I took six or seven photographs of goats in one day last year with a very elaborate photographic apparatus, the photographs unfortunately being destroyed before they could be developed, when the whole apparatus, together with my guide, went rolling down a steep incline almost into the Bridge River.

Rocky Mountain Goats

Though not worth stalking, these goats are quaint beasts and worth watching. As a rule, they live where nothing else would care to, on precipitous rock faces overhanging a stream where no grass grows, and where there is very little even to browse upon. Just at dawn you may see them crossing a wall of rock high above your camp in single file, or wending their way slowly from their feeding grounds to the timber patches in which they lie all day. They are very local in their distribution and very conservative in their habits, infesting one small mountain in great numbers and never seeming to stray into the neighbouring heights. Day after day they appear to seek the same feeding grounds, and retire to the same lairs, with a punctuality which would be becoming in a postman. Their meat is so poor that Indians will hardly eat it, and the market value of their hides is only 3s. 6d. to a tourist. They occupy only such localities as other beasts would despise, and altogether seem somewhat justified in the mute protest of their wondering regard when attacked, which seems to say as plainly as dumb beasts can speak, 'Surely you are not going to meddle with us; we, at least, are beasts of no account.' To obtain a good specimen head their haunts ought to be visited as late in the year as possible, as the coats are not so white or the beards so long in early autumn as they are in November, and a goat's head without the long patriarchal beard is a poor affair. They abound all over British Columbia, especially in such places as Bute Inlet, and I have even seen them on the islands in the Straits of San Juan, from which I am inclined to infer that they had swum over from the mainland. An old billy which I shot girthed 56 ins. round the chest after he had been skinned, and the longest horns of which I have any record measured 11½ ins. from base to tip. The accompanying plate gives a better idea of the queer old-world appearance of the Rocky Mountain goat than any word-painting of mine could do. In old days, the Indians used to make blankets of their fleece, but the industry appears to be nearly dead, now that English blankets have become cheap and plentiful in British Columbia, so that there appears to be no reason why the white goat should not be allowed to remain unmolested for many years to come. I have seen *Haploceros* in Alaska as well as in British Columbia, and expect that my friend Mr. John Fannin, curator of the British Columbian Museum, is right in inferring that the goats go as far north as the mountains do. The skin, measured by Mr. Fannin, and mentioned in his article upon goats in the 'Big Game of North America,' is far and away the largest I have ever heard of, a skin 5 ft. from horns to tail, by 40 ins. from side to side, being an exceptionally large one, whereas Mr. Fannin's large skin measured 7 ft. by 4 ft. 10 ins.

The track of the goat is not unlike that of a large bighorn ram, but squarer and blunter.

VII. THE PRONGHORN ANTELOPE
(ANTILOCAPRA AMERICANA)

The scheme of these volumes does not allow for a full and detailed account of the shooting of every variety of game found in each country. It may therefore suffice to say of this antelope that it may be killed as any other antelope is killed, either by stalking, the shots being taken as a rule at long ranges, or by coursing. There are very few parts of America, if any, in which the antelope has been so little hunted as to allow the old ruse of flagging (i.e. of attracting them within range by the exhibition of strange objects which arouse their curiosity) to be practised with success. Ten or fifteen years ago, antelope might be seen from the windows of almost every train running west of Chicago, but now their range is vastly curtailed, and though a few small herds may still be found in most of their old haunts, they are not really abundant except in Texas, in the neighbourhood of the National Park, and in Assineboia, where in 1893 I saw two considerable bands in April from the carriage windows of the Canadian Pacific Railway train.

Antilocapra americana

C. Whymper

In Texas, a friend who was there in November 1892 wrote me: 'There seems to be plenty of antelope round here, as they are frequently brought into town, sometimes by the cartload to be shipped.' In California antelopes have been almost exterminated, and the same may be said of Oregon, whilst in Colorado the districts in which they occur are not numerous, nor even in these does the beast exist in any numbers, except where it has been preserved. It seems likely that the pronghorn will be the next of the American mammals to disappear before the arms of the white man. Like the buffalo, the antelope is a dweller on the plains, seldom seeking refuge either in the timber or in the high mountains, although he is found at a very considerable altitude on the high tablelands near Gunnison, Colorado, for example (6,000 to 7,000 ft. at least above sea level). The season for antelope shooting should be from August to the middle or end of October, after which time the oldest of the bucks will have shed the shell-like covering of their horns. The rutting season lasts for about six weeks, beginning in September and ending in October. The pronghorn, though an inhabitant of the great plains, is not a wanderer as most denizens of such countries are, but seems to attach himself to a certain district, and to remain there or near there until his tribe has been exterminated. For instance, there is a small band which may be seen almost any day in winter within a few miles of one of the big cities of Colorado. The band grows smaller year by year, but it never alters its winter quarters in consequence of man's persecution. The pronghorn has, moreover, other enemies to contend against besides man and his Winchester, the great eagles of the North-West occasionally taking toll from the herds. An instance of this was seen by Mr. A. Pike in Colorado last year, when the buck, after dodging the eagle's attacks for some time, escaped into some brush; but such attacks are said by the plainsmen to be fairly frequent and often successful.

A Herd of Pronghorns

C. Whymper

Mr. Rowland Ward gives 15¾ ins. as the length of the longest horn of the pronghorn within his knowledge.

VIII. THE DEER OF AMERICA

Judge Caton, an authority upon the deer of his own country, describes eight well-defined species as inhabiting the North American continent. These are the wapiti (*C. canadensis*), the moose (*C. alces*), the woodland caribou (*C. tarandus*), the Barren Ground caribou (*C. tarandus arcticus*), the mule deer (*C. macrotis*), the Columbian black-tailed deer (*C. columbianus*), the Virginian or white-tailed deer (*C. virginianus*), and a little-known beast called by Caton *C. acapulcensis*.

With the last-named a sportsman is likely to have very little to do, as its range is extremely limited and its size insignificant ('weight from 30 to 40 lbs., height 24 ins. at the shoulder, and length from the end of the nose to the root of the tail 44 ins.'; cf. Caton's 'Deer of America,' pp. 121, 122), whilst its antlers, though quaint, are hardly worth taking as a trophy. Caton gives a cut of the antlers of a full-grown buck of this species. Of the originals of that cut Caton says that they measure in length 7 ins. and 3 lines, in circumference above the burr 2 ins., and that they are more palmated than the horns of any other American deer except moose and caribou. For further information on this deer the reader is referred to Caton's work, which should be in the library of every man interested in natural history. Of the other seven species of American cervidæ there is much to be said, and little space left to say it in.

(1) Moose (*C. alces*)

The Record Head

From a photograph

Of all deer extant to-day, the moose is the largest. Of all earth's animals, except perhaps old *Haploceros*, he bears most plainly still the impress of Nature's 'prentice hand when she made things huge and roughhewn, and had no time to polish her work and smooth off the corners. Evolution does not seem to have affected the moose, for to-day he wanders along that great chain of lakes from the Arctic to the Atlantic, from the mouth of the Mackenzie River to the St. Lawrence—a survival of the earth's dawn rather than a commonplace nineteenth-century deer. All sorts of stories are told as to his weight and size. Caton, who is always careful not to exaggerate, puts the weight of a bull moose at from 700 to 1,400 lbs., and his height at 6 ft. at the withers. The largest pair of horns of which we have any authentic record (the cut is from a photograph of them) measures in span 66 ins. (or 5 ft. 6 ins.) from tip to tip, but a recent writer in an American work upon sport and natural history (Mr. Hibbs) describes a moose which he saw dead in the Teton Basin, whose antlers spanned 8 ft. 6 ins. from tip to tip, making an arch when inverted under which a man 'slightly stooping' could walk. This Titan of the Tetons stood, '*without his legs under him*, 15 hands high,' so that, allowing for the fact that a moose has, according to Caton, 'very long legs, to which he is indebted for his great height,' he must have stood in life, *with his legs under him*, from 8 to 9 ft. high at the withers. This seems rather tall, even for a moose from the Rocky Mountains. As before stated, this great deer ranges from the Arctic Ocean to the St. Lawrence, and in spite of the persecution of man still abounds as far east as the provinces of Quebec and Ontario; is reported to exist in large numbers on the head-waters of the Clear Water River, in Idaho; is found in Montana and Wyoming, and flourishes exceedingly in the North-Western portions of British Columbia as well as in the adjoining territory of Alaska.

With great wisdom the Legislatures both of Canada and the States have taken the moose under their protection, but the great deer would be in no danger of extermination even if the law had overlooked him, as he has haunts still remote, and except in deep snow can take very fair care of himself; indeed, even as lately as 1887 I could have killed seven bull moose in six days' hunting in Ontario had I been butcher enough to do so, whilst in 1891 I saw two canoes (big freight canoes) come down loaded with magnificent moose horns from a district where almost the only residents are a few Siwashes (Indians) and some Chinese miners! Where Chinese kill game, game must be fairly plentiful still.

Although as big as a haystack, the moose is not quite as easy to hit, nor is he everybody's 'meat.' His favourite haunts are the dense thickets round lakes and about river-bottoms, the dark balsam groves, hardwood hills, and brulé patches of Ontario, and wherever the lily pads, moose wood, swamp maple, alder bushes, coarse grasses or mosses upon which he feeds are most luxuriant.

By some strange fatality, wherever things are most convenient for the moose they appear to be least convenient for the hunter. The scrub over which the moose looks without raising his ugly head closes over and drowns the unfortunate biped who tries to follow him; the fallen trees and huge logs which the moose takes comfortably in his stride must be climbed by the hunter, and yet, in spite of his size, when the big bull has answered your call and has come crashing through the alder and swamp tea to within twenty yards of you, he is likely enough to halt in the shadow, detect the fraud, and steal away without a sound.

Moose at Home

C. Whymper

Like other deer, the moose seems slow to identify objects with his eyes, but there is no doubt about the keenness of his other senses. If it pleases him to answer your call, though his answer may be all but inaudible to you, you need not call again unless you like. Through a mile of brush which to you appears a pathless tangle he will steer straight to the square yard from which your call came, unless a bough should scrape against your overalls or a tiny puff of wind carry the faintest suggestion of your presence to him. If either of these things happen, the moose will make up his mind without stopping to think. In addition to the keenness of his senses the bull moose is credited with considerable pugnacity when pursued and 'cornered,' and he undoubtedly is a bit of a strategist, choosing his couch, for instance, invariably in such a position as to command the country all round. The Indians, when following a moose's track, will, oftener than not, keep describing a succession of semicircles, so that, instead of walking in the bull's tracks, they cut them from time to time. This is done to outwit the bull, who, they say, when he means to lie down will turn aside and walk back parallel to his trail, and lie down with his head towards his back tracks, so that either his eyes or his nose must give him warning of anyone who attempts to follow him.

There are three principal methods of hunting the moose besides the foul practice of snaring him with a loop in his run ways or of butchering him in his yards (i.e. in those camps and feeding grounds which moose stamp out for themselves in the deepest snows of winter). The favourite method (in Canada, at any rate) is 'calling,' a birch-bark horn being used night and morning to imitate either the cry of the bull or of the cow, and so lure a would-be mate or rival (as the case may be) to his ruin. September is the season of the rut in Lower Canada, and during the earlier part of this season the bull seems nearly beside himself with rage and unrequited passion, wandering constantly in search of a mate or a rival, and filling the woods with hoarse calls or hoarser challenges. About one man in a million is clever enough to mimic these calls, and if you are lucky enough either to be that man or his employer, you may take advantage of the moonlight and lie out behind some log or bush watching the skyline and listening while the half-breed (it will probably be a French half-breed) grunts and roars upon the horn, imitates the thrashing of the bull's antlers amongst the alder-bushes. Experts disagree as to the amount of skill required to call a moose. Some say that any noise is good enough when he is really on the war-path, that the chopping of an axe or the bray of a donkey will 'fetch' him; others again affirm that the nicest accuracy is necessary in imitating every call, and I am bound to admit that, though I have never met a man who had seen a moose drawn to his ruin by the sound of chopping, I have more than once known that a moose owed his life to the fact that my overalls were made of a peculiarly harsh material from which the brush in passing managed to elicit a very penetrating sound.

If all goes well with the caller, it may be that at last he will hear, faint and far off, a hoarse response from the depths of the swamp below him, a response repeated from time to time, and growing each time nearer, until at last, if he can hear anything but the beating of his own heart, he will hear the scrub crunched under the foot of the advancing monster. As long as all goes well, the quiet night betrays the bull's every movement to the hidden man, almost as clearly as if the hunter could watch the whole play with his naked eyes. Now the bull comes crashing up from the swamp through the alder-bushes, now he is standing listening half in doubt as to whether to come on or go back, but the half-breed is prepared for the emergency. Good as he is, he dare not try a call at such close quarters, but he strikes the horn against the scrub and the bull comes on again, thinking that he has heard the rattle of his enemy's weapons.

When at last, with strangely little warning it seems to you, and much closer to you than you had expected, that monstrous form looms up against the half-light, remember to *look at its shoulder*, and try not to merit my Indian's reproof to me when a bullet went six inches too high—'All same again, you allus look at the horns instead of the bull, cap.'

Moose calling has almost every attribute of true sport. To succeed, a man must know the habits of his quarry and have admirable opportunities for studying them; if he 'calls' himself, he must have an excellent ear and be a perfect mimic, and for him the morning and the evening, moonlight and the grey of dawn, lend their beauty to the beauty of the silent woods. But for some men, 'calling' hardly gives the man enough to do. To these men I recommend still hunting over the hardwood hills about the time of the first snowfall, when there is enough snow to track in, with a good French Canadian half-breed as a guide. To my mind there is hardly any better sport on earth than to follow the great tracks through the new-fallen snow, through woods beautiful beyond all description with the beauty of a Canadian winter, over hardwood hills, and through patches of brulé, and then down into a bed of frozen willows, silvered by the frost, and jewelled by the sun, through swamps of tea-bush off which the frost falls in showers of crisp scales, until late in the afternoon you run up to your beast in a heavy grove of balsam, looking intensely black against the blinding purity of the snow. But for this sport you want young limbs and strong ones, and the wind and endurance of a temperate and clean liver. You want these for any sport worth the name.

There is yet another way of hunting moose, when the snows are down and the crust upon them is strong enough to bear a man on snow-shoes, but not strong enough to carry the moose. Of course, all the odds are against the animal, but still this is exciting sport, making tremendous demands upon the man's endurance; and it is moreover when pursued in this way that the moose is said to turn 'ugly' and sometimes hunt the hunter. Provided that a man only kills old bulls, and not too many of them, I see no objection to this form of pursuit. The percentage of men who can run to within shooting distance of a bull moose when trying to escape through his native forest, even when the snow is at its worst for the bull, will never be very great, and the excitement of the sport must be intense. I have never yet had a chance of trying it.

Even when a man is in the best of luck, what he generally has to shoot at, and that in a hurry, is not a beast 8 ft. high, weighing 1,400 lbs., standing broadside on in the open, but a small piece of brown passing between the boles of the pine-trees in deep shadow, one or two hundred yards off. The Indian may tell him that what he sees is a moose. Nine men out of ten would not have discovered the fact for themselves.

(2) The Wapiti (*C. canadensis*)

The creatures of the nineteenth century are the children of the earth's old age. The days of the giants are over, and the days of the pigmies are upon us. When our naked forefathers were armed only with bows and arrows, there were elk in Ireland whose antlers spanned 11 ft. from tip to tip, and even in the more recent days of the Hudson Bay musket, there were (so men say) wapiti in Wyoming whose antlers when inverted formed arches under which a six-foot man might pass without stooping.

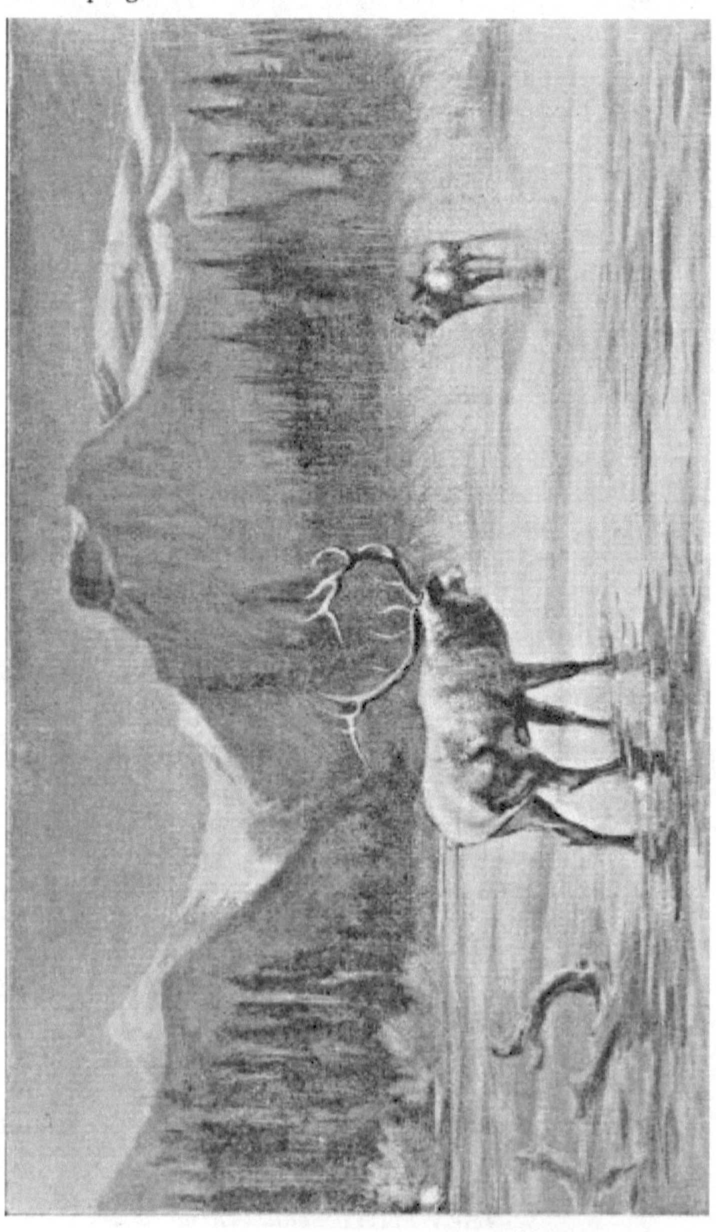

Wapiti in the Emerald Pass, British Columbia

C. W., from a photograph

Alas! there are no such wapiti nowadays, and indeed, although there are scores of men in the States who will assure you that they have themselves walked under such arches, it is very hard to believe that they are not mistaken, in the face of the fact that a *four-foot man* could not walk under the largest head known to be in existence at the present moment, though the longest wapiti head in the American Exhibition of 1887 (belonging to Mr. Frank Cooper, and numbered 89 in the catalogue) is described as measuring 62½ ins. along the back of the beam from base to tip of the longest tine, with an expanse between the antlers of 48½ ins.

It is not easy, either in America or elsewhere, to find a head (dead or alive) which will beat this by an inch in any direction; and yet, if this head were inverted, no *four-foot man* could walk without stooping under the arch so made. During several years spent in wandering about Canada and the States, I have heard again and again of gigantic wapiti heads; I have even met men who own such trophies, and have actually bought them for $500, the money to be paid when the 'head' was delivered. Unfortunately, my cash was never claimed, and I confess that I never expected that it would be, yet some of the trophy-owners wanted money 'in the worst way.'

But though the 'bull elk' of to-day is neither as large as the Irish elk nor as the 'elk' of pioneer legends, he is still a magnificent beast, not quite as big as the moose and not carrying a very much larger head on the average than the Caucasian stag; but still, take him all in all, he is the grandest stag left on earth. To an unscientific eye, the wapiti differs from the Scotch red deer in three points only: he is larger of course, his antlers as a rule lack the cup peculiar to the Scotch royal, and his call in the rutting season is a whistle, whilst the red deer's is a roar. His range in America is still a wide one, although the encroachments of civilization are driving him ever further and further back into that dense timber of which he is always too fond. It is this love of the timber which has enabled the wapiti to outlive his old comrade the bison, and will probably enable him to survive the antelope, which seems likely to be one of the next animals wiped off the face of the great American continent. In the mountain forests of Wyoming and Montana, of Idaho and Colorado, wapiti are still fairly plentiful; in California, I have heard that there are a good many in the red-wood districts, though of this I have no certain knowledge; but there is no doubt that the home, *par excellence*, of the wapiti to-day is in the dense timber of the Olympian range, in Washington Territory, in Oregon, and to a certain extent in Vancouver Island, British Columbia. In the early part of this century there were wapiti on the mainland of British Columbia, and their bones may still be found pretty frequently in the Chilcotin country; but the animals themselves are said to have been exterminated by the Indians or starved to death during an exceptionally severe winter sixty or seventy years ago. Be that as it may, there are no wapiti on the mainland of British Columbia to-day, nor are there anywhere (unless it be in the fastnesses of the Olympian range) any vast herds of this splendid beast such as we read of in the books of the pioneer sportsmen of the North-West. For this change for the worse we have to thank the meat-hunter, the skin-hunter, and the ranchman about equally, although perhaps the advent of cattle does more to drive deer out of a country than anything else. As an example of what *was* as compared to what *is*, I may cite the case of my old camp man, Sam Wells, who, when the Union Pacific Railway was being built to the west of Cheyenne, killed, in his capacity of meat-hunter to the construction party, 84 antelope, 24 elk, and 18 deer during one autumn; whereas this year, in the best bit of country known to him in Colorado, our camp was many days without meat, and myself and my friend were looked upon as exceptionally fortunate in having secured three good heads (wapiti) in three weeks' hunting. It is fair to add that the country hunted, although comparatively little disturbed, was very near to a good-sized town.

It is said that before the advent of the white man the wapiti frequented the plains, where the rich bunch grass helped to build up the enormous antlers of which we hear so much and see so little. Nowadays men and cattle have driven the wapiti from the bunch-grass plains, and he has become almost entirely a denizen of the dense timber districts.

In Colorado, where I hunted wapiti in 1892, we found our game in the timber at an elevation of 10,000 ft. above sea level, but I have shot them in equally dense timber on Vancouver Island at little above sea level. Speaking broadly, the habits of the wapiti and of the Scotch red deer are identical, except for the former's detestable predilection for timber. About the beginning of September the 'bull elk,' as all Americans insist on calling him, has rubbed the velvet off his antlers, and ten days later these antlers are dry and hard and fit for fighting. The rubbing, or 'fraying,' is generally done against the stem of a quaking asp or young green pine, the wapiti never using a dry stick for his rubbing-post. As soon as his horns are dry, the bull begins whistling or bugling, this whistling being kept up until about the middle of October. I am inclined to think that the whistling (i.e. the rutting) season varies a good deal in different districts according to the seasons and the altitude at which the bulls find themselves. In Colorado in 1892 we heard the first whistle on September 16th, and the last about three weeks later; and although our old guide considered 1892 an exceptionally early season, I fancy that from the middle of September to the middle of October may be looked upon as the ordinary rutting season of *Cervus canadensis*.

There is nothing about the wapiti more characteristic or more striking than his whistle, a call wild enough and weird enough to harmonise with the savagery of the beast's surroundings. I have never yet met a man who could imitate the whistle or even adequately describe it; but if I must attempt to give some idea of it, I should say that it was a long flute-like sound, sometimes rising and falling, and ending more often than not in two or three hoarse, angry grunts. Like the Scotch red deer, the wapiti carries his horns until March, my friend Mr. Arnold Pike having seen two old bulls with good heads on the 29th of March of this year. In Colorado, as in Vancouver Island, each band of wapiti seems to confine itself pretty closely to a particular district, never moving more than twenty or thirty miles from one place, but travelling on occasion from one side to another of its domains with a rapidity which is exasperating to the hunter who has to follow with a pack train. Early in September the principal food of the wapiti appears to be the pink-flowered fireweed (*phlox*), which grows in rank luxuriance amongst the burnt timber; and later on, when the frost has nipped the tops of the young elder bushes, these seem to attract a good deal of the great deer's attention. But *Cervus canadensis* is a somewhat promiscuous feeder, all grasses and most weeds and bushes seeming to be included in his list of things to be eaten. The young tops of the quaking asp, of the willow, and of a low creeping shrub locally known as elk weed, all seem favourites in their season.

On such food as this the wapiti grows to prodigious proportions, of which the following measurements, supplied by Mr. Andrew Williamson, give the best idea. Mr. Williamson killed sixteen bulls in one season in Colorado in 1878, of which the largest measured 9 ft. from the tip of the nose to the tail, stood 17 hands at the shoulder, and girthed 6 ft. 8 ins. round the heart. The average measurements of eight out of the sixteen bulls were as follows: Length from nose to tail, 8 ft. 5 ins.; height at shoulders, 16 hands and 5/8 in.; girth round the heart, 6 ft. 1 in. Compare these measurements with those of the largest racehorse on record, and you get some idea of the size of the wapiti, though even then the figure which you will conjure up will be small compared with the apparition which sometimes confronts a Western hunter upon the skyline, or to a 'bull elk' at bay with his head down, his bristles up, and his eyes glaring angrily at the insignificant collie yapping round him. The average length of the antlers of Mr. Williamson's bulls is given as 53 ins., and the span of these antlers, measured *inside* the beam, as 44 ins. As to the weight of a wapiti, it is unfortunate that the man who kills one has very rarely any apparatus at hand for weighing his prize; and even Mr. Caton, the great American authority upon the *Cervidæ* of North America, gives neither measurements nor weights of full-grown bulls.

In his work upon the deer of America, this writer mentions a bull once in his possession which when killed, as a *five-year-old* weighed 900 lbs. live weight; and adds that 'as the elk grows till he is eight or nine years old, he (this bull) would, had he lived to his full age, have attained to the weight of 1,000 or 1,100 lbs.' Colonel Dodge, in his 'Plains of the Great West,' puts the weight of an average 'elk' at only 500 lbs., although he qualifies this by adding that one has been killed which weighed 800 lbs.; while Mr. Andrew Williamson, in his 'Sport and Photography in the Rockies,' guesses the weight of his big bull at 1,200 lbs. But most of this is guesswork. The nearest approach to an accurate record of weight in my possession is taken from a statement made to me by an old Western meat-hunter in whose truthfulness I have every confidence. This man told me that the hind-quarters of the largest bull he ever killed ('and I cut 'em off pretty high up,' he added) weighed, when taken into town, a little over 400 lbs. From this it would appear that the live weight of the whole animal could not have fallen far short of Mr. Williamson's estimate of the weight of his big bull.

In spite of the fact that no large areas of food pasture are known on Vancouver Island, the wapiti found upon it do not, in point of size, fall far short of those upon the mainland of the American continent. I have myself, at the head of the Salmon River on this island, shot a bull which measured rather over 16 hands and 1 in. at the shoulder, and appeared to be a heavy stag for his size. Indeed, if the wapiti of Vancouver Island vary at all from deer of the same species on the mainland, it is in their antlers, which have always seemed to me to be peculiarly heavy in the beam and narrow in the span, whilst amongst them I have more than once noticed specimens having cups similar to those of a Scotch royal: a somewhat remarkable fact, as this formation is exceptionally rare amongst the wapiti on the mainland of America.

To anyone who has read this chapter thus far believing what he read, it must appear that *Cervus canadensis* is as fine a game animal as the heart of a hunter could desire. But I have only presented hitherto the fair side of the picture; of course it has another. The wapiti is superb, but his habits are beneath contempt. While the gallant mountain ram lives out on the open hill-tops, staking his life boldly upon the keenness of his own senses, the great 'bull elk' sneaks about in the shadows of the densest timber he can find just below the edge of the sheep ground, pottering about the beds of mountain streams, poking his head noiselessly through the thickets of willow round the parks, picking his way gingerly over chaotic windfalls of burnt timber, and dozing by day on the top of some woodland ridge which a shadow in moccasins could hardly reach unheard.

But 'what's the good of gassing?' as old Sam Wells would say. Come away to my camp in Colorado and see the bull elk for yourself. And first let me warn you that here in his own land, *Cervus canadensis* is 'elk,' or 'bull elick' on occasion, but never wapiti. The 'boys' don't know what a wapiti is; never 'heerd tell on him' as like as not. *Cervus canadensis* is, of course, the wapiti of the naturalists and a few thousand Englishmen and scientific gentlemen, just as the buffalo is the bison of the same well-informed circle; but to sixty or seventy millions of white men these beasts are elk and buffalo, now, henceforth, and for ever. The 'boys' round camp are rude enough to say that '*they* know what a bull elk is, and if they don't, who the — — does?' and as I hate arguing (where arguments are sometimes six-chambered), it may be as well to call *Cervus canadensis* by his local name for the next few pages.

Our camp, then, is pitched at an altitude of nearly 10,000 ft. above sea level, on the edge of a great park or 'open' of rank yellow grass, through which a mountain stream twists and turns. Years ago, before Sam Wells cleared them out, beavers had dammed this stream, and the park stills owes a good deal of its richness to their operations. Above the park in a great circle the dark ranks of the pine-trees close in; whilst above them again rise the bare ridges and strangely castellated tops of the 'divide.'

In the early summer the elk may have wandered upon those bare ridges (their tracks prove it, and a natural desire to avoid their insect tormentors accounts for it), but they are not upon those ridges now. As the rutting season approaches the elk come down from the high places, and in September every one of the forty or fifty beasts which live all the year round in this little district is within that dark belt of timber, worse luck to it!

Since June there has been no rain in the State of Colorado, nor can even the most sanguine of us see any promise of rain to come in the crystal clear vault above us.

By day the sun is hot enough to make men sit about in their shirt-sleeves, but by night the frost makes us draw our blankets closer, and almost wish for another pair. It is perfect weather for picnicing in the woods, but it is impossible weather for still hunting.

Between them, sun and frost and mountain air have made the woods dry as a chip and crisp as a biscuit. The woodland solitudes are more noisy than Chinatown at New Year: the leaves rattle like dead men's bones, and the twigs seem to explode like fire-crackers under your feet.

But it is September; the hunter's moon has begun, and now and again, just about dawn or towards evening, there is a hollow whistle from the depths of the pine forests, followed by a succession of hoarse choking grunts. This is the love song of the great bull, and for the moment he is careless of rustling leaves and snapped twigs, and, being in love, is as great a fool as a biped under similar circumstances. Nor is love the bull elk's only excuse for imprudence just now. In summer the great woods are still, but for the hum of insect life; in winter they are still as death; but now, in late autumn, they are full of sounds. Winter is coming, and everything that has breath is busy laying in stores for the approaching snow-time. All day long there is a rattle among the brush as creatures bustle through it; all day long the great fir-cones come thumping down from the pine-tops, while the squirrels who are gathering them chatter and swear at one another with the vigour and bitterness of rivals in business. Chipmunks, engaged in the same work of harvest, skip like long-legged streaks of light along the logs, and the short-tailed grey rats are as busy as either squirrels or chipmunks. As you cross the hillside, your foot sinks deep into the light soil, for the earth is full of little tunnels, and every tunnel is choked with garnered pine-cones; whilst in the high places amongst the rocks you come now and again upon a miniature haystack, neatly cut, and made of dried Alpine flowers and grasses, prepared for winter use by one of Nature's invisible workers.

As you lie upon the hillside in the warm sun at noon, with the timber all below you and a good day's work behind you, you will have time to note these things; but just now, though the stars are still visible, you should not be 'foolin' around camp' any longer, if you want to get a shot at a bull before sundown.

It is no good pleading that you have toiled for a fortnight and seen nothing; that your limbs ache, your clothes are torn to rags, and your hands and feet wounded by the beastly dead timber. Such heads as bull elk wear in Colorado can only be earned nowadays by early rising, long patience, and honest hard work; so off with you, while the rime is on the sage brush, in spite of the temptation to stop until Sam has cooked just one rasher of sow-belly. The first crossing of the brook, before you are a hundred yards from camp, will effectually wake you up and make you step out, unless you want to 'freeze solid,' for the stepping-stones at this early hour are coated with ice, and neither courage nor caution, neither moccasins, nails, nor even sand, can save you from a cold plunge. Great Cæsar's ghost! how cold it is; and how warm even the woodland bogs strike after that running water!

Here, within half a mile of your camp, is the first sign of elk; a great wallow made in the marsh late yesterday evening, and running from the wallow is a trail, well beaten, which leads, as you know, by a very circuitous route to that bare patch of red mud where the elk lick for alkali. But we have no time to follow the trail to-day, more especially as the elk seem to leave the lick before dawn. Our hunting-ground is in a belt of burnt timber very near the top of the divide, and to reach it in time we must climb straight up one ridge after another without staying to look for trails and easy places. From camp the belt of timber looks as if it lay upon a smooth, gently rising hillside. Once within it, you learn that the belt is composed of densely timbered ridges rising one behind another like waves in a choppy sea, and as you toil through and over these ridges, you wish, if you are an ordinary man, that you had never heard of elk.

Everywhere the trees crowd one another for light and breathing room, but so long as they are standing (unless they are young green pines) a man may walk at ease among them. It is when fire and wind have swept through them and left them in chaotic tangles upon the ground that the trouble begins. Then it is that the elk hunter has to rival the squirrel or Blondin, tacking from point to point along the pine logs, now straining every muscle to get a grip on the slippery trunk of a pine which offers a bridge uphill across the prone carcases of its fellows, now manfully suppressing an oath as his feet slip and he sits down inadvertently upon the 'business end' of a rampike.

For an hour, perhaps, or two, there is little or no change in your work. Your road may lie through dense green timber at one moment, through half-lit mossy glades at another, and the next through hollows full of burnt timber, amongst which the elk tracks are thick, and the pink fire-flower blooms; but it is always uphill work, and almost always in places where still hunting is impossible. Now and again there is something to cheer you up and encourage you to make fresh exertions. Now it is a great track like a deer's, but larger and blunter; now it is the stem of a young quaking asp with its bark hanging in ribbons, which makes your heart beat quicker; or perhaps it is only the freshly nibbled buds of a young elder bush. There is no doubt that there are elk about, and a good many of them, and as you stretch in vain to reach the scars upon the quaking asp, you realise that there are big bulls among them; but what is the use of the biggest bull if you are never to see him within two hundred yards? Once to-day you heard a bough break several hundred yards below you, and a few minutes later you saw the warm lair from which an elk had stolen away; but you never saw him, never even heard him, until he was well out of range.

'Hang the luck!' you mutter; in another hour the wind that rises about noon will get up and then the odds will be doubled against you. Will the luck never change? Well, yes. Just as you are deciding for the twentieth time that you never will hunt elk again, there is a long hollow whistle among the pines below you. The whistle is faint and far off, and if you had not been sitting down and at rest you would never have heard it. You have, as a matter of fact, failed to hear two or three similar whistles during the morning—whistles which a better woodsman would have heard, and which even you would never have missed had you taken Sam's advice and gone slow, 'settin' down once in a while to listen.'

You are not likely to see a motionless stag when you are scrambling through the brush, or to hear a bull's stealthy tread upon the trail, or his distant call, whilst you are forcing your way through a barricade of burnt timber.

Well, luck, which after all counts for more in hunting than all the skill and experience of the best hunter—luck has favoured you at last, and there the whistle comes again, and directly after it another, followed this time by deep, hoarse grunts, so deep and hoarse and so close to you that, as Sam puts it, 'your hair almost lifts your cap off your head.' That last bull was within five hundred yards of you, and there can be no doubt about his size. Creeping forward, you look cautiously over the brow of a little ridge on to a flat, where amongst the black, burnt stems of the dead pines the tall jungle of fireweed is vivid with every shade from fresh green to royal purple, scarlet, and orange, and even as you look, without a sound, a great head is pushed out from a bunch of quaking asp. For what seems to you an age the cow stares straight at you, and then, when you are almost in despair, moves quietly into the open followed by her calf. In another moment the bull appears on the cow's trail, without any display of that caution shown by her. There are others, you think, still in the timber, and a gleam of brown moving between the pine stems convinces you that you are right; but there is no doubt that this is the master bull of the herd, and you fairly catch your breath at the sight of his vast antlers.

As he stands there, sounding again his weird, unearthly challenge, you realise that you are looking upon one of Nature's masterpieces set in a fitting frame. When your finger presses the trigger it will destroy the picture, and yet if you hesitate much longer all your labour will be lost, and you will have no royal trophy to remind you of this day, when the good rifle is rusting with disuse and your limbs are stiff with old age.

For my part, if I could get a camera which would do good work at a hundred yards, I would rather press a button than a trigger. However, like the rest of us, the bull must die some day; if you don't kill him there is a 'prominent citizen' somewhere who made a pile in hardware, who will give a hundred dollars for those splendid antlers, and the bar-tender in the same city (a gentleman 'way up in the Order of the Elks') will give five dollars apiece for his tushes, so that, after all, you may as well fire the shot and take the spoils yourself.

For a moment the woods ring with the report; the other elk vanish like the figures of a dream, but the bull stands unflinching, as if he had neither heard the shot nor felt the sting of the bullet.

A little shiver creeps over him, and he seems to draw himself together. A moment he stands a royal figure amongst the grey mosses of his native forest, above his head a haze of golden aspen leaves, like drops of pale gold in a sea of deep amethyst, and then he staggers and crashes down amongst the giant pines lying dead like himself athwart the forest floor.

The sport is over; there is nothing left to do but butcher's work; the forest which a moment ago seemed full of moving forms is empty and still again—and are you quite sure that there is no reproach in the silence? It seems almost a pity that sport must end in the death of such a noble victim.

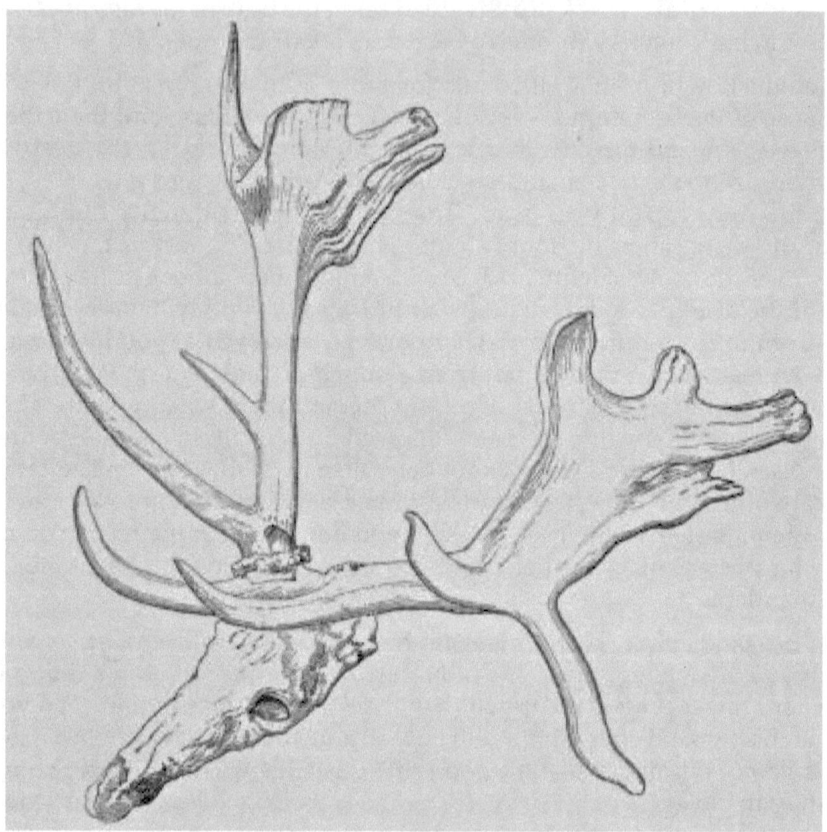

Abnormal Palmated Wapiti Head

The largest wapiti head of which I have been able to obtain trustworthy dimensions belongs to Messrs. Schoverling & Daly of New York. This head measures in length along the beam, 64 ins. (left) and 65 ins. (right); its greatest width is 48 ins. The circumference of the beam is 7⅝ ins. It is a head of 14 points. A cut of an abnormal wapiti head from Boseman is here given, and it is perhaps worth mentioning that this apparent tendency to become palmated is not rare in the horns of wapiti. An exceptionally fine head in the possession of Mr. G. B. Wrey is a good instance of this tendency and has also the remarkable girth of nearly 9 ins. in the beam. The beast was, I believe, killed in Montana.

(3) WOODLAND CARIBOU (*C. tarandus*).

If we except *C. canadensis*, the woodland caribou comes next in size to the moose, amongst American *cervidæ*. Luckily I have been able to obtain some accurate measurements of a bull caribou, taken while the beast was still in the flesh by a man who knew the value of precision. This bull, killed in 1890 by Mr. John Fannin, measured from the nose to the root of the tail 6 ft. 7 ins.; stood 4 ft. 5 ins. at the shoulder, and 4 ft. 7 ins. behind the saddle on the rump; his girth just behind the forelegs was 5 ft. 1 in., and the length of his neck (measured along the top) was 1 ft. 5 ins. His weight was never accurately ascertained, but a fair estimate would be 400 lbs. live weight. These dimensions seem to me to give a better idea of this long, low, heavily-built beast than any which I could pen, but I freely confess that one of them comes as a surprise to me. I should never have imagined that a caribou stood higher behind than he does in front, but I know my authority too well to doubt his accuracy in such a matter. Our British Columbian caribou is reputed to grow larger than the caribou of Eastern Canada, and those heads which I have seen in the east were certainly not nearly as fine as heads which I have seen out here. It is said, too, that the British Columbian caribou is darker in colour than his eastern cousin: a bull killed here in September is nearly as black as a bull moose, and a cow set up in the British Columbian Museum is even blacker than the bull. This seems worth noting, as Caton says of *C. tarandus*, 'the colour lighter than any of the other deer.' The head figured is from a photograph of one killed in British Columbia, and may be considered fairly typical, except perhaps that it is too symmetrical, and that the ploughs are too even. As a rule, one plough is large and much palmated, whilst the other is a mere spike. A large British Columbian caribou head measured 3 ft. 6 ins. in length, 3 ft. in span, and 6 ins. in circumference above the big tine, but I have no record of any exceptional head. As most men know, both male and female caribou have antlers, but the antlers of the cow are light and insignificant compared with those of the bull. The antlers are clear of velvet some little time before the rut, which begins in British Columbia when the first snow begins to fly (in September) in those high upland districts which the caribou inhabit.

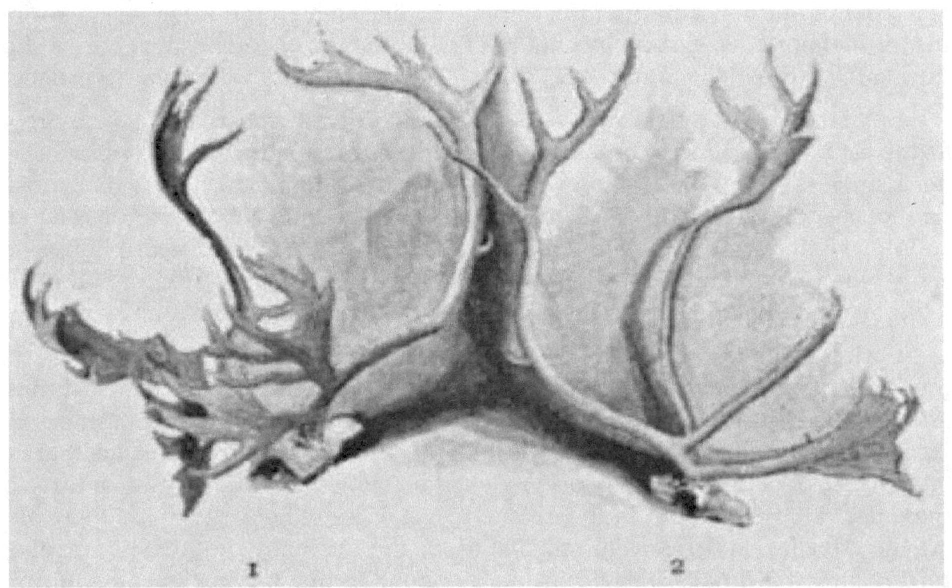

Woodland and Barren Ground Caribou Antlers

1, Woodland Caribou; 2, Barren Ground Caribou Antlers

C. Whymper

The two or three haunts of this deer known to me in British Columbia are all similar in character, lying very high at the top of the timber-line, where dark groves of balsam and other conifers, hung with immense quantities of beard moss, alternate with open glades of yellow swamp grass. The snow in these districts remains unthawed in the timber till late in May, and begins to fall again about the middle or end of September, but the exposed tops of the rolling highland above the timber are said to be free from snow a little earlier than the timber. In early summer the caribou frequent these high grassy downs, lying close to the large patches of snow left in the hollows, seeking as far as may be to avoid that pest created for their special annoyance, the caribou fly. Later on, in August, the caribou are hard to find, having left the hills and sought (so the Indians say) the seclusion of the densest brush to rub off their old coats, clean and burnish their antlers, and generally make ready for the rut. The best time to hunt the bulls is in the rutting season, when they are a little less cautious than usual, and when there is generally a good 'tracking snow' to help the hunter, who requires all the help he can get in his match with the keenest-scented beast on earth. Dull-witted the caribou may be, and I very much doubt whether his eyes are any better than a man's, but his nose is, as our neighbours say, a 'holy terror.' I have seen a caribou allow a man to walk almost up to him in very thin covert, and have had his congener, the Spitz-bergen reindeer, walk straight *back to me* when I crouched (after 'jumping' him) to see what I was. I shot him at ten paces to save myself from being run over by the inquisitive fool. The last caribou shot by friends of mine out here were killed by the lazy one of the party, while satisfying an inordinate appetite at the unreasonable hour of midday, and in camp. Captain L., like an honest hunter, was scouring the hills; Major P. was feeding contentedly in camp. L., of course, never got a shot during the expedition, but three caribou walked up to lunch with P. and were shot.

But if the eyes of caribou are not very trustworthy, their ears are about as good as the ears of other forest beasts, and their noses are matchless. I have known a herd strike the track of a man in the snow a day old, and turn as if their noses had touched hot iron; and once a caribou has satisfied himself that there is a man about, he will not stop travelling for half a day; good feed won't tempt him, deep snow won't stop him, snow-shoes can't catch him—in fact, the hunter had better look for another, and keep on the right side of him when he finds him.

Caribou feed upon very much the same food as the moose, browsing for the most part, and depending largely during the depth of winter upon beard moss and other lichens for support. Caribou hunting in British Columbia is sufficiently fascinating in itself, but for some of us it has an added charm from the fact that the best chance of getting a grizzly occurs when the bones and offal of two or three of these deer are lying about in the upland forest. Where the caribou are, there also are the grizzlies, in British Columbia at least; and the man who revisits a caribou carcase after a few days' absence is likely enough to find big tracks going in front of him, and a big, bad-tempered beast suffering from a surfeit of venison lying not far from the body.

Mr. Rowland Ward mentions a head 60 ins. long, with a span of 41⅛ ins., having 15 tines on the one side and 22 tines on the other.

(4) Barren Ground Caribou (*C. tarandus arcticus*)

Almost all that I know of the Barren Ground Caribou (*C. tarandus arcticus*) has been derived from the writings of my friend Mr. Warburton Pike, who has enjoyed exceptional opportunities of studying this beast recently in its native haunts, the barren lands of Upper Canada. According to him, the Barren Ground caribou is about one-third smaller than its woodland cousin. This seems fairly conclusive, coming from a man who has seen and shot so many Barren Ground caribou as Mr. Pike has.

The range of this beast is, according to my authority, 'from the islands in the Arctic Sea to the southern part of Hudson Bay, while the Mackenzie river is the limit of its average western wanderings.'

The Barren Ground caribou appears to rut at about the same season as the woodland variety, and masses up into those huge herds known locally as 'la foule' for its winter migration southwards, late in October. A month later the males and females separate, the latter beginning to work their way north again as early as the end of February; they reach the edge of the woods in April, and drop their young far out towards the sea-coast in June. The males stay in the woods until May and never reach the coast, but meet the females on their way inland at the end of July; from this time they stay together till the rutting season is over, and it is time to seek the woods once more. The horns are mostly clear of velvet towards the end of September, and are shed by the old bulls early in December.

As to hunting this beast, Mr. Pike says in his 'Barren Ground of Northern Canada,' 'It is no hard matter to kill caribou in the open country, for the rolling hills usually give ample cover for a stalk, and even on flat ground they are easily approached at a run, as they will almost invariably circle head to wind and give the hunter a chance to cut them off.'

(5) Mule Deer (*C. macrotis*)

To my mind the best deer we have in North America for sport is the beast whose head is here represented, *C. macrotis*, the mule deer of British Columbia and the naturalists, and the Black-tail of Colorado and elsewhere in the States. More than any other of his kin in this country, *C. macrotis* haunts the open uplands, the largest bucks being found oftener than not right up by the little snow patches, in and on the edge of the sheep land, or if not there, then in the small patches of starved and moss-grown forest at the top of the timber range. Thanks to his predilection for high places and the open, it is often possible to stalk *C. macrotis* in 'old country' fashion, instead of crawling about after him in choking timber as a man must after *C. columbianus* or almost any other American deer; but to get mule deer a man should rise early in order to see them moving up to their beds for the day.

The mule deer ruts about the middle of October, his horns being clean as a rule about a fortnight earlier, although I have seen a big buck very high up (10,000 ft.) in Colorado who had not *begun* to rub in the third week of September.

Typical Mule Deer (C. macrotis)

From a photograph

One of the writers in a recent book on American big game speaks of the *whistling* of this deer during the rutting season; but though I have spent many seasons amongst mule deer, in British Columbia and elsewhere, I have never yet heard them whistle, nor heard any mention of this habit from the natives or white hunters. However, I am not prepared to say that they do not whistle.

More than any other American deer with which I am acquainted, *C. macrotis* migrates with the seasons, passing in large numbers from his summer feeding grounds on the uplands to the green timber districts of the lower country. This migration seems to begin with the first heavy snows, but it is not an invariable rule, for I have seen big bucks in the Chilcotin country, nearly as high up as they could climb, at the beginning of December, with snow a foot deep and the thermometer 10° below zero. There is no deer in the country, I fancy, whose antlers are subject to such great variation as those of *C. macrotis*. The pair figured on p. 419 is typical, although distinctly above the average in size (25½-in. span); another pair (obtained by Mr. H. A. James in Colorado) had 41-in. span, but the abnormal head figured on p. 420 is that of a mule deer, and it has no fewer than 59 points in place of the ordinary 10 points. This stag was killed in British Columbia. I have also seen another pair, old and thick and covered with well-marked pearls, with no tines at all except at the top. The average weight of a male mule deer is about 200 lbs., though they sometimes run much larger, individuals having been killed weighing as much as 250 and 300 lbs.

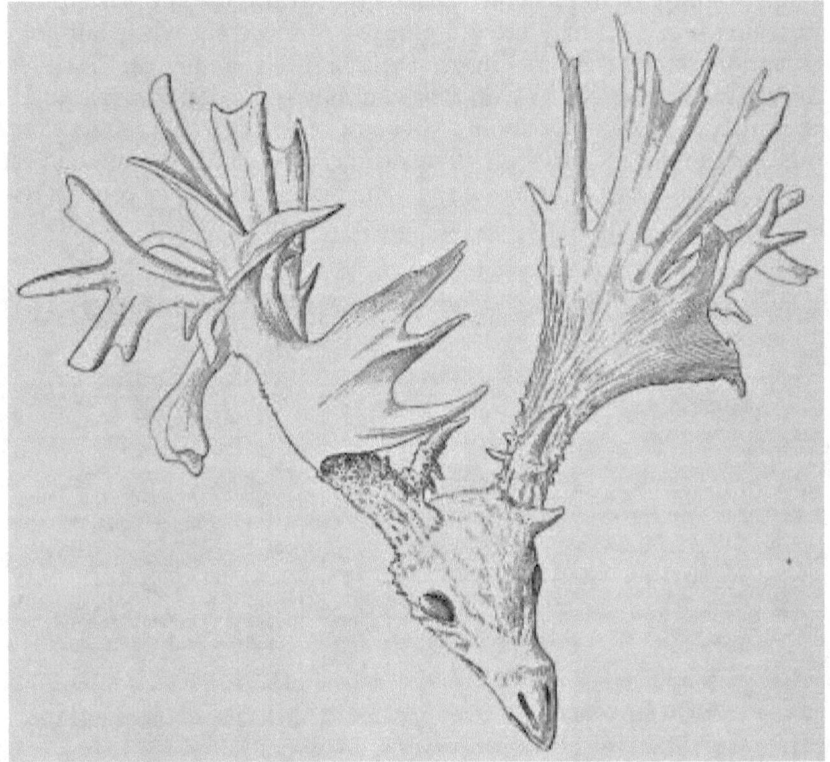

Abnormal Head of Mule Deer

Some idea of the number of these deer in British Columbia may be gathered from the fact that in one district I have had a chance of killing seventeen separate stags in an hour's still hunt, whilst one settler in the Similkameen country fed his hogs on deer-meat through a whole winter.

(6) The White-Tail (*C. virginianus*)

Of the White-tail or Virginian deer I have very little to say. Every quality which a deer ought not to possess from a sporting point of view this exasperating little beast possesses in the most highly developed form. He lives very often in close proximity to men, and seems to have caught some of their cunning. His habitat is from the Atlantic to the Pacific, his haunts are in river bottoms, in choking, blinding brush, and his habits are beastly. No one need ever expect to *stalk* a white-tail. If you want to get one, you must crawl about in places where the big boughs swing back and lash you across the eyes, where the rampikes catch in your clothes or rise up under your feet and trip you more cleverly than a professional wrestler, where hidden logs break your shins, and every other device of inanimate Nature is found to obstruct and annoy you with what seems almost live personal malice. After a long course of such sport as this, after having become dumb because you have no more 'swear words' left to say, after having grown sick of hearing that abominable 'thump, thump,' which means that you have jumped another buck without seeing him, you may catch a glimpse of a waving white tail going over the logs, and if you are a good wing-shot with a rifle you may get the beast which wears it, but the betting is you won't; or you may some day be astounded by the sight of a creature, apparently about as big as a good-sized jack rabbit, *close to you,* sneaking along under the brush, with its head craned forward, intent on escaping observation. If you move to fire, that sneaking beast will at once convert itself into the white-tailed timber jumper you have seen once or twice before.

The White-tail's Haunt

C. W., from a photograph by J. Lord

Let me be honest to the little beast. On nearly every occasion *C. virginianus* has got the best of me (I never hunted him with dogs or torches, or any other such abomination, and never mean to), but once on a red-letter day I caught a big buck of his kind dreaming on a hardwood hill. He was two hundred yards off, and though the bullet from my Express broke his foreleg, he jumped 'at a stand' a log by his side over which I could not look, though I stand nearly six feet in my boots, and gave me an hour's excessively hard work before I killed him. I should think that about 150 lbs. would be the extreme weight of the largest bucks of this variety when cleaned, but there are stories of exceptionally large white-tail bucks in the Okanagau district of British Columbia, and the heads which come from that country are certainly very fine. Mr. Rowland Ward gives 27⅛ ins. as the length and 19 ins. as the span of the best head of this deer known to him.

(7) The Black-Tail (*C. columbianus*)

Although not quite so exasperating an animal as *C. virginianus*, this, the common deer of Vancouver Island, of the islands all along the Pacific coast from Victoria to Alaska, and of the Pacific slope generally, is desperately fond of thick timber and the deep jungles of noisy sal lal bush. In size *C. columbianus* is considerably smaller than the mule deer: a buck which would weigh 175 lbs. would be a big buck for Vancouver Island, and I am not aware that the deer of this island are smaller than those of the mainland. But if *C. columbianus* is small, he is at least abundant. A week from the date of writing this, a friend of mine and myself saw fourteen deer in two days' still hunting within a drive of Victoria, and a grateful memory of my dinner reminds me that the venison of a yearling buck hung for one week is as good meat as any Esau ever brought home to Isaac. In 1892 a couple of half-breeds sold over eighty bucks in Victoria in two months, and in 1893 the same two (excellent shots and woodsmen) are reported to have killed twenty-two deer in one day. But to hunt deer or anything else upon Vancouver Island a man must be a born woodsman. Where the deer are thickest the woods fairly swallow a man up: every rolling hill is exactly like its neighbour, high peaks are scarce and landmarks very few.

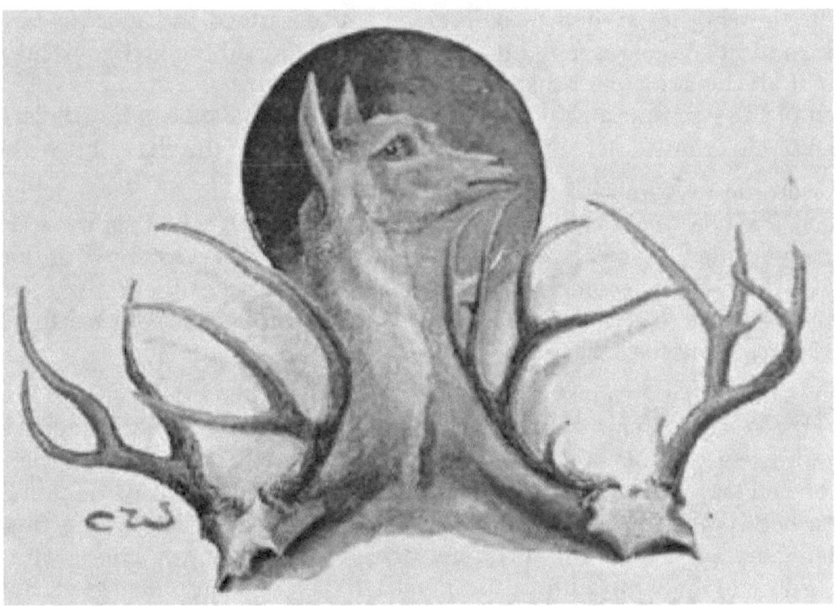

Guanaco, C. paludosus, C. columbianus

Guanaco,

C. paludosus,   *C. columbianus*

C. Whymper

Fortunately the island deer are not as wary as the white-tail, and will generally stand to gaze for a moment after having jumped from their lair amongst the sal lal.

Early in the season the neighbourhood of swamps is the likeliest place to find deer, but during the rutting season (middle of October) the old bucks seem to keep to the higher grounds. Like other deer, the black-tail browses on all manner of shrubs and deciduous trees, and, unfortunately for farmers, has a decided weakness for growing crops.

The largest head I have seen was shot in 1892 near Cowitchan Lake, Vancouver Island. It measures along the beam from skull to extreme point 21 ins., and in span it is 19 ins. from tip to tip. A typical head appears in the illustration on the next page.

Mr. Rowland Ward records a head of this deer measuring 28⅝ ins. in length, with a span of 26 ins.

NOTE ON CENTRAL AND SOUTH AMERICAN BIG GAME

There is no lack of game either upon the Pampas or in the forests and along the river-beds of Central and South America, but as yet very few English sportsmen appear to have visited either the seas of grass or the luxuriant tropical forests of Patagonia, Paraguay and the Amazon. Admiral Kennedy, indeed, in his recent book, 'Sporting Sketches in South America,' is, I fancy, the first sportsman pure and simple who has visited these regions and described the sport to be found therein, and it is to be regretted that even he has not had the luck to secure specimens of all the principal beasts known in the country. Others have, of course, written of the Amazon and of the Pampas, but they have been naturalists, who cared more to secure a new mouse than mere trophies of the chase, however fine.

According to Admiral Kennedy, the game list of South America includes the guanaco, five kinds of deer, the ostrich or rhea, the jaguar, puma, tapir, wild cattle, and the wild pig. The last two species are, of course, representatives of domestic animals which have become wild, but, unless report belies them, there are wild cattle in the world (e.g. in the Galapagos Islands) which are as well worth hunting as the biggest buffaloes.

The jaguar, though a much larger beast than the puma (identical with the panther of the West), appears to be anything but a sporting beast, haunting river jungles and dense swamps, and being unable, according to Mr. Hudson (the 'Naturalist on La Plata') to hold his own even against his smaller cousin, the puma, who is described by the same authority as a 'bold hunter,' invariably preferring large to small game, which he kills as a tiger does, by dislocating the neck. The puma is, according to the same authority, a persistent persecutor of the jaguar. Both Mr. Hudson and Admiral Kennedy seem agreed that the puma is a very dangerous enemy to the guanaco, and a scourge to everything living upon the Pampas, except man and the gama (*C. campestris*), which protects itself as the skunk does, by its unpleasant smell. Mr. Hudson's stories of the strange affection of the puma for man, although calculated to excite incredulity at first, coincide somewhat strangely with some of the Western stories of the panther (or puma) already narrated; but it must be borne in mind that the panther of the West does attack man in a few rare instances, according to the evidence of Mr. Perry.

Of all the beasts in South America Admiral Kennedy writes most enthusiastically of the guanaco, an animal nearly allied to the camel, weighing about 180 lbs., abundant from the Rio Colorado to the Straits of Magellan, and affording good sport to the stalker.

But a beast which carries no 'head,' which, according even to its admirers, 'neighs like a horse' when giving warning of danger, and 'quacks like a duck' when alarmed, seems to one who knows neither guanaco nor ciervo a very unattractive creature compared with the really fine deer, *C. paludosus*, which is found upon the Chaco of Paraguay and in the Argentine Republic. This deer somewhat resembles the red deer of Scotland, but grows to large dimensions. The horns figured are from some in the British Museum.

Besides the ciervo, South America boasts, according to Admiral Kennedy, of four other species of deer, the gama (*C. campestris*), a beast rather larger than the Scotch roe deer, common all over the Pampas, the ghazu vira or swamp deer, the ghazu colorado, and the venadillo. It is a pity that some enterprising sportsman does not devote a year or so to sport in South America. Jaguar and ciervo (to say nothing of the possibility of bagging deer almost unknown to his brother sportsmen in England) should be bait enough to tempt some one to more thoroughly investigate the sporting possibilities of South America.

For a fuller knowledge of South American game beasts, the reader is referred to Admiral Kennedy's book, and to Mr. Hudson's 'Naturalist on La Plata.'

Musk Ox

CHAPTER XIX

MUSK OX

BY WARBURTON PIKE

In a work dealing with the sport of the present day there is no necessity to inquire into the past history of the Musk Ox (*Ovibos moschatus*), or to speak of its extensive distribution during the early ages of the world. It is enough to pay a visit to the South Kensington Museum and wonder at the specimens of musk-ox heads dug out of the brick earth at Maidenhead and Ilford, differing but slightly from the bleached heads that may be picked up any day in the Barren Ground, and leave to scientists the task of describing the methods by which prehistoric man hunted the musk ox in what is now the pleasant valley of the Thames. I shall only attempt to describe the musk ox of to-day, and give a short account of the manner in which many of them are annually killed by the Northern Indians.

Whoever invented the word *ovibos* to classify the musk ox hit the nail squarely on the head, and this single word describes so exactly the strange mixture of sheep and bull that there is little left to be said upon the subject. I am indebted to Messrs.

Rowland Ward & Co. for the following dimensions, which were taken from an adult bull, not a particularly large one, but a fair average specimen:—

	ft.	ins.
Length from nose to tip of tail	6	0
Height from ground to shoulder	4	2
Height from ground to top of rump	3	10
Height from ground to belly	1	10
Round body over hair	5	9½
Depth of base of horn	1	1¼
Length of hair under neck	1	10
Length of hair under belly	1	0

The long hair is never shed, but underneath it lies a thick fleece, which comes off every year and hangs in sheets from the rocks and small bushes against which the animals have been rubbing; and herein lies the distinction between a prime musk-ox robe and one killed out of season. The hair varies from brown to black in different parts of the body, but a saddle of light yellow shows up very conspicuously in the middle of the back. The cows are smaller than the bulls, and their horns never grow together into the solid boss that is to be seen in the case of a bull at the age of six years. In the young, the horns grow straight out from the head after the manner of a barn-yard calf, and do not show the downward curve till the second year.

The present range of the musk ox is limited to the North American continent and the outlying islands in the Arctic Ocean; it is perhaps best defined as lying to the north and east of a line drawn from the mouth of the Mackenzie river to Fort Churchill on Hudson Bay. Latitude 60° is generally accepted as its southern boundary, whilst the musk ox seems capable of existing very far north, as some are recorded to have been killed on Grinnell Land, latitude 82° 27′, within a mile of the winter quarters of H.M.S. 'Alert,' in July 1876, but I can find no record of any having been seen in Greenland.

Now, all these places are necessarily hard of access, and to make a successful musk-ox hunt means spending many months in northern latitudes, and undergoing the hardships and risks which Arctic explorers have found only too plentiful in crossing the Barren Ground. A mistaken theory exists among the officers of the Hudson Bay Company, that the musk ox come into the woods in the winter; but as a matter of fact the Indians have to push out far beyond the timber, hauling wood for fuel on their dog-sleighs, and as the robes are not prime till the snow has fallen and the cold is intense, it will be easily understood that the difficulty of getting out to the musk-ox country, finding a band, and hauling in the robes, is a thing to be well considered before starting. In addition to this, it must be remembered that if a party of men and dogs fail to find their game when they are far from timber, the chances are ten to one that nobody will reach the woods alive, as the caribou which roam the Barren Ground in vast herds during the summer seek the better shelter of the thick forest directly the winter sets in, and it is perfectly impossible to haul sufficient provisions for men and dogs in addition to fuel.

My personal experience of the musk ox is derived from two expeditions, one in the autumn and early winter and the other in summer, which I made with some half-breeds from Fort Resolution, a Hudson Bay trading post on the south shore of the Great Slave Lake. We left with canoes in the middle of August, and after travelling 150 miles towards the north-east end of the lake, portaged over a range of mountains on the north shore, and passing through a chain of small lakes reached the end of the dwarf timber by the middle of September. At this point, roughly three hundred miles from Resolution, we established a permanent camp, and, reduced to four in number, set out on foot into the Barren Ground, expecting to find musk ox at any time. We travelled hard towards the north, but only fell in with two solitary bulls, both of which were killed; the rutting season was just coming on, and the bulls were apparently seeking the cows. Winter was approaching, the small lakes were frozen up and the ground covered with snow; we were unprovided with dogs and all the outfit necessary for winter travel, and were forced to abandon the hunt, reaching our camp after three weeks' absence early in October. On this journey we found the caribou plentiful, and had little trouble from short rations.

The next five weeks were passed at the edge of the woods, and it was well on in November when we started on another expedition; this time I went with a band of Yellow Knife Indians, as most of the half-breeds had deserted. Six sleighs hauled by twenty-four dogs carried a supply of firewood sufficient for three weeks with the strictest economy, and a little dried meat which was to last us till we reached the musk ox. Luckily, we had left a few meat caches on our first trip, or I think we could hardly have made a successful hunt, as men and dogs require more than the usual rations in the excessive cold which prevails in the Barren Ground during the early winter. After ten days' fair travelling, with some delays from wind storms and the trouble of cutting the meat caches out of the ice in which we had stored them, just as we had come to the end of our provisions two bands of musk ox were discovered. By rough guessing, one band contained a hundred and the other sixty animals, bulls and cows of all ages. The usual methods of winter hunting were employed, and a wholesale slaughter began; the dogs let loose from the sleighs rounded up as many of the animals as they could hold, and, going close up, we killed them as easily as cattle at the shambles.

The musk ox took no notice of the men, and seemed to suppose that the dogs were their only danger; and it is to be presumed that by herding together in this manner they resist the attacks of wolves, which follow the caribou, and probably make an attempt on the musk ox when the more timid caribou are scarce. The animals we killed were all in good condition, and an examination of their stomachs showed that they had been feeding on the different mosses that grow in profusion in the Barren Ground. The snow had drifted away from the ridges, leaving the ground bare in many places, so that the moss was easily obtainable without pawing away the snow.

We killed over forty, as the Indians were, of course, anxious to get as many robes as they could haul, to trade for ammunition and blankets at the Fort, and after we had loaded the sleighs with skins and meat we made the best of our way back to the woods, which we reached on December 2, after various mishaps through getting lost and the dogs playing out in the soft snow. Shortly afterwards we fell in with the caribou again, and reached Fort Resolution a few days before Christmas.

The short Arctic summer was at its height when I saw the musk ox again, at the head waters of the Great Fish river, after a long and tedious journey with dog sleighs, and as we spent six weeks in the heart of the Barren Ground I had every opportunity to notice the habits of these strange animals. Between the hunting grounds of the Yellow Knives and those of the Esquimaux, farther down stream, lies a debatable land of perhaps sixty miles in width, which affords the musk ox a sanctuary, and here there were scattered bands in every direction. At this season the big bulls were usually found alone, the cows and calves keeping together in small bands of ten to twenty. Their natural increase seems to be small, and calves were scarce in proportion to the number of cows. The Indians told me that a cow only calves once in two years, and this is probably true, as among the animals that we killed for food we found none that had lost a calf.

I have often been asked whether the flesh of the musk ox is good to eat, but people do not reflect that in the north, where the supply of provisions is uncertain, any kind of food is good. A fat cow killed in the fall hardly smells or tastes of musk, and I think its flesh would be palatable anywhere; but an old bull, especially in the rutting season, is a thing to be palmed off on your neighbour if there is any choice in the matter. The flesh of the calves we found insipid, and, eaten as it was without bread or vegetables, it failed to satisfy the appetite or to keep up the strength.

In the summer the musk ox live almost entirely on the green leaves of the small willows that grow in patches in the Barren Ground, and do not in this part of the country confine themselves entirely to moss all the year round, as I have seen stated. They fatten up in a wonderful manner during the short time they have for feasting, and begin the winter in splendid condition, though, according to the Indians, they are poor enough at the time of the spring hunt in April.

In summer hunting no dogs are used, but the still more destructive method of driving the musk ox into the water is often put into practice. When a band is discovered, a convenient place is chosen for the slaughter, and piles of rocks adorned with coats and gun-covers are set up a short distance apart, at right angles to the small lake that has been selected. Men are stationed at intervals to head the animals off, while others, making a détour, start the band in the right direction. On coming to the barricade the animals are afraid to pass the line of rocks, and, seeing themselves surrounded, take to the water as their best chance. Then the little canoes are launched and the whole band is quickly exterminated. The musk ox is a poor swimmer. He seems to have some difficulty in keeping his head above water, and never leaves the land except under compulsion.

If the animals are at a long distance from water, or only one or two are required for meat, they are easily approached under cover of the rolling ground, and, being naturally of an unwary disposition, are a sure prey for the Indian if he can persuade his long muzzle-loader to go off at the right moment. It might naturally be supposed that the musk ox is being rapidly exterminated, but I doubt if this is really the case. The head of the Great Fish River has always been the summer hunting ground of the Yellow Knives; and yet their chief told me that he had never known these animals more numerous than at the present day, and certainly a great many were killed while we were waiting for the ice in the river to break up. But this is only the edge of the musk-ox country: the rocky wilderness stretches far towards the north and east to the Arctic Ocean, uninhabited except by a few wandering Esquimaux close to the coast. Into this desert the winter hunters can never penetrate, as it lies too far beyond the tree-line to admit of wood being hauled on dog-sleighs. It is true that the number of hides exported by the Hudson Bay Company is greater than it used to be, but this is easily accounted for by the fact that the robes have increased in value, and the price now paid to the Indians in the north is sufficient to encourage them to haul the skins to the Fort, instead of using them for moccasins, as was formerly the case.

In spite of the many stories that the Indians told me, and the evident dread in which they hold the musk ox, I could not see anything to justify the belief that it is a dangerous animal to attack. I never saw anything resembling a charge, although I have often been close up to a badly wounded bull on purpose to see if there was any truth in these reports. But the Indians are given to superstition, and attribute miraculous powers to the musk ox, and probably the ferocious appearance of an old bull has worked upon their timid imaginations till they are ready to believe thoroughly in these traditions.

On expeditions of this kind there is really no sport in the ordinary acceptance of the term, and under any circumstances the musk ox is so easily approached that one soon tires of the slaughter; the same thing applies to the caribou, which are sometimes found in almost incredible numbers in the Barren Ground in summer or the woods in winter. But it is never a certainty that the game will be forthcoming when most required for meat, and the knowledge that starvation, even to the last extremes, may come upon you at any time, goes far to counterbalance the tameness of the sport when once you have reached the land of plenty. Sufficient excitement and danger will always be found in penetrating the little known desert of the north to satisfy the most enthusiastic sportsman explorer.

Vignette

H. Willink

INDEX

Y

Z

Lector House believes that a society develops through a two-fold approach of continuous learning and adaptation, which is derived from the study of classic literary works spread across the historic timeline of literature records. Therefore, we aim at reviving, repairing and redeveloping all those inaccessible or damaged but historically as well as culturally important literature across subjects so that the future generations may have an opportunity to study and learn from past works to embark upon a journey of creating a better future.

This book is a result of an effort made by Lector House towards making a contribution to the preservation and repair of original ancient works which might hold historical significance to the approach of continuous learning across subjects.

HAPPY READING & LEARNING!

LECTOR HOUSE LLP
E-MAIL: lectorpublishing@gmail.com

www.ingramcontent.com/pod-product-compliance
Lightning Source LLC
LaVergne TN
LVHW091521170726
843492LV00004B/1004